Prisoner Reentry in the Era of Mass Incarceration

Prisoner Reentry in the Era of Mass Incarceration

Daniel P. Mears
Florida State University

Joshua C. Cochran
University of South Florida

Los Angeles | London | New Delhi
Singapore | Washington DC

Los Angeles | London | New Delhi
Singapore | Washington DC

FOR INFORMATION:

SAGE Publications, Inc.
2455 Teller Road
Thousand Oaks, California 91320
E-mail: order@sagepub.com

SAGE Publications Ltd.
1 Oliver's Yard
55 City Road
London EC1Y 1SP
United Kingdom

SAGE Publications India Pvt. Ltd.
B 1/I 1 Mohan Cooperative Industrial Area
Mathura Road, New Delhi 110 044
India

SAGE Publications Asia-Pacific Pte. Ltd.
3 Church Street
#10-04 Samsung Hub
Singapore 049483

Acquisitions Editor: Jerry Westby
Editorial Assistant: Laura Kirkhuff
Production Editor: Kelly DeRosa
Copy Editor: Lynn Weber
Typesetter: Hurix Systems Pvt. Ltd.
Proofreader: Sue Irwin
Indexer: Scott Smiley
Cover Designer: Scott Van Atta
Marketing Manager: Terra Schultz

Printed in the United States of America

Cataloging-in-publication data is available for this title from the Library of Congress.

ISBN: 978-1-4833-1672-7

This book is printed on acid-free paper.

SFI® Certified Sourcing
www.sfiprogram.org
SFI-00453

14 15 16 17 18 10 9 8 7 6 5 4 3 2 1

Table of Contents

About the Authors

Daniel P. Mears is the Mark C. Stafford Professor of Criminology in the College of Criminology and Criminal Justice at Florida State University.

Joshua C. Cochran is assistant professor in the Department of Criminology at the University of South Florida.

Preface

The idea for this book emerged from several different sources. Prison populations have grown by historically unprecedented amounts in recent decades. Accordingly, scholars increasingly have focused their attention on this growth. Some work has examined the factors that contributed to mass incarceration. Other work has focused on desistance from offending. One particular focus to which scholars have devoted substantial attention has been prisoner reentry. During the 1990s, researchers highlighted that much remained unknown about prisoners and individuals' experiences both during and after incarceration. Previous scholarship focused on "reintegration."

The newer generation of research has centered on the idea that reentry is a process. Inmates leave prison and experience a range of challenges, and they return to diverse and difficult social contexts. Concerns about recidivism are, of course, prominent. But the burgeoning literature on reentry also has highlighted that recidivism constitutes only one of a range of outcomes—there are others, such as unemployment, homelessness, and family reunification—that warrant attention from policy makers, practitioners, and scholars. This literature has also highlighted that a discussion of reentry is incomplete without an understanding of mass incarceration and the "punitive turn" in criminal justice.

Our own interest and involvement in the study of prisoner reentry stems from a number of experiences. Daniel has spent almost two decades studying the causes of crime, evaluating crime and criminal justice programs and policies, and investigating many aspects of reentry as a social problem. He brings with him a sociological background and an emphasis on the use and development of social theory to understand offending and responses to it. At the same time, he brings a strong appreciation for the unique insights that those "on the ground"—community residents, practitioners, law enforcement agents, and court and correctional system personnel—have for understanding criminal behavior and how to effectively respond to it. In part, this sensibility comes from his experience working with delinquent youth. It also comes from his evaluation research experiences, which served to highlight how theory can be developed from the ground up based on practitioner accounts as well as from the top down based on insights from social science.

For Joshua, the interest in reentry stems from immersion in research on inmate prison experiences and their consequences for behavior during and after incarceration. When he began conducting research on these experiences, it became clear that far too little is known about what happens to inmates and the relative effectiveness of different types of sanctions. These lines of research contributed to his focus on reentry and the fascinating but troubling issues that attend reentry and, more broadly, punishment.

His interest stems, too, from personal experiences. His father worked in law enforcement and then as a clinical addictions counselor. As a result, Joshua grew up around homeless and drug-addicted populations, the bulk of whom had spent substantial time in jails and prisons. His father provided assistance to these individuals, mostly men, which involved helping them to find jobs as dishwashers, cooks, and custodians and directing them to social services and health care. However, many of the men remained addicted and unemployed and eventually returned to jail or prison. In most cases, one could point to personal failings as well as to social disadvantage as causes of these outcomes. What in particular, though, leads individuals to offend and to do so even after they have been incarcerated several times? Answering this question is central to advancing theories of offending and to improving public safety.

A somewhat more eclectic range of factors led Daniel to his interest in reentry. The interest stems in part from being cold, thinking about reality television shows, having worked at residential facilities, and collaborating with criminal justice practitioners. It stems, too, from a desire to advance criminological theory. An explanation is in order.

Although I (Daniel) grew up in New Hampshire, I can't say that I enjoyed the cold. For that reason, I should have enjoyed Austin, Texas, where I undertook my graduate studies. I did. Even so, Austin was a cold place. Really. The university spared no expense when it came to air conditioning. I wore a sweatshirt on a regular basis, then would take it off when I went outside. I have never liked the cold, not in New Hampshire and not in Texas. My brother, David, could wear no gloves in freezing weather and his fingers would be fine at the end of a run. Mine would require hours of exposure to the wood stove before they would thaw, and that was after wearing huge, wind-resistant gloves. Whatever toughness I may have, it is not "cold tough."

Why does that matter? When I worked in Washington, DC, at the Urban Institute, it was a rare day that I did not see homeless people. In the winter. In the cold. On the street. I had a long shirt, sweater, coat, hat, and more on. I would have worn a wrap-around electric warmer if such existed. The selfless part of me was, and remains, angry and pained by the scale of homelessness that exists in DC and in many metropolitan areas. The selfish part of me wondered how I would fare out on the street, in the cold.

What is the connection to reentry? When I arrived at the Urban Institute in 2001, policy makers, practitioners, and scholars were just beginning to come to grips with understanding the fall-out of the rapid increase in incarceration during the 1980s and 1990s. Jeremy Travis, in his capacity as the director of the National Institute of Justice, had special insight into the problem given his position and the research funded through his agency. He joined the Urban Institute and, along with a team of wonderful people, sought funding to support studies to illuminate a phenomenon—reentry—that was little understood. Basic questions remained largely unanswered. For example, who exactly comes out of prison? What are their experiences as they transition back into families and communities? Yes, recidivism studies existed. But little systematic theoretical or empirical research had been targeted toward understanding the profile of the ex-prisoner population, the challenges that they faced upon release, and how best to ensure not only that they stopped offending but also that they became contributing members of society.

I began to help with some of these studies and then led several. Around this time, "survival" television shows became popular. Individuals would be subject to challenges; if they could overcome the challenges, victory was theirs. It dawned on me that the challenges of reentry would not likely be overcome by your average, or even above-average, citizen. The challenges would daunt the most type A personalities out there.

A pause—when we talk about people in prison, it is important to recognize that they committed a crime. There were victims. Accordingly, the focus of this discussion and book does not require liking ex-prisoners or feeling sorry for them. Rather, all that is needed is a pragmatic mindset. If individuals consistently fail upon release from prison, then we as a society have a problem. Failure in a reentry context typically includes recidivism. That means more crime, more victims, and more cost. Such problems concern conservatives and liberals alike and, indeed, most everyone.

Back to ex-prisoners. As I reviewed scholarship about ex-prisoners, I thought about the youth at the facilities at which I had worked. They invariably had experienced hardships that, fortunately, most of us do not. The hardships included sexual and physical abuse, abandonment, mental illness and learning disabilities, neglect, and more. Most of these problems had gone unaddressed. It can be easier for us to feel more strongly about these issues when we contemplate children and young teenagers. These individuals, however, grow up, and their backgrounds do not magically disappear. That is why the profile of ex-prisoners can be so dismaying—serious family dysfunction, a history of abuse, limited education, spotty work histories, drug addiction, homelessness, residency in areas of concentrated poverty, and more.

Let us return, then, to the survival television show. Imagine you are a contestant. Your situation is as follows. You have no money. You have no more than an eighth grade education. You have a learning disability. You have a mental disorder. You have a lousy work history. In addition, you have a felony conviction, which means that you may not be able to vote, you may not be allowed to live in subsidized housing (where your family likely resides), and you are not allowed to work in certain occupations. An added bonus: During the previous two years, you received little to no rehabilitative programming, little to no education, and little to no training in or experience with the types of work or work skills that would assist you in a job search. Also, you likely have had to endure physical and verbal assaults and threats from inmates or officers. Contact with family and friends? No.

That is your reality television starting point. The goals that you must achieve if you want to win the prize? Find safe and affordable housing, secure gainful employment, and obtain treatment for a drug abuse problem.

When I first framed the issue to myself this way, the problem of reentry took on a new cast. Years earlier, I had been in the Peace Corps. That involved doing without the typical supports that most of us enjoy. It was challenging, but I had friends, some funding, training, and everybody seemed focused on helping you. Even so, I could hardly have been described as a success story for the Peace Corps. This experience came immediately on the heels of trying to find my way in college. In high school, everything came easily, but college was a different story. I struggled, and my ego took a beating. In the end, though, I bounced back from these experiences, bruised but wiser and stronger. Years later, sitting at my desk in D.C., I reflected on my past experiences and wondered what life would be like to be confronted with constant, repeated failure. Never succeeding but instead failing again and again, with no outside supports to help you.

I thought, too, about being cold. It turns out that the first few weeks after release from prison are among the hardest. Not surprisingly—given the profile of the typical inmate and the challenges faced during reentry—many ex-prisoners become homeless. And homeless people not infrequently live in the cold.

So, in our television survival show, we begin with many deficits, experience threats and violence, find ourselves out in the cold with few if any financial or social resources. And yet we are tasked, if we wish to win, with finding employment, housing, and treatment. That is a contest that many of us would lose. Remarkably, though, this situation confronts hundreds of thousands of people each year as they leave prison. It is not reality television; it is, rather, real life.

The consequences of failing to address this situation means that, in the end, society loses through more crime, victimization, homelessness, and cycles of violence and dysfunction within families and communities. Ultimately, society pays in a myriad of ways for this failure. Can we build our way out of this situation through more incarceration? The answer from research appears to be a resounding no. Are there solutions? Yes.

This book is motivated by the critical importance of reducing crime and the suffering and costs that accompany it and by the fact that many opportunities exist to create smarter, more effective systems of justice. We do not advocate a "silver-bullet" approach to improving reentry. Indeed, we argue against a one-solution mindset. In its place, we advocate capitalizing on a wide range of opportunities to improve the criminal justice system, corrections, communities, and the ways that we sanction and intervene with individuals who go to and leave prison. There is, at the same time, the opportunity to advance criminological theory on offending, families and communities, crime policy changes, criminal justice processing, and corrections. Indeed, the study of reentry offers many different ways to develop and test theory, as we will discuss. Theory sometimes can be bad. It can put blinders up and too narrowly delimit our focus. Even so, even the most pragmatic views from those "on the ground" implicitly involve recourse to theoretical accounts of reality. Indeed, for that very reason, incorporation of the insights of the individuals who work in or shape the criminal justice system is essential for creating more accurate accounts of crime and justice.

I worked at a residential facility that housed delinquent youth, and I have worked for years evaluating programs and policies designed and implemented by well-meaning individuals who strive to promote public safety and to help people. These experiences inform the research that I have undertaken, my views about the use and development of theory, and the importance of recognizing and incorporating the insights of the individuals on the ground into research and policy-making efforts. They result, too, in a sensibility that places a premium on viewing crime and justice from different vantage points. When I conducted my first study on sentencing, I interviewed prosecutors, judges, and defense attorneys. Almost invariably, it was the individuals who had worked in all three of these capacities who seemed to offer the most balanced, insightful views about problems in criminal justice and solutions to them. When we view the prisoner reentry landscape from diverse perspectives there are, yes, many problems, but there also are many solutions, ones that go well beyond building more prisons.

To identify and implement these solutions will require considerable effort by many different groups. That includes the public, who ultimately determine how government operates; students, who will go on to make the world a better place; policy makers and practitioners, who work to create approaches to improving the criminal justice and correctional systems; and scholars, who strive to understand and explain crime, criminal justice processing, correctional systems, and what can be done to improve public safety and the administration of justice. All of these groups will be needed to solve more effectively and efficiently the problems associated with crime and reentry.

We owe a debt of gratitude to Jerry Westby for encouraging this effort. Without his prompting and guidance, there would be no book! Jerry, thank you. We owe thanks as well to Denise Simon and the reviewers. They provided thoughtful suggestions that greatly helped to improve the book. We owe thanks, too, to many others. Emily, Eli, and Ashley provided no end of enthusiasm and support. They are tolerant (fortunately), curious, and wonderful people. Eli every day teaches Dan more than Dan teaches him, which is the way it should be. Our thanks to Meghan Ogle, who provided research assistance in developing the tables for Chapter 9. We thank the Sentencing Project for permission to use data from their 2012 report by Christopher Uggen, Sarah Shannon, and Jeff Manza on felon disenfranchisement to create Figure 2.4. Throughout the book, we have drawn on arguments or ideas that we have touched on in our other works. The use accords with author copyright rights, but we nonetheless want to acknowledge and thank the following presses and organizations for publishing the original works: the American Correctional Association; Blackwell Synergy; the Center for Juvenile and Criminal Justice; Elsevier; Oxford University Press; Sage; Taylor and Francis; the University of California Press; the University of Houston Law Center; the Urban Institute; and Wiley-Blackwell. Not least, we thank our colleagues, who have provided support, insight, and more.

CHAPTER 1

Introduction

Prisoner reentry—several decades ago, it barely registered in the public consciousness. Yes, crime control had featured prominently in presidential elections since the 1960s and, in particular, in President Lyndon Johnson's campaign against Barry Goldwater.[1] Johnson appointed a commission of high-profile researchers and, in 1967, received the commission's report and recommendations. In 1968, Congress, informed by the report and cajoled by Johnson, enacted the Omnibus Crime Control and Safe Streets Act. Since that time, crime has received top-priority attention from presidents.

What has changed, then? It is not the attention to crime. Rather, a tough-on-crime era arose, beginning in the 1970s and ascending into prominence in the 1980s. This era ushered in unprecedented emphases on punishment over rehabilitation and, in particular, intensive use of incarceration. Put differently, the quality and quantity of punishment changed. The country turned away from rehabilitation and toward incapacitation and deterrence as the way to reduce recidivism. It turned, too, toward retribution and the development of an ever-expanding array of strategies for achieving it. Social exclusion rather than inclusion of those who offend constituted the "new penology."[2]

In some ways, the logic seems simple and straightforward. If rehabilitation does not work—as the famous Robert Martinson report, published in 1974, suggested—and if crime stands to overrun society, recourse to no-nonsense punishment should be pursued.[3] And it should "work." That is, it should signal to all Americans the country's moral code. It should reduce crime rates by educating would-be offenders about this code and simultaneously by scaring them away from even considering a criminal lifestyle, a mechanism typically referred to as general deterrence. It also should reduce recidivism in a similar manner. A tough stint in the "slammer" should induce fear among those released from prison and so induce a specific deterrent effect.

Missed in all of this simple and straightforward logic were the kinds of insights that might have led to a more careful and considered approach to crime control and punishment. Prisons, of course, cost money. Once built, they typically remain in place. Few politicians, for example, can successfully run on a campaign of reducing prison capacity. The potential to be painted as "soft on crime" sits there and, as Governor Michael Dukakis learned in his 1988 presidential campaign, can contribute directly to losing an election.[4] Accordingly, any increase in the capacity to incarcerate should not be undertaken lightly, precisely because it obligates taxpayer dollars almost indefinitely. Put differently, investing in a prison is tantamount to obtaining a mortgage from which one cannot escape.

Finances, however, barely scratch the surface when we consider incarceration. As decades of scholarship now establish, the intensive pursuit of incarceration has created ripple effects of unintended harms that, to date, do not seem counterbalanced by benefits that may have accrued from the investment. This problem, and the need to do something about it, provides the motivation for this book. Any solution, however, requires first understanding the nature of the problem, its causes and contours, and the range of possible strategies for intervening. Simply calling for less incarceration will not suffice. Indeed, it is not appropriate. Crime hurts people. Punishment, including incarceration, stands as a time-honored way to address that harm. But it is not the only or even necessarily the best way to do so.

As we discuss below, the scale of changes in the country's use of incarceration demands attention. For scholars, innumerable opportunities exist to develop a better understanding of crime and offending. For policy makers, practitioners, and the public at large, the situation is cause both for optimism and for utmost concern. On the optimistic side, numerous opportunities exist for improving punishment policy in the United States. The concern, however, is that the failure to take advantage of these opportunities will result in immediate consequences in the form of more costs, more crime, and more suffering.

MASS INCARCERATION AND REENTRY

After decades of relatively consistent, low-level increases in prison populations, the United States embarked in the late 1970s and early 1980s on the equivalent of a policy that has come to be called "mass incarceration." States and the federal government built prisons. Lots of them. And they filled them, so much so that America's use of incarceration exceeds that of almost all other countries.[5] As inspection of Figure 1.1 shows, after adjusting for population size differences, the United States incarcerates more individuals per capita than any other country in the world. Counting both jail and prison populations, the United States incarceration rate is 716 per 100,000 residents. By contrast, Russia's incarceration rate is 475, the United Kingdom's is 148, and Germany's is 79. The United States stands at the top of this list even if all countries, not just those in the figure, are included.[6] The world incarceration rate is estimated to be 144 per 100,000 individuals.[7]

In absolute terms, the number of inmates in state or federal prisons in the United States soared from 500,000 in 1980 to over 2.3 million in the course of just over three decades, with only a slight tapering off in recent years. The increase well exceeded what would be predicted by changes in population and, as will be discussed, crime rates. Figure 1.2 shows that, in 1980, the United States incarcerated 139 individuals in state or federal prisons per 100,000 adult residents; by 2012, that rate increased to 480. (International comparisons typically include jail populations, hence the higher United States incarceration rate shown in Figure 1.1.) Put differently, over this time span, incarceration rates increased by approximately 250 percent.

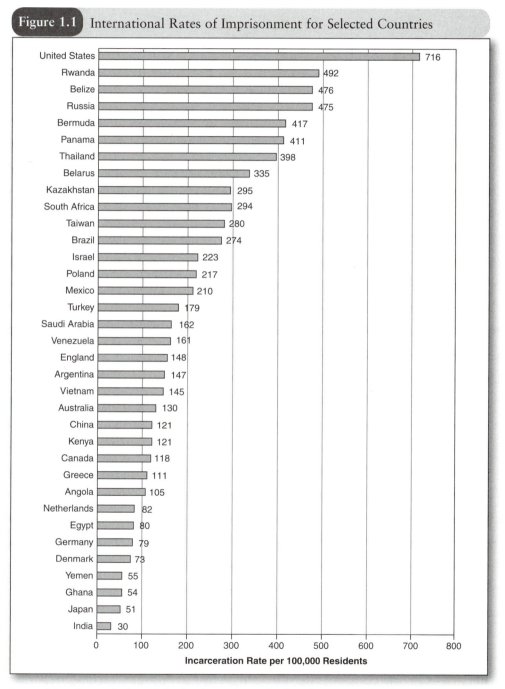

Figure 1.1   International Rates of Imprisonment for Selected Countries

Country	Rate
United States	716
Rwanda	492
Belize	476
Russia	475
Bermuda	417
Panama	411
Thailand	398
Belarus	335
Kazakhstan	295
South Africa	294
Taiwan	280
Brazil	274
Israel	223
Poland	217
Mexico	210
Turkey	179
Saudi Arabia	162
Venezuela	161
England	148
Argentina	147
Vietnam	145
Australia	130
China	121
Kenya	121
Canada	118
Greece	111
Angola	105
Netherlands	82
Egypt	80
Germany	79
Denmark	73
Yemen	55
Ghana	54
Japan	51
India	30

Incarceration Rate per 100,000 Residents

Source: Selected countries from Walmsley (2013). A complete list of countries and updated statistics is available through the International Centre for Prison Studies (http://www.prisonstudies.org/world-prison-brief).

Figure 1.2   Incarceration Rates in the United States, 1980–2012

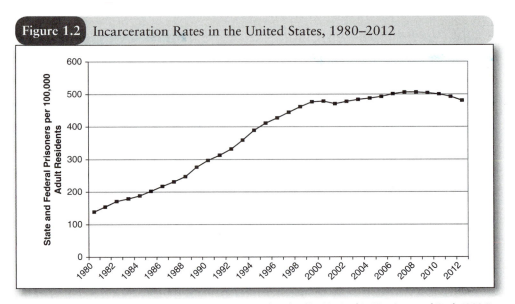

Sources: Bureau of Justice Statistics (2000); Carson and Golinelli (2013a, b); Harrison and Beck (2006).

During this same time period, the correctional system, which includes individuals on probation, in jails and prisons, and on parole, expanded from 2 million to over 7 million individuals.[8] For example, probation populations increased from just over 1 million to well over 4 million.[9] The reentry population grew, too, despite lengthier terms of incarceration. Nothing short of life sentences for all inmates can change the fact that, in general, over 93 percent of all inmates return to society.[10] The end result, as shown in Figure 1.3, is that between 600,000 and 700,000 individuals are released annually from state and federal prisons back into society. By contrast, in 1980, the country released 154,000 individuals from prison. This steady and dramatic increase in the correctional system occurred for three decades. It did so despite several economic downturns that led observers to speculate that the expansion simply could not continue. But it did. And it left the country in a position where, even with a leveling off or even a moderate tapering of the prison population, a commitment to mass incarceration—and its many intended and unintended consequences—remains.

Indeed, the end result involves much more than the release of individuals from prison. Release is but the start of a complicated process for ex-prisoners, one that is built on an equally complicated set of practices, policies, and social conditions. The reentry of prisoners into society has far-reaching consequences that implicate not only ex-prisoners but also their families, the communities to which they return, states, and the country. More than a decade of research on reentry highlights this fact and underscores that mass incarceration has imposed, and will continue to impose, substantial costs on society with benefits that remain largely speculative. For example, from 1982 to 2011, total state corrections spending increased from $15 billion to $53 billion in real dollars.[11] That estimate does not reflect the significant increase in costs for law enforcement and the courts or the costs that victims, families, and communities incurred

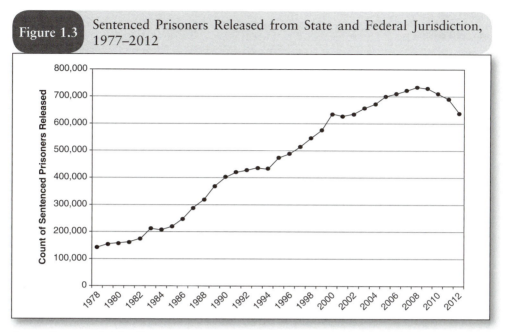

| Figure 1.3 | Sentenced Prisoners Released from State and Federal Jurisdiction, 1977–2012 |

Source: Carson and Golinelli (2013).

during this period. There are other consequences associated with mass incarceration as well. These include the potential for increased offending or crime rates, declines in neighborhood cohesion and labor markets, and other quality-of-life indicators.[12]

There is no evidence that rates of recidivism declined during the era of mass incarceration.[13] A national assessment of recidivism rates among prisoners released from thirty states in 2005 found that, within 5 years of release, 77 percent of prisoners were rearrested for a felony or serious misdemeanor (rearrest rates did not vary appreciably by type of crime), 55 percent were reconvicted of a new crime, and 28 percent were sent to prison for a new crime (see Figure 1.4).[14] An even more sobering picture emerges when we recognize that over half of prisoners (55 percent) were reincarcerated within 5 years of release; some returned due to new prison sentences while the rest returned due to technical violations (e.g., failing a drug test, missed parole officer appointments, or the like).[15] The initial months after release constitute the period when individuals are most at risk of recidivism: Rearrest occurs for over one-fourth (28 percent) of prisoners within the first six months of release. Thereafter, the likelihood of recidivism increases, but at a slower rate. The high levels of recidivism do not constitute evidence that incarceration worsens offending, but they raise critical questions about its effects.[16]

Other consequences of mass incarceration exist. To use one prominent example—the widespread and increased use of supermax incarceration, including the military's reliance on the prison facility at Guantanamo after the September 11, 2001, attacks, led to international condemnation of the United States. The emergence and use of supermax housing occurred in the absence of any credible empirical research documenting its benefits.[17] Throughout the

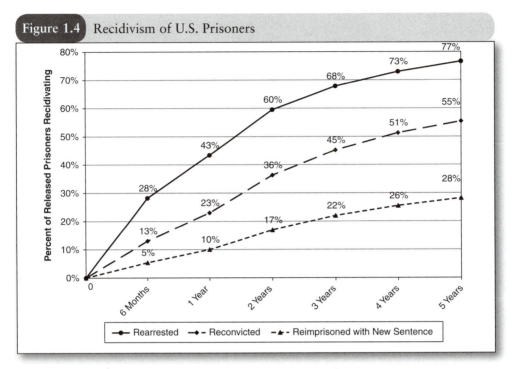

Figure 1.4   Recidivism of U.S. Prisoners

Source: Durose et al. (2014:8, 15).

book, we will discuss other examples. What we will emphasize here is that the country achieved, in but a few decades, historically unprecedented growth in incarceration. By so doing, it placed enormous demands on taxpayers while simultaneously limiting opportunities both to punish and to promote public safety through other potentially more effective and efficient approaches.

If the benefits of greater use of prison outweighed the costs, there might be cause for celebration, especially if benefits greatly exceeded costs. Yet review of the literature on mass incarceration, reentry, and punishment suggests just the opposite. Research indicates that large-scale incarceration and the more general "get-tough" shift in punishment have harmed communities. They have created or amplified racial and ethnic disparities and tensions and disenfranchised large swaths of the American populace. In addition, although in some places mass incarceration and "get tough" punishment may have modestly reduced crime and recidivism, considerable evidence suggests that elsewhere they have increased crime and recidivism relative to what otherwise would have occurred.[18]

That bleak assessment, one found in many scholarly accounts, suggests substantial cause for concern. Perhaps it overstates the case, or maybe it misses the mark altogether. Maybe large-scale investment in incarceration in recent decades needed to happen and created benefits that have yet to be fully appreciated. Is such an assessment accurate? How would we know? These are critical questions that should interest us all—citizen, policy maker, practitioner, and scholar alike. To avoid simplistic assessments requires careful consideration of many facets of mass incarceration and its end result, mass reentry.

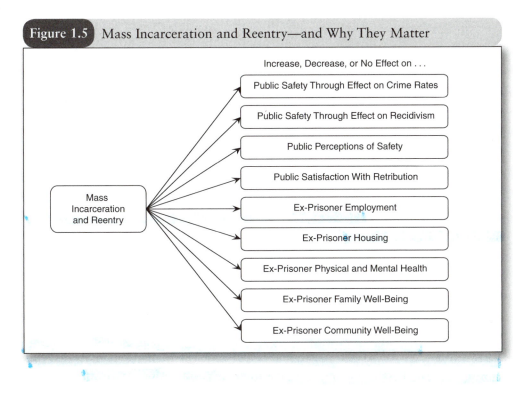

Figure 1.5 Mass Incarceration and Reentry—and Why They Matter

Figure 1.5 illustrates the point. On the left stands mass incarceration and reentry. To the right stand a range of community outcomes that may be affected by them. These include increased public safety through reduced crime rates or reduced recidivism, or both; increased public perceptions of safety, which may or may not directly accord with actual crime rates or incarceration rates; public satisfaction with a central goal of punishment, namely, retribution; and other dimensions that may seem at first blush to lie outside the purview of criminal justice and yet may be affected by incarceration. Imprisonment, for example, may affect ex-prisoner employment prospects and access to subsidized housing. It may affect mental or physical health. It may affect families, who bear additional burdens when individuals leave prison without the possibility of employment and with physical or mental illnesses that place demands on or affect other family members. Not least, it may influence communities in a myriad of ways, from increased crime rates to reduced quality of life. The net sum of the benefits and costs along each of these dimensions ultimately determines whether mass incarceration, or any other approach to punishment and public safety, is effective.[19]

Swirling in and around the many considerations that emerge when we investigate such questions are opportunities to pursue avenues of research of long-standing relevance to social scientists. What, for example, are the causes of offending? Historically, the bulk of criminological theory on offending derived from a focus on delinquents and youth populations. With the advent of mass incarceration, a logical shift to understanding offending over the life course emerged, as did theorizing that incorporated insights about changes in psychological and social development and context as individuals age.[20] Studies have turned, too, to examining the effects of incarceration on macro-level crime rates and the causes of the "punitive" turn in American punishment.[21] Such work creates the potential to answer interesting and important scholarly questions and to develop more theoretical insight into offending, crime, and social control efforts. Just as relevant, it holds the potential to contribute to discussions about and evidence for policies, programs, and practices that can more effectively and efficiently promote public safety and well-being. By "effective," we mean here that significant improvements in outcomes (e.g., reduced recidivism) occur, and by "efficient" we mean here that these improvements arise from relatively little cost or, alternatively, from the least necessary cost.

A silver lining, then, to the emergence of mass incarceration and reentry consists of the opportunities to advance policy and scholarship in mutually reinforcing ways. Any such benefit, however, rests on appreciating the character and complexity of reentry. There is no single explanation of mass incarceration to which scholars adhere.[22] There is no one "silver-bullet" solution to reducing crime or the recidivism of prisoners. The best prison program, for example, cannot control or shape the community and social conditions to which inmates return. Accordingly, efforts to reduce recidivism ideally focus on individuals not only while they are incarcerated but also after they leave prison. Such efforts should address many other factors that contribute to pro-social outcomes. Likewise, no single criminological theory will reshape reentry policy or will do so effectively. Offending results from a multitude of factors. Efforts to focus only on one or two simply will not succeed or do so "to scale"—that is, in a way that substantially reduces offending for the bulk of people sent to prison. There is, too, no single best way to integrate the on-the-ground insights of criminal justice and corrections administrators and practitioners into the creation of effective and efficient policy and practice or to have such insights inform research. Rather, many ways exist to do so.[23]

THE GOALS OF THIS BOOK

This book is motivated by these opportunities and observations. In writing it, we are well aware of the excellent accounts of prisoner reentry that exist.[24] We necessarily cover some similar terrain, such as discussion of trends in and the profile of prison populations. However, we depart substantially from prior work in developing several interrelated arguments about reentry theory and research and how to improve policy and scholarship. A strength of the ever-growing body of work on reentry lies in the illumination of important facets of mass incarceration and its consequences for individuals and society. At the same time, the risk is that we lose sight of the forest for the trees.

In this book, our focus centers on both the forest and the trees. Without an understanding of the broader contexts and factors that affect reentry, it is difficult to appreciate the significance of particular empirical findings. Even so, narrowly focused studies can illuminate significant issues that have far-reaching consequences and that give color to abstract arguments. For example, the fact that little is known about the amount of time that inmates spend in supermax housing points to broader concerns about the lack of systematic analysis of prison system operations and their effects.[25] The broader patterns are, however, critical. One significant trend in reentry policy over recent decades consists of a greater focus on individual offenders. Change the individuals, through deterrence or some other mechanism, and society will be safer. Such an approach, however, neglects the role that the criminal justice system plays in creating a population of prisoners and affecting their potential for offending. It neglects, too, the role that communities play in contributing to crime and other social problems.

At the broadest level, then, our goal is to contribute to our understanding of and policy on reentry and, in turn, criminal justice. We argue that substantial improvements in criminal justice broadly—not just within the prison system or in parole or community supervision—are needed to understand and to improve reentry. This argument builds on Jeremy Travis's advocacy of a "reentry framework" for thinking about and questioning many aspects of criminal justice, including law enforcement and sentencing practices, correctional system operations, release policies, and, more generally, how we as a society approach crime prevention and justice.[26] Here, the strength of our argument rests in large part on the examination of reentry from different perspectives, including the historical context of recent incarceration trends, the salience of in-prison and post-prison contexts and experiences for reentry, variation in the experiences that different groups have during reentry, the complicated nature of recidivism prediction and management, and the range of outcomes relevant to assessing reentry policy. In this book, we examine reentry through these perspectives, each addressed in separate chapters (described below). We do so because in our view the perspectives are important to understand in their own right. However, the perspectives provide a strategic benefit as well—they enable us to advance the goal of the book by developing several related arguments, as depicted in Figure 1.6.

First, we argue for the necessity of diverse perspectives if we are to understand reentry processes, including their causes and consequences, and to improve reentry outcomes. An increase, for example, in the incarceration of individuals for drug-related crimes points to the potential need to investigate whether this shift

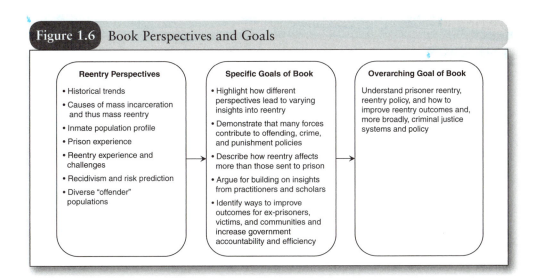

Figure 1.6   Book Perspectives and Goals

Reentry Perspectives	Specific Goals of Book	Overarching Goal of Book
• Historical trends • Causes of mass incarceration and thus mass reentry • Inmate population profile • Prison experience • Reentry experience and challenges • Recidivism and risk prediction • Diverse "offender" populations	• Highlight how different perspectives lead to varying insights into reentry • Demonstrate that many forces contribute to offending, crime, and punishment policies • Describe how reentry affects more than those sent to prison • Argue for building on insights from practitioners and scholars • Identify ways to improve outcomes for ex-prisoners, victims, and communities and increase government accountability and efficiency	Understand prisoner reentry, reentry policy, and how to improve reentry outcomes and, more broadly, criminal justice systems and policy

is appropriate. If it is, how do we best reduce offending among this group relative to, say, murderers or sexual offenders? In a related vein, to the extent that the characteristics of inmates vary and that this variation is related to in-prison and post-release behavior, policies must address these characteristics to improve outcomes. We argue that the substantial heterogeneity of the inmate population indeed requires such policies; the risk otherwise is a costly investment in imprisonment for little to no effect.

Second, we argue that improvements in reentry outcomes require efforts that address the broad array of forces that contribute to offending and crime and to punishment policies. For example, prison in and of itself may do little to affect recidivism. Rather, the experiences in prison and the conditions in the communities to which ex-prisoners return may exert a significant if not greater influence.[27] Understanding such possibilities, which is easy to do when we examine reentry from different vantage points, constitutes a central avenue by which to improve reentry outcomes and to advance scholarship on the causes of offending.

Third, we argue that such perspectives highlight the importance of looking beyond the individuals who go to prison to the other individuals affected—such as victims, families, and communities—and examining the panoply of considerations that arise when we do so. For example, an exclusive focus on prisoners neglects the fact that the growth in incarceration institutionalizes more of an offender-based rather than a victim-based system of justice. In so doing, it potentially deprioritizes victims and, indeed, the very concept of justice. Certainly, punishing individuals may satisfy some victims and communities, but it frequently can do little to restore the harm that these groups experience. A focus on prisoners, too, neglects the fact that the United States embarked on a set of policies that prioritized punishment rather than the equivalent of a balanced portfolio of financial investments. Put differently, we can focus on more and tougher incarceration or we can seek approaches that may satisfy better the many demands of the criminal justice system, including the call to increase public safety and achieve that ephemeral but no-less-important goal of justice. And we can seek approaches that achieve these outcomes while minimizing costs and harms to prisoners, victims, communities, and society at large.

Fourth, we argue that further substantial advances in reentry policy and scholarship require a better integration of insights both from practitioners and from scholars. Here, again, when we examine reentry from different perspectives and when we attend carefully to the insights from the research that has accumulated in recent years, it is evident that a significant disjuncture between theory and practice exists. As but one example, a considerable amount of risk prediction occurs with little guidance or insight from criminological theory. At the same time, hewing to one theory or another will not likely assist much with informing decisions about which inmates or ex-prisoners warrant more supervision or specific services or treatment. Better linkages between the efforts of those who work in corrections and those who work in academia can help to bridge the gap and result in policies and practices that may be more effective. We do not hew toward a primarily theoretical orientation or practitioner orientation. Rather, the book is informed by and argues for the systematic integration of theoretical insights from criminology and other disciplines and the insights that policy makers and practitioners have about criminal justice and corrections.

Finally, building on these arguments, we argue that a wide range of different approaches can be used to effectively reduce crime and recidivism and to improve other reentry outcomes, such as increased employment and reduced homelessness and drug abuse. We also argue that viable approaches exist to improve cost-efficiency and government accountability and to create justice that focuses not only on felons but also on victims and communities.

CRIMINOLOGICAL "VERSUS" CRIMINAL JUSTICE THEORY AND RESEARCH

In this book, we draw on theory and research to arrive at insights about reentry and, more generally, criminal justice and corrections. We also seek to identify ways in which theory—the more formal statement of how or why certain phenomena occur—might be advanced by a focus on reentry. Theory, research, and policy should, in our view, go hand and hand, but they do not always do so. We should be focused not only on crime but also on policy responses to prevent and respond to crime.

Criminology emerged in part from a focus on applied, pragmatic questions about controlling crime and promoting public safety. This emphasis reflected the origins of the American Society of Criminology (ASC), which emerged in 1941 largely through the impetus of August Vollmer, who had been a police chief.[28] Criminology transitioned into a discipline of academic standing by emphasizing questions about the causes of behavior and, in particular, of offending. In so doing, it sought to become less of a professional enterprise and more of a scholarly one that addressed basic scientific questions rather than pragmatic, or applied, policy-relevant questions.[29]

In recent decades, it seems that the field has moved to a middle ground. We can see it reflected, for example, in the fact that ASC presidential addresses frequently call for bridging the worlds of theory and practice.[30] We can see it, too, in the observations of those who receive the ASC's Edwin H. Sutherland Award, which is given to those who have made "outstanding contributions to theory or research in criminology on the etiology of criminal and deviant behavior, the criminal justice system, corrections, law, or justice."[31] In his Sutherland Award essay, for example, David Garland expressly called for greater attention to understanding changes in penal policies.[32] And in Francis Cullen's Sutherland Award essay, he called for scholarship aimed at using a science of offending to develop evidence-based approaches to reducing offending.[33]

Even so, a tension exists in the field, one reflected by the names of programs. Some refer to themselves as departments of "criminology" or of "criminal justice" or, in an attempt perhaps to be more inclusive, of "criminology and criminal justice." Such distinctions matter to faculty. For example, some prefer to see themselves as scientists who pursue pure knowledge and equate such efforts with "criminology." Others view themselves as focused on the nitty-gritty problems of policy and professional practice and relate more to the term "criminal justice." This tension can be seen in the names of the two prominent criminological associations in the United States—the ASC (with the emphasis on "criminology") and the Academy of Criminal Justice Sciences (ACJS) (with the emphasis on "criminal justice").

Our view is that the divide makes little sense. Theory is implicated in all that we do, whether as scientists or individuals in our day-to-day lives. We may not always call our efforts to understand the world "theories," but they are just that, theories. The most theoretical study frequently is motivated by, and may have direct or indirect implications for, policy and practice. Conversely, even the most avowedly exploratory empirical study of some aspect of the criminal justice system involves theory. The selection of topics, measures, independent variables, control variables, and the like all require recourse to theory, whether it is articulated or not.[34] That is all to the good. The history of science provides repeated instances of advances in knowledge that arrive from many directions, whether they be efforts to develop better measuring devices, create better bridges, or test theories that seemed fanciful at best until someone devised a way to evaluate them.[35]

In our view, greater scientific advances in criminology and criminal justice occur when all areas of study, theoretical or applied, are embraced as opportunities simultaneously to develop theory and to improve policy and practice. Accordingly, we see little need to distinguish between "criminology" and "criminal justice." Even so, such phrasing permeates academic writing and institutions and agency descriptions. For example, Peter Kraska has emphasized that for many scholars, "'theory' is . . . assumed to be concerned with crime and crime rates," while the study of criminal justice is "tacitly, and sometimes explicitly, relegated to the narrow role of evaluative and descriptive scholarship."[36]

We view criminology and criminal justice as investigating the same universe of questions. These include questions about the causes of offending and of variation or changes in crime rates, the effectiveness of different sanctions on offending (at the individual level) and crime rates (at the macro level), the emergence or continuity of varying types of punishment regimes, organizational operations in corrections and why actors or groups within them act as they do, and more. We are not alone in this view. For example, *Criminology,* the flagship journal for the ASC, publishes studies not only on the causes of offending but also on the causes of variation in sentencing. *Justice Quarterly,* the flagship journal for the ACJS, regularly publishes studies on these same topics. Accordingly, notwithstanding the claims of some scholars, the actual practice of research by "criminologists" spans a wide range of topics.

A focus on reentry illustrates why we and others take the above stance. Reentry clearly involves a focus on offending. The criminal justice system arrests, convicts, and sentences people who commit crimes. Certainly, scholars and practitioners alike can embrace an effort to understand the causes of offending, what traditionally has been viewed as a "basic" scientific pursuit. The scholar might focus primarily on theorizing offending and testing competing theories, while the practitioner might focus on implications of a given theory. But scholars have long held an interest in understanding the use of formal and informal social control in society. Indeed, that focus generates a steady stream of scholarship in criminology, sociology, law and society, and other related disciplines. It, too, stands as a form of "pure" science. Yet the focus could not be of more relevance for policy. When we understand why a given penal practice targets some groups more than others, we have a basis for informing discussions about changing it.

What, though, of studies of the police, the courts, jails, prisons, probation, parole, and other dimensions of criminal justice or correctional systems? Here, again, an endless array of questions exist, many of which focus directly or indirectly on offending or law-making or some aspect of organizational practice or decision making. In each instance, scholars may tack into the questions from overtly theoretical directions or on-the-ground policy-and-practice directions. The end result remains the same: Studies occur and we gain some form of insight into the world of crime and justice. Sometimes large strides in theory or practice occur, and sometimes not. Betting on which type of study—theoretical or applied—will yield noteworthy increases in knowledge or will yield improvements in policy will not likely succeed, not if the history of science is any indication.

With these observations made, we will say that many pragmatic questions about the criminal justice system have been neglected by the field. In academic settings, greater acclaim frequently goes to those who develop or test theories, and "theory" often is equated with the study of crime and crime rates.[37] That has much less to do with objective scientific merit than with sociological influences on topic selection, available data, methodologies, and the like.

Here, again, a focus on reentry proves instructive. On the face of it, no objective basis exists to determine which of the following questions is more important for science or policy: What causes some individuals to specialize in offending? Why do some convicted sex offenders recidivate at high rates while others do not? Why do some courts frequently employ prison sentences while others avoid them? Why do some states pass laws that seem to affect disproportionately, whether intentionally or not, minorities? What affects inmate culture or correctional officer culture, and how do these cultures influence behavior or system-wide patterns of order? Under what conditions do particular administrative approaches to operating prisons create greater order or disorder? Why are the people who are least likely to be victims of crimes sometimes the most punitive in their policy preferences? Why do some policy makers or states or agencies attend more to a balance of ideological and evidence-based considerations in devising policies and practices while others give greater weight to ideology? More broadly, what affects the decision making of individuals throughout the entire criminal justice system?[38] What makes some communities better able to adopt anticrime efforts, to withstand large declines in economic conditions, or to adapt to large increases in returning inmate populations?

In our view, science and policy are equally well advanced by attending to all of these types of questions. For that reason, we approach the topic of reentry in this book from many perspectives to understand it better. We do so, too, to argue for research that seeks to create theory about and greater insight into all aspects of crime and the criminal justice system. At the same time, we argue for a line of research that seeks to shed light on the myriad questions and challenges that confront policy makers, criminal justice and corrections officials, and the many individuals in the trenches who seek to improve the effectiveness and efficiency of our federal, state, and local justice systems. In every instance, the scientific bar remains the same—use the best theory and research methodologies to investigate questions. The end goals are, however, broader. They include knowledge creation ("science for science's sake") and insights that policy makers and practitioners can use to inform their decisions.

TERMINOLOGY AND SCOPE

In this book, we focus broadly on prisoner reentry. That includes a focus not only on prisoners who are released and their future criminal behavior but also on changes in reentry trends and policies, the factors that give rise to them, the different effects of reentry on those who leave prison, and their families and the communities to which they return, as well as victims. The reason is simple: Reentry involves much more than the release of prisoners into society. It entails a discussion about how the country arrived at a place where it leaned, in historically unprecedented ways, on incarceration as a mode of punishment. It entails a discussion about the good but also the bad that can result from incarceration and about consequences that go well beyond recidivism and that affect groups other than ex-prisoners. To focus only on ex-prisoners would be too narrow an approach. In addition, we would miss an opportunity to examine critical questions about what we expect from punishment, the operations of the criminal justice system, the effectiveness of decision making throughout this system, the ability of the criminal justice system to affect society through diverse mechanisms, and more.

What exactly, though, is "reentry"? It can be defined variously.[39] No one definition is more correct than another, just more or less encompassing. When we discuss reentry, for example, we might refer to virtually anyone who has ever been in prison, whether the incarceration occurred a year earlier or 50 years earlier. We could focus only on individuals coming out of prison and not jail. We could focus only on those released to some form of supervision. In this book, we take an inclusive approach, with reentry referring to the release of individuals from some form of incarceration and the experiences and impacts that arise during the days, weeks, months, and even years after release. These impacts may occur among ex-prisoners or others, including their families and communities. The bulk of empirical research to date has focused primarily on prison releasees, but that is slowly changing. In addition, most research examines reentry for delimited periods of time, such as the experience of individuals in the year or two after release. That, too, is changing. In the discussions that follow, we will not be limited by empirical research. We will draw on it where relevant and go beyond it where it does not exist. In the latter instance, important theoretical, conceptual, or pragmatic policy questions will be examined even if research does not yet allow us to identify answers.

This point warrants emphasis—one of the central contributions of scholarship on reentry in recent years lies in the identification of important new questions, many of which have profound implications for policy. As but one example, scholars have highlighted the ways in which reentry may differentially affect communities. What is this variable effect? How and why does it arise? How might reentry be structured in ways to minimize harmful effects on communities? Such questions may seem straightforward. Basic. Yet they previously remained largely unasked.

What else is meant by "reentry"? Reentry refers, too, to a process or set of experiences.[40] It is not a goal or an outcome. By highlighting that individuals who leave prison go through experiences, the term draws our attention to the potential for those who leave prison to affect or to be affected by the settings to which they go and the people with whom they come into contact. Reentry is a dynamic event, not a static moment. Those who leave prison, for example, do not necessarily have a constant level of risk of offending. Rather, the experiences that they face may alter that risk in favorable or unfavorable ways. These experiences, too, may affect or interact with one another in contributing to finding a home or a job, successfully returning to family, and more.

Reentry does not here refer to "reintegration." Scholars employ the latter term to mean a variety of things. It typically refers to the idea that an individual returns to their social network or community and their established place in society. The image that comes to mind consists of individuals hard at work. They are part of a pro-social family. Yet they commit a crime and so are sent off to prison to be rehabilitated. Then they reintegrate. That is, they pick up where they left off. In many ways, though, the term leads us astray. For example, many people who go to prison were not "integrated" in the first place. They may not have had jobs or housing, they may not have been in the running for parent-of-the-year or friend-of-the-year awards, and they may not have been well-equipped to function in mainstream society. Accordingly, *re*-integration seems a bit of a misnomer. At the same time, while it may lead us to ask questions perhaps about treatment needs, educational needs, and the like, it does not lead us to view the matter much like an anthropologist might: What happens to these people when they leave? What conditions or experiences makes for successful transitions? What ripple effects arise when ex-prisoners return to communities? By contrast, a focus on reentry—the process of reentry—leads more directly to asking such questions and, by extension, seeing the nuances, complexity, and the fuller range of consequences of incarceration.

What terminology should we use when discussing the people who go to prison? The risk in labels is that they carry a great deal of baggage. To be called a "criminal" is to conjure up many associations. Movies help (or hurt) us here. The scary offender who lacks remorse comes to mind. But someone who commits a crime is more than a "criminal." We all occupy many social roles, each with connotations and assumptions that may be correct but frequently fall short. The man walking through the grocery store with a 9-year-old having a pleasant conversation presumably is a father, and presumably a nice one, too, given the tenor of the conversation. That same man without his son—who is he? What is his character? Here we flounder and search for any cue that might tell us something about him. The problem, of course, is that our assumptions may be wildly off target. When they are correct, we give them greater weight and trust our judgment more. When they are incorrect, we write it off to the fact that, well, it was just a guess.

We all know, in short, that labels matter and that each of us consists of more than what any one classification suggests. That holds as well for the individuals who go to prison. They are more than "criminals" or "inmates" or "ex-prisoners." The "more than" is important here. It helps to humanize these individuals so that we can see ourselves in them, understand them better, and potentially devise policies that may be more effective. It is important, too, so that even if we cannot relate to or understand them, we can see the potential for a range of social forces to affect them. Without such recognition, we are left with a shell—a "criminal" who is criminal in character and intent. What we fail then to see is the fact that criminal behavior by this individual does not have to be a foregone conclusion and that many factors may contribute to his or her offending. Homelessness, unemployment, neurological impairments, and more may be at play.

None of these factors need constitute grounds for sympathy or provide grounds for in any way excusing crime. Rather, they simply point to a pragmatic issue that almost all of us, regardless of political orientation, can agree is important. If a given factor affects offending, if it does so in a sizable way, and if we can do something about it, well, then, we should consider the factor when devising policies that punish, reduce offending, and benefit society in other ways if possible. There is nothing inherently liberal or conservative in such a statement. Indeed, given how divisive and ideological debates about crime policy can be, our avowed intention throughout the book is to remain on the pragmatic, non-ideological question of what can be done to improve reentry outcomes that benefit society. Productive debates about policy are more likely, in our view, when policy makers and the public focus on evidence about what works rather than on ideologically based preferences that lead to assumptions about what must be effective.

For these reasons, we endeavor here to vary the terminology in the book. To refer to "individuals who are released from prison" has the virtue of avoiding the label "inmate" or "prisoner." It also is cumbersome. So, we also will use shorthand terms—offenders, inmates, prisoners, ex-prisoners. However, we emphasize here that the terms serve only to identify groups of individuals, not necessarily characteristics associated with them. Indeed, in the book, we emphasize that although a general profile of the "typical" person who goes to prison can be identified, considerable variation in this profile exists and has important consequences for what the reentry experience will be like and what outcomes may result.

A final observation—the book focuses on reentry, and in so doing focuses on reentry to society after a period of incarceration. What, though, of individuals who are convicted and sentenced but who received some other sanction? Many convicted felons, for example, receive a sentence to probation rather than to prison. Do they experience reentry? That is, do they undergo experiences similar to what individuals released from prison experience? Perhaps. For example, they face similar "invisible" punishments, such as restricted rights to vote and limited access to public housing. They may face barriers to employment due to having to report a felony record. There may be stigma associated with the felony record that affects them. In these and other ways, as we discuss in Chapters 6 and 9, there may be parallels to what ex-prisoners face after release. This focus serves to highlight a more general question of central relevance to the book: What do we gain by primarily get-tough approaches to crime?

ORGANIZATION OF THE BOOK

The remainder of the book is organized into eight chapters, each with discussion questions that can be used to reflect on the material or to guide discussion of it, and a concluding chapter. Full disclosure should be made up front: This book is about reentry, but it is also about something more. The focus on reentry serves a strategic purpose. It provides a lens through which to highlight the need for criminal justice and correctional system policy that more cost-efficiently achieves justice and improves public safety and well-being. Put differently, if we want to understand the reentry experience and how to improve reentry outcomes, we need to know what happens well before prisons release inmates. At the same time, if we want to understand crime and correctional policy, we need to understand why reentry has become a critical policy problem in recent decades. We therefore begin the book by describing the historical context that has given rise to "mass reentry" and the reasons for this change. With that context established, we then focus more directly on reentry. The specific chapters proceed as follows and culminate with an assessment of what needs to happen to improve not only prisoner reentry but also criminal justice and corrections.

Chapter 2 discusses historical trends in prisoner reentry and reentry policy. In so doing, it highlights the considerable changes that have occurred. This discussion situates mass incarceration and reentry in a historical context and at the same time highlights the varying approaches used to combat crime. In turn, it establishes a framework for identifying ways to understand and improve punishment and a range of outcomes associated with reentry.

Chapter 3 discusses the causes of mass incarceration and how many of these factors, more than any science-based rationale, have contributed to investment in a less-than-ideal portfolio of sanctioning. The chapter extends prior work in several ways, including identifying how systems-level forces contribute to reentry and problems associated with it.

Chapter 4 provides a profile of the inmate population, the "typical" inmate, and the salience of this profile for reentry. The primary focus here centers on reasons why we should care about the inmate profile as well as the importance of identifying and monitoring not only inmate characteristics but also the factors that influence the profile of the prison and reentry population. The chapter highlights the considerable disadvantage of the prisoner population and of the communities from which they come. It highlights, too, the use of tougher and more incarceration for certain groups, such as drug offenders. Not least, it highlights that silver-bullet solutions to reentry do not neatly fit with the heterogeneous set of characteristics and problems associated with different reentry groups. These observations align with the argument that understanding reentry and improving reentry outcomes requires systemic, nuanced approaches that draw on evidence about what works. It requires an understanding of the lives and contexts of the individuals sentenced to prison. It requires, too, understanding the social forces that contribute to changes in the types of individuals flowing into and out of the prison system.

Chapter 5 describes the prison experience and how it may affect reentry outcomes. In so doing, it points to the heterogeneity inherent to the prison experience. We argue that different types of prison experiences can affect in-prison behavior (e.g., misconduct) and reentry outcomes (e.g., recidivism). Despite the increased attention given to mass incarceration, relatively little scholarship exists that systematically describes inmate experiences and how these may affect behavior during and after incarceration. The chapter addresses this issue directly and investigates questions that emanate from a focus on the prison experience. For example, how do inmates and ex-prisoners perceive themselves and the prison experience, and why do such perceptions matter? Also, prison should punish, but what exactly should the punishment involve? Of central policy relevance, what effect does incarceration in fact have on recidivism? What types of accountability exist to ensure that abuses, which are likely in coercive settings, do not occur? The chapter examines the prison experience to address such questions and to identify tensions in punishment policy in America. For example, punishment that leads to more recidivism is clearly problematic. Why spend money for more crime? At the same time, we punish to obtain some measure of retribution. But how do we know when we have the appropriate amount or retribution and reduced recidivism, especially if trade-offs between the two are involved? In a related vein, what exactly do we, as a society, want the prison experience to entail?

Chapter 6 focuses on the reentry experience and challenges that ex-prisoners face upon release. Scholarship has identified many facets of the reentry experience that create grounds for concern. Homelessness within the first few weeks of release from prison is, for example, problematic. It runs counter to what most citizens would seem to want from punishment. It places a burden on communities. And it reduces the life chances of those who wind up homeless. However, obtaining housing stands as but one of a long list of challenges ex-prisoners face. We can choose not to care about these dimensions. The individuals who come out of prison committed crimes after all. But if society pays the cost of unsuccessful reentry, then we all should care. The chapter advances this argument. In so doing, it examines the logic of invisible punishments and the many barriers to successful reentry that exist. As part of this discussion, we describe the reentry process and its implications for ex-prisoners, families, communities, and, in turn, the criminal justice system. The discussion provides the groundwork for identifying ways to improve reentry outcomes and to advance scholarship on the causes of desistance from, for many ex-prisoners, a lifetime of offending.

Chapter 7 examines an issue central to almost any criminal justice policy discussion—recidivism and efforts to predict who will reoffend. On the face of it, scholarship on recidivism would seem to be advanced. There have been, after all, many decades to study it. In fact, though, the understanding of desistance remains very much a nascent science. As but one illustration, risk prediction instruments frequently accord little with criminological theory and include few if any measures that capture an individual's prison behavior. Put differently, in making a prediction about future behavior, states and local jurisdictions frequently ignore immediate past behavior, even though it may be a good predictor of the future. They ignore, too, how local community conditions may influence the likelihood of recidivism. The result is less accurate risk prediction. Another important result is that we are led to focus exclusively on the individual rather than his or her social context when designing interventions. Other outcomes besides recidivism—such as homelessness, unemployment, mental illness, and more—warrant attention. Even so, recidivism constitutes a central defining outcome of interest when discussing criminal justice. The chapter discusses these issues and argues that effective reentry practices require careful consideration of multiple factors. At the same time, it highlights the importance of ties between practitioner and scholarly communities. It also highlights that risk prediction leads us primarily to focus on offenders when, in many instances, a focus on improving our criminal justice and correctional systems, as well as our laws, may be the route to greater increases in public safety.

Chapter 8 examines a diverse set of reentry populations to highlight the need for policies that reflect the distinct backgrounds, needs, prison experiences, and family and community contexts of these varied groups. In part, the chapter serves to debunk myths perpetuated in media accounts. Contrary to many such accounts, criminals come from a variety of backgrounds and the causes of their offending vary greatly. Their incarceration experiences vary. The effectiveness of incarceration for different groups may vary as well, along with their reentry experiences and challenges. The chapter examines several demographic groups (the young, females, and minorities) in detail and then discusses several other groups, including supermax inmates, drug abusers, those with mental illness, and those with learning disabilities. It does so to illustrate one of the book's central arguments—that get-tough sanctioning has had unintended effects that remain largely unappreciated and that undermine the goals of the criminal justice system.

Chapter 9 discusses reentry policy and what can be done to improve reentry outcomes. The good news is that remarkable advances in scholarship have led to considerable insight about policies, programs, and practices that *don't* work, those that are promising, and those that *do* work. The bad news is that much more progress needs to be made, including less investment in ineffective and costly policies that create collateral consequences. There is, as well, far too much investment in approaches that rest on weak theoretical foundations and limited to no empirical research.

In this chapter, we discuss the good news and bad news and end on an optimistic note concerning the many different possibilities for improving knowledge and reentry policy and practice. In so doing, we argue *against* relying on silver-bullet solutions, such as mass incarceration or specific types of programs that are used exclusively. At the same time, we argue *for* relying on a diverse portfolio of strategies. Any such portfolio should focus on policies, programs, and practices that can be promoted by different stakeholder groups and that can target diverse areas, such as drug abuse, education, and employment, to improve public safety and reentry. The chapter highlights the need not only for effective reentry strategies but also for those that improve outcomes at the least costs. That idea is common sense. But common sense has not featured prominently in federal and state punishment and reentry policy making, though exceptions certainly exist.

We argue, too, for broadening our focus from one that centers primarily on reentry policy to one that underscores the need for a system of justice that serves victims and communities as well or better than it serves offenders. America has no "victim justice systems" or "community justice systems" at present. Rather, it has a "criminal justice system" that focuses primarily on crime and criminals.

The end goal, however, of a criminal justice system lies in advancing broader interests like achieving justice, reducing crime and recidivism, and supporting victims, families, and communities. Any discussion focused on improving reentry policy necessarily, in our view, requires considering how the entire criminal justice system can be improved to fulfill its broader and arguably more important set of obligations. It requires, too, investing in research that can fulfill policy-maker calls for promoting government accountability.

Finally, Chapter 10 returns to the book's central argument and ends optimistically. In it, we emphasize that, as earlier chapters demonstrate, a wide range of approaches can be pursued to improve punishment policies, prisoner reentry, and, more broadly, criminal justice and corrections. These approaches will not be magically well-implemented or successful. Indeed, they will take considerable effort and will require policy making and practices that prioritize research. No silver-bullet approach will work that is so effective in theory—or from a "common sense" perspective—that we need no or minimal research to defend it. Mass incarceration serves as a cautionary lesson in support of that assessment. The solution? Careful, sustained, research-based policy making and practice. Many local, state, and federal agencies have taken steps in that direction, and that truly is grounds for optimism.

CHAPTER 2

Historical Trends in Corrections and Reentry Policy and Practice

In this chapter, we examine historical trends in prisoner populations and in reentry policy and practice. The chapter provides context for understanding and examining contemporary approaches to punishment and, in particular, the annual reentry back into communities of between 600,000 and 700,000 former inmates. In so doing, the chapter highlights that in the past several decades, the United States entered an era not only of "mass incarceration" but also, more generally, of "mass corrections." We discuss the fact of large-scale quantitative changes in punishment in America and highlight that they constitute only part of changes that have occurred.

More broadly, new restrictions and changes to felons' rights—such as the elimination of the right to vote or to access public housing—created an era of punitive punishment, what has been described as the "punitive turn" in American criminal justice or, as Jeremy Travis has characterized it, the "resurgence of retributivism."[1] The result? Before, during, and after reentry a series of forces, including heightened surveillance and decreased assistance, seemingly conspire to inhibit the possibility of ex-prisoners becoming pro-social, contributing members of society. As we will discuss, the underlying theme that unites the various changes involves an almost religious commitment to specific and general deterrence and to retribution. Scare offenders, punish them and then punish more, and they and others will refrain from offending. Concomitantly, society will feel satisfied that retribution has occurred. Such beliefs have a solid logical basis. Indeed, perhaps because they seem intuitive it can be difficult to see where the reasoning goes awry.

One problem, which we touch on here and examine in subsequent chapters, is the flawed reasoning and lack of solid scientific evidence. There exists little credible empirical research that shows even moderate crime-reducing effects of incarceration, much less of lengthy terms of incarceration, or that demonstrates what types and amounts of punishments lead the public to feel that "sufficient" retribution has occurred. We know little, too, about the precise conditions under which deterrence operates. The situation may be likened to one where physicians have strong opinions about what works but lack evidence about what in fact effectively treats an illness. Many medical treatments may be ineffective or even worsen outcomes under certain conditions. Consider the flu vaccine—if administered to healthy individuals, it can help to prevent influenza or an intense bout of it. If given to small children or those with weakened immune systems or certain allergies, the vaccine can be deadly. Scholars have begun to amass knowledge about conditions that may lead to improved outcomes for offenders, but much remains unknown and uncertain.[2]

In addition, a near-exclusive focus on deterrence and retribution may blind us to factors that may offset their benefits. Punishment, for example, that eliminates the ability of an individual to obtain gainful employment may increase rather than decrease recidivism. It may also create harms for that individual's family members, particularly their children.[3] A central task, then, lies in identifying the precise conditions under which desired outcomes occur and adverse outcomes do not occur or are minimized.

The discussion highlights that there is nothing necessary or "natural" about mass incarceration or a range of related get-tough policies that have emerged since the 1980s. In a very real sense, the country chose to embark on a set of deterrence-based and retribution-based policies in a context in which many other possible crime control and punishment approaches could have been pursued simultaneously. It did so, notably, or ironically, at the very same time that calls for greater government accountability and evidence-based practice became common. And these policies have arguably locked the country into ineffective and expensive punishment that will take decades to be "right-sized."[4] More balanced approaches to justice can be found, and many states have been moving in such a direction. But a "tidal" force exists that inhibits the rate at which right-sizing can occur. If, for example, a state quadruples its prison system and then seeks to pursue a more balanced approach to sanctioning, it remains constrained by the fact of the fourfold increase in incarceration.

To make these points and to set the stage for discussions in subsequent chapters, we first discuss prominent changes in corrections and in reentry policy and practice. We then discuss the theory, or causal logic, of mass incarceration and of sanctions that aim to be "tough on crime." As a logical corollary, we examine the implications of the sizable changes in corrections and reentry that have occurred in recent decades. Juxtaposed against this discussion lies the broader question of what the public wants from punishment and what is realistic to expect from it.

TRENDS IN CORRECTIONAL POPULATIONS: THE ERA OF MASS CORRECTIONS

In the previous chapter, we highlighted that the state and federal prison population increased fourfold over a 30-year period beginning in 1980. With over 2.3 million individuals in prison or jail and an incarceration rate higher than that of any other country in the world, the United States stands alone in its intensive reliance on imprisonment. This change has spurred on a now-voluminous literature on mass incarceration.

In addition to mass incarceration, there has been a concomitant rise in the use of probation—the workhorse of the correctional system—and parole, as can be seen in Figure 2.1. Close to 5 million individuals are on these two forms of correctional supervision, and 4 million of them are on probation, the main alternative sanction to prison. Probation alone, which went from approximately 1 million in 1980 to almost 4 million in 2012, thus has served as the main driver of national corrections trends and, in turn, of what we are calling "mass corrections."[5]

These numbers do not tell the full story. As David Garland has written, "Whereas in other nations, and in earlier periods of American history, probation and parole aimed to promote rehabilitation and resettlement (or 'reentry' as it is now known), in America today they are oriented toward surveillance, policing and risk management."[6] Put differently, probation and parole populations have greatly expanded in recent decades, and they have done so at a rate that far exceeds increases in crime rates. At the same time, the nature of probation and parole changed. Instead of the historical dual emphasis on supervision *and* assistance, the emphasis has turned primarily to supervision.[7] This change has occurred alongside of an increasingly tougher set of sentencing laws and courts that are more focused on retribution.

In short, over a span of just thirty years, America transformed its correctional system, making it at once much larger and more punitive.[8] This era of mass corrections constitutes the equivalent of a national and state-level experiment whose effects on crime, communities, and other state functions, such as education and social welfare, remain yet to be fully understood.

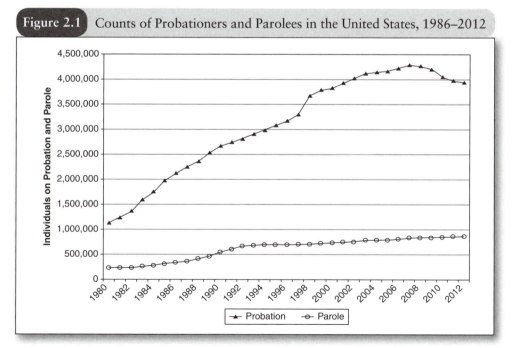

Figure 2.1   Counts of Probationers and Parolees in the United States, 1986–2012

Sources: Glaze (2011); Glaze and Parks (2012); Glaze and Herberman (2013).

The implications of this experiment for American society will likely gain considerably more attention from researchers and policy makers in the coming years.

But the era of mass corrections holds special relevance for reentry. Why? As we discuss below, states did not just expand their prison system capacity. They revoked those on probation and parole more aggressively, thereby fueling further prison growth. Among parolees, the shift in the nature of supervision altered not only potential recidivism patterns but also other outcomes, such as unemployment and housing. Below, we discuss these changes as well as a wide range of additional policy shifts that altered the nature of corrections and, in particular, reentry for those coming out of prison.

TRENDS IN REENTRY POLICY AND PRACTICE

To this point, we have focused primarily on the fact that the last three decades have been witness to large-scale growth in prisons and, more generally, correctional systems. The emergence of mass incarceration, and, in turn, mass reentry, stands of interest in its own right. It signals, for example, a punitive turn in American criminal justice.

In reality, though, this shift can be seen not just in prison growth. It can be seen, too, in punishment and social policies more broadly.[9] As Alex Ewald and Christopher Uggen have emphasized, tougher punishments and restrictions apply not only to those who have felony convictions but also to those who fall short of conviction.[10] For example, in New York City, a prosecutor may evict individuals from public housing when they issue an arrest warrant if they believe that the individuals are engaging in narcotics activity.[11]

Here, we focus on additional punishments and restrictions that have emerged in recent decades, emphasizing those that directly affect or implicate the individuals who go to and leave prison. Many of these punishments and restrictions have fueled prison growth. However, they can be viewed, too, as independent indicators of the punitive turn in American penology. Individuals no longer "do time" in prison and reenter society with a fresh chance. Instead, as Joan Petersilia has observed, they, along with other convicted felons, face "consequences that continue long after a sentence has been served."[12] The consequences are many and stem from efforts by the federal government and state governments over the past three decades to enact what Travis and others have termed "invisible punishments" that aim both to punish and to control felons.[13]

Trend 1: Sentencing Policies

Sentencing laws and practices in the United States have varied greatly over time. Contrary to some accounts, sentences were largely fixed in colonial times, that is, judges had little discretion in modifying sentences. That changed. Eventually judicial discretion emerged as central to the sentencing of criminals, as sanctioning came to emphasize individualized treatment that would incorporate rehabilitation as a means of reducing offending. By the 1980s, the pendulum had swung back, due in part to concerns about inconsistency and unwarranted disparities in sentencing.[14]

The shift was dramatic. The federal Sentencing Reform Act in 1984 spurred states on to develop various types of sentencing guidelines or systems. Fundamentally, this change involved a transition from indeterminate sentencing to determinate sentencing. No longer would it be possible for two similar cases to result in highly dissimilar sentences. That, at least, was the hope of proponents for the changes.

But the shift did not only involve a move toward determinate sentencing. It involved a call for more severe punishment, including lengthier prison terms. Policy makers achieved their goal. Figure 2.2 shows that the average time served by the time of release among state prisoners increased throughout the 1990s before then stabilizing. For example, from 1990 to 2000, the average time served increased by over 30 percent, from 22 months to 29 months.

Sentencing reforms also eliminated or reduced judicial discretion in sentencing. They mandated specific ranges of prison terms depending on the type of offense, presence of a gun, history of previous offending, and other such considerations. "Three-strikes" laws, which require extended prison sentences if an individual has committed two previous felonies and is convicted of a third, and "truth-in-sentencing laws," which require completion of longer percentages of prison sentences in actual incarceration, illustrate the trend. These laws targeted so-called habitual and violent offenders but also swept

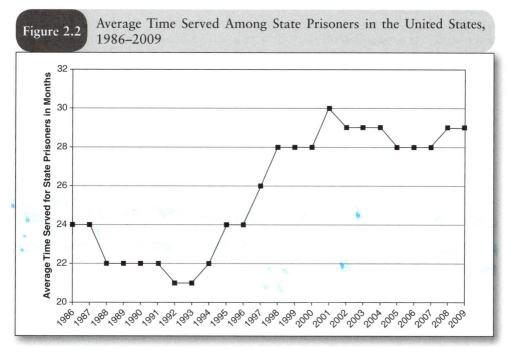

Figure 2.2 Average Time Served Among State Prisoners in the United States, 1986–2009

Source: Bonczar (2011).

into their purview those who committed other crimes, such as burglary and any of a wide range of felony offenses. Specific statutory sentences thus replaced judicial discretion.

Actually, prosecutorial discretion replaced judicial discretion. By introducing sentencing guidelines, policy makers gave greater authority to prosecutors, who typically have considerable leeway in determining the charges to file. Courts resolve the vast bulk of criminal cases through plea bargaining. The end result was that prosecutors assumed a far greater role in sentencing, essentially exercising both executive and judicial authority in the handling of criminal cases.[15]

This situation affected the front end of the prison system and also the back end. Sentencing reforms ushered in an era in which parole boards enjoyed less discretion about when individuals should be released. Indeed, some states eliminated parole board decision making by having release decisions governed by law.[16]

Mass incarceration and reentry, then, have been spurred, or paralleled, by a shift in sentencing philosophy that affected criminal sanctions and responses to parole violations. Indeterminate sentencing and the discretion of judicial and parole boards—which previously emphasized rehabilitation and reintegration and were guided by an ideal of individualized justice—have largely been supplanted by a fundamentally different approach. As articulated by lawmakers and reflected in legislation, the emphasis has turned toward retribution and "tough" responses to violations of parole as well as probation.

Figure 2.3 illustrates the change. It presents trends in state and federal prison admissions over the past 35 years. We can see that the percentage of admissions to prison stemming from a violation of supervision conditions rose steadily during the 1970s, 1980s, and 1990s before then tapering off. Since the 1990s, approximately one-third of state and federal admissions have resulted from parole violations. Indeed, estimates by Steven Raphael and Michael Stoll suggest that if parole failure rates had remained constant between 1980 and 2003, the incarceration rate in 2003 would have been approximately 20 percent lower.[17] What happened? States and the federal government toughened their approach to parolees. Where previously a technical violation might result in a warning or some type of intermediate sanction, it was likely instead to result in a return to prison. Since 2010, however, the percentage of new admissions due to parole violations has decreased, perhaps in response to efforts among states to reduce their prison populations.

To put the changes in perspective, it helps to consider the many goals that we have for sentencing. First, we typically want some measure of retribution, or "just desserts"—punishment for punishment's sake.[18] Second, we want public safety through reduced offending among those who are sanctioned and among those who are not. How such reductions arise can vary. The theoretical mechanisms include the following. (a) Sanctions can incapacitate individuals, at least for the period during which they reside in custody or are supervised or subject to various restrictions. (b) They may reduce offending through specific deterrence and general deterrence, respectively. (c) They may do so through rehabilitation of sanctioned offenders. (d) They may do so through restorative justice mechanisms, including "reintegrative shaming." (e) Not least, they may

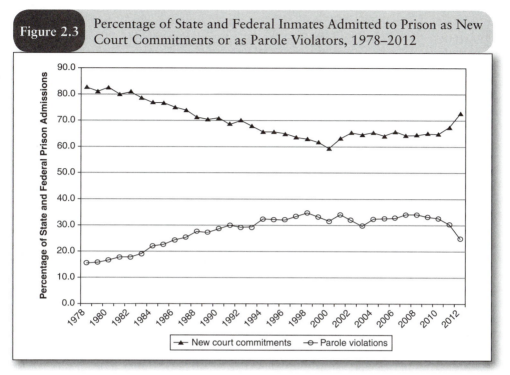

Figure 2.3 Percentage of State and Federal Inmates Admitted to Prison as New Court Commitments or as Parole Violators, 1978–2012

Source: Carson and Golinelli (2013a, b).

do so through educating the public about laws, what is referred to as an educative effect. Here, punishment serves to clarify and reinforce the importance of specific values or beliefs.[19]

The challenge for states and the federal government lies in how to balance the goals of retribution and public safety and the different strategies for achieving them. In a very rapid period of time, beginning in the 1980s, the country appeared to prioritize increasingly retribution and, simultaneously, two strategies for achieving the goal of public safety—incapacitation and deterrence. This punitive turn toward mass incarceration and reentry constituted but one part of a larger cultural and political shift in the exercise of state power and in the strategies used to sentence criminals, whose causes we discuss in the next chapter.

Trend 2: Criminalizing Drug Use

One of the central driving forces of correctional system growth in the United States stemmed from criminalizing the use of a wide range of drugs and creating enhanced penalties for illegal drug use. In one of the first assessments of system-levels contributions of drug offenses to prison growth, Alfred Blumstein and Allen Beck attempted to examine which offenses and which processing decisions (e.g., arrest, conviction given an arrest, incarceration given a conviction, time served) contributed most to the state and federal increases in incarcerated populations.[20] Examining trends from 1980 to 1996, they found that drug offenses emerged as the single-largest driver of the prison population. This situation arose from dramatic increases in drug arrests and the conversion of arrests into sentences to prison.[21] By 2010, drug offenders constituted 17 percent of the state prison population and 52 percent of the federal prison population.[22]

The focus on drugs—whether as a moral, health, or crime problem—has a long history in the United States, dating back to Prohibition and, indeed, well before then. In the 1980s, however, concern about illegal drugs, especially crack cocaine, crescendoed.[23] Considerable debate arose about the magnitude of the problem and how to address it. Proponents of get-tough measures viewed illegal drugs as the source of violent crime and cultural decline. From their perspective, the crisis required emergency steps to rein in the threat to the social fabric.[24]

By contrast, others viewed drug use as a problem, but one most accurately understood as a health rather than criminal justice issue. Indeed, federal judges such as Lois Forer resigned from the bench precisely because they took this stance and because they felt that mandatory sentencing guidelines coerced them into becoming participants in mistreatment.[25] Judge Forer identified many problems that led to her decision. These included the placement of sentencing discretion with prosecutors rather than judges, the elimination of individualized sentencing, the violation of the "principle of proportionality," and the lack of a clear justification for sentences relative to putative public safety benefits.[26]

The emphasis on illegal drugs largely accorded with the general tough-on-crime trend. However, it received an additional boost from efforts to increase drug treatment. Indeed, drug offender treatment emerged as one area where rehabilitation was "in play," but, notably, treatment was tied directly to tougher supervision. Drug courts, for example, surfaced in the early 1990s and became widespread over the next decade. They embodied the dual emphasis on treatment and tougher and more intensive supervision. The punitive turn thus can be seen in the emphasis on drug offenders, not only in sentencing laws but also in the emphasis on control-oriented treatment efforts that could result in a greater detection of violations and, in turn, a greater likelihood of being sent back to prison. Thus, while some drug courts may have effectively reduced recidivism, their broader aggregate impact may have been to expand the web of social control wider.[27]

Trend 3: Getting Tough on Sex Offenders

Sentencing laws and reforms largely centered on violent, chronic, and serious offenders and secondarily on drug offenders. Another group that garnered attention was sex offenders. Several incorrect assumptions contributed to the emphasis. Policy makers and the public appeared to believe that sex offenders in general, not just serial sex offenders, could not be effectively treated and that sex crime had increased.[28] States turned their focus to creating a wide range of new laws and policies aimed expressly at sex offenders.[29] These included enhanced sentencing penalties, sex offender registries, community notification laws, residency restrictions, lifetime supervision laws, driver's license notations, chemical castration, and civil commitment. Such changes, like those targeting violent, chronic, or drug offenders, signaled a dramatic departure from the approach taken in prior decades. And they just as clearly signaled a primary emphasis on retribution as a goal and on incapacitation and deterrence as strategies for achieving public safety.

Trend 4: Law Enforcement, Courts, Probation, Parole, and the Web of Social Control

In the 1970s, significant concern arose about net widening.[30] The deinstitutionalization and diversion movement contributed to this concern. Deinstitutionalization efforts focused on removing individuals from prisons and supervising and treating them in communities instead. Diversion efforts focused in part on the use of services and treatments to address problems that non-serious offenders might have and to ensure that less restrictive and costly sanctions were employed. The ideas seemed sound, but scholars soon identified problems. For example, the potential for the courts to exert control over ever-larger numbers of individuals emerged. In the juvenile justice system, for example, concern emerged that the court—whether out of a mindset focused on rehabilitation or on tough-love punishment—was using diversion to intervene in minor cases that in the past might otherwise have been dismissed.[31]

Net widening presents a problem in criminal justice because it creates more costs for unclear gain. It also amplifies the effects of decision making in various parts of the justice system. Consider that if no changes in arrest rates or time served in prison occurred, expanded use of diversion might well increase probation populations or referrals to treatment or rehabilitative services but not affect rates of incarceration. Here, no amplifying effect occurs. However, diversion in a different context could well affect prison populations. Consider, for example, a context of increased arrest rates, convictions given an arrest, prison commitments, and aggressive enforcement of the conditions of probation and parole. In this situation, diversion efforts might well contribute to a large-scale ramping up of the prison population. Indeed, a critique of diversion efforts lies in the possibility that an individual previously may have received no sanction but now, under some type of diversion policy or approach, is subject to a minor sanction that opens the door to supervision and thus receiving a more serious sanction in the event of a violation.[32]

This situation aptly characterizes the situation that arose in the 1980s and in subsequent decades. As discussed above, probation and parole populations greatly increased. At the same time, funding for law enforcement agencies and the courts skyrocketed. For example, spending on police increased from $20 billion to $100 billion from 1982 to 2006 while spending on the judiciary increased from $8 billion to $47 billion during this same time period.[33] The hiring of more police and court officials along with significantly expanding the capacity of the probation and parole systems contributed to prison growth. As Garland, echoing the assessment of many other scholars, has emphasized, "violation of parole license has become a major basis for imprisonment, with states such as California attributing most inmates received into custody to this source."[34]

Here, as with the other policy shifts discussed in this chapter, the increased investment in these formal social control functions reflected an emphasis on punishment and control. There was not, for example, a commensurate increase in spending on crime prevention, public health measures targeting crime, or rehabilitation. In addition, expansion of law enforcement, court, probation, and parole capacity was paralleled by a qualitative shift that illustrated this trend. In each instance, less support for and investment in treatment or rehabilitation existed, supplanted instead by a focus on more and tougher supervision.

Trend 5: More Punitive Handling of Supervision, Violations, and Recidivism

When placed on probation or parole, individuals have to abide by certain conditions—meeting with officers at established times, avoiding contact with criminal associates, providing urine specimens for testing, remaining at home during certain hours, participating in educational, vocational, or rehabilitative programming, engaging in no threatening behavior toward intimate partners or others, paying supervision fees, and so on. Historically, however, community supervision included a social welfare or rehabilitative function.[35] Supervision officers served dual roles—law enforcement agents, on the one hand, and social workers, on the other. In the 1970s, this philosophical approach to supervision came under attack. Parole board decisions, for example, came to be seen as arbitrary and unfounded.[36]

States thus reduced parole board discretion, much as they had reduced judicial discretion in the handling of criminal cases. Throughout the 1980s and beyond, states placed parolee supervision oversight with agencies located in departments of corrections. The changes were, as Travis has written, ironic:

> At the same time that legislatures placed severe restrictions on discretion exercised by judges and parole boards, they greatly expanded the realm of official discretion by placing more people than ever under the supervision of parole officers, government employees with far more discretion and far less accountability for the exercise of that discretion than judges and parole board members.

One might characterize these changes, however, as more than ironic—they resulted in large numbers of parole violators contributing to prison growth. Whereas in 1980, only 17 percent of new prison admissions consisted of parole violators, by 1999 that figure rose to 35 percent. In two-thirds of these cases, the return to prison stemmed from a "technical violation" (e.g., missing an appointment with an officer or treatment provider, having a positive drug test) rather than commission of a new crime.[37] In short, the punitive turn in American criminal justice can be found not only in sentencing laws and the targeting of select groups of offenders but also in changes to system practices.

Trend 6: Reduced Investment in Treatment and Rehabilitation

"Most prisoners do not participate in prison programs, such as education and vocational programs, and the rate of participation has dropped over the past decade."[38] James Lynch and William Sabol rendered that assessment in 2001. Examining Bureau of Justice Statistics survey data, they found that the percentage of soon-to-be-released inmates who had participated in vocational programming not only was low but also had declined. In 1991, it was 31 percent and by 1997 it was down to 27 percent. Similarly, during this time period, the percentage of inmates reporting that they had participated in educational programming declined from 43 percent to 35 percent. Extrapolating such changes to the total inmate population, Lynch and Sabol estimated that the effects of such changes would result in an additional 85,000 inmates in 1997 who did not receive vocational programming. Perhaps more notable, however, are the low rates of programming. For example, the alternative way of presenting the 1997 statistics is to say that 73 percent of inmates received no vocational programming and 65 percent received no educational programming.

In contemporary times, this situation remains largely unchanged. Michelle Phelps, for example, examined data from the 1970s to the present and found that "programming rates have been quite modest and in most cases fairly consistent over time."[39] Certainly, states have invested in drug and mental health treatment and reentry programming. However, program opportunities for inmates have been historically modest, even during the "rehabilitative era." This situation means that most inmates leave prison having received little education, training, treatment, or preparation for the transition back into society. In addition, although examples of well-designed and implemented programs can be found, more examples of poor program design and implementation exist as well.[40] The dramatic growth in correctional populations and accompanying case-processing pressures as well as the general cultural shift toward greater emphasis on retribution lead to the inference that the typical situation involves weak rather than strong program design and implementation.[41]

Trend 7: Housing and Residency Restrictions

Alongside of these trends are a range of invisible punishments that ensure additional retribution and control of felons long after they complete their prison sentence or term of probation or parole.[42] In Travis's analysis of federal statutes, for example, he found that Section 8 housing—that is, public-supported housing—could be denied to "any drug-related or violent criminal activity or other criminal activity which would adversely affect the health, safety, or right to peaceful enjoyment of the premises [by others]."[43] States and correctional systems contribute to housing challenges for ex-prisoners as well. Indeed, according to Petersilia, "parole officials say that finding housing for parolees is by far their biggest challenge, even more difficult and more important than finding a job."[44]

The barriers to housing are numerous. They include incarceration in facilities far away from home communities, which makes transition planning difficult; little assistance finding housing upon release; vouchers that provide only a few weeks of housing; supervision conditions that limit association with criminal associates, which can limit potential housing opportunities; shelters that limit the number of days an individual can reside at them; housing markets that are cost-prohibitive; long waiting lists for affordable housing; landlords who don't accept tenants with a criminal history; restrictions on public housing; and geographical limitations on where some ex-prisoners, especially sex offenders, can live.[45] As a result of these barriers, many inmates end up homeless within weeks of release from prison.[46]

As is the case with many aspects of reentry, there is much that remains unknown about the housing experiences of inmates upon release.[47] Although we know a great deal about the barriers to housing and the experiences of homelessness that occur as a result, we have little systematic empirical documentation, state by state, of the housing arrangements of ex-prisoners in the days, weeks, months, and years after release.[48] That state of affairs stands out in part because it illustrates a pattern or characteristic of the punitive turn. Retributive policies arose with seemingly minimal attention to the potential adverse consequences that those policies would have. At the same time, they proceeded from an assumption that a deterrence-based logic necessarily would yield beneficial outcomes for public safety.

Trend 8: Employment Restrictions

Just as they did with housing restrictions, states and the federal government enacted policies that restricted opportunities for released inmates to obtain employment. Most prisoners have spotty work histories. Consequently, their prospects for gainful employment lag far behind that of the general public. Employment programs have constituted a focus of many correctional systems precisely because of the belief that enhancing employment eligibility will improve life outcomes and reduce offending.[49] The evidence for the effectiveness of these programs in fact is mixed.[50] However, well-designed and implemented programs may improve outcomes.

Employment prospects for ex-prisoners are dim for relatively straightforward reasons.[51] The individuals who land in prison have weak work histories. The experience of prison may sever ties to individuals who could assist with finding work, and it may erode labor market skills and an individual's work ethic. Ex-prisoners also have poor educational histories and often suffer from mental illness or drug addiction. In addition, they tend to return to areas where the local employment context and community conditions are poor.[52] When they do find work, they tend to earn less than they did prior to incarceration.[53]

Added to this constellation of factors are policies that limit employment for ex-prisoners. The stigma of a felony conviction constitutes a critical barrier. Ex-prisoners, as well as any individual with a felony conviction, regardless of whether they were incarcerated, must report their felony record on employment applications. Doing so can reduce the likelihood of being hired. Employers may be unwilling to assume the risk liability associated with criminal activity or harm that may result if they hire ex-felons. Increasingly, too, during the punitive turn, laws were enacted that bar ex-offenders from a wide range of occupations, including certain jobs in child care, education, medicine, real estate, barber and beautician trade, and more.[54]

Some restrictions make sense at face value, such as a sex offender not being allowed to work with children. However, in other instances, as Petersilia has observed, "there is no rational connection between the restriction placed on an ex-offender's occupation and the crime she committed."[55] In addition, ex-prisoners sometimes participate in vocational training programs but then are disallowed by law from working in the vocation for which they were trained. Felons, too, may not obtain government work in many states.[56] If they do not have a driver's license—which can occur when convicted of a felony drug crime—they will have difficulty obtaining work. In cases where a clearly rational basis exists for anticipating risks associated with hiring ex-felons, there remains the fact that these individuals will have difficulty obtaining employment and the likelihood that, without jobs, they may end up homeless or continue to offend.[57]

Here, again, then, we see a similar pattern. State and federal policy makers enacted get-tough measures that sought to expand punishment and to achieve public safety through, in this instance, deterrence or incapacitation. If, for example, individuals cannot work in certain jobs, they cannot commit crimes at them, according to this logic. As with housing restrictions, however, in the area of employment we see that an emphasis on retribution risks unintended adverse consequences that may worsen rather than improve public safety.[58]

Trend 9: Welfare Restrictions

In 1996, during President Clinton's administration, Congress passed welfare reform legislation—the Personal Responsibility and Work Opportunity Reconciliation Act (PWORA)—that encouraged states not to provide federally funded assistance or food stamps to individuals convicted of drug crimes.[59] Some states chose not to adopt this provision, but many others embraced it. The legislation also required temporary termination of benefits to individuals who violate conditions of probation or parole. [60] Because much of the growth in corrections over the past 30 years resulted from get-tough punishment of drug-related offending, welfare and other restrictions focused on drug felons have affected large swaths of the correctional system population.

A central strategy the federal government used to promote adoption of welfare and other restrictions consisted of using block grant funding, termed Temporary Assistance for Needy Families (TANF), that involved "purse string" ties. That is, only if states adopted certain provisions could they receive full funding. To see that states, independent of the federal government, embraced the punitive turn in punishment, we need look no farther than restrictions on welfare benefits. For example, almost half of states opted to permanently ban drug felons from welfare and food stamp benefits for life.[61]

As with other invisible punishments, this imposition created ripple effects for felons and for their families and children. As Petersilia has emphasized, "ex-offenders have historically relied on public assistance to pay for food and housing. Since welfare and food stamps often helped fund room and board in alcohol and drug treatment programs, ex-offenders now find it increasingly difficult to pay for their treatment programs."[62] In addition, incarceration of parents, as Naomi Sugie has observed, can inhibit the likelihood of families being able to receive welfare benefits.[63] Such ripple effects only begin to scratch the surface, however, and highlight the importance of identifying collateral consequences associated with the punitive turn in American crime policy.

Trend 10: Restrictions on Voting, Driver's Licenses, Educational Loans, and More

Housing, employment, and welfare restrictions are among the most conspicuous ways that the federal government and states have sought to punish and control felons. However, many other related efforts have been undertaken. Disenfranchisement laws, for example, have been adopted in almost every state, as Figure 2.4 reveals.[64] The laws vary greatly, with some states eliminating voting rights while a convicted felon is on probation or parole and/or while he or she is in prison and others retracing their right to vote for life.[65] Estimates indicate that 2.5 percent, or roughly 6 million individuals, of the voting age population in the United States was disenfranchised in 2010; the rate of disenfranchisement among blacks is estimated to be four times greater than that of whites.[66] Figure 2.4 highlights that disenfranchisement occurs at a higher rate in some states than others. In Florida, for example, 10.4 percent of the voting age population is disenfranchised, while in most other states less than 1 percent is.

Still other restrictions have been created. For example, Congress used financial incentives to induce states to adopt laws that would take any individual's driver's license away if convicted of a drug felony and to create sex-offender registries.[67] Although some states have opted out of these requirements, others have accepted them. In 1998, Congress enacted the Higher Education Act, which included provisions that restricted access to student loans for individuals convicted of drug crimes.[68] Some estimates indicate that participation in postsecondary educational programs in prison settings declined by 44 percent after the elimination of Pell Grants.[69] In addition to these restrictions, a criminal record typically precludes holding public office and "may also preclude their receiving government benefits and retaining parental rights, be grounds for divorce, prevent their serving on a jury, and nearly always limits firearm ownership."[70]

THE THEORY, OR CAUSAL LOGIC, OF THE PUNITIVE TURN IN SANCTIONING CONVICTED FELONS

The punitive turn in American punishment can be seen not only in mass incarceration but also in a panoply of so-called invisible punishments. Invisible punishments are restrictions to civil liberties that felons are subject

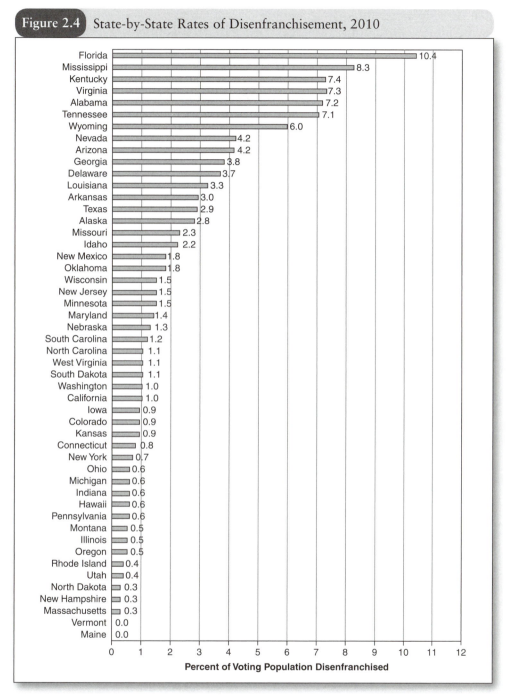

Figure 2.4 State-by-State Rates of Disenfranchisement, 2010

Source: The Sentencing Project (Uggen et al. 2012). Used with permission.

to in addition to any prison time or probation. There have always been some invisible punishments, but what is different in modern times is the much wider range and intensity of restrictions as well as the inclusion of efforts that directly affect minorities and the poor. Limitations on housing, employment, and welfare constitute the most obvious examples of this changed emphasis.

What was the logic of this effort? That is, what is the theory of the punitive turn in sanctioning convicted felons? Or, to use the language of evaluation research, what is the "causal logic" of the punitive turn in punishment?[71] For example, how does imposing additional restrictions on convicted felons contribute to such outcomes as improved public safety or increased satisfaction among the public that a desired level of retribution has been obtained? In the next chapter, we will examine factors that gave rise to the punitive turn in American penal policy at the turn of the twenty-first century. Here, we focus on the logic of greater punishment and invisible punishments, along with collateral consequences that they can entail, on a historically unprecedented scale. Specifically, how do these efforts create greater justice, retribution, and public safety?

One straightforward justification for harsher punishment and restrictions is that they protect the public. In some cases, this logic is self-evident. For example, allowing individuals who have committed sex crimes against children to work at child care centers would hardly seem to warrant debate, no more so than we might debate the merit of not allowing cigarette lighters to be used in areas housing combustible materials. Yet, frequently, the logic—seemingly self-evident at first—is unclear after careful inspection.

An Example—The Theory and Logic of Sex Offender Policies

Sex offenders provide a useful touchstone for illustrating the point. Sex offender housing restrictions would seem to be, on the face of it, a good idea. Keep sex offenders away from areas where children congregate, such as schools, and in so doing we can prevent victimization. This policy, though, is built on incorrect assumptions. Do sex offenders typically live near schools? Does child sex victimization typically occur on or near school grounds? To the extent that sex offenders prey on child sex victims, would not being able to live near a school suffice to deter them from seeking out potential targets when, say, children were a mile or two away from school or on some form of public transportation?

We have little research that directly examines such questions empirically, but in general the evidence to date indicates that the assumptions are wrong.[72] Sex offenders live all over the map and do not in any obvious way cluster near schools; child sex victimization happens in many contexts and often occurs at the homes of family members and friends. If an individual feels compelled to victimize children, a barrier such as living a few miles away from a school would be unlikely to prevent victimization.

Community notification laws seem to be an obviously smart initiative as well. Residents in a given area should know who among their neighbors broke the law and were caught and convicted. That way, they can . . . Well, what exactly *can* they do? Some communities work to push convicted felons out of their neighborhoods, but that strategy, apart from ethical considerations, rarely works.

What, then? Few of us can readily move from one home or housing arrangement to another given the costs of doing so. Our work and recreational routines may not be easily changed. Perhaps, though, we no longer walk down a street that we used to traverse. Or we watch our children more closely when they play in the driveway or at a nearby park. Those steps are possible. But why would they make us or our families safer?

With sex offenders, the image that comes to mind consists of the serial violent sex offender, repeatedly raping and murdering and incapable of changing. A monster. But the vast bulk of sex offenders do not fit that profile. They do not typically murder. Some rape while others engage in indecent exposure or they grope someone at a bar. Some victimize strangers, but most victimize known family members, friends, or acquaintances. "Sex offender," as a category, encompasses considerable variation in offending. This diversity can limit the usefulness of knowledge that a sex offender lives down the street.

Even if we do know the type of sex crime an individual committed, we are left, again, with the question of what actions we can take to make ourselves safer. Consider the mother of an 8-year-old girl who lives in public housing in an inner-city neighborhood. Within several blocks of her home may reside individuals who have committed some of the following crimes: rape, sexual abuse, incest, frotteurism, indecent exposure, groping. In many of these instances, the individuals pose no threat to the mother's child. But in cases in which the person does, there is little that the mother can do beyond what she likely would do anyway, such as lock the doors at night and seek to ensure that her daughter is well supervised before, during, and after school.

A Second Example—The Theory and Logic of Felon Voting Restrictions

Voting restrictions—if the goal is retribution, the causal logic would seem to involve reference to the notion that the public views withholding voting rights as punishment. Many individuals, however, never vote. Regardless, if we think about what type of sanction the public wants to achieve retribution, voting would not seem to be high on the list, especially with probation and prison terms as options. The science of retribution, in fact, is not well developed in criminology or in public policy.[73] Although many studies have examined public views about offense severity and whether the courts punish enough, relatively little empirical documentation exists about the precise nature and intensity of punishment that the public requires to achieve a desired sense of retribution.[74] Theoretical and empirical research to date has almost entirely ignored the extent to which the public supports additional punishments for retributive purposes, in large part because these types of punishments have not previously existed.

If the goal is deterrence, the logic somehow has to involve the notion that offenders (in the case of specific deterrence) or would-be offenders (in the case of general deterrence) refrain from committing crime because of a fear that they might lose their right to vote. Of course, among individuals who have already lost their right to vote, there is no such possibility. That situation aside, the claim on the face of it defies logic. Consider, for example, that we use prison to deter. If a prison term will not deter, why do we think eliminating voting rights would do the trick? Indeed, as with housing restrictions, it might increase the likelihood of offending by stigmatizing individuals and leading them to feel that no opportunity for redemption exists.[75]

The Flawed Logic of Deterrence in Current Penal Practices

The recent emphasis on invisible punishments consists of tougher, more severe punishment to achieve retribution and public safety. At its most general level, the causal argument reduces to the idea that if we impose punishment of many kinds, and more of each, deterrence will occur. Why deterrence? Because by and large, during the punitive turn, investment in rehabilitation and opportunity-based approaches to reducing crime declined or constituted a distant priority relative to investing in more and harsher punishment.[76] The logic of deterrence does not entirely rest on punishment severity, however. It rests, too, on the certainty and speed of punishment and on a weighing of potential costs versus potential benefits. In involves, for example, as Raymond Paternoster has pointed out, perceived versus objective punishment severity, certainty, and celerity.[77] As Paternoster has emphasized, "At its core, . . . deterrence theory is a social psychological theory of threat communication in which the causal chain runs from the objective properties of punishment through the perceptual properties of punishment to crime."[78] More complications exist. For example, deterrence may operate differently for some individuals depending on such dimensions as prior direct and vicarious experience with punishment, cognitive ability, addiction, self-control, and situational context.[79] The vast bulk of deterrence research has focused on traditional criminal justice sanctions, not the various invisible punishments that have surfaced. It remains unclear—not only for incarceration but also these additional punishments—how much they deter or, if they do, which aspects of the punishments deter.[80] A useful, if simplistic, way of viewing the matter is to examine any given tougher punishment, such as incarcerating individuals who have violated parole or eliminating the right to vote, and ask two questions: (a) How does the punishment affect the perception among sanctioned offenders or the general public of the severity, certainty, or celerity of punishment? (b) How does the objective nature of the punishment affect these two groups? As is evident in the examples above and in the analyses of the collateral consequences of incarceration and invisible punishments, the causal logic is unclear and empirical research, except in the case of incarceration, is nominal.

Even with incarceration, the assessment largely stands. For any given change in the risk of incarceration, for example, "would-be offenders would have to be aware of the heightened risk."[81] There is not, however, "much evidence in support of a strong correlation between the objective and subjective properties of punishment."[82] In addition, many aspects of deterrence theory remain open to question. For example, accounts of deterrence typically refer to celerity of punishment as a factor that increases deterrence. Yet speedy punishment may be less of a deterrent than delayed punishment, especially among individuals who prefer to receive their sanction right away rather than live in dread of receiving it at some unspecified time.[83]

In short, the causal logic underlying the punitive turn rests on shaky theoretical and empirical grounds. That does not mean that the motivation to make society safer should be impugned or that one "correct" approach to punishment exists. It does, however, indicate that the likely effectiveness of this change in punishment is limited. In general, we have greater confidence that a policy is or will be effective when it rests on a sound theoretical foundation and when credible empirical research identifies substantial improvements and few harms. With the punitive turn, we have just the opposite—little sound theoretical or empirical basis to anticipate improvements in public safety or in public satisfaction with levels of retribution. At the same time, a large body of work identifies potential harms resulting from the large-scale shift toward mass incarceration and attendant emphases on get-tough responses to crime.[84]

IMPLICATIONS OF HISTORICAL TRENDS IN INCARCERATION AND REENTRY POLICY AND PRACTICE

Scholars have raised many concerns about the dramatic shift toward retributivist sanctioning. Here, we highlight several of the more prominent concerns. In so doing, we intend no indictment of a politically liberal or conservative approach to punishment. The reality is that liberals and conservatives joined forces to create the punitive turn. And both groups express support for smarter approaches to punishment.[85]

First, tougher, more severe punishments cost money—lots of it. Taxpayers foot the bill for every new prison and for staffing new and old facilities. The costs tend to have the equivalent of a "hangover" effect. When all is said and done, once a prison is built or some type of new get-tough initiative is implemented, it typically stays in perpetuity, generating ongoing, fixed costs to taxpayers. In addition, the financial costs go well beyond investments in law enforcement, courts, jails, prisons, probation, and parole. To the extent that current sanctioning approaches are criminogenic, there may be increased costs due to increased crime.[86] In addition, the collateral consequences of mass incarceration, such as adverse effects on children, families, and communities, should be included in any cost-benefit assessment of mass incarceration and invisible punishments.

Second, the creation of a system of invisible punishments indirectly constitutes a commitment to placing punishment authority with legislators, prosecutors, and corrections officials. Legislatures create sentencing laws, of course. Historically, though, courts apply these laws and issue punishments. In contemporary times, many invisible punishments occur because of being labeled a "convicted felon." And sanctioning power—by dint of charging authority and sentencing guidelines—rests more with prosecutors rather than with judges. At the same time, correctional system officials and staff have greater authority to impose punishments, if only indirectly. For example, when parole officers aggressively impose technical violations on ex-prisoners in contexts where prosecutors likely will seek to reincarcerate the offenders, they exercise indirect control over punishment.

Third, the emergence of invisible punishments has created a form of "unchecked retributivism."[87] Many of these punishments escape public scrutiny and create opportunities for misuse. Within correctional systems, the same potential exists. For example, discretion about placing inmates in supermax incarceration—what many view as a form of additional punishment with considerable room for abuse—lies with prison officials. Yet little empirical information about administrative decisions to incarcerate particular individuals in supermax housing exists.[88] The broader concern is the lack of systematic empirical evidence about critical decision making that occurs throughout criminal justice.[89]

Fourth, despite the large-scale increase in punishment, it remains unclear that the public feels greater levels of satisfaction with the criminal justice system.[90] That constitutes grounds for significant concern. The United States has invested heavily in expanding its criminal justice systems and its punishment capacity. Ideally, there would be something to show for it in the form of public satisfaction with the justice system, including perceptions about retribution and perceived and actual safety. However, we have almost no coherent empirical guidance about the types and amounts of punishments that the public feels would provide satisfactory retribution, even though retribution constitutes a central goal of punishment.[91] It may be that some crime reduction occurred, whether due to incapacitation or deterrent effects, but there remains marked uncertainty about that assessment.[92] In addition, the central question is not whether public safety improved or how the public feels about the retribution it has purchased. Rather, the more critical question is how much public safety and satisfactory retribution has been obtained relative to other approaches that could have been pursued. We unfortunately have precious little empirical research that answers that question either. We do, however, have a large body of research, discussed in later chapters, that suggests that a more diversified "portfolio" of sanctioning strategies might produce better outcomes and fewer harms.[93]

Fifth, the emphasis on punitive approaches to crime control has created challenges for states.[94] As discussed in the case study of California, the sustained focus on and investment in retributive sanctioning for over 30 years has locked many states into a system of punishment that imposes tremendous costs. One of the more significant costs stems from the emergence of systems problems (discussed in more detail in the next chapter). For example, when states increase sentence lengths and toughen parole practices, prison populations have nowhere to go but up, and politically it becomes difficult to make certain changes, or to revert back, because doing so opens policy makers up to attacks as being soft on crime. States then get locked into large fixed costs that recur annually and that limit their ability to introduce meaningful large-scale reforms.

Chapter 2 Case Study: California and the Get-Tough Era of Sentencing

The punitive turn in criminal justice policy can be seen in, and in part resulted from, systems-level changes that reinforced an emphasis on expanded punishment. California illustrates this change and some problems it has created.

In 1994, California enacted a three-strikes law that emphasized certain and lengthy prison terms for a third felony conviction. The law contributed substantially to higher rates of incarceration and longer prison terms. It also led to large-scale reincarceration of parolees for technical violations (Travis and Lawrence 2002). By 2007, California accounted for 15 percent of parolees nationwide (Grattet et al. 2009). During this same time, California, like other states, made substantial investments in law enforcement, expanded its court system, and started building new prisons. In short, the state's policy shift exemplified the punitive turn.

How did these new policies work out? After decades of tougher punishment policies and continued expansion of the correctional system, California confronted an increasingly worrisome problem—overcrowded prisons and poor oversight of conditions within them. The situation led to a lawsuit that eventually reached the Supreme Court. The Court issued a far-reaching decision that required the state to reduce its prison population, which stood at approximately 120,000, by 10,000 inmates (Gorman 2013). It cited several concerns, including the conditions inside California's prisons and a lack of appropriate treatment for inmates' medical and mental health. These conditions, according to the Court, violated the Eighth Amendment (*Brown v. Plata* 2011).

California faced a daunting challenge—determining which 10,000 prisoners to shift from prisons to local jails, which to release outright, how to proceed with oversight of those inmates who were released, and how to punish in lieu of increasing prison populations. The sustained downturn in the economy created a context in which some common ground might be found among policy makers. Yet little agreement existed and the options were few.

One reason is that the punitive turn created a system of justice in California and elsewhere that has made it difficult to achieve a balanced approach to punishment and public safety. Each part of the criminal justice system has grown. More and more criminal cases must be decided, and typically these decisions occur with little time for careful deliberation. David Heilbroner's (1990) account of his experiences as an assistant district attorney in Manhattan provides one of the more nuanced and colorful accounts of how case-processing pressures permeated almost every decision in his office. The police and courts face similar pressures. Yet little is known about the quality of decision making that occurs throughout the criminal justice system. What we do know is that case-processing pressures lead to more errors and that these errors exist in a system where little monitoring of decision making occurs (Mears and Bacon 2009). In the end, it may take emergencies, such as overcrowding or economic recessions, to lead to significant change. At that point, we end up paying far more to achieve far less.

CONCLUSION

Punishment in America has changed dramatically in recent decades. To the extent that incarceration rates and invisible punishments serve as valid indicators, the country has emphasized retribution more so than at any other period in U.S. history. In so doing, it committed to costs that taxpayers will cover for decades to come. The investment in criminal justice and punishment infrastructure has been expanded and strengthened, and this infrastructure in turn will obligate the lion's share of criminal justice and correctional system investments for decades to come. Certainly new and innovative approaches to achieving retribution and public safety have emerged. The room, though, to introduce large-scale changes to "right-size" criminal justice is severely constrained. Interestingly, this situation parallels challenges in the American medical system.[95] In each instance, systems-level changes have resulted in skyrocketing costs, with little to show for it in the form of improved outcomes.

Here, now, we return to the arguments that we identified in the introduction. We do so to lay the foundation for observations that we will make in subsequent chapters. First, reentry is complicated. It involves far more than simply the fact that hundreds of thousands of individuals return to society annually after years of incarceration. It involves invisible punishments that have proliferated and show few if any signs of abating. It involves, too, changes in time served in prison and the reasons that individuals return to prison. Parole decision making, for example, has greatly fueled incarceration growth by returning thousands of individuals to prison for technical violations. It involves as well lawmaking and policy making preferences for punishing rather than treating drug-related offending. Understanding the diverse dimensions of reentry and their causes will be necessary for devising ways to achieve more effective and efficient punishment practices.

Second, if the country and states are to improve reentry experiences and outcomes of released prisoners, they will need to develop many different strategies. These include changes in laws, front-end decision making by law enforcement and court actors, back-end decision making by parole officers, and decision making throughout criminal justice and correctional systems. The range of invisible punishments alone highlights that, as we have argued, reentry may best be understood by placing it within a larger context of cultural shifts in punishment philosophy. Put differently, improving reentry ultimately will require improving the country's approach to punishment.

The point bears emphasis: "mass incarceration" as a phrase obscures more than it reveals. Police practices, court practices, probation and parole officer practices, court decisions—changes in these and other areas have occurred. In each instance, they may have created benefits and harms in isolation or in ways that have built on one another and contributed to ripple effects throughout the criminal justice system and society.[96] Efforts, for example, to get tough on parolees through increased violations and through reincarceration for such violations directly contributed to overcrowding in California's prison system and elsewhere.[97] Similarly, a focus on drug offending led to increases in prison populations. In turn, both of these changes contributed to greater interest in some places in using drug courts. These courts are supposed to divert individuals from prison and more effectively punish offenders while also reducing their likelihood of drug relapse and recidivism.[98] In short, reentry is part of a system of justice. Accordingly, we need to focus on that system if we are to understand and improve reentry.

Third, when discussing reentry and, at the end of the book, "what works," we can anticipate already that context matters.[99] Reentry policies and practices changed greatly over a span of three decades—the 1980s, 1990s, and 2000s—and did so during a period in which marked social and economic change occurred. At the same time, these policies and practices appear to have affected not just convicted felons but also their families, friends, and communities, a point to which we will return in subsequent chapters. For that reason, questions naturally arise about the implementation and effects of various aspects of the criminal justice system that fuel mass incarceration, reentry programs, policies, and practices, and their effects on different groups (e.g., ex-prisoners, victims, children, families, communities). Put differently, the reentry process is likely a highly dynamic one that has changed over time and that may have variable effects for different groups. Such a possibility poses direct implications for how to improve reentry. To illustrate, when unemployment rates increase, ex-prisoners must compete with more people for jobs, and they do so with the added disadvantage of a felony record.[100] Jobs programs might be more effective for ex-prisoners at these times than in times when unemployment rates are relatively low. In short, historically specific social conditions may affect reentry experiences and the effectiveness of interventions to improve ex-prisoner outcomes.

Fourth, although not directly the focus of this chapter, it should be apparent that in an era of mass incarceration, many changes have gone unexamined by scholars. Indeed, for the academic community, much of what occurs in correctional systems constitutes the equivalent of a black box.[101] Correctional system officials and staff, and practitioners who work in this system or with offenders and their families or communities constitute a critical source of potential insight into the operations of the system and how to improve it. Intriguing and effective initiatives can result when their views are tapped. Consider Hawaii's Opportunity Probation with Enforcement (HOPE) program, which was created by Judge Steven Alm in an effort to devise an approach that might more effectively reduce drug use and recidivism.[102] This effort did not emerge from a top-down approach emanating from a theory of penal policy or offending. Rather, it resulted from a ground-up approach informed by consideration of the court population and its characteristics and system capacity and opportunities. In a context of enormous systems growth, the systematic cultivation of insights from the individuals with their feet on the ground will be central to creating more effective and efficient reentry policy.

Finally, given that the punitive turn consists of a large web of punishment policies and practices implemented at diverse points in the criminal justice system, opportunities to improve reentry exist at all of them. Accordingly, diverse leverage points exist for improving recidivism, employment, housing, and other outcomes. Simply focusing on incarceration alone, for example, likely will do little to improve public safety outcomes. Similarly, simply increasing rehabilitation and treatment alone likely would do little. A more effective and cost-efficient strategy will entail undertaking a myriad of changes that target different parts of criminal justice and corrections. We might introduce new programs like HOPE. But the efforts that might be most effective for producing aggregate improvements could easily involve taking mundane steps such as relying more on data and research to assess implementation and fidelity to, say, district attorney practices or prison protocols about case management and decision making.[103] Even more effective and efficient would be strategies that target *all* aspects of crime prevention, criminal justice, and correctional system policy and practice. We will be returning to these possibilities in subsequent chapters and, in particular, Chapter 9 and the conclusion.

DISCUSSION QUESTIONS

1. Which of the trends in sanctioning policies and practices best symbolizes the cultural shifts in punishment philosophy in America?

2. What is the theory, or logic, that justifies invisible punishments?

3. How might invisible punishments combine to create worse rather than better outcomes as well as collateral consequences for prisoners and their families and communities?

4. What implications of the punitive turn present the greatest challenges for American criminal justice policy?

5. How might the punitive turn in punishment be modified to achieve an effective balance of punishment goals, including retribution, public safety, and victim assistance?

6. Why might historical and social context, including systems change, matter for understanding and improving reentry?

CHAPTER 3

The Causes of Mass Incarceration and Thus Mass Reentry

This chapter identifies some of the leading causes that scholars have put forward for the rise, over the previous three decades, of more punitive crime control approaches—the punitive turn—and, more specifically, mass incarceration. This discussion is central to our argument that any effort to understand and improve reentry involves identifying the causes of the large-scale shift in American corrections. Scholars have advanced many arguments about why the punitive turn occurred, but they agree that it arose as but one part of a much larger set of cultural and political forces that shaped diverse aspects of society, including education and social welfare policy.[1]

It is not, then, a simple causal scenario. To make matters worse, most causal accounts of the punitive turn do not readily lend themselves to rigorous empirical analysis. Accordingly, the credibility of any one account rests largely on how convincing the logic appears and how well different empirical patterns or regularities fit with that logic. A simple example illustrates the challenge here—although the United States embraced incarceration over the past several decades, states varied in the extent to which they did so. We cannot, therefore, argue that some national culture of punitiveness exists or, if it does, that it exerts an equal force among states.

Against that backdrop, our goal is to take a wide-ranging look at different potential causal factors. In so doing, we include a focus on systems-level forces that can contribute to increased prison growth and sustained investment in mass incarceration. For example, expanded parole officer caseloads can increase the law enforcement dimensions of parole and decrease the social worker dimensions of it. That, in turn, can result in a greater likelihood of parole officers meting out violations or arrests in contexts where they otherwise might issue warnings or make additional efforts to connect individuals to rehabilitative services. In a context in which laws and prosecutorial practices call for tougher punishment of recidivists, the end result can be exponential and unchecked growth in prison populations.

The chapter argues that understanding such factors is critical for developing a fuller, more accurate account of how prison growth unfolded during the last three decades and what can be done, going forward, to create a more effective and efficient approach to punishment and to improving reentry. Implicit in this approach is the belief that understanding the causes of why various policies are adopted is critical for creating improvements in them. In that sense, "looking backward" can be critical to effectively "moving forward." Many innovations in medicine, for example, have never been adopted or have taken decades to adopt even when compelling scientific evidence existed to support them. In part, that results from organizational barriers and constraints to adopting evidence-based practices.[2] Identifying when and why such barriers exist constitutes a critical part of what we need to improve policy and practice. It is especially needed for improving reentry, punishment, and justice.

CAUSAL COMPLEXITY IN UNDERSTANDING THE PUNITIVE TURN

Many phenomena in life result from multiple causes. We might become sick because of exposure to certain viruses or bacteria, fatigue and an associated decline in our defenses, compromised immune systems, poor health habits, and more. Such factors might operate in isolation, together, or in interaction with one another. When investigating why some outcome occurs, our task is much simpler if only a single cause exists. It is more complicated if two or so causes exist. It is more complicated still if five, six, seven, or more exist. And it is even more complicated if some of these factors interact with one another.

This last scenario, in our view, aptly characterizes efforts to understand the punitive turn in American corrections.[3] It is well established that this shift occurred primarily during the 1980s, 1990s, and the first part of the twenty-first century. We can see it, for example, reflected in incarceration on a scale greatly exceeding that found in other countries, a dramatic expansion of the correctional system more generally, and an array of measures, including tougher sentencing laws, that contributed to the growth and reflect a cultural, punitive shift in penology.[4]

What led to this situation? A large number of possibilities exist. Consider but one factor—changes in system capacity. Even without tougher sentencing laws, states can increase prison populations simply through expanded law enforcement, court, and correctional system capacity. As Alfred Blumstein and Allen Beck highlighted in their analysis of prison trends in the 1980s and 1990s, and as we discuss further in this chapter, a considerable amount of prison growth has resulted from "the conversion of arrests into prisoners."[5] Put differently, something as seemingly mundane as a change in processing patterns can greatly influence prison growth.[6] There is, of course, the question of what drove this processing change. The increased arrest-to-imprisonment rate may arise from tougher sentencing laws available to prosecutors, for example. But it can arise, too, from expanded court capacity to process larger volumes of cases or a cultural shift in public views of and political discourse about crime and punishment.[7]

Given the likely multicausal and causally complex nature of mass incarceration, we focus here on prominent causal factors that scholarship suggests have contributed to mass incarceration and reentry. Each of the causes are depicted in Figure 3.1 and discussed below. As the bottom of the figure highlights, there may be contingencies involved, such that one factor may have little to no effect in the absence of another variable. There may be thresholds that must be reached for a given factor to exert an effect. And some factors may have lagged effects or need to change by a certain amount to contribute to mass incarceration and reentry. As we discuss, there is, too, the possibility that these causal complexities arise at once.

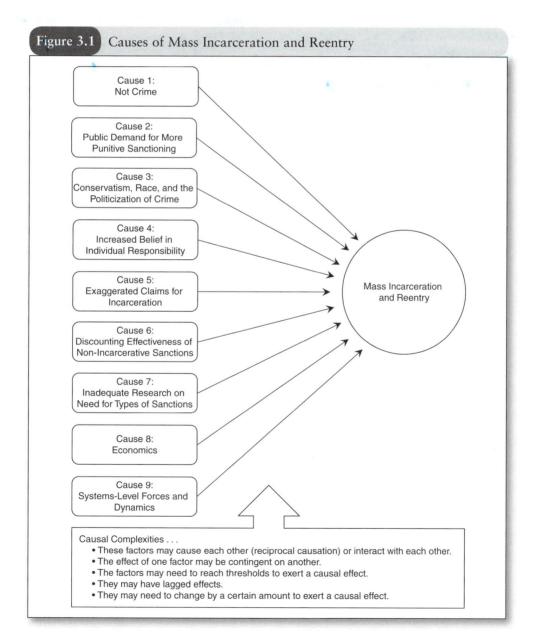

Figure 3.1   Causes of Mass Incarceration and Reentry

CAUSE 1: NOT CRIME

It would seem self-evident that crime drives punishment practices and policies. As a literal matter, without crime there can be no criminals and so no punishment of them. But the fact of crime itself does not require punishment. It does not require a certain type or amount of punishment. Nor does it require that a specific percentage of offenders be caught or that a set percentage of caught-and-convicted offenders be punished, or punished in a particular way. By extension, specific changes in crime do not dictate that specific changes in punishment occur.

The public at large may think differently. Many might assume that the police hear about almost all crime, that most offenders get caught and arrested, that it is clear who is guilty and who is innocent, that the guilty always receive appropriate punishments, and that it is clear what these punishments entail. On every count, such thinking is wrong. However, even if the public—or criminologists, for that matter—held accurate views about these processing stages, we would be left with a quantification dilemma. Specifically, exactly how many offenders does society think *should* be caught? (All of them? If so, we would need to greatly expand law enforcement agency capacity well beyond what historically has been possible, even during the get-tough era.) Convicted? Sentenced to probation? Prison? In the latter instance, for how long? How long for individuals with two prior convictions? Or three?

These observations and questions serve to highlight that crime trends alone will not necessarily tell us anything about punishment trends.[8] If, for example, "excessive" incarceration (defined perhaps based on some national survey of citizens) has been the norm for one decade, it might well be that incarceration decreases in the subsequent decade. During that time, crime may also decrease. In that case, a decrease in crime will be associated with a decrease in incarceration. However, the latter would not necessarily result from decreased crime but rather a desire to use prison less, perhaps in a way that some might perceive to be a more proportionate manner. Alternatively, after a decade of "excessive incarceration," crime might begin declining, and the public in turn might come to believe that the excess in fact was effective, thereby leading them to call for more incarceration to drive crime rates down even further.

Identifying a clear causal relationship between crime trends and crime policy thus presents many challenges. What we know, though, is that national crime trends did not in any obvious way point to the need for more incarceration. As can be seen in Figure 3.2, violent victimization in the United States was stable throughout the 1970s, declined slightly in the mid-1980s, and then steadily increased from the mid-1980s to 1994. At the peak level in 1994, the country's violent victimization rate was lower than it had been in the latter part of the 1970s. From 1994 to the present, violent crime steadily and markedly declined. After 2010, it began to increase slightly.

The story for property victimization differs. Although a claim could be made that the rise in violent crime—murder in particular—in the mid- to late 1980s fueled get-tough criminal justice policies, no such claim can be made for property victimization. The latter steadily declined prior to, during, and after the get-tough era, though in 2011 and 2012 it began to rise slightly.

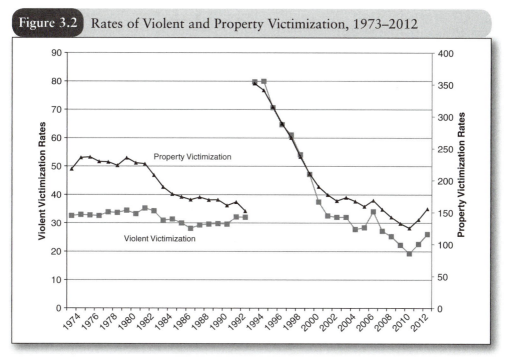

Figure 3.2   Rates of Violent and Property Victimization, 1973–2012

Source: Rand and Catalano (2007), which provided estimates of victimization for 1973–1992. Lauritsen and Rezey (2013), which provided estimates of victimization for 1993–2010. Truman et al. (2013), which provided estimates of victimization for 2011–2012.

Note: In 1993, the National Crime Victimization Survey (NCVS) implemented a new design for estimating victimization. There are different ways to display the NCVS data to account for this change. Here, we present the unadjusted NCVS estimates for 1973–1992. Estimates for 1993–2010 are based both on the new design implemented in 1993 and on the revised estimation method introduced by Lauritsen et al. (2012) that includes series offenses. The increase for violent victimization and property victimization in 2006 reflects a change in the sampling methods used by the NCVS for that year and is not reflective of a true increase in victimization.

Here, a brief detour is warranted to address an important question: Why do we see a large jump in victimization rates in 1993? The rates displayed in the figure come from estimates based on the National Crime Victimization Survey (NCVS). NCVS estimates differ for rates calculated before 1993 compared with those calculated thereafter. First, the NCVS implemented a new estimation design that started in 1993. The rates shown in the figure, prior to 1993, are based on non-adjusted, official estimates of victimization from the old design. Rates of victimization from 1993 to 2010 come from the new design and reflect a revised estimation procedure that accounts for series (i.e., repeat) victimizations. Both estimation changes caused the appearance of increased victimization and are responsible for the substantial gap that appears between 1992 and 1993. However, the victimization *trend* remains the same regardless of changes in estimation or variations in how the data are displayed.[9]

We can see that the brief spike in violent crime in the late 1980s could easily be viewed as justification for increased punishment, and the steady decline in violent crime in the 1990s could be viewed as evidence that this increase worked. Indeed, some estimates suggest that perhaps as much as one-fourth of the crime decline in the 1990s could be attributed to increased incarceration.[10] However, at least three significant complications exist here. First, property crime declined throughout this entire period. Second, it is unclear what drove violent crime up in the first place. That in turn makes it difficult to know how, if at all, the specific increases in incarceration in the late 1980s and early 1990s drove crime down. Third, scholars disagree about the causes of the crime increase and decrease. For example, Eric Baumer, in his analysis of crime trends and studies of them, has argued that we simply lack the research necessary for drawing any firm conclusions about what contributed to the crime decline in the 1990s.[11]

Our focus on crime and increased incarceration leads to a more fundamental problem—before violent crime rates began to escalate, states around the country already had started, in the early 1980s, to invest in prisons at historically unprecedented rates. At best, continued investment in prisons might have been justified once violent crime rates increased in the mid- to late 1980s. But the *initial* impetus for mass incarceration has no clear or obvious relationship to crime in the 1970s or early 1980s.[12] Accordingly, and as we discuss below, any use of crime trends to explain mass incarceration likely requires a discussion of the interaction of crime trends with other causal forces that together fueled the dramatic increase in imprisonment.

CAUSE 2: PUBLIC DEMAND FOR INCREASED PUNITIVE SANCTIONING

Policy makers like to say that they represent "the people" and, in particular, their constituents. Nationally, then, we can expect—given the emergence of mass incarceration and the punitive turn—that the public clearly, loudly, and unequivocally called for tougher punishment, especially incarceration. Oddly, we have little evidence that the public made any such call.

How policy makers learn about the public can affect how accurately they understand public views.[13] They may hear from lobbyists and different stakeholder groups who call or meet them. They also may learn about public views from newspapers from their home jurisdictions, representatives of law enforcement agencies and the correctional system who contact them, town hall forums, and so on.[14] Different groups may conduct public opinion polls, which the media may feature, and these too may inform policy maker understanding of their constituents' views. However, these sources likely do not accurately represent the views of most citizens. The aphorism "the squeaky wheel gets the grease" captures the problem—the loudest voices get heard but do not necessarily represent the views of others.

Given that policy makers must rely on non-random sources for gauging the public will, they typically cannot and do not know what most members of the public actually want. All of us are highly vulnerable to what psychologists refer to as "confirmation bias."[15] That is, we tend to see patterns in the world around us that confirm our preestablished views. If we think that New Yorkers act rudely, we will tend to focus on those New Yorkers who in fact act rudely, which will reinforce our beliefs. Medical doctors make diagnostic errors that result from this type of bias.[16] Prosecutors can make similar errors in judgment.[17] Policy makers are no exception. There may be no cure to this problem, save to call for policy makers to rely on diverse sources of information, to be aware of the potential biases in the information that they receive, and to prioritize objective sources of information. But the problem nonetheless should be recognized because it speaks directly to claims that the public demanded punitive punishments.

Before addressing that claim, a related question bears discussion: *Should* policy makers listen to the public when devising sentencing policies and considering various approaches to increasing public safety? In a democracy, such a question seems ludicrous—of course, they should. However, what really does the public know about crime and punishment? Mass incarceration has been premised in part on the argument that the United States experienced increased crime and that other options, including rehabilitation, did not work. The bulk of mass incarceration policies emerged at the state level. How much did citizens know about levels of crime in their respective states? About levels and types of punishment? Rates of punishment? For example, what percentages of offenders were caught, arrested, convicted, and sentenced to prison, respectively? How accurately did the public understand the changes that occurred along each of these dimensions? Or the costs? Or the available alternatives and their relative costs? Or, not least, what was known about their relative effectiveness for improving public safety?

In a class one of us teaches—a course on corrections—students are asked how many individuals reside in Florida prisons. The vast bulk of the students come from Florida, and typically the class consists of juniors and seniors as well as criminology majors. They do not represent the general public because, among other things, their education and major give them a head start on knowing a bit more about criminal justice facts. Regardless, when Florida's prison population stood around 100,000, students responses varied greatly. Some said that the state housed about 5,000 inmates. Others guessed 50,000. Still others guessed as high as 500,000. The point is that simply asking the public about what punishments we should mete out does not make sense if most do not hold accurate perceptions about the scale of crime or the type and amount of punishment their state imposes.[18]

It may make more sense, however, if we gauge public perceptions by asking nuanced questions that provide the public with critical information. If we ask people whether the courts should be tougher on crime and provide them with response categories, such as "strongly disagree" to "strongly agree," we will likely end up with large percentages of respondents in each category. However, the responses almost certainly will change if we first provide respondents with critical information. In studies on views about the death penalty, for example, support for the death penalty declines by approximately 20 percentage points if respondents are told that life without parole is an option.[19]

With that backdrop, then, what do we know about public support for the punitive turn? Perhaps first and foremost, we know that public opinion polls in the United States and in many other countries (e.g., Britain and Canada) pointed to increased support during the 1980s and 1990s for more punitive sanctioning.[20] Despite get-tough trends in punishment in other countries, however, available evidence suggests that the American public endorses more punitive sanctioning than what the citizenries of other Western nations endorse.[21] It is, however, variable. In the late 1980s and early 1990s, Americans expressed increasingly greater concern about crime, but then this concern declined in subsequent years.[22]

Second, we know that the public is not nearly as punitive as policy makers assume.[23] Certainly, concern about crime increased during the 1980s. But such concern did not necessarily mean that the public called for large-scale increases in incarceration or greatly expanded use of probation, tougher enforcement of probation and parole conditions, elimination of or reduction in early release options, and the like. Only when the focus of questions centers on chronic, serious, or violent offenders does the public consistently endorse a more retributive, "just deserts" approach to sanctioning.[24] Even then, support for more retributive sanctioning does not itself indicate that incarceration constitutes the best way to achieve retribution.

Third, we know that when we ask the public simplified, decontextualized questions, they respond in ways that exaggerate their views.[25] The death penalty example above is illustrative. Another example—if we ask members of the public if they support tougher punishment of violent juvenile offenders, we assuredly will learn that large percentages of respondents agree. However, if we ask them if they support rehabilitation of youth, and even tax increases to support rehabilitative programming, we again will see large percentages of the public agreeing.[26] If we rely on the first approach, the straightforward conclusion is that the public wants tougher punishment of violent youth. If we rely on the second, the conclusion is more complicated. Yes, they want tougher punishment, but they also want rehabilitation to be part of that punishment and will support higher taxes to fund it.

Fourth, researchers have documented that one of the sources of public punitiveness stems from views that crime was out of control in the 1980s and 1990s.[27] This pattern stands out because this assumption was not correct or, at a minimum, was overstated. A related source of punitiveness may have involved the view among the public that America was in "moral decline."[28] Whether the country indeed was in moral decline remains, of course, open to debate and difficult to refute or to prove.[29] Still another related source of support for punitive measures may have stemmed from racialized perceptions of crime. Whites tend to equate being black with criminal behavior and concomitantly may have been more supportive of the punitive turn.[30]

Fifth, public opinion may not so much drive policy as reflect policy maker preferences. For example, Mark Ramirez examined changes in public opinion and found that "the ups and downs of punitive sentiment are driven by important political factors such as the construction of crime by political leaders. The framing of crime as a problem of a permissive system and [also] increasing perceptions of racial integration increased public demand for punitive policies."[31] We might safely conclude that a more tempered situation exists—public opinion may shape policy maker attitudes and decisions, but the latter may affect public opinion as well.

Sixth, Americans strongly support rehabilitation and did so throughout the mass incarceration era.[32] In addition, the public has supported reduced reliance on prisons and more investment in alternatives.[33] Here, again, though, the more accurate depiction is that the public wants a balanced portfolio of approaches to reducing crime and punishing criminals.[34]

CAUSE 3: CONSERVATISM, RACE, MORAL PANICS, AND THE POLITICIZATION OF CRIME

Perhaps the most commonly identified potential cause for the punitive turn in American criminal justice is what has come to be termed the "politicization of crime." From this perspective, changes in crime have not led to heightened punitiveness, but instead crime has provided the impetus for the rise of get-tough policies. This perspective suggests that punitive policy shifts were motivated by a nefarious goal, such that the main driver for the new policies stemmed from conservative political ideologies that focused on crime less because of the public safety benefit that might accrue and more because doing so would create greater political capital.[35] At the same time, it would provide a vehicle for addressing anxieties in America that arose due to such social changes as the transformation of women's roles in the workplace and of gender hierarchies more generally, racial and ethnic tensions, concerns about immigration, and more.[36] These anxieties, the argument goes, resulted in a "moral panic" that required action. That included getting tough on criminals, especially to the extent that criminals were viewed as originating from various threatening groups.

Seeming support for this argument can be found at first blush by the fact that under Presidents Ronald Reagan and George H. W. Bush the country experienced 12 straight years of largely conservative leadership that made "lock 'em up" punishment a priority. According to the politicization argument, liberals had no recourse but to embrace tough-on-crime platforms if they wished to remain or get elected and obtain greater political clout. President Bill Clinton, for example, prioritized tough-on-crime criminal justice policies throughout his 8-year presidency. These policies included the hiring of 100,000 law enforcement officers nationwide.

The lynchpin of this argument, however, rests on the notion that policy makers did not actually care about public safety. Rather, their focus on crime emanated entirely from self-interested political gain. That position is difficult to sustain. As discussed above, violent crime did increase in the 1980s and provided more than sufficient impetus to raise concerns about how to protect the public.[37] Increases in high-profile drug dealing and drug-related offending, too, offered substantial grounds for concern about crime. A milder version of the politicization argument is more tenable—policy makers well may have been concerned about promoting public safety, but they also realized the utility of crime control rhetoric as a means of signaling their own political strength and, conversely, the weakness of the opposing party.

Evidence for this possibility can be found readily in the 1988 presidential election. Vice President George H. W. Bush ran against Massachusetts Governor Michael Dukakis using an advertisement that profiled Willie Horton, a furloughed murderer who raped a woman.[38] The advertisement effectively conveyed a simple message: Elect Michael Dukakis and it could be your friend or family member that he allows to be victimized. Alternatively, elect George H. W. Bush and you will be safe. The advertisement is widely credited with contributing to the election of Bush to the presidency. Texas Governor Ann Richards took heed of what happened and, in her 1994 reelection campaign against George W. Bush, ran television advertisements in which she walked in front of prison fences proclaiming, "If you do the crime, you will do the time."[39]

We can see further evidence of the politicization of crime in other lawmakers'—both Democrat and Republican—public speeches and pronouncements, as reflected in the following statements:

- *"[Law and order is being sacrificed] just to give criminals a sporting chance to go free."*—Barry Goldwater, Republican Party presidential nominee, 1964.[40] As with contemporary political statements, the argument boils down to the following: The opposition stands for increased crime and disorder and the rights of criminals. By contrast, a vote for [in this instance Barry Goldwater] serves as a vote for safety, order, and the rights of victims and, more broadly, law-abiding citizens.

- *"[There] isn't a cure for the career criminal, there is only one way to protect the public from violent criminals . . . and that is to lock them up. Mandatory sentences must be established."*—Senator Henry Jackson, Democratic candidate for the presidential nomination, 1972.[41] The image evoked here and in many lawmaker accounts consists of one in which the criminal justice system handles primarily career criminals who have not been punished enough. So locking them up must be the solution. Many questionable if not incorrect assumptions inhere to such statements. Criminal justice systems deal with a large variety of offenders, many of whom do not fit neatly the image of a career criminal. Many chronic offenders do receive tough punishments, including lengthy prison stays. And, although creating even longer prison terms might achieve some incapacitation, the returns relative to the costs are unclear.

- *"Piously claiming defense of civil liberties and prodded by a variety of bleeding hearts of the society, we have dismantled much of the intelligence operations of law enforcement that we must have if we are to protect society from political terrorists."*—Governor Ronald Reagan, 1975.[42] Reagan here was echoing themes found in Goldwater's 1964 campaign, Richard M. Nixon's 1968 campaign, and in Reagan's subsequent terms as president. The politicizing of crime thus has existed for many decades. At most, it assumed greater prominence in the 1980s and "resonated" because it occurred during a period when murder rates rapidly escalated.

- *"We simply cannot treat them [young violent offenders] as juveniles when their life experience has turned them into hardened adult offenders before their time."*—Evan Bayh, Democratic governor of Indiana, 1995.[43] Bayh here implied that juvenile offenders had been coddled and that no one realized that some youth commit terrible crimes. An additional implication was that some young offenders really are not truly youthful. Rather, they are adult-like, capable of horrific offenses and, accordingly, worthy of tough punishment. The efforts to transfer more youth to the adult system resulted in what some scholars have characterized as the "criminalization" of juvenile justice[44] and reflects the dramatic shift in recent decades towards a get-tough philosophy advocated not only for adult offenders but also for juvenile offenders.

- *"I can be nicked on a lot, but no one can say I'm soft on crime."*[45] Bill Clinton, Democrat, presidential candidate, 1992. Clinton went on to win the presidency and did so in part because he heeded lessons from the previous presidential race in which Democrats appeared soft on crime. Here, then, the justification for tough-on-crime policies derives from the political benefit that comes from doing so, not from any reference to objective need.

- *"Liberals do not understand this simple axiom: criminals behind bars cannot harm the general public. To that end, we support mandatory prison sentencing for gang crimes, violent or sexual offenses against children, repeat drug dealers, rape, robbery and murder. We support a national registry for convicted child murderers. We oppose parole for dangerous or repeat felons. Courts should have the option of imposing the death penalty in capital murder cases."*—Republican National Committee, 2012.[46] The explicit message is that "liberals do not understand" something as basic as incapacitation and thus cannot be relied on to keep America safe. Democrats have used such language as well. When the two political parties agree on a general policy approach, such as tough-on-crime sanctioning, the result can be successful large-scale implementation. When they do not, as occurred in 2013 with the Affordable Care Act under President Barack Obama, the result can be anemic implementation.

We can see, then, that crime control has been seized upon as a political tool for many years, not just during the 1980s and 1990s or after. At its foundation, the rational core involves the common-sense observation that crime hurts society and merits a response. The politicization of crime, however, contorts crime control discussions into political tools that enable lawmakers to get elected or to pursue broader agendas. A more benign characterization of the politicization of crime is one that views a focus on law-and-order policy making as a form of "penal populism." It constitutes "a political response that favors popularity over other policy considerations."[47] Less benign characterizations exist, however.

Some scholars, for example, have argued that the politicization of crime has allowed for the use of "crime control and its associated rhetoric and techniques as a template for governance in areas as diverse as education, housing, workplace relations, and family policy."[48] As Jonathan Simon has asserted, it enables policy makers to "govern through crime."[49] From this perspective, a focus on crime facilitates getting elected and pursuing political platforms. It also facilitates the ability to govern or control certain populations, such as the poor, racial or ethnic minorities, immigrants, and other groups. Similarly, Michelle Alexander has portrayed the politicization of crime, including the use of disenfranchisement, as a method for marginalizing blacks.[50]

The connection between the politicization of crime and race stands out prominently in accounts of mass incarceration. Blacks have been incarcerated at substantially higher rates than whites. In addition, black communities shoulder a disproportionate amount of the burden for accommodating or addressing the challenges associated with large numbers of ex-prisoners returning to them. Reentry affects these communities in ways that quantitatively and qualitatively differ—it is at once greater in magnitude and potentially more pernicious in its effects on social order. Punitive policies more broadly, not just incarceration, have been found to affect blacks adversely and more acutely. Voter disenfranchisement has emerged as one of the most prominent examples.[51] The greater use of punitive policies with blacks and the greater effect of them in black communities give credence to accounts like those articulated by Simon and Alexander. They are further reinforced by other sources. For example, studies of public opinion point to racial animus as central to support for tougher punishments. In James Unnever and Francis Cullen's analyses, for example, they found "that one of the most salient and consistent predictors of American punitiveness is racial animus."[52] Other scholarship suggests that fodder for the get-tough movement stems from members of the public equating crime with blacks.[53] From this perspective, the politicization of crime is directly tied to fear of blacks and an effort to control them through a seemingly race-neutral mechanism— punishing offenders.

We can view the politicization of crime through other lenses as well. For example, when crime control becomes subject to ideological battles, with one party heralding its philosophical stance as superior to the other, the door opens to dramatic shifts in policy. These shifts create significant inefficiency—in one fell swoop we dismiss one approach for another, as if only extremes were effective.[54] The politicization of crime, too, can lead policy makers to "symbolic gestures," calling for broad changes in policy for political gain but not attending to the complicated nuts-and-bolts planning required to design and implement effective policy. Silver-bullet solutions, for example, may be advocated even though the many causes of crime likely require many strategies and efforts to increase public safety effectively.

In short, the politicization of crime seems to be directly implicated in the punitive turn. But as a causal factor, its effect is not necessarily direct. Rather, part of its causal force likely arises from the rise in violent crime and drug-related crime that occurred during the 1980s and the concomitant rise in a new and well-articulated conservative ideology. At the same time, concern about crime appeared to coincide with concern about increased threats presented by minorities, blacks in particular. The war on drugs provided another contextual factor that served to legitimize an all-out attack on crime by sending a clear-cut message: Crime will not be tolerated. This nexus of forces created plenty of room for politics to enter into what otherwise might have been a more tempered form of debate about how best to make the country safer.

CAUSE 4: INCREASED BELIEF IN THE IDEA THAT INDIVIDUAL RESPONSIBILITY MATTERS MOST

Central to the punitive turn is a philosophy emphasizing individual responsibility, one implicit in the types of tough-on-crime policies and practices that emerged in this time period. Conservative political platforms tend to emphasize individual agency. Republicans, for example, tend to locate responsibility for personal success or failure in individual initiative, while Democrats tend to locate it in social conditions. The reality is that individuals do not live in social vacuums; at the same time, social context does not dictate what individuals do. Accordingly, extreme views distort reality. When, as discussed above, policy discussions become politicized, extreme views assume greater prominence and play a larger role in shaping policy. The salience of notions of individual agency bears scrutiny, therefore, because they not only permeated policy discussions in the 1980s and 1990s but also directly supported an emphasis on incapacitative sanctioning. There was, however, nothing intrinsic to a focus on individual responsibility that had to lead to this approach or to a broader deterrence-based focus on sanctioning.

A focus on supermax prisons illustrates the point. Supermax housing emerged in part because of a concern about prison disorder. If we accept the idea that disorder results from a multitude of factors—poor prison management, ill-equipped or untrained staff, ineffective inmate classification, extensive opportunities for misbehavior, and a ready and willing supply of individuals to act out—then we likely would call for an array of policies that addressed each of these factors. This approach would implicitly recognize that the conditions that give rise to violence and disorder in prisons stem from a range of sociological and individual-level factors. Research tends to bear out this idea.[55]

However, if we believe that misconduct results entirely from personal failings, then we logically will be drawn to focus on the individuals who engage in misconduct. We can do so in many ways. We can provide treatment, services, education, training, and the like. We also can punish more. All of these approaches are consistent with a focus on individual causation as the sole factor contributing to systemwide prison order or disorder.

How, then, do we arrive at a situation where we focus exclusively on locking certain inmates away in supermaxes with largely no treatment, services, or the like? Such an approach assumes that the sole cause of misconduct stems from some type of moral failing or problem with self-control *and* that these can be corrected through punishment. That is, it involves a belief in severe punishment's efficacy as a deterrent or form of treatment.[56]

This idea seems to resonate with the American public, and certainly with large segments of conservatives. At the same time, it runs counter to a prominent streak in American culture that emphasizes the importance of opportunities to achieve the "American dream." Hard work is requisite, absolutely. But so, too, is the chance to succeed. Indeed, this idea undergirds the logic of having a separate juvenile justice system. Creation of the juvenile court resulted from the belief that youthful offenders could change and that, with a mix of accountability, punishment, treatment, services, and opportunities, they could succeed.[57] Liberals tend to emphasize these ideas as well, but they place greater emphasis on the social conditions that some groups, such as the poor and minorities, face in trying to achieve the American dream.

The fact that many crime policies emphasized personal agency almost exclusively appears to indicate that Americans—both Republicans and Democrats—felt that, prior to the 1980s, justice system responses weighed social conditions too heavily. To the extent that such a view prevailed, a sustained period of conservative political control, such as occurred from 1980 to 1992, provided a unique conduit for amplifying this concern. In turn, such concern could be translated into policies that systematically focused not on communities and social contexts within which offenders resided but rather on individual offenders.

Such views may have resonated especially well with the American public because they emerged during a time of economic insecurity in the United States.[58] During times of economic crisis, there may be less support or tolerance for views that somehow excuse offending. For example, when individuals have lost their jobs, the notion that a young or adult offender might have committed a crime because they were neglected, attended poorly functioning schools, resided in areas of concentrated poverty and crime, and so on may carry little weight. We tend to develop short fuses when we are stressed. By extension, we may feel less accommodating toward offenders. Punitiveness and an emphasis on personal agency may come more naturally during such times. Support for that idea is reflected in the fact that welfare reforms, not just criminal justice policies, became more restrictive during the 1980s and 1990s.

Here, again, one of the challenges to simple causal accounts of the punitive turn lies in the fact that these reforms occurred under both Republican-led and Democrat-led presidential administrations. It lies, too, in the fact that the American public tends not to swing to extremes in its views about crime and punishment or personal responsibility. Rather, the swings tend to be subtle. Support for the death penalty is illustrative—views do change but typically by a few percentage points, not 30 or 40 percentage point changes in a year or two.[59]

At the end of the day, what we do know is that punishment-focused criminal justice policies reflect a more individualistic view of the causes of and solutions to crime. They proceed from an assumption that the causes of increased crime rates lie within individual offenders. By extension, they assume that large-scale decreases in crime can be obtained by sending a message to these individuals that they need to get their act together or they will experience even harsher punishment. The American emphasis on individual responsibility and initiative seems, then, to constitute a factor that has contributed to the punitive turn in punishment or that has moderated the awareness of other causal forces in creating this policy shift.

CAUSE 5: EXAGGERATED CLAIMS FOR INCARCERATION

Disenchantment with rehabilitation constituted a central contributing factor to the punitive turn and it led to interest in an effective alternative.[60] In any policy context where an existing approach falls out of favor, two options exist. The first is to map out the possible range of strategies that could be used and then to assess the relative feasibility as well as costs and benefits of each. The second is to seek recourse to simple, "common sense" solutions. When a given problem results primarily from one cause or when evidence clearly establishes that a single solution can be largely effective in addressing the problem, such an approach in fact might be aptly termed "common sense." However, when the problem results from multiple causes, when multiple potential solutions exist, when evidence for one or another approach is limited, and when, even so, we pursue one particular approach to the exclusion of others—that does not constitute common sense. Rather, it amounts to blind faith that a silver-bullet solution exists that can magically solve the problem.[61]

This situation characterizes the emergence of mass incarceration. Implicit in the dramatic expansion of prison populations is the idea that incarceration achieves such goals as reduced crime, reduced recidivism, more satisfactory levels of retribution, and increased public perceptions of safety. Actually, these expectations were not very implicit. Policy-maker statements made such claims.

Proponents of get-tough legislation argued expressly that "lock 'em up" punishment policies necessarily would achieve these goals.[62]

In recent years, some studies have suggested that increased incarceration has reduced crime rates by as much as 25 percent, whether through incapacitation, specific deterrence, general deterrence, other mechanisms, or some combination of these possibilities.[63] However, no scholarly consensus supports such assessments. Thus, the assessments may be correct, but they may not be. They may understate the effects or overstate them. Adjudicating this situation will require a much larger body of studies than what exists at this point. More salient for our discussion here, however, is the fact that such work did not exist in the 1980s and early 1990s, at precisely the time that prison system expansion occurred. As a logical matter, investment in prisons necessarily involved an assumption that empirical research would validate the belief in the ability of increased incarceration to reduce crime rates.

In a similar vein, few credible empirical studies existed to support the claim that incarceration, relative to non-incarcerative sanctions, or lengthy terms of incarceration reduce recidivism.[64] Indeed, recent reviews have emphasized that there remain few credible studies of incarceration effects. Those that exist have produced equivocal estimates, with some finding null effects, some finding beneficial effects, and most finding harmful ones.[65] Here, again, then, large-scale investment in incarceration necessarily proceeded from a belief in its effectiveness. There was no body of research then or now that provided compelling evidence that prison or lengthy terms of incarceration produce consistent or large reductions in recidivism.[66] By extension, no body of work exists that establishes that the magnitude of benefits offset the financial or social costs of mass incarceration and do so appreciably more than other types of punishments, such as intensive probation or shorter, more certain stays in prison.[67]

We also do not have much of a "science of retribution," one that, for example, could tell us how much suffering an individual experiences for a given type of sanction or how much satisfaction the public feels when offenders receive these sanctions.[68] What we do know is that the public has limited knowledge about the criminal justice system and the punishments available to the courts. Typically, they view the system as inadequate. For example, "the public tends to underestimate the severity of sentences imposed and to overestimate the proportion of inmates who are released on parole."[69] Put differently, as Julian Roberts and Loretta Stalans found in their review of public opinion research, "in the public mind, crime rates are constantly rising, and the system is always too lenient."[70] This pattern does not necessarily have to mean that the public wants more incarceration as a means of obtaining retribution. Rather, it means that existing responses appear to the public to be insufficiently retributive. Incarceration stands as one option for increasing retribution. However, we can increase retribution other ways, such as by using probation for individuals who otherwise might receive little to no sanction.

What we know more broadly is that public views are complicated and that they typically reflect a poor understanding of true crime rates, actual punishments, individuals' experiences with punishment, the effectiveness of these punishments, the spectrum of potential responses to crime, or their costs.[71] We know, too, that simplistic questions tend to distort public views. In these instances, respondents think about the worst offenders and then indicate their support for a given sanction. More nuanced approaches almost invariably change the findings. For example, after individuals receive information about specific facts concerning a given case, they become much more likely to view the resulting sanction as appropriate.[72]

Despite decades of research on public perceptions of sentence severity, relatively little research systematically documents public views about the relative retribution obtained from a diverse range of sanctions. Instead, studies tend to focus on whether the public views the courts as dealing "too harshly" or "not harshly enough" with criminals.[73] The responses thus conflate multiple issues. For example, if we view the courts as not dealing with criminals harshly enough, that might mean that the courts are not sufficiently retributive, that they are not applying the types of tough punishments that will deter certain offenders, or some combination of the two. It obscures, too, the fact that the public typically has little understanding about the relative use of various sanctions or the specific contextual factors that contributed to sentencing decisions.[74]

Policy makers tend to emphasize the importance of being responsive to the public. Accordingly, public views about the performance of the justice system constitute another dimension of potential relevance. Studies typically have found that individuals express considerable satisfaction with law enforcement agency performance but not court performance; the public tends to perceive the courts as insufficiently tough and as too reliant on plea bargaining.[75] The complicating factor, again, lies with the fact that the public rarely has an accurate understanding of local or state sentencing practices, constraints, or the reasoning behind specific sentences or processing decisions. Another complicating factor stems from the fact that public opinion changes. To illustrate, although the public expressed more punitive views in the 1980s and 1990s, contemporary views appear to be more tempered. In a 2012 public opinion poll, for example, 69 percent of Americans reported supporting non-incarcerative sentences for nonviolent offenders, even as they still supported tough penalties for violent offenders.[76]

In short, based in particular on public opinion studies and policy-maker statements, it seems likely that unrealistic assumptions about the need for and benefits of incarceration contributed to mass incarceration. That these claims lacked any clear, coherent, or systematic empirical foundation in research does not refute that idea. It does, however, raise concern that the country embarked on a highly costly enterprise with little empirical justification. In addition, it highlights that any causal account of mass incarceration requires looking beyond simplistic claims that it arose due to the need for more punishment.

For our purposes, it highlights, too, the broader context that gave rise to mass reentry and the context to which ex-prisoners return. Briefly, the individuals who leave prison face an array of constraints and additional punishments that collectively fit within a similar logic, one that says that more restrictions and more punitiveness are needed and effective. These individuals at once experience more punishment during and after incarceration and, simultaneously, less rehabilitation and support during and after incarceration. The question, to which we will return, is whether such an approach constitutes the most effective way to improve public safety, justice, and satisfaction with the criminal justice system.

**CAUSE 6: DISCOUNTING EFFECTIVENESS OF
NON-INCARCERATIVE SANCTIONS**

One of the ways that policy makers and the public could have convinced themselves that incarceration was needed and effective involved the assumption that non-incarcerative sanctions don't work. Much has been made of the influence of the 1974 Robert Martinson report in contributing to disenchantment with rehabilitation.[77] There appears to be little doubt that the report tapped into or reflected a widely held view that the rehabilitative ideal could not be attained or be effective. As recent studies have highlighted, however, this assessment was premature and in many ways incorrect.[78]

A starting point for highlighting this issue begins with Table 3.1. As can be seen, sanctioning options available to the courts vary. Punishments do not

Table 3.1   Incarceration and Types of Non-Incarcerative Sanctions

Incarceration Sanctions

  Jail or prison

  Variable sentence lengths

  Variable in-prison experiences, treatment, and services

  Variable intensity and quality of post-release supervision (parole)

Non-Incarcerative Sanctions

  Low-intensity community supervision (probation)

  Medium-intensity community supervision (probation)

  High-intensity community supervision (probation)

     and/or

  Halfway house

  Boot camp

  House arrest

  Day-reporting centers

  Electronic monitoring

  Restitution and fines

  Drug testing

  Community service

  Treatment (drug, mental health, etc.)

  Specialized courts (e.g., drug, gun, mental health, community)

Sources: Tonry (1997); Mears and Barnes (2010); Mears et al. (2011).

involve an either/or set of options—either go to prison *or* receive some type of rehabilitative intervention. Indeed, a range of options exists and in almost every instance involve both punitive or rehabilitative emphases.[79]

At the most punitive end of the spectrum (excepting the death penalty), we have jail or prison. Here, though, a menu of options confronts us: Individuals may be sentenced for shorter or longer durations than others. They may receive little to no rehabilitative treatment or services or a lot or some amount in between. They may be released to parole or not. When released to the community, they may be placed on supervision or not. And if on supervision, they may be supervised closely or not, and they may be provided substantial assistance in finding jobs, treatment, and housing, or not. Collectively, these possibilities amount to a range of punishments with varying degrees of punitiveness or rehabilitation attached to them. In short, even if we focus exclusively on incarceration, considerable variability exists.

That variability is, if anything, more pronounced when we turn to non-incarcerative sanctions. Individuals may go to halfway houses or boot camps, be placed on house arrest, be required to check in at day-reporting centers, be placed on electronic monitoring, pay restitution or fines, undergo drug testing, perform community service, receive drug or mental health treatment as a part of a term of probation, or be sanctioned through specialized courts that provide variable amounts of supervision, accountability, and treatment and services. In every instance, supervision might be intensive or relatively mild. Treatment and services might be considerable or nominal. The length of time served for any one of these sanctions, too, may vary. Notably, probation—what sometimes is referred to as the workhorse of the criminal justice system—does not have to entail mild punishment. Indeed, some studies indicate that convicted felons view probation and other supervision-based sanctions as more severe than prison.[80]

Are these non-incarcerative, intermediate sanctions effective? The short answer is yes if they are implemented with appropriate types of individuals at appropriate levels or "doses" by trained personnel, and no when these conditions do not hold.[81] However, relatively little credible research exists that provides robust estimates of the effectiveness of the diverse range of sanctions relative to one another.[82]

Even so, the prevailing view during the 1980s and into the 1990s, even among many scholars familiar with the state of research at that time, appeared to be that nothing works; and so, given increased violent crime, incarceration must constitute the best, most effective available option. This assessment overstated the case. In fact, during the 1980s, public support for non-incarcerative sanctions was considerable—and substantially greater than what policy makers and criminal justice professionals believed. In a review of research, for example, Roberts and Stalans found that both groups "tend to overestimate the punitiveness of the public sentiment."[83] They cited, as one illustration, a 1985 study in which "fewer than one-quarter of criminal justice decision makers believed that the public would support the use of alternatives to incarceration" when in fact surveys of citizens in the state (Michigan) "found that fully two-thirds of respondents approved of the use of such sentencing alternatives."[84]

As with the other potential contributors to mass incarceration, then, we can see that any causal relationship involves complicated dynamics. Here, for example, we have policy makers potentially helping to drive public opinion and, at the same time, misunderstanding it. We have policy makers discounting non-incarcerative sanctions and pronouncing that they do not work and that get-tough prison stays do. We have the fact that support for non-incarcerative sanctions then as now likely depends heavily on the types of offenders thought to receive them, with the public expressing less support if the offenders have committed violent crimes.[85] We have, too, the potential for the public to be unaware of the range of available non-incarcerative sanctions and their relative effectiveness or costs. We have the potential, not least, for their views to change markedly when presented with specific information about these and other dimensions.

Despite such complications, we are left with the fact that mass incarceration occurred with no commensurate increase in treatment or rehabilitative-focused sanctions.[86] That suggests that mistrust in the effectiveness of such approaches contributed to the punitive turn.

CAUSE 7: INADEQUATE RESEARCH DOCUMENTING THE NEED FOR SPECIFIC TYPES OF SANCTIONS

Causes sometimes consist of forces that appear. At other times, however, they consist of forces that fail to appear. One of the arguably more powerful causes of mass incarceration and reentry, and the punitive turn more broadly, lies with the absence of empirical research that carefully documented the causes of increases in crime rates and the relative use, effectiveness, and cost-efficiency of various sanctions by these jurisdictions.[87]

As discussed above, it requires little effort to assert that what we are doing doesn't work. In the 1980s and 1990s, policy makers repeatedly claimed that contemporary efforts were not effective and so new efforts, especially punitive approaches, needed to be adopted. Such claims can be easily bolstered, at any time, by the fact that there always will be horrible crimes to which we can point, as if doing so self-evidently demonstrates a failure of current policy.

This type of thinking is logically flawed. For example, if property crime declines and violent crime increases, it may well be that current policies, including sanctioning approaches, are effective but that they need to be increased. It may be that more certain punishment rather than more incarceration would be most effective. It may be, too, that an increase in violent crime stems from forces over which the criminal justice system has no control. If, for example, a dramatic economic downturn increased violent crime, then creating more punitive punishments will not likely reverse this trend. If more of a given cause creates a problem, then typically less of it will reduce it. Changing the economy would require effort, but, in this example, doing so would produce more public safety benefits than investing in more punishment.[88]

We suspect that sanctioning during the 1980s and 1990s might have looked quite different if jurisdictions provided documentation of the scope of crime problems, using not only official records data (e.g., arrests, convictions), which provide a distorted view of crime rates and trends, but also self-reported offending data. It might have looked different, too, if they had provided empirical documentation of the use of various sanctions, their costs, and estimates of best-case scenarios for what might be achieved by increased use of a given type of sanction. As it was, however, states invested considerably in incarceration without clearly documenting the need for doing so or estimating the likely returns relative to what might accrue with other sanctioning approaches.[89]

A large body of research documents that the way in which information is presented affects how we process it.[90] If the public had been presented with information about the best-guess causes of crime increases and best-guess estimates of the relative costs and benefits of various sanctions, the betting money is that they likely would not have supported mass incarceration or even the broader punitive turn. Instead, they might well have supported a more balanced portfolio of approaches to reducing crime and improving the criminal justice system.

We cannot demonstrate that such an effect would have occurred. However, it strikes us as plausible if not probable. Any such effect depends heavily on credible research. At present, however, there remains no coherent, well-funded research infrastructure nationally or among states.[91] That situation does not lend itself to the government accountability that legislators increasingly have advocated in recent decades. Only when governments start to operate with true transparency can balanced, evidenced-based approaches to justice emerge. As we argue in later chapters, opportunities exist to improve research infrastructure in ways that will enable policy makers to assess better the uses and effects of diverse criminal justice sanctions and interventions.

CAUSE 8: ECONOMICS

Scholars have suggested that economic conditions have contributed to the punitive turn. Here, though, no simple storyline exists. For example, economic declines might contribute to increased crime and in turn to greater emphasis on incarceration. Alternatively, they may have little clear association with changed crime rates. (In fact, the relationship between crime and economic conditions, including levels of and changes in them, is at best murky.[92]) To use a recent illustration, during the 2000s, the economy declined substantially and yet crime consistently trended downward rather than upward.[93] In the mid-1990s, violent crime began to decline rapidly and yet the American economy seemingly prospered. Here, then, two forces existed—reduced crime and an improved economy—that would seem to argue against mass incarceration and efforts to sustain the more general punitive turn. Even so, the punitive turn held and, if anything, increased throughout the 1990s and 2000s. And it did so even though popular and scholarly accounts indicated that prison growth could not be sustained in the face of chronically poor or worsening economic conditions.[94]

Only with a sustained decade-long downturn in the economy, alongside of ballooning correctional system costs whose drain on state coffers did not become fully apparent until well into the new millennium, did states begin attempting to slow their rate of prison expansion.[95] That, however, did not occur until around 2010, at a point when even a slowdown in prison growth or slight declines would not appreciably change state correctional system budgets.

We are left, then, with considerable uncertainty about how economic conditions contributed to the punitive turn. To illustrate but one of the more complicated set of possibilities, consider the following. During the 1980s, a conservative political movement occurred that fostered support for more punitive crime control policies. An increase in violent crime engendered even greater support for the new tough-on-crime stance. Economic conditions at the time were poor and in fact, despite increased incarceration rates, may have reined in prison growth. Then, when economic conditions improved in the 1990s, states and the federal government had more leeway to fund even greater prison expansion. This expansion stemmed in part from increased law enforcement, court, and prison capacity as well as legislatively required increases in time served. In the 2000s, as the economy faltered and even as crime rates went down, prison growth continued because the mechanisms to promote it—including the increased system capacity and tough-on-crime laws—remained in place.

David Weiman and colleagues have presented a similar account: "Combined, the tougher 'front-end' and 'back-end' criminal justice policies of mass incarceration have sustained the current high levels of imprisonment, despite the sharp drop-off in crime rates."[96] The front-end policies "increased the number of those imprisoned on a new conviction and commitment," while the back-end "'net-widening' parole policies have increased their likelihood of a quick return trip upon release."[97] Other scholars, such as Loïc Wacquant, David Garland, and Michael Lynch present different, more complicated accounts.[98] The complexities defy systematic empirical assessment. Accordingly, we are left with the likelihood that economic conditions may have influenced the punitive turn but not necessarily in any direct, linear manner. Rather, as Theodore Caplow and Jonathan Simon and others have argued, they may have interacted with other social forces.[99]

CAUSE 9: SYSTEMS-LEVEL FORCES AND DYNAMICS

Systems-Level Forces

As the discussion to this point has highlighted, an accurate causal explanation for the rise of mass incarceration and reentry likely entails multiple factors, interactions among many of them, contingent effects, and more. In addition, we argue that systems-level forces themselves contributed to the growth. They have largely cemented existing levels of correctional system capacity and constrain the ability of the system to be reduced in size or to shift substantially to new ways of punishing.

What are these forces? They include but are not restricted to the following: (a) substantially enhanced police capacity, which results in more arrests, regardless of changes in crime rates; (b) substantially more prosecutors, which results in more convictions and plea bargains to various sanctions, largely regardless of crime trends; (c) tougher sentencing laws that empower prosecutors and that are unlikely to be substantially altered if only because disempowering prosecutors constitutes a risky political platform; (d) tougher sentencing laws that require more incarceration and lengthier terms of incarceration and that, because of the political risks involved with appearing soft on crime, likely will remain in place despite recent calls to temper them;[100] (e) more punitive prison conditions and expanded prison capacity, both of which reduce the possibility of providing high-quality rehabilitative treatment and services, which in turn increases the risk of recidivism; and (f) tougher supervision policies and practices that are more police-like and less social worker–like and that thus increase the likelihood that individuals on parole who violate conditions of supervision or who commit new crimes will be caught and punished.

Systems-Level Dynamics

The magic of systems is that they can take on a life of their own.[101] Thus, once a set of causal forces creates a system, it can remain in operation even when the forces that created it recede or disappear. Of course, they need not disappear for the system to exert its own independent effect on sustaining or expanding itself. When we focus on incarceration, we can see that systems-level dynamics can exert strong effects on prison growth, as Blumstein and Beck have demonstrated.[102] These dynamics can enable even small changes to result in large increases in correctional growth. Garland has emphasized precisely that point, noting that "small variations in enacted laws or their enforcement may produce large variations in penal outcomes."[103]

Consider the highly simplified example illustrated in Table 3.2. At Time 1, we have a situation in which 100,000 arrests are made, 30 percent of them (30,000) result in convictions, and 20 percent (6,000) of the convictions result in prison sentences. In this example, we will make the simplifying assumption that each prisoner serves 1 year in prison. In reality, inmates typically serve longer than 1 year in prison. Increases in prison sentence lengths necessarily would increase the "stock" population of prisoners if admissions to prison remained constant.[104]

At Time 2a, arrests increase, but the conviction rate (30 percent) and prison-sentence-given-a-conviction rate (20 percent), respectively, remain the same. In this situation, the system processing patterns are identical to those at Time 1. However, more "inputs"—arrests—have been made; we can see that 150,000 arrests occurred. The end result is a total of 9,000 prison admissions. This increase amounts to an additional 3,000 prisoners or a net increase of 50 percent more new inmates.

Systems effects can dramatically change this situation. Times 2b and 2c illustrate this potential. In Time 2b, the same time span has elapsed as in

Table 3.2   The Amplifying Effect of Systems Forces

	Arrests	Convictions # (%)	Prison Sentences	Increase in Prisoners
Time 1	100,000	30,000 (30%)	6,000 (20%)	—
Time 2a	150,000	45,000 (30%)	9,000 (20%)	3,000 (50%)
Time 2b	150,000	60,000 (40%)	12,000 (20%)	6,000 (100%)
Time 2c	150,000	60,000 (40%)	15,000 (25%)	9,000 (150%)

Time 2a. Only the processing patterns differ. We see, again, an increase in law enforcement activity, resulting in 150,000 arrests. However, the conversion of arrests to convictions is higher, rising from 30 percent to 40 percent. Here, then, the coupling of more arrests and a higher conviction rate creates a much larger increase in prisoners. Indeed, in Time 2a (more arrests) we see "only" a 50 percent increase in the prison population. By contrast, in Time 2b (more arrests *and* tougher or more successful prosecutions) we see a 100 percent increase in the prison population (i.e., 12,000 prisoners rather than 6,000).

In Time 2c, we now add in the potential for prison sentence rates also to increase, which can happen if the courts toughen their responses to convicted felons. In this situation, we can observe the combined effects of three systems forces interacting:

- Increased arrests (from 100,000 at Time 1 to 150,000 at Time 2c)
- An increased conviction rate (from 30 percent at Time 1 to 40 percent at Time 2c)
- An increased prison sentence rate (from 20 percent at Time 1 to 25 percent at Time 2c)

The interaction of these three forces demonstrates the amplifying effects of systems forces. Instead of 6,000 prisoners, as occurred at Time 1, we now have 15,000 at Time 2c, an increase of 150 percent in the number of prisoners.

Several points bear emphasis. First, this simplified illustration is just that, a simplification, with estimates that likely are conservative. If prison sentence lengths increased, that effect would interact with the other forces and result in even greater increases in prison populations.

Second, once capacity for incarceration exists, processing patterns can and do change to meet that capacity. Net widening provides a perfect illustration of how that can happen. If we build 9,000 new beds to accommodate Time 2c, we may find in subsequent years that we have fewer serious, violent offenders to incarcerate. How, then, do we fill up the beds? We convert arrests that previously might have been dismissed, convert the arrests to convictions, and in turn convert the convictions to prison terms. In their analyses of correctional system growth in the 1980s through the 1990s, Blumstein and Beck showed, for example, that convictions and prison sentences for drug offending drove up prison populations more so than other systems factors.[105]

Of course, system actors would not necessarily or even likely think in this manner. Their collective decision making, however, could result in the functional equivalent of this type of dynamic.[106] Indeed, the sociologist Emile Durkheim long ago anticipated such a possibility.[107] As he emphasized, in a society in which a given type of serious offense eventually disappeared altogether and in which a minor offense remained relatively rare, citizens "will become more sensitive to these minor offenses, which up to then had had only a marginal effect on them."[108]

Third, systems can be affected by different changes or, put differently, may be leveraged by different internal forces. For example, Franklin Zimring and others have argued that the systems processing that drove mass incarceration initially derived from increased prosecutorial discretion that emphasized more aggressive sentencing. Then, due to national and state legislative changes, the system turned its focus to drug offending. These two changes then were followed by legislation and policies that increased sentence terms and reduced early release.[109] Collectively, such changes served to increase prison populations and did so during and well after the crime declines in the 1990s.[110] Another prominent example involves parole violations. As can be seen in Figure 2.3, the number of new prison admissions due to parole violations increased greatly in recent decades. Simply by creating tougher responses to parole violators, then, as California did, we can increase prison populations substantially, creating a feedback loop that can reinforce that very process and further drive up growth in incarceration.

Systems-Level Dynamics and External Factors

When considering the criminal justice system as just that, a system, we can see that internal dynamics—such as the extent to which arrests are converted to convictions—may affect system growth. However, external factors may weigh in as well. For example, a worsening of poverty, schools, and community cohesion might result in more crime and support for punitive sentencing. Increased crime of course constitutes a central input to the criminal justice system. New, even tougher sentencing laws constitute a central mechanism for creating a more punitive system of justice. These two external forces then may amplify the existing system of justice and at the same time, provide more cases and more of a requirement to treat them in a tough manner.

This type of systems account of prison growth lacks some of the scholarly appeal that some theoretical accounts provide. It does not require, for example, a coherent attempt by the upper classes to rule the lower classes. It does not center on the idea of racial animus and the history of race relations in America. It does not entail references to "state structures" and "state processes." At the same time, it does not preclude them and yet stands on its own as a potentially independent explanation for why the punitive turn is not a turn but in fact a new direction, a machinery of sorts, that America has developed for over three decades.

CAUSAL COMPLEXITY REVISITED

Different Types of Causal Patterns and Their Implications

As alluded to at the beginning of the chapter, mass incarceration may have resulted from any one of the above factors or some combination of them. Or it may have resulted from more complicated causal dynamics.[111] Scientists typically prefer parsimonious explanations for the phenomena they study.[112] However, based on existing scholarly accounts, parsimony does not seem appropriate in this instance. Here, we consider just a few of the potential dynamics that seemingly preclude simple, monocausal explanations for the punitive turn.

First, the punitive turn may have resulted from *reciprocal* effects, where one factor causes the other and, in turn, the other causes the first, leading to increasingly greater effects of one factor on the other. For example, a small increase in incarceration, such as the construction of one or two new prison facilities, may increase media and public attention to crime. Such attention may cause more fear of crime as a social problem. This fear in turn may lead to public pressure for further prison expansion, which then may lead to even greater awareness of crime, and so on. Reciprocal effects can lead to substantial changes and yet are difficult to identify.

Second, and in a related vein, the punitive turn may have resulted from *interactive* effects, where the effect of one factor varies depending on the level of another. To illustrate, increases in crime may spur greater investment in punitive sanctions. This effect may be greater during times of war, political conflict, or downturns in the economy.

Third, it may have resulted from *contingent* effects (a type of interactive effect), where one factor may not have an effect unless another is present. For example, conservative political platforms had zeroed in on employing get-tough responses to crime for many decades.[113] It may have been the emergence of crack cocaine, along with the end of the Cold War, in the 1980s that provided an opportunity for this platform to take full effect. From this perspective, then, political parties—and their normative preferences—do not per se cause a particular policy shift. They only do so when other conditions allow for their influence.

Fourth, it may have resulted from *threshold* effects, where a factor may have little effect until it reaches a certain level. Water does not boil until a certain temperature is reached (depending on the altitude). Similarly, support for sustained large-scale investment in prisons may have required that crime escalate rapidly. If we focus on crime in general, the trends in the 1970s into the 1980s provide little support for this argument. However, violent crime, murders in particular, increased dramatically in the mid- to late 1980s.[114] Of all the types of crime that might prompt a get-tough or extreme policy response, murder would seemingly be it.

Fifth, it may have resulted from *lagged* effects, where a factor produces an effect only after a lengthy period of time. Garland has argued, for example, that the "extraordinary levels of violent crime and disorder that characterized parts of the United States in the 1960s and 1970s, and the social, cultural, and political consequences that flowed from [it]" contributed to the get-tough penal policies that surfaced in the 1980s and 1990s.[115] In a similar vein, Alexander has argued that the civil rights movement of the 1960s created the foundation for the disenfranchisement of blacks in the 1980s and 1990s by establishing a need for a new way of subordinating blacks.[116]

Sixth, it may have resulted from *change effects,* where a change in some factor produces an effect. Change is frequently assumed in many theoretical accounts, with little attention given to *how much* change needs to occur for an outcome to arise. Perhaps, for example, increases in crime spur punitive responses. But how much does crime need to rise for such a response? Arguably, as suggested above, a threshold level of change must occur. Alternatively, a linear relationship may exist, where every increase in crime, no matter how small, results in a corresponding change—down or up—in punitive crime control measures. The latter seems unlikely but could occur. For example, a marked rise in violent crime, on the face of it, seems to have contributed to a wide range of get-tough policies. If smaller increases, or much smaller increases, had occurred in the 1980s, would we have seen small, incremental increases in prison populations? It seems unlikely. Even so, it is possible.

An Illustrative Causal Explanation

We view it as likely that causal complexity characterizes mass incarceration and, more broadly, the punitive turn. To the extent that this assessment is correct, it casts doubt on the veracity of single-factor accounts or even those that highlight a few factors. Such accounts may help to illuminate specific, nuanced ways in which a given social force contributed to mass incarceration. They also obscure the possibility that considerably more complicated sets of relationships gave rise to mass incarceration and reentry.

Consider one admittedly simplified causal account.[117] Conservative politics led to an emphasis on crime control in the 1980s. President Reagan, a prominent Republican, controlled the executive branch. For his first 6 years, Republicans controlled the Senate. Concern about illegal drugs emerged, especially a new type of drug, crack cocaine. Concern arose, too, about spikes in violent crime, especially murder. Part of the broader historical context consisted of a perception among Americans that the United States lacked a requisite level of power and control, as evidenced by the inability of the country to defuse or directly resolve the Iran hostage crisis. Many prominent accounts emerged that suggested that rehabilitation of offenders does not work. Political leaders may have come to view the country as facing an emergency—both internationally and domestically—that required emergency responses. Accordingly, they pursued last-resort social policy options on many fronts, including the building of more and more prisons. In so doing, they tapped into racial animosities and tensions, in part because changes in social welfare and crime policy disproportionately affected poor, minority communities.

With greater attention to crime, it became politically unviable *not* to campaign on crime. Whether Republican or Democrat, then, candidates included crime policy as a central part of their platforms. In so doing, they had little choice but to emphasize being tough-on-crime or risk being viewed, as Michael Dukakis was, as soft on crime. Subsequently, President Clinton, during an era when the economy dramatically improved, took heed of the political salience of crime and aggressively seized it as a central platform of his presidency. New laws were passed and substantial increases to funding for criminal justice occurred. Greater funding for law enforcement led to more arrests. Tougher laws, along with more prosecutors to enforce them, led to lengthier sentences. And tougher parole and probation systems led to more violations and reincarceration. As disproportionately more minorities entered and left prison, more opportunities arose for race and crime to become even more intertwined in media accounts.

In so doing, further support for mass incarceration emerged, fueling even greater increases in incarceration. And so on.

In this account, we can see reciprocal effects, such as a tougher response to crime that engenders greater discussion and coverage of crime, and, in turn, a felt need to respond aggressively to it. We can see interactions, such as the interplay of actual increases in the more serious type of violent crime, such as murder, along with the election of a staunchly conservative president who enjoyed the support of a Republican-controlled Senate. There are contingencies as well. It is unclear, for example, that the emergence of crack cocaine would have engendered a substantial law-and-order response had it arisen in a period in which the economy was stronger. Similarly, we can see potential threshold effects. The magnitude of the get-tough response might have been smaller, for example, if crime had not become so thoroughly politicized and thus central to election campaigns or if dramatic increases in murder rates had not occurred in the 1980s. There are potential lag effects, too. The get-tough laws of the 1980s and the increased investment in building prisons, for example, created the foundation for greatly expanding correctional system capacity in subsequent decades. Once that capacity emerged, it was used, which led to the need for further prison expansion to accommodate the ever-expanding flow of cases identified by enhanced law enforcement departments.

Causes of Mass Incarceration and Cause for Skepticism

Disentangling what exactly produced the punitive turn is, in the end, extraordinarily difficult. Why? There are many potential causal forces to which we can point. Many of them happened at once. Determining which are causally relevant and which are not presents a substantial challenge. Similarly, as we have emphasized, historical and scholarly accounts claim that many of the causal forces affected one another in a reciprocal manner. Not least, the accounts frequently posit interactions and the other types of causally complex relationships discussed above.

This situation is even more complicated because states themselves have varied greatly in the timing of their crime increases and investment in incarceration. They have varied, too—independent of crime rates—in their use of incarceration as a punishment.[118] We have a national increase in incarceration that ultimately stems from national *and* state-level forces. Some of these forces clearly seem to be common to most states. For example, almost every state in the country enacted get-tough laws in the 1980s. But these forces may be more prevalent or manifest differently in some states compared with others. And other forces may be unique to particular states. Some states, for example, have highly centralized approaches to government while others actively foster citizen involvement in governmental decision making and oversight, as Vanessa Barker's account of incarceration changes in California, New York, and Washington has highlighted.[119]

To make matters worse, capable scholars can provide equally compelling accounts that are not readily adjudicated through empirical analysis. The possibilities discussed here barely scratch the surface. Some scholars call for inclusion of many other causal forces. These include, for example, "state structures and processes" as well as legal changes and their operations within unique, state-specific historical contexts.[120] The challenges in empirically quantifying such dimensions and then examining sequential, interactional, lagged effect explanations—especially in a context where we have few data points or observations—defy overstatement. Theoretical accounts to date provide almost no foundation on which to identify how much change in various causal factors must occur for significant changes in criminal justice policy to occur. These accounts illuminate possible reasons for the punitive turn. However, we should view the accounts, even those that seem especially compelling, with considerable caution.

CONCLUSION, OR WHY UNDERSTANDING THE PUNITIVE TURN IS RELEVANT FOR REENTRY POLICY

Many of the factors that scholars believe gave rise to the punitive turn in America—such as welfare reforms, shifts to more conservative law-and-order politics, declines in the economy—can be found in other industrialized countries. In many of these places, we see increased use of punitive sanctioning. However, as Garland has emphasized, "few [nations] exhibited anything like the fourfold increase displayed by America's prison rates. And all of them continue to impose imprisonment at a fraction of the rate of that which operates in the United States."[121] There is, then, something unique about America and its embrace of incarceration.

As this chapter has highlighted, several observations can be made. First, mass incarceration likely resulted from many forces; conversely, no one force likely suffices to explain it or the general punitive climate that confronts ex-prisoners. Second, they likely exerted effects in complicated ways, including interactions with one another, contingencies, lags in the timing of the effect of a given force, and more. Third, because of such complications and the fact that many causal forces identified in the literature occurred simultaneously, there is no way to apply rigorous empirical research methodologies to disentangle which forces or dynamics truly caused mass incarceration. The likelihood of reciprocal effects further reinforces that assessment. That does not mean that we should discount theoretical accounts of mass incarceration. It does mean that we should view them with caution. Indeed, it is notable that after decades of theoretical work, historical and comparative scholars disagree about the relative salience of various factors, their interactions, critical thresholds, and more.[122]

Even so, understanding the potential causes of the punitive turn constitutes an important undertaking for many reasons. One reason is purely scholarly. If we wish to understand what led to mass incarceration and to the numerous challenges associated with reentry, we need efforts that aim to capture the diverse contributing factors. Doing so can improve "science." But it also can lead to insights of particular relevance to policy. If, for example, cultural shifts in punitive sentiments helped cause mass incarceration, it suggests that reentry for most ex-prisoners would be especially challenging because they return to communities largely hostile to them. In such a context, simply focusing on reentry programs will not suffice. The most effective reentry program likely cannot offset cultural forces, especially if these result in more control-oriented, punitive law enforcement and sanctioning. By the same token, if policy-maker and public beliefs in the ineffectiveness of non-incarcerative sanctions contributed to the punitive turn, the opportunity exists to undertake educational campaigns. These could highlight significant advances in our understanding of such sanctions and, simultaneously, the limited evidence for the effectiveness of incarceration-based policies in reducing crime.

A second and related reason is that even without consensus on the best explanation for the punitive turn in American criminal justice, greater understanding of some parts of the puzzle holds the potential to inform policy deliberations. One simple but important example involves the documentation of crime and punishment trends. Many policy makers have claimed that crime is out of control and that we do not punish offenders sufficiently. They have done so without credible empirical evidence to back such claims. Left unaddressed, these claims can be used to bolster arguments that current policies and practices don't work. Conversely, the documentation of actual trends in crime and punishment can serve as a check against unwarranted or empirically inaccurate claims.

The importance of such an approach is difficult to understate. For example, a careful reading of existing scholarship highlights that actual crime rates in no direct or isolated manner created the get-tough trend in punishment. More influential in some ways has been *perceptions* about escalating crime and inadequate punishments. Policy deliberations ideally should be clear about the precise reasons for adopting a new approach to punishment. That may seem simplistic, and it is. At the same time, allowing claims about nonexistent increases in violent sex crimes or exaggerated claims about impending waves of "super predators" to go unchecked likely results in policies of limited effectiveness and cost-efficiency.

A third, and again related, reason for seeking to understand the causes of mass incarceration is that doing so can lead to insights about the different groups who have a stake in the criminal justice system. The primary stakeholder group is the public. Policy makers and criminal justice system administrators and personnel all seek to promote public safety and justice. Even so, some stakeholder groups appear to have garnered greater attention than others. For example, the United States aggressively sought to toughen penalties for drug-related offending. In so doing, the country indirectly targeted some groups, blacks in particular, for greater law enforcement and more punishment and thus affected communities of color more so than others.[123] The get-tough measures of the last several decades also have not reflected well the desires or needs of victims. In scholarly accounts about the rise of punitive sanctioning, little mention exists of victims, or victims' rights advocates, calling for tougher punishment.[124] Rather, they typically have called for greater attention to the needs of victims and funding and implementation of diverse approaches to protecting them. Although considerable advances have occurred, we continue to have what is aptly termed a "criminal justice" system, not a "victim justice" system.[125] Get-tough policies do not necessarily or directly help victims and, indeed, can sometimes victimize them further by being unresponsive to their needs, coercing victim involvement in court proceedings, or intervening despite victim preferences not to do so.[126]

Fourth, investigating the causes of the punitive turn can help to situate reentry within a broader context that highlights the goals society has for its criminal justice system. In turn, we may be led to investigate the discussions that occur on the ground—that is, the deliberations that policy makers and practitioners engage in as they determine the contours of public safety and justice. Conspicuously absent from many accounts of the punitive turn are on-the-ground insider descriptions of criminal justice policy making.[127] These are missing, too, from accounts of the creation of rules, protocols, and practices that affect processing and sanctioning decisions as well as the prison experience.[128] Exceptions can be found, but the behind-the-scenes decision making involved in developing penal policy occurs largely out of sight. We have, for example, the emergence of supermax prisons without any coherent, systematic documentation of why they were built or how exactly they are used.[129] Policy decisions are central to why the get-tough era of mass incarceration emerged. They are central to defining, literally, what is meant by justice and the goals that we have for punishment. By focusing, then, on the causes of mass incarceration, there is the potential for shedding light on the larger questions about what society wants and should expect from criminal justice.

Finally, and not least, causal analysis of mass incarceration highlights that a focus on reentry entails a focus on crime and justice more broadly. Put differently, if we seek to improve reentry, we may want to focus on specific programs and interventions that facilitate successful transitions back into society. But we also will want to focus on the policies and practices that will best reduce crime and improve justice.

DISCUSSION QUESTIONS

1. Which factors, or combination of factors, contributed the most to the rise of mass incarceration, that is, the punitive turn in American criminal justice?

2. Which causes of mass incarceration can most likely be affected through policy making?

3. What cultural shifts in society are reflected by get-tough criminal justice policies?

4. How can the decisions and discretion of prosecutors affect incarceration trends?

5. How should policy makers heed public opinion about criminal justice, especially if the public generally knows little about the inner workings of the criminal justice system?

CHAPTER 4

*Profile of the
Inmate Population*[1]

To understand why reentry can be challenging, and why the vast majority of inmates recidivate and struggle both during prison and after release, it helps to understand who lands in prison and, accordingly, who exits it. This chapter describes the characteristics of the inmate population. Our focus here, however, centers primarily on the implications of inmate characteristics—such as prior criminal justice system involvement and demographic, socioeconomic, and health backgrounds—rather than on providing an in-depth account of these characteristics. Many books have undertaken the latter task.[2] By contrast, our main focus here lies with identifying why exactly inmate profiles matter, what forces change these profiles over time, and the implications that such change holds for understanding and addressing mass incarceration and the reentry of individuals in prison back into society.

A central theme that the book and chapter highlight is that inmates constitute a highly disadvantaged population. That does not mean that their crimes should be forgiven. It does mean that the challenges associated with creating improved life circumstances, including reducing recidivism, create substantial barriers to successful reentry. Silver bullet solutions that focus on one approach thus will not likely be effective. Indeed, they can be counterproductive. They can lead us to invest in expensive strategies that are ineffective or harmful and to miss opportunities to invest in those that can be more effective and less costly. Conversely, we can achieve more cost-efficient sanctioning and reentry if we know something about inmate characteristics and the contexts from which they come and to which they return.

WHY INMATE AND EX-PRISONER CHARACTERISTICS MATTER

Descriptions of prisoners can be found in many federal reports, journal articles, books, and media accounts. The various sources provide information about the criminal history and demographic and social characteristics of inmates, such as their age, sex, race, ethnicity, education levels, income, and more. We will touch on some of these dimensions below. However, a logical first step is to zero in on a question that frequently gets lost in descriptive accounts. Specifically, why do inmate, or, by extension, ex-prisoner, characteristics matter?

This question might seem irrelevant. People commit crime and get punished. Some go to prison. They are criminals—end of story. In fact, though, we have many reasons for taking an interest in the characteristics of people who go to prison. A business perspective alone—one advocated increasingly by policy makers—calls for understanding "clients" to ensure a fit between them and provided services. If simply housing inmates in cells were all that prisons did, this perspective would be irrelevant. In reality, however, prisons need to plan for expansion and, though it happens less often, contraction. They strive to maintain order and safety and use classification and other strategies to achieve these goals. They attempt to rehabilitate inmates. At the same time, they house individuals who may have physical or mental illnesses that need to be addressed and that may affect their behavior. They also return individuals back to society, with the hope that these individuals will fare well and, in particular, cease offending, find employment, find housing, reunify with family, and more. Not least, prisons confront the reality of social inequality and the need to ensure that it is not continued or amplified through correctional system policies, rules, or practices.

In each of these instances, inmate characteristics may play an important role in the attainment of correctional system goals. Understanding inmate characteristics helps correctional systems identify, forecast, and address prison and parole capacity needs, prisoner treatment and service needs, prison management challenges, inequality, and reentry supervision and assistance needs. By addressing each of these goals, correctional systems position themselves to achieve the broader goal of reducing crime through reduced recidivism and of improving such outcomes as ex-prisoner housing and employment.

Forecasting Prison and Parole Capacity Needs

A central challenge confronting any prison system centers on a seemingly mundane question: How many individuals will this system need to house? It is a complicated question to answer. Changes in crime rates, sentencing laws and practices, funding for courts and prison system capacity, political dynamics—these all may directly or indirectly affect prison system capacity and populations. Perhaps no need exists for a new prison, but legislators push for tougher responses to crime. That creates a perceived need for expansion, so states build more prisons. Expanded prison use becomes the new norm and can remain in place even if, as occurred during the 1990s and throughout the subsequent decade, crime declines.[3] We may see, too, changes in arrest and conviction rates for certain crimes (e.g., drug offenses) in some areas (e.g., economically disadvantaged communities). These changes, whether intentionally or not, may target younger people who come from predominantly minority communities. The end result is a prison population that may look different than in previous years. There may be more drug offenders, minorities, and young males, for example. There also may be more individuals with mental health and physical health problems. Educational deficits may be greater among new cohorts of prisoners, and many other such differences may exist.

In each instance, sentence lengths may vary depending on the population involved, especially if different groups are more likely to commit certain types of crimes *or* to be differentially sanctioned for the same types of crimes. That fact alone holds substantial implications for prison system forecasting. For example, if states disproportionately convict and sentence young, black males for drug crimes—and if these sentences tend to be longer than those meted out to other groups—then states must expand prison capacity.

They have no choice. Or, more precisely, the available choices pose considerable political risk. One choice, for example, includes shortening average lengths of stay. Historically, inmates typically have not served their entire sentence in prison. They might serve 30 to 40 percent of it incarcerated and then be released onto parole. States traditionally have varied greatly in the percentage of a sentence that inmates serve in prison.[4] In recent decades, though, states enacted truth-in-sentencing laws that increased these percentages. Reducing them can be seen as being soft on crime and creates substantial risk for political candidates. Other choices, such as introducing reforms that reduce sentence lengths or the use of incarceration for certain types of offenses, carry similar risks.

In the end, states can more effectively plan for capacity needs if they know the characteristics of the individuals who enter their prisons, how long they stay, and how likely they are to recidivate after release. These three numbers—rates of admission (including rates of parolee revocations that result in incarceration), average lengths of stay, and recidivism rates—vary across groups for a variety of reasons. If states monitor these numbers and reasons for changes in them, they have a better ability to forecast the need to expand or contract bedspace. Doing so is better than having to respond in knee-jerk fashion to brief surges in prison admissions and then be locked into greater capacity when it may not be needed in the longer term.[5]

Identifying and Forecasting Prisoner Treatment and Service Needs

Notwithstanding the early history of American corrections, contemporary prison systems typically have a legal, if not moral, obligation to address certain inmate needs, such as treatment of physical and mental health problems.[6] Conditions in prisons themselves must not amount to cruel and unusual punishment. More broadly, prison systems must provide food and protection, sanitary living conditions, some opportunity to freely practice one's religion and access reading materials, and due process in administering sanctions or withholding or allowing privileges, such as visitation or recreation.[7] Ideally, prisons, too, provide treatments and services that effectively improve inmate conduct and reentry outcomes.[8] Here, one need not take a moral stance; rather, from a pragmatic perspective, any treatment or service that might improve these outcomes constitutes a good for society, especially if the benefits outweigh the costs.

Creating a prison setting that stands up to what society expects on legal, moral, and pragmatic grounds requires considerable planning. It entails far more than simply building additional prisons. One central starting point for effective planning consists of knowing in detail the characteristics and needs of the population to be housed, supervised, treated, and served. As Benjamin Steiner and Benjamin Meade have argued, "effective programming begins with an understanding of inmates' needs."[9]

This undertaking would be straightforward but for the fact that the prison population is heterogeneous—it varies greatly and does so along many dimensions. In Chapter 8, we will discuss different prison groups. Here, consider as but one illustration female inmates. They share many of the same health problems that male inmates do, including substance abuse and addiction disorders, infectious disease, diabetes, mental illness, and more. In addition, however, female inmates face unique problems, such as separation from their infants and higher rates of sexual victimization. Historically, their needs have not been well addressed because prison facilities have been ill equipped to handle females' unique needs and because of discriminatory views and practices among correctional system staff.[10]

If a prison system identifies that a substantial increase in the number of females sent to it will occur, officials can plan accordingly to ensure that their general or specialized needs are addressed. The same implication holds for other groups. An influx of especially violent individuals, for example, likely would require changes to staffing, housing, and programming. An influx of very young offenders likely would require introducing additional educational opportunities.[11] The arrival of greater numbers of drug-addicted felons likely would require creating more drug treatment capacity. Similarly, a greater number of mentally ill inmates likely would require enhanced treatment capacity for such inmates.[12] Such observations can be made about other groups as well, including racial and ethnic groups, gang members, inmates from different religious backgrounds, older inmates, and so on.

Forecasting trends in each of these and other groups may not be easy. The starting point, however, begins with carefully profiling the existing prison population and trends in the admission of different groups of inmates to prisons in prior years. Along with analysis of some of the potential causes of these changes, such information in turn can allow for informed guesswork about what the inmate population likely will look like in future years.

Identifying and Forecasting Prison Management Challenges

A related benefit of examining inmate characteristics consists of being able not only to anticipate better the treatment and service needs of inmates but also to anticipate management challenges that may be looming on the horizon. One of the most well-known accounts of prison order, importation theory, argues that an orderly prison stems from the characteristics of inmates. Essentially, order (or disorder) is brought into the prison system.[13] Although the theoretical logic centers on the idea that inmates import cultural beliefs and attitudes or values conducive to violence, most scholarship instead has examined correlates of inmate misconduct. Research has shown, for example, that age, sex, race, ethnicity, education, marital status, prior record, gang membership, and the like are associated with misconduct and violence.[14]

The management challenges presented by different groups vary. Younger inmates, for example, may be more likely to act out defiantly to establish their street credibility within prison. They also may be more at risk of victimization by other inmates. Accordingly, an effective approach to reducing prison disorder might entail housing younger inmates separately from older inmates, monitoring them more closely, or providing more structured activities for them to reduce opportunities to engage in misconduct. Mentally ill inmates, by contrast, may not necessarily act out more than other groups, but they may act in ways that could be more disruptive. Similarly, gang leaders may be especially disruptive and engaged in organized efforts aimed at inciting violence or facilitating illegal activity within the prison walls.

Anticipating changes in the profile of the inmate population thus can be useful for identifying potential programming needs as well as administrative challenges. Extant research provides guidelines for some of the dimensions that merit attention. These include social and demographic characteristics, prior record, gang membership, and physical and mental health problems, among others. Prison systems of course can identify additional dimensions that may be viewed as especially salient for them. What then is needed is the research infrastructure for monitoring changes in inmate characteristics over time. With this infrastructure in place, prison systems can track changes in resources and be better positioned to identify management challenges and needs. Absent such information, prison systems place themselves at the mercy of unidentified inmate compositional changes that can pose a direct threat to system order.[15]

Identifying, Monitoring, and Addressing Inequality

Inequality stands as a central concern for prison systems. The inequalities that occur in free society exist in corrections. They may exist more so and serve to perpetuate inequalities among certain correctional system populations and the communities to which they return. These inequalities may fall along many dimensions, including racial and ethnic divides, gender, age, and socioeconomic class, and they can be manifest in different ways.

Perhaps the most obvious example involves differences in the sanctioning of blacks. A large body of scholarship has established that blacks are more likely— relative to the proportion of blacks in America—than whites to be arrested, detained prior to trial, convicted, sentenced to prison, and given lengthier prison terms. This work highlights that many of these differences disappear once we adjust for racial differences in the types of crimes committed and prior record.[16] That said, many exceptions exist, and complicated dynamics represent the norm. For example, prosecutorial charging and plea bargaining practices may contribute to tougher sanctioning of blacks, but it is, at the same time, an extraordinarily difficult dynamic to document empirically. In addition, tougher sanctioning may be more pronounced for young blacks, young black males in particular, even after controlling for legally relevant factors.[17] In cases where processing patterns differ for blacks, the causal explanations may be far from straightforward—they may arise from outright discrimination but may more likely arise from unconscious stereotyping and sentencing laws that penalize blacks more than whites (e.g., laws that impose tougher penalties for crack cocaine).

Inequalities do not arise solely along racial lines. Women, for example, may be more likely than men to receive lenient sentences even after controlling for differences in type of crime committed and prior record.[18] Class differences may exist, with those who come from economically disadvantaged backgrounds potentially being more likely to receive tougher sanctions compared with individuals who come from more advantaged backgrounds. Age constitutes yet another dimension that may matter. For example, younger defendants typically receive tougher punishments than older defendants.[19]

If we zero in on the prison system alone, substantial inequalities can exist.[20] Numerous historical accounts, for example, document racial segregation within the prison system and ways in which it has been used by administrators on the ground to maintain institutional security.[21] In contemporary times, such segregation can arise through different mechanisms, such as the separation of gangs into different facilities; gang membership tends to fall along racial divides, and so this approach effectively results in segregation.[22] Whether it helps to decrease violence remains largely unknown. Some accounts suggest that segregation may worsen racial tensions.[23] Regardless, the segregation of inmates raises constitutional and legal problems that prison systems typically must address.

Racial divides may occur in other ways. For example, there may be differences among blacks and whites in access to quality educational programming, vocational training, or treatment or in the use of various types of disciplinary measures, including confinement in supermax housing.[24] Similarly, there may be differences across social groups in access to such programming or in approaches used to manage or treat them.

Understanding the causes of these differences is critical. For example, racial disparities in incarceration may stem from greater involvement of blacks in violent offending. This difference in turn may result from differences in the social contexts of blacks. For example, as Michael Tonry has observed, "Black Americans much more often than whites are affected by the conditions—being raised in poverty-level, single-parent households; living in disadvantaged, socially disorganized neighborhoods; being educated in substandard schools; having limited employment prospects; lacking positive role models—that are correlated with higher levels of crime and victimization."[25] Insights about what might create race differences in offending provide the grounds for potential policy interventions; similarly, insights about what generates differences in programming or management of some groups provides the basis for identifying changes that could be implemented to reduce these differences. For example, racial segregation might stem more from inmate preferences than from policies aimed at segregating gangs. Conversely, administrative practices for managing gangs may result indirectly in segregating blacks, whites, or other groups. Each possibility raises different implications for how prisons might proceed with ameliorating unwarranted differences in the treatment or management of inmates.

The behavior of inmates may vary across social groups and result in part from inequalities in programming or treatment. Ideally, then, monitoring efforts would track variation in misconduct rates across groups and variation in the factors that may contribute to them.[26] Some studies have shown, for example, that the factors associated with misconduct among male inmates and female inmates, respectively, overlap considerably but that differences also exist.[27] Monitoring can serve, then, to identify potential inequalities and their causes.

Identifying and monitoring inequalities—in programming, vocational training, physical or mental health treatment, punishment, visitation, reentry preparation, and the like—do not necessarily result in resolution of these inequalities. However, it provides the groundwork for informing discussions about how prison systems may address them.

Forecasting Ex-Prisoner Population Supervision and Reentry Needs

Understanding different inmate populations and their experiences can also directly inform reentry planning. For example, states might monitor the extent to which different groups of inmates participate in or receive disproportionately more or less programming aimed at assisting ex-prisoners to find work or housing. They might monitor, too, the extent to which inmates return to different socioeconomic contexts that advantage or disadvantage them. Blacks, for example, may return to economic contexts that substantially reduce their likelihood of finding gainful employment.[28] In addition, their likelihood of being visited and of having sustained pro-social bonds while incarcerated may be less to the extent that they were incarcerated in facilities farther away from their homes.[29] Being aware of such differences can help states to improve reentry preparation and tailor assistance to the needs of each group.

Monitoring efforts, too, can focus on the amount and quality of supervision that different groups of inmates receive. These efforts can be used to help anticipate workload demands for new cohorts of released inmates. For example, if substantial increases in high-risk youth returning to select communities are anticipated, planning efforts can be undertaken to ensure that staffing and programming adjustments can be made as needed.

INMATE AND EX-PRISONER CHARACTERISTICS

As the discussion to this point has highlighted, many benefits can result from identifying, monitoring, and forecasting changes in the profile of inmate and reentry populations. The question then arises: Which characteristics matter and why? It depends on our goals and context.

A simple illustration underscores this point. If we want to forecast prison capacity needs, we need information about changes in the flow of individuals who have varying sentence lengths. If a given characteristic is not associated with sentence length, then it may be largely irrelevant to forecasting efforts. If it is associated with sentence length, then it may be quite helpful. For example, if blacks tend to receive lengthier sentences than whites, then forecasters would want to monitor changes in the admission of blacks and other groups into prison. Of course, information about such discrepancies could be used to identify potential unwarranted disparities in sentencing, time served, or inmate treatment as well.

Another example involves prison management. Prison officials typically have important insights into what affects their prison system. These insights can directly inform monitoring efforts. For example, officials may believe that certain types of inmates disproportionately contribute to disorder and violence (like gang members) or require special treatment (like those with mental illness). Monitoring the admission of such inmates and how they respond to different interventions can help officials devise relevant programming.

No inmate or ex-prisoner profile in and of itself is necessarily useful. Here, then, we describe with broad brushstrokes some of the characteristics of individuals who enter and leave prisons. One thing is clear: Individuals who go to and leave prison are highly heterogeneous, but they are highly homogenous in one way. They constitute a highly disadvantaged group. Their heterogeneity and disadvantaged status present many challenges to correctional system efforts to maintain order and to promote successful reentry.

Criminal Justice System Involvement

Prison systems do not typically deal with first-time offenders who have committed minor crimes. Rather, they tend to be repositories for individuals who commit the more severe types of crimes or for individuals who chronically offend. However, the percentages of inmates who have committed certain types of crimes vary from year to year and across states. That said—as shown in Table 4.1—in 2010, approximately half of state prison inmates (53 percent) nationally were incarcerated for violent crimes, roughly one-fifth were incarcerated for property crimes (18 percent), almost one-fifth were incarcerated for drug crimes (17 percent), and the remainder (11 percent) were incarcerated for public order and other crimes.[30] Although the percentage of inmates incarcerated for these various types of crimes remained relatively stable from 2000 to 2010, as reflected in the small percentage changes in the last column of Table 4.1, states can and do shift emphasis in who they incarcerate.[31] In addition, the inmate profile in the federal justice system typically differs from that of the states. For example, since the 1980s, federal prisons increasingly have housed a greater proportion of drug offenders.[32]

Substantial variation exists within these broad crime categories. When we talk about violent crime, for example, it can refer to murder, manslaughter, rape, sexual assault, robbery, or assault. Similarly, property crime can include a range of offenses, including burglary, larceny, motor vehicle theft, and fraud. Inmates are highly heterogeneous, and they are not all violent or chronically violent offenders. That insight points to the potential usefulness of offense characteristics to assist with efforts to forecast bedspace capacity, prison management, and reentry supervision and treatment needs.

National type-of-offense statistics are not nearly as helpful for states as state-level statistics are, which show likely changes in their own prison system populations For example, increases in the percentage of inmates who have engaged

Table 4.1 Type of Offense, United States Inmate Population, 2000–2010

	Prisoners Sentenced, 2000 (%)	Prisoners Sentenced, 2010 (%)	Percent Change, 2000–2010
Violent crime	*51.7*	*53.2*	*1.5*
Murder[1]	13.0	12.2	−0.8
Manslaughter	1.4	1.6	0.2
Rape	4.8	5.2	0.4
Other sexual assault	6.2	6.7	0.5
Robbery	14.3	13.6	−0.7
Assault	9.7	10.8	1.1
Other violent	2.3	3.2	0.9
Property crime	*20.4*	*18.3*	*−2.1*
Burglary	11.2	9.5	−1.7
Larceny	3.6	3.4	−0.2
Motor vehicle theft	1.6	1.1	−0.5
Fraud	2.1	2.3	0.2
Other property	1.9	2.0	0.1
Drug[2] crime	*21.4*	*17.4*	*−4.0*
Public order[3] crime	*5.8*	*10.5*	*4.7*
Other/unspecified[4]	*0.3*	*0.6*	*0.3*

Notes: Based on state prisoners with a sentence of more than 1 year. Percents may not sum to 100 due to rounding and missing offense data.

1. Includes non-negligent manslaughter.
2. Includes trafficking, possession, and other drug offenses.
3. Includes weapons, drunk driving, court offenses, commercialized vice, morals, and decency offenses, liquor law violations, and other public order offenses.
4. Includes juvenile offenses and other unspecified offense categories.

Source: Carson and Sabol (2012).

in violent acts might raise flags for prison officials because violent offenders may be more likely to contribute to prison violence.[33] Sex offenders tend to be more at risk of victimization.[34] Such groups, and others who might be at greater risk of misconduct or victimization, ideally would be monitored. However, because most offenders tend to be generalists—that is, they do not specialize in only one type of crime—the use of offense categories should be done cautiously.[35]

If we move beyond type of offense and focus on inmate experiences with the criminal justice system, we find that many inmates have extensive prior records. For example, 75 percent of state prisoners have had prior experience with the correctional system, such as having been placed on probation or having been previously incarcerated.[36] They also have had repeated contact with law enforcement. In a 2014 national study of inmates released in 2005 from thirty states, researchers found that these individuals had an average of 10.6 prior arrests (the median was 7.8).[37] In addition, they accumulated multiple arrests after release. For example, the released inmates were tracked for 5 years and analyses showed that 23 percent were never rearrested, 19 percent were rearrested once, 15 percent were rearrested twice, 12 percent were rearrested three times, 9 percent were rearrested four times, 6 percent were rearrested five times, and 16 percent were rearrested 6 or more times.[38] We might infer from such statistics that criminal justice system involvement—whether through arrest, conviction, or some type of sanction—exerts only a weak deterrent or rehabilitative effect. Indeed, the high level of recidivism suggests that, if anything, incarceration may increase rather than decrease reoffending.[39]

At a minimum, the statistics highlight that the reentry population does not consist of low-level, first-time offenders. Rather, it consists primarily of individuals who, for whatever reason, have repeatedly become involved in the justice system. That fact raises important questions about how the justice system affects individuals while they are incarcerated and what, if anything, should be done differently to manage, treat, or sanction those who have more extensive prior records. Prison systems and reentry efforts clearly encounter a diverse population, the management of which may well require tailoring administration, intervention, and sanction strategies to fit different groups. For example, individuals incarcerated for the first time may be more at risk of suicide and so require more assessment and monitoring.[40]

Another important point of heterogeneity is time served. Due to tougher sentencing laws and enforcement of these laws, time served has increased among inmates. For example, from 1990 to 2009, the average time inmates served in prison rose to 2.1 years, an increase of 9 months.[41] The changes varied by type of offense; for example, violent offenders served on average 1.3 more years in 2009 (5 years) compared with 1990 (3.7 years), property offenders served a half year more time (2.3 years in 2009 compared with 1.8 years in 1990), and drug offenders also served a half year more (2.2 years in 2009 compared with 1.6 years in 1990). Changes in time served varied greatly by state. During the 1990–2009 time period, some states, such as Florida, increased time served among inmates by over 160 percent whereas other states, such as Illinois, shortened the time served by inmates.[42]

Time served merits attention for many reasons. It highlights that many prison systems now focus on inmates who serve lengthier prison terms and who may present unique management challenges because of this change. It highlights the relative punitiveness of different states, which in turn can provide a foundation for assessing the effectiveness of different punishment regimes on recidivism.[43] And it can be used to inform forecasting efforts. If, for example, increasing percentages of violent offenders enter a prison system each year, and if time served has been increasing for them each year, then plans would need to be made to increase bedspace capacity for this group. Time served may also have implications for managing prisons; for example, inmates who serve lengthy prison terms may be less inclined to behave. Lengthier prison stays may make reentry preparation more challenging, in part because inmates may have more difficulty maintaining ties to family and friends.[44] And not least, to the extent that prison is criminogenic, lengthier prison stays may worsen reentry outcomes, recidivism in particular.

Demographic and Socioeconomic Characteristics

The demographic and socioeconomic characteristics of inmates also may be consequential for the reasons discussed above, including forecasting prison capacity needs, treatment and service needs, and management challenges; identifying and addressing inequality; and anticipating reentry supervision, support, treatment, and service needs. Here, we touch on several possibilities that illustrate this point.

The prison system is comprised of individuals who span the spectrum, from 17 and 18 years old to ages 70 and older. Table 4.2 breaks down the age variation in the U.S. prison population. About 30 percent of inmates are ages 18–29, 30 percent are ages 30–39, 24 percent are ages 40–49, 12 percent are ages 50–59, and 4 percent are ages 60 and older.

This variation matters for many reasons. For example, the youngest inmates may be more prone to engage in violence and misconduct and so may warrant more proactive efforts to reduce their opportunities for such behavior.[45] They also may require different types of programming and may be more likely to maintain their relationships with family and friends.[46] Conversely, the oldest may present different challenges. For example, with inmates serving longer sentences, the U.S. prison population is graying. In 1991, only 20 percent of inmates were forty or older; by 2011, this percentage increased to 39.[47] These inmates require more medical services and thus increase costs to prison systems.[48] From a reentry perspective, these individuals may require more attention to continuity of medical care and may face greater employment challenges given their poor work record and advanced age.

Racial and ethnic differences matter as well. Minorities, blacks in particular, are overrepresented in the prison population relative to their presence in the U.S. population at large.[49] In 2011, 34 percent of inmates were white, 38 percent were black, and 23 percent were Hispanic (see Table 4.2). As Bruce Western has observed, "The basic brute fact of incarceration in the new era of mass imprisonment is that African Americans are eight times more likely to be incarcerated than Whites."[50] This disproportionality may result from differences in offending, law enforcement, the likelihood of conviction, sanctioning, and other such factors.[51] These factors in turn may vary in their relative salience in any given state. Disproportionality and the identification of its causes constitute a central concern for criminal justice systems because of the potential for inequality to resurface or to become amplified and because of the need to develop management tools that address racial or ethnic conflict.

Prison officials also need to track gender differences. By and large, the prison system has been primarily a place that houses males. For example, in 2012, 93 percent of all prisoners in the United States were men (see Table 4.2); in addition, men are incarcerated at substantially higher rates (932 per 100,000 residents) than are women (65 per 100,000 residents).[52] Even so, the percentage of women in prison has increased greatly, as can be seen in Figure 4.1.[53] In 1978, there were almost 300,000 male inmates and by 2012, there were almost 1.5 million males in state and federal prisons. During that same time period, the number of female inmates increased from almost 13,000 to approximately 110,000, with the growth concentrated among black females and Hispanic females.[54]

Table 4.2   Profile of the U.S. Inmate Population

	Percent of Inmates
Panel A. Demographic Characteristics[1]	
Male	93.3
Female	6.7
Ages 18–29	30.2
Ages 30–39	30.4
Ages 40–49	23.6
Ages 50–59	11.8
Ages 60+	3.8
Race/ethnicity—white	33.6
Race/ethnicity—black	37.8
Race/ethnicity—Hispanic	22.8
Panel B. Educational Attainment[2]	
Less than high school diploma	39.7
Graduate equivalency degree (GED)	28.5
High school diploma	20.5
Postsecondary/some college	11.3
Panel C. Drug Abuse[3]	
Any history of dependence and abuse	34.9
Prior abuse of marijuana/hashish	59.0
Prior abuse of cocaine/crack	30.0
Prior abuse of heroin/other opiates	13.1
Prior abuse of methamphetamines	14.9
Panel D. Mental Health Problems[4]	
Any mental health problem	56.2
Recent symptoms of major depressive disorder	23.5
Recent symptoms of mania disorder	43.2
Recent symptoms of psychotic disorder	15.4

[1]Carson and Sabol (2012), state and federal inmates.
[2]Harlow (2003), state inmates.
[3]Mumola and Karberg (2006), state inmates.
[4]James and Glaze (2006), state inmates.

Research indicates that males and females commit different crimes and may experience prison in different ways. They also manage the strains associated with incarceration differently. For these reasons, gender-specific programming may be indicated for maintaining order and safety and improving reentry outcomes.[55] Women, for example, are more likely to be in prison for drug crimes and substantially less likely to be incarcerated for violent crime.[56] They may be

Figure 4.1   Total State and Federal Prison Population, by Sex, 1978–2012

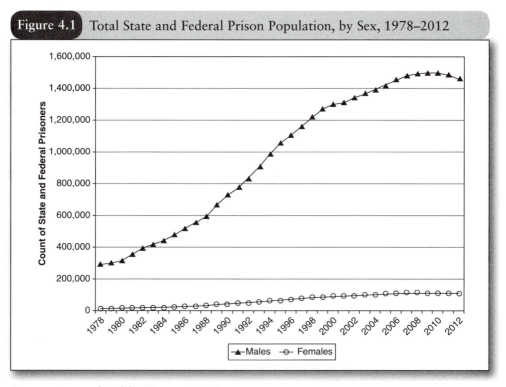

Source: Carson and Mulako-Wangota (2014).

more likely to have dependent children and to have been the primary caretaker prior to incarceration, and so may need more assistance in maintaining relationships with them.[57] They typically have more preexisting infectious diseases, have a greater prevalence of mental illness, and are more likely to have been victims of abuse.[58]

Differences in education matters as well. The individuals who go to prison lag substantially behind the general public in their education. As Table 4.2 highlights, an estimated 40 percent of inmates stop short of graduating from high school, 29 percent have a graduate equivalency degree (GED), and only 20 percent earned a diploma. Another 11 percent have some postsecondary education. These percentages have remained relatively stable over time.[59]

Research clearly establishes that inmates are considerably more likely than members of the general public to have learning disabilities.[60] Addressing educational deficits and learning disabilities constitutes a central focus for many prison systems, and it represents an approach that holds the potential for improving inmate behavior and successful reintegration after release from prison. At the same time, doing so does not necessarily address the possibility that low educational attainment itself may serve primarily as a proxy for having come from a disadvantaged background. In that case, educational programming may not necessarily produce large improvements in reduced offending. It may help, though, and also serve to improve other outcomes, such as securing employment.[61]

In fact, employment itself represents another significant social divide that characterizes prisoner and reentry populations. Estimates indicate that between 21 and 38 percent of inmates were unemployed in the month prior to their incarceration.[62] Research increasingly points to employment as a central avenue through which desistance may occur or as an activity that signals that these individuals are ready to desist.[63] In the latter instance, correctional systems may be able to use information about inmate employment histories and participation in vocational training programs to predict how individuals may behave during incarceration and after release.[64] The glass-half-empty view of this situation is that inmate employment histories are so anemic, and the challenges that they face in finding jobs so large (including a return to areas with high unemployment rates), that few prospects for improving their work opportunities exist.[65] The glass-half-full view, however, takes heed of the fact that precisely because of this situation, even small gains in employment training and readiness might improve inmate morale while in prison and job prospects after release.

Health Characteristics

Prisoners vary in their health profile too.[66] The health profiles vary across states and over time, but in general inmates are much more likely than members of the general public to suffer from physical disease, mental illness, and drug abuse and addiction. For example, inmates are five to twenty-four times more likely than members of the general public to have some type of mental disorder,[67] and over half of inmates are estimated to have used drugs in the month prior to incarceration.[68]

Table 4.2 shows rates of addiction and serious mental disorders, including major depressive disorder and psychosis, among inmates. We can see that inmates differ greatly in the types of drug and mental health problems that they have. Almost 60 percent of inmates report having used marijuana or hashish, 30 percent report using cocaine or crack, 13 percent report using heroin, and 15 percent report using methamphetamines.

This situation creates ethical and pragmatic challenges for prison systems. As a general matter, the presence of medical and mental health problems requires some type of response. The challenge lies in identifying appropriate types and amounts of treatment that can be administered within a prison system context and that can be continued during reentry.[69] Successful treatment may benefit prison systems because inmates may show increased compliance with rules. Healthier individuals likely fare better upon release, placing less of a burden on health care systems, and may be more likely to engage in pro-social behavior.[70]

Community Characteristics

Community characteristics merit far more attention than they have received in the past. Historically, the primary emphasis in risk prediction, for example, has been on individual-level factors, such as prior record, education, family context, peers, and the like, that may affect recidivism. In the past decade, however, scholars such as Charis Kubrin and Eric Stewart have highlighted the fact that when individuals leave prison, they typically return to impoverished communities.[71] In these areas, poverty and unemployment rates are much higher than that of other areas. Single-parent households are more common. Neighborhood cohesion—reflected in the likelihood that residents may look out for one another—may be low as well.

We can anticipate that anyone who returns to such a context may be more likely to become homeless, to be unemployed, to engage in drug abuse, and to recidivate. Indeed, some studies suggest that these consequences indeed result from returning to disadvantaged areas.[72] Coming from areas of concentrated disadvantage may also make it more difficult for some inmates to be visited by or maintain ties to friends and family, which in turn may adversely affect inmate behavior and preparation for release back into society.[73]

THE "TYPICAL INMATE" PROFILE

The "typical inmate" thus is an individual who is more likely to be male, black, and age forty or younger and to have been incarcerated for a violent offense. This inmate has been on probation or has been incarcerated before, has not graduated from high school, and has a history of unemployment. The inmate probably has a history of drug abuse and mental illness and comes from (and will return to) an area of marked social and economic disadvantage. Not surprisingly, three-fourths or more of inmates will be arrested for a new crime within 5 years of release from prison.[74] Knowing about these challenges can help corrections officials in their efforts to create a safe and orderly prison environment and to assist inmates in succeeding after they return to their home communities. Of course, no silver bullet solution exists for magically creating more pro-social behavior. Instead, as we discuss in later chapters, comprehensive approaches that tackle these different dimensions likely must be implemented to create long-term, appreciable improvements in the behavior and outcomes of individuals after they return home.

With that said, the typical inmate in prison is a misnomer. In reality, inmates vary along many dimensions, as the discussion above highlighted. That discussion actually understates the case. Inmates may vary in a myriad of other ways. Some may have much higher levels of self-control than others, which is relevant because of the strong association between self-control and offending.[75] The social contexts of individuals in prison and upon release vary greatly as well. Inmates and ex-prisoners vary in the types, amount, and quality of prison programming and postrelease supervision and treatment that they receive. Family context, including family support and marital status, vary.[76] Inmates are housed on average 100 miles away from home, but some inmates reside substantially closer and others reside much farther away.[77] Some inmates are visited frequently, while others are never visited.[78]

In addition, the culture and professionalism of staff among prisons may vary and thus directly create different experiences for inmates in ways that affect their behavior during and after incarceration.[79]

All of these factors and more may be critical to understanding how best to operate prisons, plan for changes to prison operations and programming, addressing inequalities, and improving reentry experiences and outcomes. They also highlight a shortfall of criminological theories of offending. Although the theories provide us with some understanding of why individuals commit crime, they leave us with a relatively narrow perspective on the causes. One of the benefits of focusing on inmate populations lies in the fact that when we examine the characteristics of these individuals, we can better discern the need for theories that identify the ways in which clusters of factors interact to adversely affect behavior.[80] Practitioners understand this idea intuitively because they do not deal with individuals who have a given causal factor "net of other factors." Rather, the individuals that they face bring with them many deficits and challenges simultaneously, as illustrated in the inmate profiles provided in the case study. That does not mean that all of these factors must be addressed to produce improved outcomes, only that addressing many of them likely will increase the chances of success.[81] Why? Because typically, human behavior, crime included, results from multiple causal factors and because, for any given individual or context, we do not know which ones matter most.[82]

Chapter 4 Case Study: Inmate Profiles and the Challenges They Present

Most inmates have problems, such as mental illness, addiction, and weak employment histories, which incarceration will not likely improve and indeed may aggravate. The rapid expansion of the prison system over a short period of time, accompanied by a sustained economic downturn over the past decade, has created substantial challenges for state and federal corrections systems and the families and communities to which prisoners return. Addressing the problems entails substantial costs. At the same time, not addressing them places society at risk through potential harms to the individuals in prison and through collateral consequences to children, families, and communities. Consider a few examples of typical inmates—in this case composites based on profiles of the types of individuals who leave prison—that illustrate the challenges that prison systems and society face in an era of mass incarceration.

Case 1: An African-American man, 40 years of age who, prior to prison, had never been incarcerated. He worked in a low-wage job outside of the inner city, which he used to support his wife and two children. In prison, he no longer has income for his family. His wife cannot afford child care and so works only part-time. The inmate received visits from his family at first, but his wife no longer could afford to

(Continued)

do so and retain her job while also looking after their children. Over time, his relationship with his wife deteriorates and they eventually divorce. He experiences psychological strain from the isolation and separation from his family. He becomes depressed and acts out in prison. Prior to and then upon release, he finds that he has underestimated the challenges that he will face finding work and reconnecting with his children. He becomes depressed, frustrated, and aggressive.

Case 2: A young white man, 22 years of age, who has been in and out of prison several times. He never graduated from high school or held a job and suffers from severe mental illness and substance addiction. Over a short time he has lost all ties to family members and friends, has significant physical health needs caused by homelessness and addiction, and is HIV positive. While incarcerated, his behavior becomes increasingly erratic and sometimes violent. Corrections officials repeatedly send him for brief stays in a mental health facility. He consistently presents a risk to the safety and order of the prison. As a result, he has limited opportunities to socialize or to take part in prison activities and programming. The tedium and isolation of his restricted prison life aggravates his conditions. Eventually, he returns to his home community, presenting more risk to others than he had prior to incarceration.

Case 3: A Latino woman, 30 years old, who is a single mother with one child and is pregnant with a second. She did not graduate from high school and, at the time of her arrest, worked part time at a fast-food restaurant. Upon incarceration, her first child, a daughter, goes to the custody of the inmate's parents, who live in another state. The mother can see her daughter during prison visits, but such visits occur infrequently. Over the course of incarceration, she requires intensive medical care leading up to and following the birth of her second child. The stress and anxiety of her incarceration jeopardizes the baby's well-being. No father surfaces to parent the child, and so her family again steps in to help; the inmate rarely sees this child. Several years later, upon release, she finds that her children do not accept her.

Such cases constitute the norm and can be found in numerous accounts, including those offered by ex-prisoners themselves, victims, correctional system personnel, journalists, and scholars (see, for example, Conover 2000; Rhodes 2004; Christian 2005; Travis and Waul 2004; Travis 2005; Comfort 2008; Hassine 2009; George 2010). Aggregate statistics obscure the fact that individual inmates have unique clusters of characteristics. The underlying common theme among the cases is the significant disadvantage that they have experienced and the fact of having committed crimes. Regardless of any of our personal views about appropriate punishment, the fact remains that inmates constitute a tremendous challenge to correctional systems and, upon release, to society. Further punishment, however much it may satisfy our retributive tendencies, will not likely resolve these challenges. A failure to address them means that we likely end up making matters worse through increased crime, poverty, and adverse effects on children, families, and communities.

WHY INMATE PROFILES CHANGE OVER TIME

Why Profile Changes Matter

To this point, our focus has been on the inmate profile and why it matters. As we discussed, it can be helpful for several reasons, including forecasting prison and parole capacity needs; identifying and forecasting prisoner treatment and service needs as well as management challenges; identifying, monitoring, and addressing inequality; and forecasting reentry population supervision and reentry needs. These goals are laudable, but they derive from a fundamentally reactive orientation. It is the equivalent of medical doctors accepting whatever patients walk through their front door and doing their best to treat them. Managing, supervising, and assisting inmates during and after release is sensible, much as it is sensible for a doctor to monitor case flows, anticipate future demand, and plan how to best address that demand.

However, such an approach stands in direct contrast to a more proactive stance. In the latter instance, we examine why, in the case of medical doctors, certain types of cases consistently show up at our front door or have been showing up more often. The proactive stance holds the potential for reducing the need for intervention in the first place. It also holds the potential for identifying how to intervene earlier and so avoid the need for costlier, less effective treatment.

Turning our focus directly to prison systems, then, the question that we face is, "What causes changes in the inmate profile over time?" Answering that question involves not only forecasting changes in prison population size but also, and more specifically, changes in the characteristics of this population. Here, again, we can undertake monitoring efforts. The monitoring, however, centers on the *causes of changes in the inmate profile.*

Any discussion about inmate profiles would seem to be all to the good—it enables the country and states to identify precisely who goes to prison and whether the reasons are defensible. A medical analogy illustrates the point. In some regions of the country, obstetricians may perform more C-sections on a per-pregnancy basis than in other parts of the country. The question is whether higher C-section rates are appropriate and constitute effective intervention. As with many medical practices, physician decision making may be driven by normative judgments about what is appropriate and assumptions about the relative effectiveness of a given approach compared with another.[83] Only by identifying variation in medical practices does it become possible even to begin systematically examining and discussing what is appropriate and the assumptions that undergird decision making. By extension, only by identifying when and why there may be increased percentages of young adults, sex offenders, drug offenders, and so on in the prison system can we then deliberate on whether the changes appear warranted.

Another illustration—if we put candy machines in schools, we might well see a rise in cavities among the student population. We could focus our attention on changing students' eating habits and dental hygiene. That would constitute a reactive approach. Alternatively, we could investigate the wisdom of a policy that makes candy widely available to students. The latter approach holds the potential to reduce substantially the problem and so reduce the need to employ interventions. Normative judgments clearly may matter. Some individuals and businesses may feel that students should have a right to eat candy and that financial benefits to the school offset any harms. Empirical evidence, too, may matter. Different camps may hold different assumptions about the relative costs and benefits of making candy available to students. Without research, a battle of assumptions dictates the discussion. With it, the possibility of an evidence-based approach to deciding the appropriate and cost-effective course of action emerges.

To date, what we know with certainty is that states vary greatly in the composition of their inmate populations; within and across states, the composition of this population varies over time. The composition of the federal prison system, too, varies over time. For example, from 1980 to 2010, the proportion of federal inmates consisting of drug offenders doubled, rising from 25 percent in 1980 to 52 percent in 2010.[84] We know that a variety of factors contributed to this variation. Ultimately, however, state-specific analyses provide the only credible foundation for determining which factors contribute to a given state's prison population characteristics and whether such influences appear to be defensible on normative or evidence-based grounds. Such analyses can be used as well to inform forecasting efforts. If, for example, increased get-tough policy making aimed at drug crimes led to a 30 percent increase in a given state's inmate population, and if even tougher reforms are expected to occur, states can anticipate that their prison systems will need to expand. They can anticipate, too, an accompanying need for, or potential benefit of, expanding drug treatment in prisons. In considering such changes, states may consider reversing course and undertaking alternative approaches to reducing drug crime.

Some Factors That Influence Changes in Inmate Profiles

What, then, affects the composition of inmate populations? Here, we briefly identify some of the contenders suggested by research, including crime, philosophical shifts in views about crime and punishment, drug wars, police and court size and emphases, and sentencing guidelines. The possibilities extend well beyond what we list. In addition, complicated processes, detailed in many studies, affect the salience of each potential cause. Our primary goal, therefore, consists of illustrating the range of possible causes of variation in inmate population characteristics. In so doing, we seek to highlight that variation in crime rates alone—a seemingly obvious explanation for why prison populations might change over time—does not account for these changes. Indeed, in many instances, they may exert little influence.

Crime. Do changes in crime affect calls to the police, and who gets convicted and sentenced? In general, the answer appears to be yes. However, the dynamics can be complex.[85] For example, property crime was declining for many years and violent crime had been stable or declining when, in the early 1980s, the country began to enact a series of get-tough sentencing laws. In addition, these laws continued to be passed and funding to enforce them expanded throughout the subsequent two decades. That occurred even though violent crime declined from the mid-1990s forward. The violent crime spike in the mid-1980s through the early 1990s helps to explain increases in prison populations, but the other patterns do not. At the state level, similar seemingly contradictory processes have unfolded. That does not mean that crime changes are irrelevant, only that the link to incarceration trends and the characteristics of the inmate population may be indirect and complicated.[86]

Philosophical Shifts in Views About Crime and Punishment. Public and policy-maker views—and, more broadly, philosophical or cultural shifts in views about crime and punishment—may affect criminal justice system activities, including processing and sentencing. As we discussed above, this idea runs counter to what the public may think occurs. The public typically thinks that the police learn about most crime, that all arrests where a conviction is possible in fact result in conviction, and that decisions about who to incarcerate are straightforward. In reality, many crimes never come to the attention of the police, which stems in part from the nature of some offenses, such as burglary, but also from the extent to which the public feels comfortable calling law enforcement and from the size of law enforcement agencies.[87]

More generally, no absolute rule dictates the percentage of offenders who should be caught, the percentage who should be arrested, the percentage of those arrested who should be convicted, or the percentage of convicted felons who should be incarcerated for a given length of time. We can see evidence of this in the fact that states vary greatly over time and among themselves along these dimensions.[88] Some states have incarceration rates in excess of 600 per 100,000 residents while others have incarceration rates that are 200 or 300 per 100,000. Such variation stems not just from differences in crime in these states. It stems as well from normative judgments about how willing we should be to rely on incarceration as a sanction. Unfortunately, crime is ubiquitous, and there likely will always be extreme cases that catch the public imagination and lead to swings in policy.[89] That situation gives rise to the potential for philosophical or cultural shifts in punishment views to affect sentencing. In turn, states can witness their prison populations expand rapidly in a short period of time.

In America, support for rehabilitation clearly declined in the 1970s for a variety of reasons, not least of which was the belief that rehabilitation achieved little save for coddling criminals.[90] Public concern about crime escalated considerably in the 1980s. Simultaneously social policies nationally shifted toward a more individual-focused emphasis, one that placed more importance on personal responsibility. That shift, when coupled with increased disillusionment with rehabilitation, appears to have contributed to a more punitive approach to sanctioning. However, more severe punishment for retribution's sake was not the only emphasis. Policy makers appeared to believe that increased punishment and less rehabilitation necessarily would produce specific and general deterrent effects. In another era, prevailing views might have led to different punishment policies and potentially less rather than more incarceration. The end result, too, might have been variation in the characteristics of the individuals sent to and released from American prisons.

The War on Drugs. Philosophical shifts in views about punishment may influence which types of offenses receive more attention. The war on drugs that began in the 1970s under President Richard Nixon led to more arrests, more convictions, and longer sentences for drug offenders.[91] Black drug offenders faced especially tough penalties because crack cocaine, used more so among African American groups, was penalized more than powder cocaine, used more so among whites, even though the two substances share similar pharmacological properties.[92]

Police and Court Size and Emphases. Police and court capacity alone can substantially affect arrest, conviction, and sentencing patterns. A simple thought experiment illustrates the point. We can have two cities, identical in all respects except one: police size. In one city, there might be twice as many police officers as the other. The end result? More arrests. Such variation exists not only among states but also over time.[93] Under President Clinton, for example, the Violent Crime Control and Law Enforcement Act of 1994 provided funding to hire 100,000 police officers. Considerable debate exists about the effect of this increase on crime, but in the short term its most immediate consequence was an increase in arrests.[94] During the peak period of the get-tough era, funding for the criminal justice system grew dramatically, rising from $19 billion in 1982 to almost $100 billion in 2006, and in so doing created the infrastructure for more capacity to arrest, convict, and incarcerate.[95] When such capacity is coupled with philosophical shifts toward greater punitiveness, the end result can be a marked increase in incarceration and changes in the composition of the inmate population. As but one example, with increased funding for law enforcement and the allocation of police to primarily high-crime areas, the indirect result can be a greater percentage of minority and low-income groups in prisons.[96]

Sentencing Guidelines. Another element of the get-tough era was the emergence of sentencing guidelines. During the 1980s, the federal government and states moved aggressively in the direction of creating laws that removed discretion from the court.[97] The change partially resulted from concern that similar cases received disparate treatment within and across courts. Such "informal rationality" would be supplanted by "formally rational" sentencing, in which only legal factors, such as prior record and type of offense, and not race, ethnicity, or sex, would affect court decisions. What appears instead to have happened is that discretion simply shifted from judges to prosecutors, and so indirectly placed greater weight on punishment.[98] Regardless, the emergence of new sentencing regimes—such as "three strikes and you're out" laws and enactment of mandatory minimum statutes that require sentenced individuals to serve a specific percentage of their sanction in prison—created a foundation for increasing the use of incarceration in ways that appeared to have affected drug offenders and minorities more so than other groups. This effect could arise even in cases where crime declined, as occurred during the past decade.[99]

In addition to these different factors—crime, philosophical or cultural shifts in punitiveness, the war on drugs, police and court size and emphases, and sentencing guidelines—many others can be identified as potential causes of changes in the inmate profile, like changes in the economy and in political emphases. No monitoring effort likely can track every possible factor, but the cost of developing tracking systems pales in comparison to building and using even one prison that may not be needed. Tracking systems can be developed by compiling data from correctional systems, law enforcement agencies, state agency databases, and data from such federal agencies as the U.S. Census Bureau and the Bureau of Justice Statistics.[100]

A simple example illustrates how such monitoring can be helpful. A state may see a marked increase in prison admissions. It undertakes an analysis of county-by-county changes in sentencing practices and discovers that, coinciding with the election of a new district attorney, a near doubling of admissions for assaults and drug crimes occurred. That information in turn allows for greater investigation and discussion of whether the increase is warranted or effective. No change need necessarily occur. However, the opportunity arises for key stakeholders, including the district attorney, to determine if the increased use of incarceration fits well with state resources and with what is available to sanction and treat offenders most effectively. The end result might well be a reduction in the use of incarceration and a greater reliance on intensive probation.[101] In turn, the state refrains from building prison capacity that, once it exists, would impose great costs for decades to come.

CONCLUSION

In this chapter, we briefly described some of the characteristics of the "typical" inmate and focused intensively on a question that descriptive accounts of prisoners typically leave unaddressed. Specifically, why do inmate characteristics matter? As we discussed, they matter for many reasons. They can be used to understand better how to forecast bedspace capacity in prisons. They can be used to identify and monitor potential social inequalities involved in sentencing individuals to prison and releasing them back into society. They can be used to inform decisions about appropriate prison-based and reentry treatment and services. Not least, they can serve as a foundation for understanding better the risks, needs, and challenges unique to specific social groups who return to society. The chapter also explored causal forces that can contribute to changes in inmate population characteristics and the usefulness of focusing on such forces for informing research and policy. Here, now, we step back and connect themes in this chapter to the broader goals of the book.

One goal of the book and of this chapter is to argue that if we want to understand reentry processes and to improve reentry outcomes, we need to know about the characteristics of the people who enter and leave prison. Effective education typically requires tailoring materials and instruction to the learning styles and abilities of a given individual. Similarly, our ability to assist or deter individuals in prison and after they leave requires tailoring approaches to reflect the real-life trajectories of these individuals. For example, an individual who enters prison as a drug addict will face additional challenges upon release from prison. Relapse in particular stands as a paramount concern. Similarly, individuals who have been separated from their children face the unique challenge of trying to reconnect with them. The mentally ill may have difficulty in maintaining continuity of care. Inmates released from supermax facilities may be ill equipped to handle even the most basic day-to-day interactions with others. These and many other possibilities exist and affect not only the experience of reentry but the potential for interventions to deter individuals from reoffending and to help them obtain work and housing.

This chapter highlighted the diverse array of deficits that characterize inmate populations. Many inmate problems existed prior to incarceration and may have even led to incarceration. They present challenges to maintaining safety and order in prisons, will likely be exacerbated as a result of incarceration, and in turn will enhance the challenges that inmates face when they reenter back into society. The end result of a prison stay thus can be an increased propensity to reoffend rather a decreased one. That does not mean that prison may not deter. It may for some inmates, but that is far from a foregone conclusion.[102] It means, too, that incarceration may have effects that permeate outward to families and communities.

A second goal is to emphasize the need for multifaceted interventions rather than "one size fits all" approaches. The individuals who go to prison constitute a diverse lot, and the causes of their offending may vary greatly. Not least among the sources of variation are the socioeconomic contexts to which the individuals return and how well equipped they are to negotiate them. If we want to reduce recidivism and improve other reentry outcomes, we need approaches that will work with specific types of individuals in the specific types of settings to which they will return.

A third goal is to argue that understanding reentry and its consequences requires looking beyond offenders and examining how incarceration and reentry affects other groups, including victims, families, and communities. The considerable heterogeneity of the individuals who go to prison may not, on the face of it, seem to support this argument. However, closer investigation of the issue suggests otherwise. Perhaps the most prominent example involves racial and ethnic disparities in incarceration, since minority families and communities bear more of the brunt of mass incarceration and reentry. Another example: We know that many inmates have children. In some cases, removing parents from children can be helpful, but it carries risks as well. Families may lose their sole wage earner and children may have to be placed in foster care. By understanding more about the people who go to prison, we establish a foundation for identifying groups—especially inmate families and their home communities—who may be at risk of harm because of select incarceration policies.

A fourth goal of the book and of this chapter is to argue that insights are needed from practitioners and those on the ground if we are to understand and improve reentry. The diversity of the prison population highlights that we can reasonably anticipate that inmates have diverse backgrounds and different experiences in prison and after release. Who is best suited to identify these differences? Researchers certainly can offer insights, but typically the insights stem from one-time studies, such as a survey of inmates at a given point in time. In the meantime, we have prison staff and community residents who arguably know more about what inmates need while in prison and after, what can be done to help and deter them, and what can be done to reduce harms to victims, families, and communities. To gain access to this insight, however, requires developing a research infrastructure that has the capacity to collect and organize information from these groups and make it readily available to policy makers, administrators, and practitioners. It also means creating the capacity to examine the factors that contribute to policy-maker decisions. Their choices ultimately affect the entire criminal justice system. Understanding more about the pressures they face and their perceptions of crime, its causes, and the effectiveness of extant laws and programs can provide a foundation for placing policy decisions on stronger, empirically based grounds.

A final goal of this book and of this chapter is to argue that different approaches can be used to improve reentry outcomes and, at the same time, improve government accountability, cost-efficiency, and justice. This chapter establishes some of the foundation for supporting this argument. In particular, the diversity of the inmate population highlights that no single approach to punishment or reentry—no silver bullet—will be appreciably effective. Inmates and ex-prisoners simply vary too much in their characteristics and the areas from which they come. Accordingly, and in anticipation of later chapters, we need multifaceted approaches to sanctioning if we are to improve public safety in a cost-efficient, just manner.

The chapter highlights, too, that what we should "do" about reentry is complicated by the fact that we likely should attend not only to certain inmate characteristics but also to the *causes* of changes in these characteristics among inmates. The most prominent example consists of enactment and enforcement of tougher drug sentencing laws. A *reactive* policy approach consists of developing drug treatment interventions within the correctional system. However, a more *proactive* approach likely involves examining whether these laws—and, simultaneously, their tougher enforcement—constitute effective policy. If they do, then we are left with the reactive approach. If they do not, then logically we need to focus less on large-scale investment in criminal justice system-based drug treatment, drug courts, and the like, and more on diverting certain types of individuals from the justice system entirely, ideally to settings where their health needs might more effectively and cost-efficiently be addressed.[103]

This reactive versus proactive tension permeates discussions of punishment policy and reentry. Indeed, they cannot easily be disentangled. At the end of the day, societies use incarceration as a prominent type of punishment. Accordingly, they will continue to have individuals with specialized characteristics who present unique challenges to prison systems and, upon release, society at large. Yet it is possible to restrict substantially the population to whom incarceration gets applied, provided alternative punishments exist. When they do, we likely incur fewer costs and retain a greater ability to leverage family and community resources to improve life outcomes among those involved in the criminal justice system. No neat solution here exists, save to use punishment carefully and selectively and to understand the characteristics that most affect inmate behavior and reentry outcomes.

DISCUSSION QUESTIONS

1. What is the profile of the "typical" inmate?

2. Why are the characteristics of inmates relevant to a discussion of the prison experience and prisoner reentry?

3. Which characteristics of inmates warrant monitoring and forecasting? Why?

4. Which characteristics of inmates appear most likely to contribute to adverse experiences while in prison and upon release? Why?

5. What factors contribute to changes in the inmate population profile? Which seem most justifiable? Which seem most amenable to policy control?

6. What are the likely consequences of ignoring variation in prisoner characteristics for managing inmates and improving reentry outcomes, including public safety?

CHAPTER 5

The Prison Experience

This chapter examines the prison experience. Many accounts in the prisoner reentry literature have focused extensively on what inmates face when they return to society. That constitutes an important endeavor in its own right. However, this focus neglects the fact that what inmates "import" into prison may affect their behavior upon release, as we discussed in the previous chapter. It also neglects the fact that what they face while incarcerated—what we term here "the prison experience"—also may affect greatly reentry outcomes.[1]

Accordingly, here we describe how prison provides a setting that involves different types of experiences and why understanding these experiences matters. One reason is that the experiences may contribute to inmate misconduct and criminal activity while incarcerated. Another is that they may affect recidivism and other postrelease outcomes such as housing and employment. Not least, they may affect families and communities. For example, when inmates cannot visit with their children, there arises the possibility that the children become more rather than less at risk of criminal activity themselves.

The chapter describes two prominent theories of inmate behavior—importation theory and deprivation theory—that together provide a powerful framework for understanding both what happens to inmates and how their characteristics and experiences can contribute to misconduct and recidivism. It then describes aspects of the prison experience, including prison programming, visitation, victimization, and solitary confinement, that illustrate how what happens in prison may influence inmates and reentry success. In so doing, we emphasize the importance of understanding how inmates perceive themselves. Finally, we close with a discussion of what is known about the effects of the prison experience writ large. In particular, what is the effect of incarceration on recidivism? In what ways might it help or hinder the process of desistance?

Consistent with several themes in the book, this chapter highlights the complexity of reentry. Imprisonment serves to punish. But what really do we expect when people go to prison? What experiences, beyond simply the deprivations that accompany not being in free society, should happen to create the type or amount of retribution that the public wants? At the same time, what experiences should happen to achieve the desired amount of retribution, deterrence, or rehabilitation? What types of prison experiences lead to reoffending, and by contrast what experiences lead to desistance? What steps can be undertaken to improve order and safety in prisons? What role, if any, does government accountability play in the operation of prison systems and the creation of more successful reentry outcomes? By examining the prison experience, we may not answer these questions fully, but we can shed light on what needs to occur to answer them. And we can identify the consequences of failing to do so.

WHY WHAT HAPPENS IN PRISON IS RELEVANT FOR UNDERSTANDING REENTRY

Incarceration constitutes such a different experience from that in free society that it almost assuredly affects individuals. Incapacitation and retribution stand as two prominent goals of incarceration. However, prisons ideally create public safety benefits by deterring would-be offenders in society ("general deterrence"), by deterring future criminal behavior among sanctioned individuals ("specific deterrence"), or by rehabilitating these individuals or otherwise intervening in ways that reduce their likelihood of recidivating.[2] The precise goals of prisons have changed over time.[3] Even so, in contemporary times, we typically view them as effective when they achieve some amount of retribution and public safety, whether the latter occurs through incapacitation, deterrence, rehabilitation, or some other mechanism.

Concern arises, however, when we realize that over three-fourths of incarcerated individuals will be rearrested within 5 years of release.[4] One source of concern is that incarceration may worsen rather than improve public safety.[5] Instead of reducing recidivism, for example, it may harden individuals into more highly skilled, socially isolated, chronic offenders who become increasingly less responsive to any type of intervention. This idea has gone largely unrecognized in the shift toward more punitive sanctioning, which has assumed that individuals "get the message" after they receive lengthy prison sentences and so go on to become pro-social, contributing members of society. Little evidence supports that assumption. Indeed, policy makers and scholars increasingly have voiced misgivings about incarceration as a mechanism for doing much more than temporarily incapacitating individuals (and even this benefit is uncertain[6]) and, of course, doing so at great economic and social cost.

Notwithstanding this assessment, the fact remains that we have limited knowledge about the specific aspects of prison life that contribute to incarceration effectiveness in reducing recidivism. A review by Daniel Nagin and colleagues of research on incarceration effects highlights this very point. Few credible empirical estimates exist of how incarceration influences recidivism and fewer still show how aspects of the prison experience contribute to the likelihood of offending.[7]

We argue in this chapter that a host of in-prison dimensions may be especially salient in affecting incarcerated individuals and that these dimensions may exert different effects depending on the characteristics and contexts of particular individuals. For example, an individual who, prior to prison, faced bleak prospects of finding a job or getting an education and was seemingly destined to a criminal career may be deterred from crime by opportunities to reform during and after incarceration. By contrast, an individual who enjoyed relatively promising life circumstances—such as supportive family members and secure housing and a job—may be more likely to be adversely affected by the general prison experience or by specific aspects of it, such as abuse, victimization, or social isolation.[8]

What types of prison experiences are helpful or harmful? The implications of some experiences seem fairly obvious. We can anticipate, for example, that actively engaging in serious misconduct or crime in prison may increase recidivism. Such conduct may signal an underlying propensity to offend, but it also may create adverse experiences, such as being labeled a "chronic offender," that exert additional criminogenic influences.[9] Similarly, the development of serious mental illness in prison, especially if poorly treated, may exert harmful, long-term impacts. That does not mean that mentally ill individuals necessarily commit more crime. However, their illness may contribute to experiences, such as reduced unemployment opportunities, that may increase the likelihood of offending.[10] By contrast, effective drug treatment or addiction counseling may be helpful in directly or indirectly reducing recidivism.[11] Still other experiences may have uncertain benefits. For example, being visited by friends or family members in prison may help individuals to maintain social ties and manage the strains associated with incarceration, both of which should improve behavior.[12] But what if a visit results in fighting and arguing? Or to receiving drugs in prison? Or to maintaining criminal ties? In these instances, visitation may do more harm than good.

Building on these observations, we seek to highlight a central insight about prisons—there is no single, uniform prison experience that exists or that affects individuals in the same way. Although in this book we use the term "the prison experience," individual backgrounds, organizational conditions, such as how a given prison operates, and family and community context, all may create a different prison experience for any given person sent to prison. It is not that some commonalities do not exist. A five-star hotel typically will offer special perks not offered by a three-star hotel. Yet how individuals experience each hotel may vary a great deal. Similarly, substantial variation may exist in the operations and culture of different prisons and the types of individuals housed in or working at them. A critical challenge thus lies in sifting through the myriad events, circumstances, and experiences that inmates encounter in their day-to-day lives and over the course of a prison term. A related challenge lies in identifying those that may be most beneficial or harmful, those that present moral and ethical dilemmas, and, not least, those that may be most easily and cost-efficiently implemented by prison staff to improve inmate behavior and life chances.[13]

THE IMPLICATIONS OF IN-PRISON CRIME AND MISCONDUCT

Why In-Prison Crime and Misconduct Matter

Crime and misconduct that occur merit attention for several reasons. First, it constitutes behavior that concerns society. Crime leads individuals to become incarcerated, but the fact of incarceration does not terminate society's interest in having individuals conform with the law.

Second, prison administrators are primarily concerned with maintaining order and safety in their institutions. Crime and misconduct undermine their ability to achieve this goal. Although not all forms of misconduct would be considered illegal in free society, any conduct that undermines prison staff authority can lead to further disorder within prisons.[14] Disorderly prisons present safety risks and legal liabilities.[15] Prisons with high rates of disorder and violence are underperforming, even if we do not know the cause of the poor performance.

Third, crime and misconduct in prison may predict or affect reentry outcomes. In many respects, engaging in crime and misconduct while incarcerated can signal to corrections officials that an individual will continue offending upon release.[16] That information may be useful for criminologists seeking to identify different groups of criminals (e.g., chronic offenders) and for practitioners seeking to identify which groups require more supervision, treatment, or some type of intervention. It also may be useful for exploring whether there may be some way to structure the prison experience to interrupt what otherwise will be sustained criminal activity during and after release from prison.

The Heterogeneity of In-Prison Crime and Misconduct

In-prison offending, like crime in free society, is heterogeneous. It varies widely in severity and frequency and in its causes. Some offenses occur against other inmates or guards; others are victimless. Some offenses are more easily detected by prison staff or more likely to be reported. Some individuals engage in more crime and misconduct than others. Some crimes occur more in isolation by individuals acting on their own; others require group activity, such as the coordinated actions of gang members.

Although extreme violence and riots occur infrequently, prisons are less safe than what most citizens encounter in free society. National estimates suggest an average within-facility assault rate of roughly 16 per 1,000 inmates, compared to .44 per 1,000 persons in the general (free) population.[17] It is difficult to accurately estimate sexual victimization, but national estimates suggest prison populations face greater risk—7.5 percent of state inmates report some type of sexual victimization compared with less than 1 percent of persons in the general population.[18] A range of other offenses exist that present significant concerns and management challenges, including but not limited to drug use and distribution, theft, threats, fraud, arson, smuggling, gambling, escapes, bribery, hate crimes, and prostitution.[19]

Theories and Factors That Predict In-Prison Crime and Misconduct

What factors lead to in-prison offending, or reduce its likelihood? In Figure 5.1, we highlight different pathways to in-prison misconduct. Some of these pathways may lead to increased misconduct but others may exert a misconduct-reducing effect. These dimensions can also be linked directly or indirectly to recidivism.[20] Consideration of these different pathways is important for understanding the needs, deficits, and challenges inmates bring with them to prison and how to address them.

Figure 5.1   Pathways to Prison Misconduct and Violence

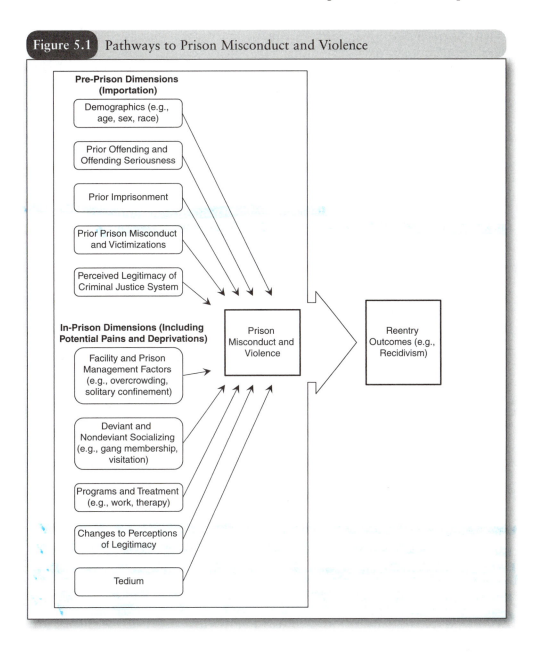

Scholarship on inmate behavior has centered on two theories, both of which emerged from an attempt to explain "prisonization," a phenomenon identified by Donald Clemmer in which incarcerated individuals acquire the folkways and culture of prison. These theories sought more broadly to explain why inmates act out and violate prison rules.[21] The first, importation theory, was developed by John Irwin and Donald Cressey and built on Clemmer's insights. It argues that pre-prison characteristics may influence the behavior of an individual in prison and do so in part by importing a belief system conducive to crime and misconduct.[22] A host of pre-incarceration characteristics may be related to in-prison offending, including age, gender, race and ethnicity, perceptions of legitimacy of the criminal justice system, prior offending patterns, offending severity, and prior victimizations.[23] Many of these factors have been found to be associated with inmate behavior and so are of practical use to prison administrators for identifying higher-risk inmates.[24] Such efforts carry their own risk, however. For example, knowing that a given factor may be associated with misconduct does not tell us *why* that association exists.[25] What is it about age, for example, that may lead a younger inmate, on average, to engage in more misconduct? Risk classification without information about how to structure supervision or intervention does not provide prison systems with much insight about what to do with higher-risk versus lower-risk individuals.

An alternative perspective, deprivation theory, argues that the experiences of incarceration itself affect the likelihood of crime and misconduct.[26] Gresham Sykes argued that the pains of imprisonment give rise to an inmate culture that itself is criminogenic. These pains and deprivations include loss of liberty, goods and services, heterosexual relationships, autonomy, and security.[27] Deprivation theory is reinforced by other theoretical accounts, such as those that emphasize the salience of being treated fairly. Fair and humane treatment, according to this argument, should be more likely to result in orderly and safe prison environments. Conversely, unfair or inhumane treatment should contribute to disorder and violence.[28] The more general argument, one advanced by Anthony Bottoms and other scholars, reduces to the idea that prison conditions or ecology affect inmate behavior.[29] These conditions can run the gamut, including prison administrative styles, staff-to-inmate ratios, prison culture, program and treatment availability, opportunities for visitation, and more.[30]

In recent years, scholars increasingly have argued that substantial empirical support exists for both theories and that more powerful explanations of inmate behavior require combining the two perspectives into an integrated model. This model points to the idea that inmate behavior results from a constellation of characteristics that individuals import into prison settings, the conditions in prisons, and the interaction of these two sets of factors together.[31] Accordingly, any given individual characteristic or prison condition may have (a) a direct effect on inmate behavior; (b) an indirect effect, in which a given characteristic or condition contributes to an experience or event that in turn contributes to inmate behavior; or (c) an interactive effect, in which a given characteristic or condition interacts with another, such that it has a greater or lesser effect depending on the presence or level of the other characteristic or condition.

In-Prison Crime and Misconduct as Predictors of Recidivism

Studies have found that in-prison infractions, violations, and criminal activity positively correlate with recidivism.[32] Why might in-prison crime and misconduct lead to recidivism? Several possibilities present themselves.

First, it may not per se be a causal relationship. Rather, engaging in these behaviors may simply reflect an underlying propensity to engage in offending. That propensity itself may stem from a wide variety of factors identified by criminological theories of criminal behavior.

Second, rule violations may result in sanctions, including disciplinary confinement, which may hinder participation in rehabilitative programming. Here, the effect is indirect. By adversely affecting the chances of receiving or participating in rehabilitation-focused interventions, inmates miss an opportunity to become more pro-social through changes in attitudes, beliefs, and habits.

Third, these violations may result in inmates self-labeling themselves as somehow inherently criminal or in others applying such a label. In turn, inmates may internalize these labels and, in accordance with labeling theory, be more likely to offend.[33]

Fourth, misconduct and various violations may result in additional strains, such as missed opportunities to visit family, which in turn elevate the risk of recidivism. In this example, there is the potential for these behaviors to sever ties to family and so reduce social bonds that inhibit offending.[34] Inmates, too, in accordance with social learning theory, may learn how to commit crime or become more committed to a criminal lifestyle while incarcerated.[35]

Fifth, and not least, involvement in crime or misconduct while incarcerated may signal that something about the individual or his or her environment is creating a greater likelihood of offending.[36] The signal consists of just that—a sign that increased risk exists. It does not tell us necessarily why that risk exists. It could be due to the pains of imprisonment, perceived injustice, or any number of prison conditions or stressful or traumatic personal events. To know more about what the signal itself represents or what gave rise to it, we need to know more about what happened to the individual while he or she was incarcerated.

PRISON EXPERIENCES THAT MAY HAVE IMPLICATIONS FOR PRISONER REENTRY

Apart from in-prison offending and misconduct, what other prison-based experiences or events might affect inmate behavior and have implications for prisoner reentry? Table 5.1 lists a wide range of possibilities. Even so, the list is far from comprehensive. We seek here simply to illustrate that many prison experiences can be influential. Below we provide a more in-depth discussion of several of these experiences to ground the more general observation that what happens in prison may be critical to understanding inmate behavior and how individuals fare when they leave prison. In developing this idea, we draw on a large and rich body of qualitative and quantitative studies that provide valuable insights about life in prison, including ways that inmates cope with social isolation and how they navigate prison culture, abuse, and victimization.[37] Despite such research, little systematic empirical scrutiny exists that examines how the experiences and conditions identified in the table contribute to successful reentry.

Prison Programming

Prison facilities typically offer some type of programming, although it may not be widely available or provided in sufficient doses or quality to have much of an effect.[38] Program types may be educational, vocational, work, recreational,

Table 5.1   Prison Experiences That May Affect Reentry

1. Facility and Prison Management

Overcrowding

Racial and ethnic composition

Physical condition of facility

Design of the facility

Staff abuse

Rates of violence and misconduct

Custody level

Location of facility

Characteristics of prison staff

Clarity of rules and regulations

Perceptions of legitimacy

Punishments

    Solitary or supermax confinement

    Transfers to other facilities

    Visitation restrictions

    Loss of "good time" credits

    Fines, restitution

    Verbal reprimand

2. Programming and Treatment

Work and vocational programs

Educational programs

Recreational programs

Family programs and counseling

Substance abuse treatment

Mental health treatment and counseling

Physical health treatment

3. Socialization on the Inside

Inmate–staff relationships

Inmate–inmate relationships

Gang membership

Deviant peer groups

Nondeviant peer groups

Sexual activity

Recreation and games

In-prison enemies

4. Socialization with the Outside World

Contact with family and friends

    Visitation

    Conjugal visitation

    Phone calls

    Internet video calls

    Letter writing, emails

    Victim–offender contact

Participation in outside educational classes

Legal case work with lawyers

Contact with volunteers, clergy, etc.

5. Sentencing Dimensions

Sentence length

Risk classification

Anticipated postrelease sanctions

Early release eligibility

Determinate vs. indeterminate sentence

6. Victimization

Sexual victimization

Violent victimization

Property victimization

Witness to sexual victimization

Witness to violent victimization

Witness to property victimization

7. Misconduct

Sexual misconduct

Violent misconduct

Property misconduct

Disorderly conduct

8. Amenities and Privileges

Ease of access to services and treatments

Ease of access to outside contact

Provision of useable recreation equipment

Quality of life (e.g., air conditioning)

religious, substance abuse, psychological, and cognitive behavioral.[39] Each type includes programs of varying quantity and quality. For example, educational programs can entail many classes, including basic literacy, graduate equivalency degree (GED), vocational training, associate degree, bachelor's degree, and law or graduate degree classes or programs. In addition, within these education categories there can exist even more variation. For example, inmates might take college courses through a community college or from a state university, classes might be in person or online, and the specific degrees and majors they work towards can vary. Similarly, inmates may participate in vocational training that provides experience in any number of fields. Religious programs, too, vary greatly, from those that entail bible-study classes or visits with pastors to immersion programs that provide a wide range of faith-oriented or faith-informed activities.[40] In-prison drug treatment programs and interventions vary tremendously in design, implementation, and effectiveness as well.[41]

Many inmates will receive little to no significant exposure to programming, while others will receive modest exposure. One source of variability in the prison experience thus centers on this difference. Among inmates who receive more than a nominal amount of programming, the question we face is, "So what?" Is it effective in achieving intermediate outcomes—such as improved anger management, reduced drug use, improved mental health, educational progress, and so on—and longer-term outcomes, such as improved in-prison behavior and reentry outcomes? Ideally, for example, we want participation in programming to result in intermediate outcomes that in turn result in postrelease success, including obtaining housing and employment and engaging in pro-social rather than criminal behavior.

Extant research provides a mixed picture. By and large, effective programs exist that have been shown to improve intermediate and longer-term outcomes.[42] But even the best programs are only as good as their implementation. Often prisons offer too little quality programming to achieve substantial reductions in recidivism.[43] Certainly, individual programs achieve marked success.[44] However, achieving a 10 percent reduction in recidivism among 1,000 inmates in a system of, say, 100,000 inmates is simply not enough to significantly improve public safety.

The variation in the types of programs that exist, when coupled with the fact that many of these variants have not been well evaluated, adds another layer of complexity. Consider prison work programs. Studies suggest that half of all inmates work in some type of job while incarcerated.[45] The work may involve maintenance, groundskeeping, laundry, food service, barbering, public works, woodworking, and more. These work-related activities, as with vocational training programs, may provide inmates something to do during prison, thus reducing opportunities to act out and a way to feel productive.[46] Work also can help inmates to learn useful vocational skills and to instill discipline and normative behavior. Research in fact suggests that inmates who work in prison have reduced likelihoods of recidivism compared with those who do not work.[47] Even so, substantial questions exist about the effectiveness of a broad range of employment-focused programs.[48]

Drug use is, as discussed in Chapter 4, highly prevalent among those admitted to prison. For that reason, drug treatment constitutes one of the most common programs in prison settings.[49] In part, policy makers and practitioners may subscribe to the belief that drug use causes offending. That idea holds considerable appeal because it leads to the inference that curing this problem will greatly reduce recidivism. It seems like the perfect silver-bullet solution. However, the causal relationship between drug use, abuse, and addiction, on the one hand, and offending, on the other hand, is uncertain. Drug problems simply may reflect or result from many criminogenic factors. In that case, addressing these factors arguably constitutes the more effective path.[50] Regardless, drug treatment serves as one obvious target for intervention. A wide range of programs exist, including detoxification approaches, professional and peer counseling, cognitive-behavioral modalities, and specialized intensive efforts such as therapeutic communities. Prisons struggle, however, to ensure that drug-involved individuals get matched with programming that fits their specific needs and problems.[51]

It seems self-evident that some types of programs should improve inmate behavior and life on the outside for ex-prisoners. We know, though, that often what seem to be the most common sense approaches do not always translate into effective outcomes. In the case of prison programming, we simply know too little about what prisons actually provide, the amount and quality of programming, or its effects on an array of outcomes to state with confidence their effectiveness or cost-efficiency.[52] We know only that some effective programs do exist but currently not on a level that would create large-scale, enduring reductions in recidivism.

Visitation

Social isolation from family and friends constitutes one of the biggest fears that inmates express.[53] From a policy perspective, the fear appears well grounded—isolation may be criminogenic. Conversely, visits from family, friends, and community members may help to improve inmate behavior and reduce recidivism.[54]

The social isolation that inmates experience represents, of course, an inherent part of what it means to be incarcerated. The pains of imprisonment include isolation.[55] In many respects, it literally defines the prison experience. It does not have to do so, however. One could be deprived of many liberties and yet still be housed in settings that allowed and promoted frequent contact with family and friends. The fact that this approach has not been taken, by and large, in American corrections suggests implicitly that, in the United States, the very idea of a prison sentence should include social isolation. Inmate ties should be severed or diminished. That seems logical, especially if we think about criminal associates exerting harmful effects on a prisoner. At the same time, humans are social beings by nature, and social networks and relationships can play a substantial role in helping ex-prisoners to establish a pro-social life.[56]

Scholars and practitioners alike have identified several theoretical pathways through which visitation may help to reduce recidivism.[57] It can help to reduce the strains of imprisonment. It can help individuals maintain ties to family, friends, and other members of their social networks. And it can increase the ability of inmates to access social resources necessary for successfully navigating the reentry experience. One study by Mark Berg and Beth Huebner found that inmates who maintained ties to outside social networks were more likely to gain employment upon release.[58] Visitation—or, more generally, letters or phone or video calls—may help, too, to improve employment prospects as well as access to drug and mental health treatment, transportation, social welfare services, and housing.[59]

Studies typically find that few inmates experience in-prison visits. Estimates suggest that roughly one-third of inmates receive visits over the course of incarceration.[60] Contact patterns, however, likely vary across subgroups, such as those who are younger or older, or who have more or fewer intimate social ties on the outside. Some studies suggest, for example, that younger inmates are more likely to be visited.[61]

We might expect that prisoners with children would experience relatively high rates of visitation if only to foster sustained ties between parents and their children. Scholarship suggests that children of prisoners may be more likely to be arrested or incarcerated.[62] Accordingly, visitation—and, in turn, sustained ties with children—may help to interrupt a cycle of crime within families. However, Figure 5.2 shows that nearly 60 percent of U.S. inmates with minor children never receive personal visits. Other forms of contact, though, happen more frequently. For example, more than 50 percent of inmates with minor children report contact via telephone, and nearly 70 percent report contact via mail.

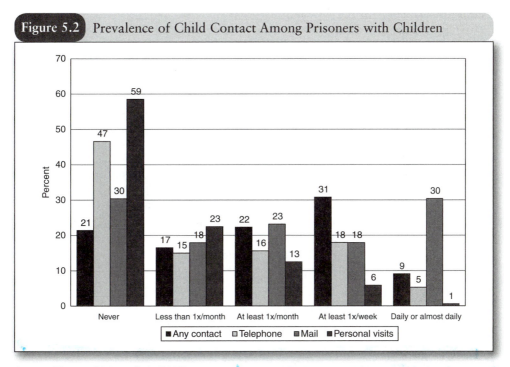

Figure 5.2 Prevalence of Child Contact Among Prisoners with Children

Source: Glaze and Maruschak (2008).

Studies of visitation effects are limited in number. Those that exist typically find that inmates who are visited engage in lower rates of misconduct and are significantly less likely to recidivate.[63] Thus, visitation appears to count as a largely beneficial experience, one with implications for inmate behavior in prison and during reentry and implications in turn for their families and possibly their communities. Dig a little deeper, however, and we find that visitation is a more complex and nuanced prison experience than studies to date indicate. For example, visitation experiences vary, and this variation likely influences the effectiveness of visitation.[64] For example, visitation can vary by type of visit. Inmates might be visited by parents, spouses, children, or other family members. Visitors might come from an offender's community, a religious group, or a local volunteer organization. There might be different patterns of visitation. Inmates might be visited regularly or seemingly randomly. They might be visited early on during incarceration or at the end of a prison term.[65] In addition, the effect of visitation may depend on events that occur during a visit (e.g., fighting, arguing, signing divorce papers).

Although visitation may help inmates maintain or strengthen their outside social bonds or relieve the strains of isolation, variation along these dimensions likely changes this relationship. Consider an inmate who is visited by a girlfriend every week. Over time, visits become fewer until they no longer occur at all. It is reasonable to believe that, although having been visited might constitute a beneficial experience at first, the cessation of visitation or the expectation of visits that never occur may create greater strain and increase misconduct and recidivism.[66] Consider, too, a situation where visits occur regularly. Such visits may provide a way to hold the prison system accountable and to establish and support a viable reentry plan.[67] By contrast, infrequent or irregular visitation may be insufficient for such support.[68]

Juxtaposed against such considerations are inmate and visitor accounts, which highlight that they want to visit but frequently cannot due to a variety of barriers. Visitation requires finding transportation, traveling long distances (sometimes over 100 or 200 miles), taking time off from work, paying for child care, and navigating complex administrative requirements for visiting.[69] Facilities may be off-putting and lack amenities, such as games or books, that would make parents feel more comfortable bringing their children along on a visit. In addition, many inmates come from highly disadvantaged socioeconomic contexts; their families and friends may lack the resources to overcome the barriers to visitation.

Visitation is, in short, a prison experience that holds considerable potential for influencing the lives of inmates and their families. Although evidence has accumulated that it can reduce misconduct and recidivism, empirical research that more clearly establishes the precise conditions under which it helps rather than harms is needed. The broader point echoes the argument that runs throughout this chapter—aspects of the prison experience likely shape the experience of reentry and the likelihood of recidivism.

Victimization

The prevalence of victimization is two to ten times higher for inmates than for individuals in the general population.[70] Victimization of any kind raises moral, ethical, and legal concerns for prison officials. It also raises important questions about how inmates will cope with the resulting trauma and how well they will make the transition to free society.[71]

Studies suggest that several forms of victimization occur among inmate populations. Analyses of self-report survey data indicate that 10–20 percent of inmates report some type of violent victimization in prison.[72] A number of studies have found that roughly 4–10 percent of inmates report experiencing one or more incidents of sexual crime in prison.[73] Even if inmates do not themselves experience victimization, they likely witness it. For example, in a recent study of the experiences of 1,616 released inmates in Ohio, 98 percent of those interviewed reported witnessing the victimization of another inmate; the victimization events included theft, physical assault, verbal assault, and sexual victimization.[74]

Victimization events themselves can vary not only by type (e.g., physical assault, theft) but also within type. For example, sexual victimization varies greatly. Table 5.2 presents descriptive statistics of the sexual victimization experiences reported in a national sample of former state prisoners to illustrate this point. In panel A, we see that among those surveyed, 10 percent reported experiencing sexual victimization when they were last in a prison, jail, or community treatment facility. Roughly half of those victimizations involved another inmate, and the other half involved a prison staff member.

Panel B provides details reported by those inmates who were victimized about the specific incident, including whether or not the incident involved different types of coercion and physical injuries, the location of sexual victimizations, and the number of perpetrators. (Inmates may be repeatedly victimized, hence the percentages do not add to 100.) Over half (59 percent) were forcibly coerced into sex or engaged in sex due to a threat. Serious physical injury occurred in 23 percent of the cases and in 4 percent of the cases broken bones resulted. Over 60 percent of the time, victimization occurred in the victim's cell, 37 percent in the shower or bathroom, and 24 percent in another inmate's cell.

What does victimization portend for reentry? Empirical assessments of the association between victimization and reentry outcomes are scant. However, existing studies indicate that violent victimization is associated with depression, post-traumatic stress symptomatology, other types of mental disorders, substance abuse, and worsened perceptions of the legitimacy of the prison system.[75] In a study focused specifically on inmates, Shelley Listwan and her colleagues found that inmates who scored higher on a coercion index, based on victimization experiences and perceptions of the prison environment as threatening, were more likely to reoffend. Similarly, experiencing a violent victimization or simply witnessing a sexual victimization in prison was associated with a higher likelihood of rearrest or reimprisonment after release.[76]

More research is needed to determine how repeated victimization or specific types of victimization may affect individuals during and after prison stays. For example, property victimization may harm individuals less than sexual victimization. However, frequent property victimization may adversely affect mental health. A sense of violation and anger may persist or grow and in turn carry over into the community upon release.

Table 5.2   Self-Reported Sexual Victimization Experiences of Former State Prisoners

Panel A. Prevalence of Sexual Victimization	Percent of All Former Inmates
Any reported sexual victimization	9.6
Inmate-on-inmate victimization	5.4
Staff-on-inmate victimization	5.3
Panel B. Characteristics of Victimization Incidents	Percent of Inmates Reporting Inmate-on-Inmate Sexual Victimization
Selected types of coercion	
Involved coercion by force or threat	58.6
Involved coercion by bribing/blackmail	25.6
Involved coercion by drugs/alcohol	9.0
Involved financial coercion (paying off a debt)	8.2
Prevalence of physical injury and selected types	
Any physical injury reported	29.7
Bruises, cuts, sprains, etc.	28.6
Serious physical injury	22.9
Anal/vaginal tearing, severe pain, or bleeding	11.7
Knocked unconscious	8.4
Internal injuries	6.3
Knife/stab wounds	4.4
Broken bones	4.3
Most common locations of victimization	
Victim's cell	61.9
Shower/bathroom	36.7
Another inmate's cell	24.3
Yard or recreational area	21.8
Workplace	17.9
Number of perpetrators	
1	53.8
2	25.4
3 or more	20.8

Note: In the survey, former prisoners were asked to report whether sexual victimization occurred during their most recent period of incarceration in any of the following facilities—jail, prison, postrelease community treatment facilities—and to provide details of incidents. Percentages for prevalence of physical injury and victimization location do not sum to 100 percent because respondents were permitted to report multiple responses.

Source: Beck and Johnson (2012).

Solitary Confinement

Prison wardens and staff employ both sticks and carrots to reinforce good behavior and to deter bad behavior. In the punitive shift of recent decades, the use of sticks has become more common, reflecting a belief that individual behavior results primarily from individual characteristics, such as motivation, more so than environmental characteristics, such as how prison officers treat inmates. It reflects, too, the decreased availability of rehabilitative programming that might be used to incentivize inmates to conform to prison rules and expectations.

Solitary confinement epitomizes the get-tough trend in criminal justice policy and in corrections. As with other punitive crime and corrections policies nationally, its use has increased greatly in recent decades.[77] There are several categories of solitary confinement: (a) punitive segregation (temporary isolation as punishment for misconduct); (b) protective segregation (temporary isolation as a means of protecting vulnerable inmates); and (c) administrative segregation (long-term isolation as a means of managing certain inmates), or what scholars frequently refer to as "super-maximum" (or "supermax") housing.[78]

Supermax housing involves single-cell confinement for 23–24 hours each day with little to no programming or contact with others. Its logic in some ways harks back to the Walnut Street Jail in the late 1700s and the Quaker emphasis on silent contemplation. However, as a modern-day management strategy, it represents a distinct move away from the emphasis on dispersing troublesome inmates throughout the prison system to concentrating them in one place. Accounts of supermaxes typically characterize the strategy as one of placing the so-called bad apples in one place. Prior to 1980, states did not have supermax housing, but since that time, almost every state has created such housing. Conservative estimates indicate that 25,000 or more inmates reside in supermax housing, and some spend half or more of their prison term in it. Estimates suggest that 100,000 inmates or more are in solitary confinement at any one time.[79]

Time spent in solitary confinement has been associated with a range of adverse health outcomes, including anxiety, depression, psychosis, social withdrawal, hallucinations, and suicide.[80] Inmates likely face significant challenges adjusting back into the normal prison population, and back into society, after spending significant amounts of time in isolation without social contact.[81] To date, the use of solitary confinement in the United States has raised concerns because many believe it constitutes unjust and immoral treatment of inmates, it entails considerable costs, and its effectiveness in creating greater systemwide order and safety or in facilitating successful returns to society has not been established.[82]

Few studies have examined the effect of supermax incarceration in particular on recidivism. Two that have done so—one by David Lovell and colleagues and another by Daniel Mears and William Bales—have found that inmates who experience supermax confinement reoffend more than those who do not experience it.[83] That constitutes weak grounds for indicting supermaxes, but it does suggest that supermaxes may poorly prepare inmates for reentry and indeed may worsen the chances for a successful return to society.

Why? Accounts of supermax incarceration indicate that inmates feel that solitary is unfair and oppressive. As a result, they may resent prison authorities and society at large more and thus feel unconstrained by conventional norms. Typically, too, solitary confinement in practice precludes participation in rehabilitative programming and visitation. It also may cause mental illness or amplify existing mental illness. These possibilities and more point to the likelihood that those who experience solitary confinement, and supermax incarceration in particular, may find reentry to be challenging.

HOW INMATES PERCEIVE THEMSELVES AND THE PRISON EXPERIENCE AND WHY IT MATTERS

Incarceration exposes individuals to a range of pains and deprivations but also to beneficial experiences and interventions. Here, we turn our focus to inmates' perceptions of themselves in prison and the implications of these perceptions for their incarceration and reentry trajectories.

A number of theories and studies point to the salience of self-perception on behavior. Labeling theory, for example, argues that how we view ourselves affects our behavior, and how others label us does so as well.[84] Shadd Maruna's work, which involved interviewing ex-prisoners, has found suggestive evidence that labeling processes appear to feature prominently in contributing to desistance.[85] This work points to the salience of identity scripts in which ex-prisoners come to view the former self as an offender but their new, truer self as a pro-social person. In Maruna's study, such transformations typically required significant investment by at least one person who believed in and supported them.

In a related vein, some studies have identified a positive relationship between individual perceptions of stigma or shame and future criminality.[86] Conversely, individuals who leave prison with greater optimism about reintegrating back into their families and communities appear to be more likely to desist from offending.[87] An important cause of optimism appears to involve social ties. When ex-prisoners can sense that others care about and believe in them, they feel less skeptical about their ability to desist from future crime.[88]

If self-perception affects recidivism, then we are led back to the prison experience. Consider, for example, the following scenario. An inmate joins a gang, attacks another inmate, and subsequently, as payback, is himself victimized. He loses touch with family members and his children. He may or may not come to regret his crime, but he may feel considerable guilt and shame about how his incarceration may have affected his family and his relationship with his children. He engages in some work, but it primarily consists of repetitive tasks that require little skill and will not likely result in improved job prospects. Some officers treat him fairly, while others taunt him and issue disciplinary reports for minor incidents.

We may well not feel sympathetic toward this individual, especially if his crime involved serious harm or injury to another person. At the same time, we may well understand how this situation might feel and how difficult it would be to feel that it was possible to become a good person, one who could or should be valued by family, friends, or, indeed, anyone. Ironically, returning military soldiers, the seeming antithesis of criminals, may experience similar feelings.

They have engaged in acts that their friends and family may not be able to understand; they may feel ashamed of what they have done and, indeed, others may be ashamed of them; and they may find it difficult to know how to fit in and resume a normal life after exposure to events that most civilians will never experience or understand. Inmates, too, have experiences in prison that few of us may readily appreciate. That in no way forgives the crimes. It simply recognizes that self-perceptions, and a sense of purpose and possibility, can serve as powerful influences on ex-prisoner decisions, motivation, and commitment to overcoming barriers to success.[89]

This observation suggests that prison experiences should be structured in ways that promote pro-social identities and a sense of possibility. Jeremy Travis, for example, has written about the idea of reentry courts and the notion of a welcome-back type of ceremony. The court and the process essentially tell the individual that they are desired and that support exists to help place them on a trajectory of pro-social behavior and success.[90] Punishment does not take a back seat; rather, the emphasis on reentry augments the punishment, or retribution, and serves as a forward-looking aspect of sanctioning. Various programs—educational, vocational, and the like—and treatment also can serve to create a sense of purpose and possibility.[91] They may not always be effective.[92] If designed and implemented well, however, they may be.[93]

Only research will tell. In the meantime, we are left with the likelihood that backward-looking punishment, and the attendant emphasis primarily on retribution and deterrence through severe sanctions, will not yield recidivism reductions commensurate with sanctions that include forward-looking elements. Part of a forward-looking approach to sanctioning involves structuring the prison experience in ways that facilitate a positive identity as well as optimism about becoming a contributing member of society. Critical to any such endeavor is the recognition that those in prison typically have harmed individuals. The victims may well not want ex-prisoners to ever succeed. That, however, does not characterize the views of many victims.[94] And it ignores the fact that individuals can be held accountable for their actions while also being required to take steps to compensate victims and society.

THE (LACK OF) EVIDENCE ON THE EFFECTIVENESS OF INCARCERATION

When we consider the dramatic expansion of the prison system and the substantial fiscal costs, it seems outlandish to suggest that limited research exists to suggest that incarceration effectively reduces crime and reduces recidivism. Yet that is in fact the case.[95]

Evidence for the aggregate effectiveness of incarceration on crime rates is mixed. Some studies identify effects that range from reductions in violent crime of less than 1 percent to reductions of up to one-third.[96] Almost all studies of aggregate crime rate effects run into the challenge of arriving at credible, robust estimates of whether and how incarceration may affect crime.[97] The situation stems in part from simultaneity problems—many changes occurred during the past three decades and did so alongside of the dramatic growth in prisons. Attempting to net out the specific effect of prison growth, or particular levels or rates of incarceration, presents substantial methodological challenges to researchers.

Evidence of substantial effects of incarceration on public safety through incapacitation of offenders is as, if not more, limited and finds largely null effects.[98] Here, again, methodological challenges arise. Incapacitation estimation depends on having a credible estimate of the types and amounts of crime that individuals would have committed if they had not been incarcerated. Making such estimates brings with it substantial error. In addition, incapacitation effects necessarily only arise during the period of incarceration or correctional supervision. Accordingly, incapacitation effects are not constant over time and indeed may vary depending on the length of incarceration. Incapacitation effects also are always relative to what otherwise would have happened. That scenario does not always consist of nothing. Rather, it might consist of various intermediate sanctions that themselves may have incapacitative effects. In addition, crimes occur inside prisons. These events must be counted as well in estimating incapacitation effects. Not least, offenders typically age out of crime. This aging-out process means that even without incarceration, an individual's likelihood of offending would decline.

When we turn to recidivism, more studies exist, but they paint a bleak picture. To date, research has focused primarily on the effects of prison versus probation. Few examine the effect of sentence length or ways in which incarceration experiences influence recidivism.[99] For example, a systematic analysis conducted by Daniel Nagin and colleagues reviewed all existing studies of the effects of imprisonment on reoffending.[100] The authors discovered that only a small handful of rigorous, quasi-experimental studies existed that assessed the impact of incarceration, relative to other sanctions, on recidivism. (For understandable reasons, few experimental studies exist.) Among the existing studies, critical methodological problems could be identified. Nagin and colleagues emphasized that in these cases, the problems sufficed to raise substantial questions about the credibility of the estimates and thus the ability to draw firm conclusions about prison effects on recidivism.

In the end, their primary conclusion zeroed in on the methodological problem—too few credible studies exist to feel confident in arriving at an estimate of incarceration effects on recidivism. A second finding was that most studies found either null effects or criminogenic effects of incarceration on recidivism; at the same time, some studies indeed have found modest recidivism-reducing effects of incarceration.

Not surprisingly, given this state of evidence, scholars have called for systematically examining prison experiences and their implications for recidivism and other reentry outcomes, including housing and employment.[101] What can be anticipated is that research may identify the conditions under which incarceration, specific incarceration terms, and various incarceration experiences give rise to reduced offending.[102] For example, incarceration may be criminogenic when it entails minimal programming, disrupted mental health or drug abuse treatment, inmate abuse and victimization, and little to no contact with family or reentry preparation. Conversely, it may reduce offending when appropriate programming and treatment occur, when officers and entire prisons operate with a culture of professionalism, when abuse and victimization occur rarely, when ties to family are supported, and when reentry plans are developed, well implemented, and revised to adjust to an ex-prisoner's changing life circumstances.

Central to advancing research and contributing to evidence-based policy will be the accumulation of studies that identify the specific prison experiences that most contribute to improved outcomes and that cost the least to implement on a large-scale basis across prison systems. Alongside of such research is the need for empirical assessments of what exactly the public wants from incarceration and, as we discuss below, of how retribution can be achieved while helping rather than worsening recidivism outcomes.

CONCEPTS OF WHAT THE PRISON EXPERIENCE SHOULD BE

In considering the prison experience, a question surfaces: What exactly should prison be like? For example, when someone is sent to prison, how much suffering should occur? How exactly should that suffering be achieved? Is isolation from family and friends enough, or should other freedoms also be restricted? How can retribution be achieved without at the same time increasing the likelihood of recidivism? We can ignore such questions, but in so doing we presumptively end up assuming that sentencing laws and the "black box" of prison operations necessarily reflect public will. Indeed, it may do so, but without empirical evidence that claim rings hollow. Many public opinion studies highlight that citizens typically want a balanced approach to justice, not "just" retribution and deterrence-based sanctioning and not "just" rehabilitation. Yet sentencing laws and correctional practices have reflected a more extreme approach, one that increasingly has emphasized almost exclusively a punitive orientation.

These questions entail philosophical debates about the very nature of punishment.[103] Let us assume that incarceration should entail some suffering. A crime was committed and some form of retaliation seems in order. But how do we measure the appropriate amount of suffering for the offender? A 20-year-old woman with no children may commit the same crime as an older mother of three, but the same sentence—say, a year of incarceration—will create substantially more pain and suffering for the mother of three than for the 20-year-old because of ripple effects like the loss of her children to foster care and emotional harm to her children. Society has meted out equal sentences but not equal suffering.

In the quest for retribution, we need to think more precisely about what punishment should entail. Should prisons be dark and poorly lit? In some European countries they are not. Is a dark, overcast setting what we want to achieve retribution? Is it what we believe will create a painful prison experience capable of creating a deterrent effect or of inspiring reform? What about the atmosphere of prison? Should it be militaristic or nurturing, what might be characterized as the "inmates are people, too" approach?[104] Norval Morris, in his account of Alexander Machonochie's approach to reforming prison operations on Norfolk

Island in the mid-1800s, illustrates how the pendulum has swung between these two extremes for centuries. It can be seen, as well, in accounts of different administrative approaches taken at the Guantanamo facility operated by the U.S. military.[105] An administrator determines that inmates are out of control and decides that a rigid system of rule enforcement and punishments must be implemented. A new administrator determines that this approach clearly has not worked and so implements more of a carrots-and-sticks incentives-based approach.

Research can provide some guidance about what the public truly wants from sanctioning.[106] Peter Rossi and Richard Berk, for example, surveyed the public about their views concerning the appropriateness of different sentences for different types of offenses.[107] Criminologists have long investigated the complexities of public views and preferences for various sanctions or sanction approaches. And scholars have undertaken many studies of sanctions and interventions that can reduce offending. None of this work collectively provides specific concrete suggestions to individual states in how they should proceed. It does illustrate, however, that states could undertake empirical studies on a regular basis to gauge public preferences for how to address crime and punish offenders in ways that balance the goals of retribution, public safety, victim restoration, and the ephemeral notion of justice. Such work could include estimates about how much the public is willing to pay for certain approaches.[108] It also could include investigating dimensions of the prison experience that they may prefer be emphasized (e.g., employment preparation, mental health treatment, life-skills training). Such preferences would not need to be substituted for empirical evidence about what works. At the same time, it would help to address normative considerations about what ultimately involves philosophical and cultural views about the nature of punishment.

MAKING GREATER ACCOUNTABILITY HAPPEN

The substantial room for variability in the prison experience raises concerns about government accountability. In recent decades, policy makers have emphasized the notion of accountability repeatedly.[109] Part and parcel of this notion is the importance of government using taxpayer dollars wisely and ensuring high-quality implementation of government-funded efforts. Here, then, we find an irony—prisons constitute the most costly part of the American correctional system and yet the vast bulk of what occurs inside prisons goes unseen, unmeasured, unmonitored, and unevaluated.[110] Indeed, prison growth writ large has occurred without much evidence that it was needed to reduce crime or that the public preferred it as an approach against other strategies. For example, intensive probation can be substantially cheaper than prison and used with far more individuals, thus increasing the potential for larger and more cost-effective reductions in recidivism. Even so, intensive probation may not always be effective. Indeed, as with any intervention, its effectiveness ultimately rests on using it with the appropriate types of individuals and implementing it well.[111]

Going forward, one central avenue for increasing accountability—for documenting what prisons do and which activities and experiences yield the greatest returns for the least amount of cost—is to create database systems that assist not only with day-to-day administrative decisions but also with monitoring efforts. These monitoring efforts can be used to ensure that prison officials and staff comply with regulations. They can be used to operate facilities in accordance with legal or correctional administration requirements. They also can be used to conduct evaluations of activities, such as visitation or specific management styles, that most effectively create order and improve reentry outcomes. This approach increasingly has been used in the medical field to ensure quality implementation and to help identify what works.[112]

In many states, rich administrative data sets already exist. Typically, though, the data lend themselves more readily to making administrative decisions—about such matters as when inmates need to be transferred to one facility or the other—than to undertaking research. Even so, the data provide numerous opportunities to illuminate what happens in prisons and how to improve in-prison and post-release outcomes. These data can be easily augmented with survey data from inmates, staff, and wardens. Doing so provides a built-in capacity, as we discuss in Chapter 9, to draw on the insights of practitioners to identify potential problems in different facilities and to identify corrective steps that might be taken to address the problems.

CONCLUSION

This chapter argues that a systematic examination of the experiences of individuals is important for understanding the potential implications of mass reentry in the United States. In particular, if we want to develop a better theoretical understanding of the causes of offending and how prison may or may not reduce crime, the prison experience constitutes a critical area of inquiry. At the same time, for policy debates and discussions to proceed in a rational manner, there ideally should be a better understanding of what society wants the prison experience to entail. We need, too, a better understanding of how willing we are to make trade-offs between retribution, public safety, and the relative costs of different punishment approaches to achieving these goals.[113]

Prison experiences constitute a natural focus of inquiry for understanding what we want incarceration to do and its effects on the individuals placed in them. For the study of reentry, the focus is natural as well—incarceration experiences have consequences that reach beyond the prison's walls and follow individuals as they make the transition back into society. Indeed, a growing body of qualitative and quantitative research has identified direct and indirect links between in-prison experiences and long-term outcomes. The examples provided here—including prison programming, visitation, victimization, and solitary confinement—illustrate the diverse experiences that inmates have and their potential implications.

Together, the salience of prison experiences underscores the pressing need to pay closer attention to what actually happens in prisons. Scholarship increasingly has highlighted the significance of both importation *and* deprivation processes. What inmates bring with them into prison, including their beliefs, attitudes, and culture, likely interact with the conditions in prisons, including how they are operated, their culture, and the programming and level of order and violence in them. Despite the seeming scholarly consensus that this model best accounts for inmate behavior, there remains remarkably little empirical research that systematically assesses it. There remains, too, little research that explores how different inmate experiences contribute—directly or in interaction with inmate characteristics and backgrounds—to prison order and inmate behavior.[114]

With greater insight into the prison experience there is the possibility of developing a more powerful theoretical account of inmate behavior and a better understanding of the benefits and harms that result from incarceration. In so doing, research can provide information for assessing the validity of correctional theories that inform punishment policies.[115] It also can help contribute to a greater understanding of how inmate perceptions—their views of themselves and the correctional system—affect prison experiences and behavior. Different theories of crime argue that how individuals perceive themselves affects how they act. If they view themselves as criminal, for example, then they more likely continue to offend after incarceration.[116] Some theories argue that perceived injustice may increase offending.[117] Prison settings provide many opportunities for self-labeling ("I am criminal") or other-labeling ("You are criminal") as well as abuse and injustice to occur.[118] Further research on such possibilities and how they relate to diverse prison experiences holds the potential for expanding knowledge of how to punish effectively.

At the same time, the heterogeneity of the inmate population—when coupled with the heterogeneity of prison experiences and of the contexts to which ex-prisoners return—underscores the importance of punishment and incarceration policies that carefully consider individual differences. Effective sanctioning likely requires systematic consideration of how each individual will respond to and act in prison and how they will fare after release. To do so may require the establishment of an organization or agency whose purview extends from court processing through release back into the community.

A focus on improving prison experiences alone will not suffice. Consider a drug-abusing inmate who receives effective treatment while in prison but then returns to a family and community where illegal drug use is highly prevalent. Arguably, the in-prison drug treatment represents a wasted investment unless it occurs along with postprison interventions aimed at assisting ex-prisoners to avoid relapse. Courts tend to focus primarily on sentencing. Prison systems tend to focus on what happens inside them. And parole agencies tend to focus only on parolees and conditions of supervision. An agency with a broader purview would not necessarily replace these organizations. However, it would be charged with helping to implement sanctions and experiences that best achieve retribution and public safety and that create the least harm and most benefit for victims, families, and communities.

This observation leads to a related one. We need to think more about what the prison experience *should* look like. Prison does not have to entail lengthy terms of confinement, though it can. It does not have to entail prison programming, or it can. It does not have to entail housing in bleak conditions, with minimal contact with family or friends, though it can. Put differently, there is nothing obvious about how incarceration experiences should be structured. That fact can be seen in part in the history of incarceration worldwide. Within the United States alone, over the past 200 years, approaches to incarceration have run the gamut from extreme isolation for most inmates to an emphasis on congregate activities and work to still other approaches.

The broader questions here center on what society wants and what is effective. What prison experiences most effectively achieve desired levels of retribution, maximum increases in public safety, and desired levels of victim and community satisfaction that justice has occurred? Conversely, which experiences undermine achievement of these goals? How does incarceration compare in its achievement of sanctioning goals relative to other approaches?

What we know to date is that prison likely increases recidivism or exerts little to no effect on it, whether through deterrence or other mechanisms; a small number of studies indicate that there may be some reduction in recidivism.[119] At the same time, large-scale incarceration appears likely to reduce crime rates, though the effect via incapacitation appears minimal and the effect through other mechanisms remains uncertain. Few credible estimates of the crime reduction benefit exist, but those that do point to modest reductions and raise questions about whether the returns offset the costs, especially in comparison with what would arise through other sanctioning approaches.[120]

A focus on the prison experience highlights another issue—government accountability. In recent decades, federal and state officials increasingly have called for greater accountability.[121] The idea is that government-funded endeavors should be designed and implemented well. Notably, however, prison systems operate largely in the functional equivalent of a black box.[122] We know little about the typical inmate experience, the types of programming that they receive, how well-implemented such programming is, or how frequently inmate-on-inmate or officer-on-inmate abuse occurs. This oversight stands out in part because prison settings provide numerous opportunities for abuse. That does not mean that prison officials or staff support or engage in it, only that a priori we know that abuse likely occurs.

To be consistent with calls for accountability, states and the federal government ideally would implement database systems that allow for monitoring inmate experiences. Doing so would increase both accountability and statistical evidence about the experiences that most contribute to improved outcomes. This type of undertaking could be used to determine whether such experiences as inmate visitation or programming constitute cost-efficient ways to improve inmate behavior and to reduce recidivism. As we have argued throughout, this possibility underscores further the idea that improved reentry outcomes can be achieved through numerous avenues and leverage points throughout corrections.

Is it possible to increase understanding of the inmate experience and how it influences in-prison and post-release behavior? Absolutely. Numerous ways exist for research to unpack the black box of prison experiences and to examine the effects of these experiences on inmate misconduct and recidivism as well as on their victims, families, and the communities from which they come.[123] Here, we emphasize as but one example the importance of tapping the on-the-ground perspectives of inmates and officers. These individuals occupy unique positions from which to gain insight into the problems, challenges, and solutions to effective prison governance and operations and to effective reentry. Their views have been examined in different scholarly undertakings. However, states do not regularly or systematically compile data on their views. This oversight is unfortunate but can be corrected through low-cost surveying of inmates and different practitioners, including wardens and prison and parole officers. If conducted regularly, such surveys could provide insights into how prison experiences might be structured to increase inmate conformity with rules and participation in programming while also increasing successful reentry. Information from the surveys could be combined with other data sources, such as prison administration records, to shed even further light on how to achieve these outcomes. In short, states can cost-efficiently compile information on inmate experiences and how these may affect inmate and ex-prisoner behavior. There is everything to gain by doing so.

DISCUSSION QUESTIONS

1. Why is it helpful to understand what happens in prison?

2. How does understanding the prison experience have the potential to inform theory and policy aimed at improving prison order and prisoner reentry?

3. Among the different types of experiences that individuals in prison have, which seem most likely to affect inmate misconduct and reentry experiences and outcomes? Why?

4. What types of prison experiences are likely to be criminogenic? Why?

5. How do inmates typically view themselves and the prison experience? How do their views potentially affect their behavior while in prison and after release?

6. What does research indicate about the effectiveness of incarceration in reducing crime and recidivism?

7. How do we best balance the goals of retribution with public safety, especially given that incarceration (a) involves unknown retributive benefits, (b) is financially costly, and (c) achieves little to nothing in reducing recidivism and uncertain crime reduction benefits? What alternatives to incarceration exist that might better provide a balance between these two goals?

8. How can prison systems be held accountable?

CHAPTER 6

The Reentry Experience and Reentry Challenges

This chapter details the experiences and challenges that individuals face after release from prison. Scholars have identified many hurdles that ex-prisoners confront, including difficulties obtaining employment, housing, and drug or mental health treatment; reintegrating with children and family; and regaining or simply having a sense of civic identity. The chapter provides an overview of the process and experience of reentry. It then describes the logic of introducing additional, or invisible, punishments for convicted felons after they have been released from prison. These additional punishments constitute one source of challenges that make reentry difficult for ex-prisoners. Our discussion then turns to a description of some of the specific reentry challenges individuals face upon release from prison and discusses their implications for ex-prisoners, families, communities, and the criminal justice system.

One of our central arguments is that reentry entails complicated processes and challenges and has diverse consequences. The move to mass incarceration, for example, brought with it a decreased emphasis on the social work dimensions of parole and an increased emphasis on supervision. Even so, many inmates now leave prison and receive virtually no supervision. Whether supervised or not, individuals who leave prison typically come from impoverished backgrounds and have accumulated a diverse set of in-prison experiences, some helpful and some harmful. They then return to communities that may not welcome them. In addition, they continue to be punished and to experience restrictions that are historically unprecedented. These invisible punishments and constraints can create challenges for ex-prisoners and result in collateral consequences for them, their families, and their communities. Ultimately, the risk is that these punishments and constraints worsen crime, labor markets, and family and community well-being. In the conclusion, we return to this idea and discuss its implications for policy.

THE REENTRY PROCESS AND EXPERIENCE

Ex-Prisoners, Returning Soldiers, and Reentry

In the conventional view of prison, individuals go to prison, realize that they made a mistake, change their attitudes and beliefs, and commit never again to engage in criminal activity. When they leave prison, individuals pick up where they left off, only now they have the tools and proper attitude for leading a pro-social life. If we are watching a movie, the final scene shows someone leaving a correctional institution, embraced by a spouse and family. If we are watching a political ad, such as the one Ann Richards, a Democrat, ran during her 1994 gubernatorial campaign against George W. Bush, a Republican, we hear, "You do the crime, you do the time," with the attendant implication that somehow the punishment will unquestionably deter would-be offenders from criminal activity.[1] In short, go to prison, leave, and reenter society as a better person, one with moral strength of character, a greater appreciation of the law, and a commitment to helping rather than harming society.

The reality of reentry differs greatly from this scenario. To gain insight into why, it can help to look far afield from criminals and focus instead on a group who, on the face of it, could not be more different—soldiers. When we compare and contrast ex-prisoners and returning soldiers, we in fact can see many instructive parallels.

In both cases, individuals have undergone experiences to which few people in mainstream society can relate. For example, inmates may have witnessed or participated in extreme violence. They may have done so out of frustration, fear, or a commitment or perceived need to support other inmates. Soldiers, too, see and commit violence that most of us have never seen or undertaken. Typically, the violence is legally sanctioned and, indeed, expected or demanded. Sometimes, the violence accords with what the military allows. Other times it may not and, indeed, may be criminal. Whether legal or not, participation in violent acts can be a source of considerable psychological strain, which can be amplified when one returns to a setting where few others can understand or relate to engaging in these acts.[2]

For both inmates and soldiers, time away from family and friends constitutes a significant source of strain. It can create greater emotional distance that, in some instances, leads to separation or divorce. Relationships with children can deteriorate. In addition, and perhaps more dispiriting, inmates and soldiers typically lack much if any control over the lives of their families. They cannot easily help them, for example, in their day-to-day activities, provide support during emergencies, or ensure that food and housing are in place.

Reentry involves similar challenges. Reestablishing intimacy with loved ones and bonds with children, family, and friends can be difficult. One's previous roles in various social networks may have been clear-cut, but now no longer are. Finding gainful employment and stable housing may be challenging. Homelessness constitutes a risk for both groups. Also, addressing mental health problems or physical limitations can be difficult.

More parallels can be drawn, but those above suffice to highlight the simple but no less important insight that reentry entails many complications and challenges. With soldiers, we have little difficulty appreciating this idea and readily endorse the provision of support services to help them make a successful transition back home. With ex-prisoners, however, such an insight seems more difficult to sustain. Somehow criminals must be different. The fact of having committed a crime creates a master status of sorts that privileges the fact of having committed a crime over that of other characteristics of the individual or of actions that he or she may have undertaken. Compared with the soldier, they are "less." In particular, they lack an appreciation for the law. Accordingly, after teaching them a lesson by putting them in prison, we can release these individuals back into society and all will be well. If they face challenges, so be it. They chose to commit crime, they will need to confront the consequences.

We focus here not on the moral implications of this view but rather on its pragmatic consequences. Let us assume that the individuals who go to prison are bad people and that we should not sympathize with them. It is a faulty assumption in many instances. People who go to prison typically have redeeming characteristics and are not necessarily on balance worse people than most of us. Even so, in many instances we all might agree that sympathy might be ill placed. Regardless of whether those who leave prison are "bad" or "good," the risk to society remains—reentry experiences may contribute to worse, not better, outcomes for ex-prisoners and their families and communities.

With returning soldiers, the concern is that, absent support, they and their families and communities suffer. With ex-prisoners, the concern is that reentry may contribute to further homelessness, unemployment, crime, and adverse outcomes for families and communities. Although we may find the notion of providing support unpalatable, failing to take supportive steps might lead to adverse effects.

The Process of Reentry

What is reentry? Broadly, we can understand reentry as a process of returning to society and attempting to engage in the life activities that define most of us. These include becoming enmeshed with family and friends, living in stable housing arrangements, finding meaningful employment, managing our health, and so on. The essential defining dynamic of reentry involves a return. (Almost all individuals who go to prison will return to society.[3]) When we already live somewhere, have a job, and a daily routine that involves other people, there is no return. However, when some event interrupts our lives—going to war, serving overseas in some capacity, or, in this instance, going to prison—then reentry can happen. The interruption creates distance that influences us on many levels. We forget routines and learn new ones, which in turn may become the habits to which we adhere unconsciously. Others may forget about us or move on with their lives in ways that prioritize new friends or family and make it difficult to include us when we return. We may lose assets or resources to which we once had access. The longer the duration of the interruption, often the more difficult the return.

Reentry thus is not a rapid-fire event in which an individual instantly resumes their place in society, much as they would if they had a twenty-four-hour illness and returned to the land of the living the next day. Instead, it requires time and ingenuity to resume relationships, find housing and work, address health problems, and more. These challenges would be daunting to most of us. They are all the more daunting for ex-prisoners who face additional barriers such as having to indicate felony convictions on employment applications.

In addition, reentry requires us to negotiate the ways that others see us. Soldiers who return from war experience this challenge, especially when the people with whom they come into contact disapprove of war in general or the particular war in which the soldiers served. They do not necessarily return to welcoming arms but instead may encounter acute social disapproval. Similarly, ex-prisoners face social disapprobation. The social isolation itself raises questions for ex-prisoners about their very place in society and whether they belong.

The challenge ex-prisoners thus face is, in part, existential. In particular, how do I, as an ex-prisoner, define myself, and how do I let others define me? Shadd Maruna's interviews with prisoners who desisted from crime have highlighted the salience of these questions and of social support in answering them. His research has found that desisters tend to have support from at least a few individuals who believe that they have a good, or redeeming, side.[4] These individuals did not necessarily reject the fact that they committed illegal acts. They did, however, focus not only on this fact but also on the idea that these acts alone did not define them. They were more than these acts. The support of others who believed in them helped to sustain this view, which led to desistance from crime.

Ex-prisoners, like soldiers, face, too, the challenge of managing the experiences that they had while away from conventional society. Most of us have been frustrated by having experiences that we cannot share with others, and have felt relieved when we can talk with someone who has been there and gets it. Support groups of all kinds exist that aim for this shared understanding. They may be groups focused on having experienced cancer, alcoholism, depression, or any of hundreds of challenging events in life. Soldiers and ex-prisoners typically have experienced, participated in, or witnessed violence and abuse and often need support to manage the psychological aftermath.

If we view reentry as a dynamic process, we necessarily implicate other considerations. We focus not only on recidivism but also on the ability to obtain housing and employment and to return to families and communities that ideally help rather than harm them. We focus not only on ex-prisoners but also on their families and the communities to which they return. We focus, too, not only on short-term success but also on longer-term success. The goal is not a reduction in recidivism for 1–2 years but rather desistance over the life course and reductions in crime rates for many years. This longer-term focus is critical if we wish to make meaningful strides in improving social outcomes. Many studies show, for example, that communities that experience high levels of poverty and crime become isolated. Concentrated disadvantage in these areas make it increasingly difficult to alter their trajectories and improve the lives of the residents in them.[5]

Finally, reentry is not the same thing as reintegration. The latter term has been used for decades and suggests that individuals previously were integrated into many aspects of society and now simply need to return to their previous position. They may not have been well integrated into society at all, though. A similar problem arises with the term "rehabilitation." It suggests that an individual once was "habilitated" and needs simply to be returned to that former state.

In the end, concepts are not correct or incorrect but rather more or less useful. Here, we follow the lead of many scholars who, over the course of the last decade, have relied on the concept of reentry to highlight that leaving prison is, as Jeremy Travis has emphasized, a process.[6] This process involves many challenges to becoming a pro-social member of society. It does not only involve reintegration or rehabilitation. These may contribute to or be part of the reentry process. However, that process involves much more. It may involve achieving a level of integration or habilitation that exceeds what the individual had prior to incarceration. For example, an individual who was homeless before going to prison ideally will find stable housing when he or she returns to society. Indeed, reentry entails just that—a process of returning to society, overcoming a range of obstacles, accessing services and treatment when needed, and more. If successfully negotiated, the process may result in reintegration and rehabilitation; if unsuccessfully negotiated, it may result in recidivism and adverse outcomes.

Survival Shows and Barriers to Reentry

One of the problems that plague criminal justice policy discussions is that we view the individuals who commit crimes as fundamentally different from us. We are law-abiding; they are not. We are persistent and hard workers; they are not. We have strong moral fiber; they do not. We confront barriers in life head-on and overcome; they do not. We tend to assume, too, that these individuals—the ones who differ from us so much—respond in a straightforward way to punishments, such as incarceration.

Such assumptions likely are wrong. The individuals who go to prison do not necessarily differ from us, at least not in a few key respects. In addition, research typically finds that those who leave prison do not intend to commit crime. Rather, they want to lead a pro-social life and anticipate that they will do so.[7] That they will encounter substantial barriers seems to bypass many inmates, who frequently think that upon release their lives somehow will fall into place.[8] Differences do exist, of course. From research, we know that many individuals in prison, more so than members of the general public, come from highly disadvantaged backgrounds, have lower levels of intelligence and self-control, and have spotty employment records. Such differences distinguish them from the average citizen. Yet they also typically have family and friends who support them and have levels of intelligence and self-control that do not dictate that a life of crime need necessarily occur. In these respects, they are similar to the average citizen.

The relevance of these observations lies in the fact that if we want to improve reentry processes and outcomes, it can help if we understand what reentry might be like. It can help, too, if we understand that members of the general public, who have considerably more individual and social capital compared with those who go to prison, likely would have a difficult time reentering society after a term of incarceration. Imagine a prison survival reality show, for example. The goal, as with many survival shows, consists of overcoming a series of challenges better than the competition. With reentry, though, the challenges involve not just a series of activities that must be undertaken or barriers that must be cleared. They also include accepting a change in one's personal characteristics or resources. They include, too, confronting a variety of invisible punishments that create additional obstacles to achieving such goals as obtaining a job, housing, and the like.

Consider the following scenario that might serve as the basis for a survival-of-the-fittest reality television show. First, you have hurt someone. Perhaps you feel guilty. Perhaps not. But it constitutes one fact about your past that defines you, that may influence how you see yourself, and that likely will affect how others see you.

Second, you must accept a substantial lowering of your intelligence and self-control. In essence, you start out hungry, sleep-deprived, and fatigued.

Third, you spend a year in prison. You see violence. Occasionally, you participate in violence, perhaps out of frustration or because you feel that you must do so to protect yourself. Or perhaps your impulsiveness leads you to resort to violence to resolve conflict even though alternative approaches might be more effective. You are bored for a great deal of the time. You rarely if ever see family. Friends who said that they would visit do not. Your spouse or partner, if you have one, is upset with you, rarely visits, and runs into a number of challenges, such as paying the rent, which you cannot resolve. Some prison officers taunt you on a regular basis.

Fourth, you return home. Employers do not want to hire you because you have a lousy work history and you have been convicted of a felony. You cannot live with your family because they live in subsidized housing and you have been convicted of a felony drug crime. You have no savings and so cannot rent an apartment or pay for food. The family and friends who said that they would help you try to do so, but they have little to no extra money or assistance to offer. Jobs, social services, and treatment opportunities in your home community are few and far between.

Your mission? Find a job, find housing, obtain treatment for depression, support a child in attending school regularly, develop a noncriminal sense of identity, ignore any social disapprobation that you experience, and, of course, do not commit a crime.

Even the most self-confident among us can see that this situation presents a test of character well exceeding that which most of us have ever confronted. Yet this situation characterizes precisely what the vast bulk of the 600,000 to 700,000 or more individuals who leave prison each year confronts.

We in no way need to forgive people for the crimes that they have committed or sympathize with them. We can choose to do so or not. The policy challenge remains the same in either instance: How do we punish in a way that achieves what we want punishment to do and not worsen social outcomes? How, when we incarcerate individuals, do we structure the incarceration and reentry experience in ways that improve rather than worsen social outcomes?

THE LOGIC OF "INVISIBLE" PUNISHMENTS
AND THEIR CONSEQUENCES

In Chapter 2, we touched on the idea of invisible punishments, many of which create barriers to the successful reentry of ex-prisoners back into society and have collateral consequences, such as the potential for increased recidivism as well as harms to families and communities.[9] What is the logic of punishments that extend outside the prison walls and that, strictly speaking, affect not only the felons who go to and are released from prison but also any individual who has a felon status, regardless of whether he or she experienced incarceration? Here, we return to this idea and explore it in more detail, focusing in particular on the reentry process and specific challenges to reentry. As we will discuss, the individuals who leave prison face a daunting set of challenges that greatly reduce the likelihood that they can become pro-social, contributing members of society. That does not mean that they somehow deserve our sympathy. Perhaps some do, and perhaps some do not. As a pragmatic matter, however, we should care because higher rates of offending, unemployment, homelessness, poor parenting, and more affect all of us in one way or the other.

Before describing these challenges, we focus first on the logic of invisible punishments, such as restricting the rights of felons to vote. Not all of the challenges that ex-prisoners face consist of these types of punishments. For example, many inmates leave prison and have few if any financial resources on which to draw. That does not constitute a punishment. It does, however, create a challenge that will make reentry difficult.

Even so, many of the challenges stem from imposing invisible sanctions. What is the logic of punishments that extend outside the prison walls and that, strictly speaking, affect not only the felons who go to and are released from prison but also any individual who has a "felon" status, regardless of whether he or she experienced incarceration?

As shown in Figure 6.1, one reason is retribution. We send people to prison to punish them for punishment's sake. Of course, even if we toughen punishments, that may not result in increased public satisfaction with the criminal justice system. The public, for example, may not feel that sufficient retribution has occurred. Indeed, additional retribution without educating the public that penalties have become more severe likely would do little to satisfy the public. During a period of increased incarceration, it is possible for the public to feel that too little has been done to punish offenders.[10]

During the bulk of the twentieth century, probation and incarceration constituted the primary means of punishment and retribution. Incarcerated individuals would receive supervision and services upon release to help keep them on the straight and narrow and to rehabilitate them. However, these postrelease efforts centered on reducing crime, not on imposing more punishment for punishment's sake.

In the latter part of the twentieth century and into the twenty-first century, the United States shifted toward a retributive stance, what scholars have described as the "punitive turn."[11] One obvious place to impose more punishment was to institute sanctions, restrictions, and requirements that might be applied to individuals after they leave prison and, more broadly, to convicted

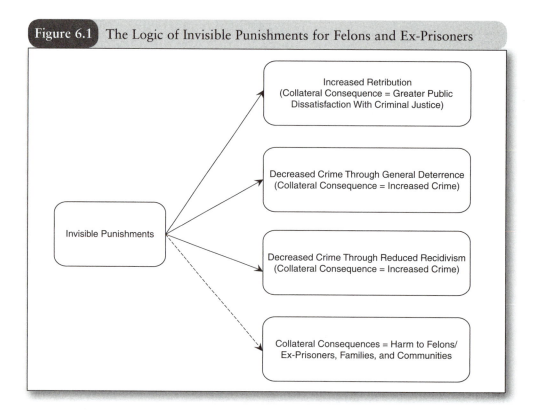

Figure 6.1   The Logic of Invisible Punishments for Felons and Ex-Prisoners

felons. What might be targeted? Well, we might extend terms of supervision. We might reduce rehabilitative intervention services and treatment. We might make it easier to identify the criminals in society through the use of registries and labels. And so on.

From a retributivist perspective, almost any effort that imposed a pain or burden on felons would suffice. One might call this emphasis on ever-greater punishment the seductive logic of retributivism. Why? Because, on the face of it, additional punishments seem not to require evidence that they work. When we bar felons from holding certain jobs or obtaining student loans, doing so seems reasonable, enough so as to obviate the need for empirical evidence that these steps are effective. At the same time, who really wants to defend criminals or argue for less punishment? Moreover, if few interventions work to reduce recidivism, then why not accomplish something else? Taking retributivist steps is easy. They allow us to feel that we are taking action. In that sense, the punitive turn can be seen as a form of action bias that leads to an intervention—more punishment—that seems necessarily effective.[12] We can create more and more punishment with the assumption, largely unchecked empirically, that doing so will lead to a more appropriate or culturally desired amount of retribution.

A second logic that justifies additional punishments, restrictions, and requirements is that they make the public safer. How? They may reduce crime through general deterrence or recidivism through specific deterrence, limited opportunities to offend, and the like. For example, allowing convicted sex offenders who targeted children to work at child care centers clearly does not make much sense. To date, however, we have little empirical evidence that the various additional punishments, restrictions, and requirements yield beneficial outcomes.[13] Rather, ironically, what we have instead are studies that point to harms that such efforts cause to felons and ex-prisoners and to the families and communities to which they return.

This point bears emphasis. Ideally, policies have strong theoretical and empirical backing. We then can trust more that a policy, if implemented well, will produce improved outcomes. What research highlights, however, is that many invisible punishments lack a clear theoretical or empirical foundation. Deterrence theory, for example, provides no clear guidance about what we should expect if we take away an individual's right to vote. Perhaps it serves as the type of punishment that strikes fear into the heart of would-be offenders. They then refrain from further criminal activity. Perhaps, though, it makes them frustrated and angry. That leads them to feel that they can never belong in society. In turn, they may cease trying to belong and resume committing crime.

Other collateral consequences may occur as well, including increased unemployment, homelessness, and drug abuse. These consequences may affect felons and ex-prisoners as well as their families and communities. Such effects presumably are not intended (as indicated by the dashed line in Figure 6.1), but the very logic of invisible punishments can be expected to produce them. These harms may be small. Alternatively, they may be so large that they offset the hoped-for benefits of punishment. Legislators typically seek to promote the public good. However, action bias that builds on poor theory and research can lead to a situation where policymakers inadvertently worsen the very outcomes that they seek to improve. Such effects may arise through many mechanisms. In criminal justice, the efforts may directly worsen recidivism and other reentry outcomes. Perhaps, for example, having to check off "convicted felon" on an employment application reduces the likelihood of being hired and, in turn, contributes to further offending. The efforts may indirectly do so because attention and funding is focused on ineffective policies rather than effective ones.[14] At the same time, the efforts may create financial obligations that persist over many decades and further cement an inability to fund more effective approaches to sanctioning. For example, tougher supervision can result in reincarceration for noncriminal violations of parole conditions, in turn imposing more pressure to expand prison system capacity.

Ultimately, the litmus test for any policy is whether it improves society. The logic of imposing additional punishments, restrictions, and requirements unfortunately suggests that we cannot be sure that society benefits when felons, and ex-prisoners in particular, receive additional invisible punishments. We explore this idea further below and highlight how some of these punishments may adversely affect felons and their families and communities.

SPECIFIC CHALLENGES DURING REENTRY

The individuals who leave prison typically come from impoverished backgrounds and return to areas characterized by marked disadvantage. Many want to succeed, but most will not. They may lack the motivation, the skill set, or support to succeed, or they may face challenges that all but preclude success, including having a job and housing, health, family, and friends and not engaging in antisocial or unhealthy behavior. Any one of these hurdles might be a sufficient obstacle to success; the presence of so many hurdles are, as Thomas LeBel and Shadd Maruna have emphasized, "all interrelated in the lives of ex-prisoners."[15]

Challenge 1: Disenfranchisement ("Not Really a Citizen")

We begin first with the disenfranchisement of ex-prisoners. As Figure 2.4 highlighted, almost every state has enacted laws that either eliminate or limit the rights of convicted felons to vote. Some states ban inmates from voting for life.[16] Current estimates indicate that approximately 6 million voting age members of the U.S. population is disenfranchised; blacks are four times more likely than whites to be unable to vote.[17] Disenfranchisement laws and policies have resulted in many other restrictions on civic engagement. Depending on the type of offense, and on federal and state law, many felons cannot have a driver's license, access student loans, receive government welfare benefits, retain parental rights, hold public office, serve on a jury, or own a firearm.[18] Not surprisingly, ex-prisoners feel stigmatized because of their criminal record and a sense that they will never be seen as anything but a criminal.[19]

The effect of these efforts to disenfranchise felons signals to these individuals that they do not belong and that their identity as a criminal is fixed. This problem is often compounded by racial or ethnic discrimination or a drug-involved past.[20] Again, while we may not be sympathetic to the plight of ex-prisoners, society suffers if disenfranchisement creates a sense of hopelessness and a lack of care or respect for conventional society. Such changes can increase recidivism and impose more social harm on others. LeBel and Maruna's research, for example, along with that of other scholars, such as John Laub and Robert Sampson, indicates that a sense of self-efficacy and optimism can be essential to helping ex-prisoners desist from offending.[21]

Challenge 2: Housing

Separation from family constitutes one of the top concerns among prisoners.[22] Perhaps for this reason, approximately three-fourths of released inmates initially reside with their families upon release from prison.[23] In part, though, the reason is more mundane and pragmatic—when inmates leave prison, they typically have no money in their pockets, no savings, and no established housing save for what their family or noncriminal friends might provide.[24] They also face legal restrictions, depending on the type of crime for which they were convicted, that preclude access to public housing. They may have vouchers for a few weeks of housing, but then must pay for the housing themselves. Shelters typically limit the amount of time individuals can reside in them. Although family may allow ex-prisoners to live with them, the stay may be temporary, especially if their ties to the individual have weakened or if his or her presence poses a threat to housing stability for the family.[25]

Not surprisingly, then, some estimates indicate that up to one-fourth of ex-prisoners end up homeless; metropolitan areas experience higher rates of homelessness among the ex-prisoner population.[26] Parole officers indicate that finding housing is one of the hardest challenges that the individuals on their caseloads face.[27] Here again the concern is that society ultimately pays when difficulty in finding stable housing contributes to recidivism and to difficulty obtaining employment.[28] This problem may be amplified in some areas, especially those with high levels of social and economic disadvantage where few resources exist to assist ex-prisoners and where drug crime and other illicit activities predominate.[29] Perhaps for this reason, if inmates return to new neighborhoods, whether to protect family or to start life anew, their recidivism risk may decrease.[30]

Challenge 3: Finances and Employment

When inmates leave prison, they normally have $50 to $200 in gate money, one pair of clothes, and a bus ticket.[31] They almost invariably will have no savings or other material assets on which to draw. They therefore will lean heavily on family and friends for support. However, the willingness of family and friends to do so indefinitely may wane. Ex-prisoners then must find alternative sources of support or risk becoming homeless.

The lack of financial resources stands out as a prominent barrier because it constitutes such a tangible nuts-and-bolts issue for ex-prisoners seeking to reestablish themselves. It creates, too, an immediate pressure to find employment, and employment prospects for felons are bleak. They typically come from impoverished backgrounds, have a less-than-stellar employment record, and reside in areas of marked disadvantage. They may have drug abuse and addiction problems as well as mental health problems and learning disabilities. And the felony record itself blocks many employment opportunities. As Angela Hattery and Earl Smith, for example, found in their study of ex-prisoners, "the process of disclosing their status as a felon was, at least in their minds, the *key factor that prevented them from obtaining employment*."[32] Other studies have come to the same conclusion. Checking "felony conviction" on an employment application all but precludes employment.[33] As many accounts have documented, a felony conviction, or a felony conviction for certain types of crimes, legally precludes employment in certain occupations and does so even when no clear or empirically based rationale exists for imposing this barrier.[34]

Employment barriers highlight how multiple challenges typically exist for ex-prisoners and especially those convicted of a felony. These individuals may not have driver's licenses, savings, housing, or basic life skills; they may have mental or physical illnesses; they face discrimination; they may have low self-control; their education is limited and they may be ineligible for student loans; and more. The imposition of employment barriers thus serves more as a factor or dimension that further cements the likelihood of failed reentry. Indeed, the constellation of deficits that individuals who leave prison possess and the many invisible punishments and restrictions that they face may help to account for the limited effectiveness of many in-prison and postrelease employment programs.[35] Even so, evidence suggests that ex-prisoners who find employment, especially higher-quality work that includes a living wage and job security, have a lower risk of offending.[36]

Challenge 4: Family Reunification

Humans are social beings. For that reason, one of the most painful aspects of incarceration can be separation from family.[37] The bulk of inmates receive no visitation from family during incarceration. For example, in a study of Florida prisoners, William Bales and Daniel Mears found that 58 percent of released inmates experienced no visitation in the year prior to release.[38] Their study echoed that of others in showing that incarceration does not just deprive inmates of their liberty, it deprives them of the ability to maintain meaningful relationships with family. Even when visits occur, they can be infrequent and present a hardship for families, especially when they must travel a long distance, find child care, and take off time from work.[39]

Contact with family may occur through telephone calls and mail, but many inmates receive no calls or mail. Even when some contact occurs, the interactions can be strained and difficult. In this regard, those in prison do not differ appreciably from the rest of society. Without frequent contact, it can be difficult under the best of circumstances to maintain our ties and commitments to others. Accordingly, when prisoners—who clearly do not reside in the best of circumstances—return home, they can find that reentry to family holds more tension and challenges than they anticipated. Inmates typically express more optimism about their life chances upon release than is realistic.[40] The let-down can be considerable when they discover that family, including children, may be less than welcoming. It can be devastating to learn as well that they constitute a burden through their inability to find work or parent effectively.

One challenge for inmates involves their legal status as a parent. Many inmates have their parental rights terminated and, upon reentry back into society, must meet certain requirements—such as obtaining housing and having a source of income—to regain those rights.[41] In addition, ex-prisoners, especially those convicted of felony drug charges, may not be eligible for subsidized housing and, at the same time, face employment barriers that make it difficult to obtain a job and thereby help to demonstrate to the court that their rights should be restored.

Do such barriers matter? Research suggests that they do. Studies have found that "feelings of being welcome at home and the strength of interpersonal ties outside prison help predict postprison adjustment."[42] Individuals who leave prison and remain with family have been found to be more likely to desist from offending.[43] Such benefits may be offset by residing in a high-crime area or returning to families who have drug problems or are actively involved in criminal activity.[44] Even so, they underscore the potential importance of developing ways to ensure that families maintain their ties with offenders during and after incarceration.[45]

Challenge 5: Drug and Mental Health Treatment

Estimates indicate that approximately half of state or federal prisoners meet the criteria for drug abuse or dependence and that they are five to twenty-four times more likely to suffer from a mental disorder.[46] Drug use and dependence is strongly correlated with recidivism, although the causal connection may not always be clear.[47] For example, among those who recidivate, many other problems, such as housing, employment, family conflict, and more, typically exist. Regardless, drug involvement clearly may contribute to offending and recidivism, and treatment can serve as a critical component of successful reentry. Many programs may not be especially effective. However, evaluations have found that some programs, especially those with a coherent intervention model and postrelease aftercare, can contribute to reduced drug use and addiction and to reduced recidivism.[48]

The challenge during reentry lies with continued treatment or with accessing treatment when relapse occurs. In many communities, few resources exist to meet the demand for drug treatment among ex-prisoners.[49] The same challenge arises with mental health services and treatment. Although few studies exist that document the precise magnitude in the gap between needed and available services and treatment, most reviews indicate that it is large.[50] In short, a perfect storm of sorts exists—large percentages of individuals leave prison with drug and mental health problems, but few will receive needed services and treatment. Many states and cities have recognized this problem and have sought to create networks that allow for continuity of care from in prison to the community, but they face considerable challenges.[51]

Challenge 6: Welfare Benefits

Changes in welfare laws and policies illustrate another invisible punishment that creates collateral consequences for ex-prisoners. Recent welfare restrictions imposed new barriers on felons, especially those convicted of drug crimes, by limiting their ability to obtain food stamps or housing assistance. As Chapter 2 discussed, this policy affected large swaths of the reentry population because much of the get-tough movement in American corrections in recent decades focused on increased criminal prosecution and incarceration of drug offenders. Welfare benefits historically had enabled some felons to pay for treatment programs.[52] Without them, then, treatment prospects for ex-prisoners have diminished. At the same time, welfare reforms have affected families by limiting the ability of released prisoners to live with those families who reside in public housing.

Challenge 7: Supervision

Surprisingly, the supervision of those released from prison may itself constitute a barrier to successful reentry. The more law enforcement–oriented focus of parole has led to increased revocations; indeed, revocations that result in a return to prison constitute one of the primary drivers of mass incarceration.[53] The emphasis on revocations illustrates the punitive turn and the emphasis on deterrence as a seeming panacea to crime and reduced recidivism. Notably, studies do find that parole can reduce recidivism. On the whole, however, the literature on supervision effectiveness has produced mixed findings.[54]

The mixed findings likely reflect the complicated nature of supervision. Some parole officers may be, or may be perceived as, helpful to ex-prisoners in finding services, treatment, employment, housing, and the like. They also may hold ex-prisoners accountable. However, the reverse may be true as well. The officers may exercise excessive control, impose unreasonable burdens on ex-prisoners, and foster ambivalence and hostility among those supervised. As some scholars have argued, "When people 'get out,' they want to *be out*. Any compromise or half-measure, any 'hoops' or hassles places in their path, breeds resentment."[55] In an era in which supervision increasingly has assumed a more punitive emphasis rather than a rehabilitative one, a greater potential exists for such effects and, in turn, increased recidivism.[56]

What about the effects of a lack of supervision or assistance? One irony of get-tough laws has been the release of individuals who serve their entire sentence in prison and so are released with no supervision. This is concerning both because these individuals present a risk to the community and because they likely need assistance and services to find housing, employment, treatment, and more. A lack of helpful supervision likely constitutes a better situation for released inmates than a release to a control-oriented form of supervision. The absence of the latter, however, constitutes a barrier to successful reentry in its own right.

IMPLICATIONS OF REENTRY CHALLENGES FOR EX-PRISONERS AND FAMILIES AND COMMUNITIES

The return of thousands of individuals from prisons back into communities each year has ripple effects on families and communities. When, for example, a barrier to successful reentry limits the ability of an ex-prisoner to find employment, families may be more at risk of homelessness and communities may be more at risk of experiencing higher unemployment rates and poverty. Below, we highlight these and other risks of imposing barriers to successful reentry and, conversely, failing to take steps to ensure that successful reentry occurs.

Implications of Reentry Challenges for Ex-Prisoners

The punitive turn of recent decades has contributed to a range of unintended adverse outcomes: less civic engagement, homelessness, unemployment, less family involvement or support, continued or worse physical or mental health problems, continued or worse drug problems, difficulty obtaining educational or vocational training that would pave the way for gainful employment and civic engagement, more rather than less recidivism, and social stigma that can influence all of these outcomes, among others.[57]

Large bodies of research have provided convincing evidence of these adverse outcomes. To illustrate, studies have found that those who go to prison face a 10 percent to 30 percent wage penalty upon release.[58] Employers typically conduct criminal background checks and convicted felons under federal or state law cannot work in certain occupations, both of which greatly reduce job prospects for released prisoners. Similarly, studies indicate that inmates become less healthy over the course of their incarceration.[59] Typical health problems include a substantially higher prevalence of infectious diseases, including tuberculosis, hepatitis C, and HIV.[60] Not least, prison itself may be criminogenic and increase recidivism.[61] Difficulties during reentry then either may independently increase recidivism or amplify the criminogenic effects of incarceration.

No systematic empirical assessments exist on a state-by-state basis of these effects. Such an assessment, and monitoring of a wide range of reentry experiences and outcomes, would require a greater investment in data and research than what has occurred to date in most states. In some states or communities, beneficial effects may arise or adverse effects may be minimal, while in others substantially greater adverse effects may occur. What we are left with then is a body of theory and research that suggests that mass incarceration and reentry at best serve to incapacitate and punish but not, on average, to improve these outcomes. Indeed, they may worsen them.

Implications of Reentry Challenges for Families

The individuals who go to prison do not, of course, come from unpopulated islands. Rather, prior to incarceration, they reside within social networks, such as families. Thus, as with any social network, when an individual leaves, ripple effects result, especially if the departure occurs suddenly. In a two-parent household, for example, the detention and then incarceration of one parent immediately creates repercussions. One person is left responsible for working, paying rent, buying groceries, getting children to school, arranging child care, and so on. These difficulties do not mean that punishment should never happen. It does mean that punishment without attention to its consequences may well leave society worse off rather than better off.

A simple example, from a case handled in a Federal District Court in Manhattan, illustrates this issue.[62] A single mother with five children pleads guilty to serving as a lookout for several men who rob a bank. Court testimony reveals that, under the mother's care, the children regularly attend school and have been performing quite well. If she goes to prison, the children likely will go to foster care. They may be separated from one another and the foster care may result in neglect or abuse of the children. Many foster care placements result in support, nurturance, love, and improved outcomes for children. But many do not and, indeed, may provide just the opposite. In the end, the judge sentences the mother to prison.

In this situation, the judge ultimately ignored the fact that the children may suffer and focused purely on the crime. A compelling argument exists for this decision. A serious crime occurred. Also, why should someone be punished more leniently than someone who does not have children? At the same time, the potential harm to the children constitutes a very real prospect that ultimately may affect society.

Punishment practices would seem to require that the courts take that possibility into account. They do, in part. For example, although courts typically must focus primarily on the offense that occurred, they can weigh mitigating circumstances on a case-by-case basis. That practice itself, however, raises questions about fairness in sentencing. In addition, in an era of get-tough punishment, institutional pressures exist to limit consideration of mitigating factors.

In an ideal world, we would be able to devise punishments that achieved the various goals that we want for it—justice, retribution, and public safety, for example—and do so with minimal harm to society. If we achieve some of these goals but leave society less safe and increase homelessness, child abuse, or the like, then on balance we take a step backward. If it were a medical decision, and if the harms were sufficiently large, then the clear implication—following a "do no harm" edict—would be not to intervene. Or it would be to intervene in a way that would result in less harm. In the example of the mother who served as a lookout, we might consider a term of intensive probation. We may disagree about the precise sanction, but we can agree that we want sanctions not only to serve a retributive purpose but also to improve public safety and minimize the production of more social harm. Intensive probation might not be the answer, but a wide range of sanctions exist that might be more effective than prison and result in less harm to families.

If little basis existed to anticipate harms to families, this issue would be moot. A substantial body of work exists, however, that suggests that incarceration can harm families and that the return of ex-prisoners to families can be harmful. How?

While incarcerated, individuals can no longer provide much in the way of meaningful support for their families. For example, they can not provide financial support and they can not help to take care of children or dependents. Of course, many individuals who go to prison failed to offer such support prior to their incarceration. Others may have provided substantial support. In these cases, families are at risk in multiple ways. Caregivers may find that they can no longer work and simultaneously take care of their children or dependents. Alternatively, they may work longer hours and so have less time to care for or supervise them. The latter issue becomes especially problematic when children are involved because the loss of a parent or guardian may be traumatic and may contribute to acting out behaviors or a greater involvement in peer groups that engage in criminal activity. Estimates indicate that over half of inmates are parents, and approximately one-fourth have three or more children.[63]

Upon return to a family, many challenges can arise. If the family lives in public housing, then, depending on the type of crime for which the individual was convicted (e.g., a drug offense), he or she may not be able to live with the family.[64] This situation may benefit some children. However, research indicates that outcomes such as delinquency and educational attainment among children of incarcerated parents, and by extension outcomes among those whose parents can not return to live with them, worsen.[65] Homelessness, too, is more likely among children of incarcerated parents. It in turn makes family reunification during reentry difficult.[66] Family dynamics are problematic as well given that many children will have been under the care of foster families and these arrangements may continue even after the parent has been released back into society.[67] If the parent does regain custody or seeks to become involved in the lives of his or her children, doing so can be difficult. The ex-prisoner may face considerable ambivalence from a child who is angry about the separation or who may not remember much about their parent.[68]

More broadly, any problems an individual has when they leave prison, including ones that may be caused by the prison experience itself, can affect families. When an inmate leaves prison with a drug abuse problem, this problem poses direct risks for his or her family. When he or she has a mental health problem that goes unaddressed, the result can be increased stress and strain for the families to which they return. When an inmate has learned attitudes and behaviors conducive to surviving in prison, they bring these with them back into their families in much the same way that soldiers may bring attitudes and behaviors necessary for surviving in war back home. Some returning prisoners and soldiers may adapt so that this problem does not arise, but it constitutes a challenge for many of them. Effective punishment and reentry practices ideally would minimize these harms or avoid them altogether.

Implications of Reentry Challenges for Communities

As with families, the challenges of reentry have consequences for the community as well. One obvious risk is higher crime. When large numbers of a community's members go to prison, that can leave families at risk of homelessness and with fewer caretakers to look after children and teenagers. Here, again, exceptions certainly exist—in many cases, families will be better off without, say, an abusive adult who is drug-addicted and does not work. On the whole, however, the risk remains that communities spiral into decline or remain mired in disadvantage when large swaths of working-age individuals are taken away.

At the same time, when these individuals return to the communities from which they come, they may be more likely to recidivate and less likely to find gainful employment.[69] In addition, the higher levels of residential mobility associated with mass reentry can reduce trust and social capital in communities.[70] The end result? More crime and more social disadvantage occurs that becomes increasingly difficult to address. As Robert Sampson's work has highlighted, communities that experience concentrated social disadvantage typically cannot easily reverse course.[71] Indeed, any community confronted with the removal of sizable proportions of its residents—and with the return of these individuals after they have become less employable and potentially more prone to engage in crime—likely would face the risk of higher crime rates.[72] This creates a vicious cycle in which ex-prisoners engage in more crime, younger people may be less likely to view employment as a typical life event, families may face increased burdens without sufficient resources to offset them, and so on. Concerns about these types of harms stem from studies that have investigated the consequences of mass incarceration and prisoner reentry for particular communities.[73]

Such studies do not provide a definitive empirical portrait of reentry effects on communities. They do suggest, however, that reentry can directly and indirectly affect communities in multiple adverse ways. When unemployment rates and homelessness rise, for example, poverty increases, placing greater demands on social welfare programs and raising concerns about delinquency and the education, care, and well-being of children.[74] The removal and return of men may have implications for community demography such as family structures and marriage rates. Single ex-prisoners may be less likely to be viewed as marriageable, thus contributing to single-parent households that may face greater financial insecurity.[75]

In addition, mass incarceration and, by extension, reentry, can negatively affect ex-prisoners' and other citizens' perceptions of the legitimacy of the criminal justice system.[76] In predominantly African-American communities, there can exist significant mistrust of law enforcement and a belief that sentencing laws, and the enforcement of these laws, unfairly target minorities. For minority communities, then, reentry may amplify such mistrust and concern.[77]

Not least, the disenfranchisement of felons can result in the disenfranchisement of entire communities. Sasha Abramsky documented one account, for example, of a politician who stated that there were some precincts where campaigning made little sense because few individuals in them could vote.[78] Jeff Manza and Christopher Uggen undertook a study that suggested that some U.S. senate races, as well as the 2000 presidential election, may have been affected by the fact that many individuals with a criminal conviction could not vote.[79] As they suggested, the effects of reentry processes and policies, including invisible punishments, do not involve only the right to vote. They influence, too, the very nature of American citizenship. Specifically, "people who are under no form of community supervision but cannot by law serve in the military, vote, own a firearm, sit on a jury, drive a car, receive governmental benefits, or work in numerous professions are no longer full citizens."[80] By extension, neither are the families and members of communities to which these individuals belong.

CONCLUSION

In this chapter, we sought to highlight ways in which prisoner reentry constitutes a process, one that would challenge even law-abiding citizens who have plenty of resources at their disposal. Individuals who go to prison operate with a number of deficits, including poor work histories, a history of drug abuse, and residence in areas of concentrated disadvantage. In prison they may have had minimal opportunities to engage in rehabilitative programming and considerable exposure to violence and abuse. And they may return to families and communities with few assets or resources to assist them and to a range of barriers and invisible punishments that may impede success, whether that be defined as finding a job or housing, refraining from criminal activity, or adversely affecting some other life outcome.

Historically, parole involved a supervision emphasis and a social service emphasis that would serve broadly to facilitate successful returns back into society. In recent decades, however, many individuals leave prison with no oversight from the correctional system. Among those placed under some type of community supervision, the primary emphasis has shifted to supervision. There is, then, little to no attention accorded to treatment or rehabilitation or to providing social service assistance or linkages.

The end result for society? We invest heavily in placing people in prison and, on balance, likely end up no better off or perhaps even worse off. No doubt, there likely were reductions in crime during the ascendance of mass incarceration.[81] There is little evidence, however, that sustained record-level incarceration rates continued to provide this benefit or do so today. There is little evidence, too, that prison provides specific deterrent or rehabilitative benefits. At the same time, studies suggest that incarceration worsens recidivism or has no effect. They suggest that removing large swaths of young adult populations from communities and returning them to these communities after prison may result in more harm than good, whether through increased crime, lower employment rates, increased family dysfunction, or other adverse social outcomes.[82] There is the concern, then, that the process of reentry and an attendant array of invisible punishments largely preclude desistance, employment, and stable housing for all but a relatively small percentage of those who leave prison.

Against that backdrop, we close by making several observations that return us to the book's goals and its overarching arguments. First, as we have argued at the outset, substantially improving reentry outcomes requires understanding the reentry process and doing so from different perspectives. One such perspective, detailed in this chapter, involves examining the process of reentry and the challenges that attend to it. When we view reentry as a process that builds on pre-prison and in-prison experiences, one that involves encountering a range of barriers and invisible punishments, we can easily see how prison may be criminogenic and adversely affect the lives of ex-prisoner families and communities. Second, and in anticipation of the next chapter, we can see, too, that risk prediction likely would benefit from including information about what happens to individuals during reentry. The challenges individuals face during reentry may themselves be criminogenic. They increase the risk of offending again, resulting in more victimization and more costs to society. Accordingly, improvements in risk prediction, and in intervening effectively so as to reduce that risk, may come from developing database systems that monitor postrelease experiences and the contexts to which individuals return. Such improvements would allow for analyses that could result in real-time adjustments in supervision and assistance that might prevent recidivism.[83]

Third, when we examine reentry as a process, it implicates families and communities. By and large, most individuals who leave prison return to their families and home communities. They can be a threat or burden to these families and communities. They may be more likely to offend, less likely to work, and may end up homeless or mired in drug addiction that precludes any type of positive trajectory for themselves or others. And, of course, released offenders return to the areas where they victimized others. These victims have a fundamental stake in criminal justice sanctions and the consequences of these sanctions.

Fourth, these insights highlight the importance of developing an on-the-ground understanding of reentry processes and their impacts. What are the experiences of ex-prisoners in particular locales? What are the experiences of families and communities who receive the most ex-prisoners? What services exist to help these different groups? What services most help and do so for the least cost? Scholarly research on the causes of offending nationally or in any given state will provide little help in answering such questions. Rather, what we need is research infrastructure at the local level that enables criminal justice officials and practitioners to tap into the views and insights of ex-prisoners and their families as well as members of the community and those who seek to improve outcomes for these different groups.

Fifth, as we discuss in Chapter 9, opportunities exist to improve this situation. These opportunities include developing laws that restrict incarceration to those situations where it can best and most cost-effectively achieve such goals as retribution and public safety. They include, too, developing reentry supervision and support that targets not only those who leave prison but also those who may be affected by these individuals. We cannot simply identify high-risk ex-prisoners, place them under intensive supervision, and expect much in return. Doing so will do little to nothing to address the range of barriers and challenges that make up the reentry experience. Few of us want costly and complicated policy approaches. In the end, though, a more nuanced approach to sanctioning and to improving reentry likely can result in less expense and greater public safety and quality-of-life returns for society.

DISCUSSION QUESTIONS

1. How is the concept of reentry different from the concept of reintegration?

2. In what ways are the reentry experiences of ex-prisoners similar to those of soldiers?

3. What is the process of reentry and what makes it challenging?

4. What is the logic of imposing invisible punishments on convicted felons, and what are the consequences of these punishments?

5. Which of the many reentry challenges that ex-prisoners face seem most likely to contribute to increased offending rather than desistance? Which ones seem most amenable to policy intervention in ways that would improve rather than worsen reentry outcomes?

6. How does reentry affect families and communities?

CHAPTER 7

Recidivism and Risk Prediction

This chapter zeroes in directly on the issue of recidivism. Although many outcomes are relevant to discussing crime policy, and punishment in particular, recidivism stands out as a central priority. Accordingly, the chapter begins first by discussing mass incarceration as a policy for reducing crime and how reducing recidivism fits into the incarceration-to-reduce-crime equation. Here, we critique mass incarceration as resting on a largely atheoretical platform. We then shift gears and identify theoretically predictable, adverse consequences of incarceration for recidivism. These discussions form the foundation for focusing our attention directly on recidivism—the problem that it represents and the use and success of different risk prediction approaches in identifying those who may merit intervention.

Although substantial grounds exist for feeling encouraged about risk prediction improvements, substantial concerns also exist about the ability of correctional systems to predict accurately or to use predictions to improve ex-prisoner (or felon) management, supervision, or assistance. We have little interest in harping on each and every challenge to risk prediction. However, the challenges nonetheless merit attention because they underscore the considerable need to exercise caution in undertaking prediction efforts. On a more positive note, we discuss ways that risk prediction can be improved. Some avenues for improving prediction come from drawing on criminological theory and using information about prison experiences and the community contexts to which ex-prisoners return. A more systematic reliance on the insights from theory and from practitioners holds great promise for improving recidivism prediction as well. Finally, we present the argument that a novel way to improve recidivism reduction consists of focusing on other outcomes and, perhaps more important, the performance of agencies, organizations, programs, and units responsible for reducing crime among convicted felons.

THE ATHEORETICAL FOUNDATION OF MASS INCARCERATION

The reliance on large-scale investment in prisons to achieve criminal justice goals rests on a relatively flimsy theoretical foundation. One certainly can point to different theories to support punishment in general. Deterrence theory emphasizes punishment. Strain theory emphasizes the use of noxious stimuli (e.g., punishment) or positive stimuli (e.g., rewards or incentives) to reduce negative behavior. Social learning theory emphasizes decreased exposure to criminal associates and increased exposure to opportunities to learn pro-social behavior. And so on. None of these theories, however, explicitly states or argues that incarceration effectively reduces crime. Indeed, many of them do not even emphasize the notion of punishment. For example, from a strain theory perspective, we might emphasize teaching individuals about a range of coping strategies that might be more effective than criminal behavior. Similarly, from a social learning theory perspective, we might emphasize any number of educational interventions to change thoughts, attitudes, and beliefs conducive to criminal behavior.

Of course, we punish not simply to reduce crime but to achieve retribution. A science of retribution remains to be developed, but even if we allow retribution to enter into our discussion, we are confronted by the fact that there is nothing intrinsically obvious about using incarceration to achieve retributive goals. Punishment for punishment's sake might be achieved through other sanctions. For example, tarring-and-feathering might create a greater sense of retribution among some of us, though it also likely would violate the moral sensibilities of others. In contemporary times, we do not rely on such measures, or, more generally, corporal punishment (save for the death penalty). We do use incarceration, but it does not constitute our sole punishment option. In addition to prison, we use probation, house arrest, and various types of intermediate sanctions. Notwithstanding this palette of options, we land back in the same spot where we started—no theory and no science of retribution exists that dictates that incarceration constitutes the retributive option of choice for Americans, much less how much retribution we achieve through specific lengths of confinement or specific conditions of confinement.

Apart from retribution, we use incarceration to lower crime rates. Perhaps mass incarceration has achieved some level of crime reduction in recent decades, or did so during the 1990s. Scholars continue to debate this issue. As we have discussed, the best estimates suggest that perhaps as much as one-quarter of the crime decline during the past decade or so can be attributed to prison growth. Now, however, we are left with a level of incarceration that well exceeds that of other countries as well as that used historically by the United States. Perhaps the current level will buffer the country from crime increases or reduce the magnitude of the increases from what they otherwise would be. It will be difficult to know because no other countries provide a close counterpoint to the United States.

Our focus here, though, is not on retribution or crime rates but rather on recidivism. Specifically, how, in the end, does mass incarceration make the country safer through reduced recidivism? Does it? As our earlier discussions in Chapters 2 and 3 highlighted, it remains unclear that incarceration has improved public safety through this mechanism. Indeed, the best available evidence suggests that, if anything, incarceration may have worsened public safety by increasing recidivism relative to what would have occurred with other sanctions. (Of course, such a harm might be offset by reduced crime rates, to the extent that incarceration creates general deterrence or incapacitation effects.)

That situation bears closer scrutiny. Why exactly would incarceration reduce recidivism? No clear answer exists. Only if we vaguely allude to the notion that more severe punishment should deter do we arrive at a perhaps seemingly defensible theoretical stance. Clearly, being sent to prison constitutes a severe sanction and should deter. Yet it should be emphasized that no criminological theory, or any theory, points to incarceration as an effective way of changing human behavior. Rather, incarceration constitutes an idea that came into use and, over time, became normative. It today is what many societies use to achieve various and sundry goals, including retribution, general deterrence, and reduced recidivism.

To put the situation in perspective, we can start with a situation where no prison exists, only a wide range of non-incarcerative sanctions. Here, we will put aside retribution as a related but difficult problem. So, too, we will put aside crime rates and efforts to achieve justice through incarceration. How retribution and justice can be achieved remains nebulous at best and clearly does not have to involve incarceration.

Instead, we focus on an immediate policy challenge—we wish to reduce the offending of those who have committed a crime, and we want a sanction that will achieve this goal more effectively than our current sanctions achieve. To identify a solution, we convene a work group consisting of experts from all walks of life. Someone mentions that perhaps putting an individual in a cell by himself or herself all day, or most of the day, will work.

The recidivism-reducing work group pauses to consider this idea. Questions percolate. Why would that reduce offending? Very quickly, the adept members of the committee start raising ideas that flow from contemporary criminological theories. For a brief moment, some members of the group experience a sense of gratifying satisfaction. Here is a new policy and it has theoretical support.

However, more questions begin to bubble up. How many days should someone be in confinement before we can expect a reduction in offending to occur? If we cannot totally eliminate their likelihood of offending, can we at least reduce it substantially by putting them in this new type of cell for a week or two? How about a year? If we do that, how much will we reduce the likelihood of that person offending?

More conversation ensues. What should it be like in these cells? Dark? Light? Boring? Should these cells be put together somehow? Someone pipes up that this idea defies reason. Why put criminals together? A few of the more efficiency-minded members point out the benefits of scale. More cells will be cheaper to build if they are together at one place, what the members begin to refer to as a prison.

Some of the members observe that any design considerations should be aimed at maximizing reduced recidivism. The group stops. They consult with criminologists. They review criminological theory. Nowhere do they find clear guidance about any of these questions. A few criminologists express avowedly liberal views, and they summarily get dismissed. So, too, the avowedly conservative ones. The work group only wants to hear the science, not personal predilections or political agendas. Once, again, however, they receive no clear guidance.

THE A PRIORI, THEORETICALLY PREDICTABLE CONSEQUENCES OF INCARCERATION

The situation becomes murkier. As the work group members review criminological theories, it becomes evident that many of them emphasize causal factors that do not in any obvious way respond to incarceration. Indeed, incarceration might worsen them.[1] Strain theory suggests, for example, that strain-inducing experiences should increase, not decrease, offending. Social learning theory suggests that exposure to criminal others might worsen offending. The same pattern surfaces with other theories. To put a further damper on the proceedings, biological theorists point out that little about incarceration addresses the causes of offending that their work highlights. Many of the theories can be combined in ways that lead to even more dismay over the idea that incarceration will be effective.

A bit of a crisis develops. It turns out that equally compelling theoretical arguments can be made for incarceration worsening recidivism as for it improving it. Indeed, it seems easier to identify harmful effects. Worse, still, no empirical evidence provides clear or compelling grounds for incarceration as a recidivism-reducing sanction.

One member mentions that rehabilitation can work. Rehabilitation? What is that, the other committee members want to know. The member reports that it consists of treatment, services, and assistance designed to help individuals achieve a level of psychological and social functioning that better approximates that of conventional, law-abiding citizens. (One member of the committee is a professor and ponders how well university faculty would fit this latter profile, but of course says nothing.) Much excitement ensues. Why? These interventions could be structured in ways that address some of the causes of crime that criminological theories highlight. Education and vocational programming, cognitive-behavioral counseling, anger management classes—these and more might reduce strain, promote positive behavior, and lead to other desirable outcomes. The air is electric! Incarceration could reduce recidivism through deterrence, but it also could do so through other mechanisms emphasized by different criminological theories.

An old-timer, highly pragmatic and more of a nuts-and-bolts type, raises the question: How much rehabilitation of each type would be necessary for an inmate? During a 6-month or 12-month prison stay, would different rehabilitative services be necessary? Can rehabilitation really be effective when it occurs inside a prison? Do changes that occur inside prison walls necessarily carry over to society? The member comments that practicing a game against no real opponent provides little insight into how the team will play against real opposition. An inmate (the work group devolves on this term) might learn to change their thinking while in prison, but can that change really be sustained once the individual returns to his or her family, friends, and community? A few members, chastened, nod their heads in agreement. Several others point out that the work group soon must move on to other policy matters. One member moves to a vote on whether to build a prison. The motion passes. Members vote. The vote carries. (The retributivist and justice work groups continue their own deliberations down the hallway.)

In this fictionalized example, it should be readily apparent that not only does incarceration not in any obvious way rest on a theoretical foundation, there also are theoretically predictable consequences of incarceration that point in the direction of it worsening rather than improving recidivism. Strain theory, for example, points to strain as a central cause of crime. Few experiences in life are more strainful than prison. The strain extends along many dimensions. Enduring isolation and a severing of social ties can be psychologically strainful. Attempting to return to a social world that may have forgotten you or moved on can be strainful. And so on.

For many criminological theories, the clear theme is as follows—provide interventions during and after incarceration that speak directly to the causes emphasized by each theory. Doing so might reduce future offending. Fail to do so and expect little by way of crime reduction. Indeed, if prison experiences adversely affect the causes of crime identified by these theories (e.g., strain, social bonds, self-control), then anticipate that recidivism will worsen.

This situation poses direct implications, as we discuss below, for risk prediction. Ultimately, we want risk assessments to help us identify those who most likely will reoffend and to know how best to reduce their offending. To undertake such assessments accurately, however, requires knowledge of the causes of offending, the dimensions of the prison experience that may have addressed these causes, and the dimensions of an individual's social context after prison. Context matters because it may affect an individual and, in turn, his or her offending. Do current risk assessment practices achieve this type of accuracy? The short answer: no.

RECIDIVISM RATES—A DEPRESSING PROBLEM

Recidivism constitutes a tremendous problem for corrections, especially the prison system. As we have discussed earlier, national estimates indicate that 77 percent or more of released prisoners will be rearrested within 5 years of release.[2] That is just rearrest, not actual reoffending. Getting arrested takes some work. You have to be apprehended. Many crimes occur, however, that go unnoticed or unreported. Even when reported, crimes frequently will not result in an arrest. So, from the true universe of reoffending, arrest only captures some part. It is reasonable, therefore, to anticipate that 80 percent or more of people released from prison go on to commit more crime.

This situation creates substantial grounds for concern about the problem of *churning*.[3] In many experiences in life, repeating an effort that previously failed, and then repeating it again and again in the face of failure, constitutes grounds for needless frustration. When we focus on prisons, we can see clear grounds for frustration. We have individuals who go to prison repeatedly. They do not really go; rather, our courts send them. Yet, on the face of it, prison appears to achieve little, given that over three-fourths of released prisoners will be rearrested and that an even higher percentage reoffend.

The concern only increases when we realize the limited utility of a binary measure of reoffending—or rearrest, reconviction, or reincarceration—as a way of assessing incarceration effects. For example, if, prior to incarceration, an individual committed 10 crimes per year and then, after prison, committed only five crimes per year, a significant improvement has occurred. Yes, offending still occurred, but the *amount* of criminal activity clearly declined. This idea constitutes a central insight of scholarship on desistance. The interest, from a desistance perspective, lies with identifying turning points in the amounts of offending over time.[4]

Regardless, we remain left with the problem that, however measured, recidivism occurs with regularity among the vast bulk of ex-prisoners. There should be little surprise at this fact. The individuals who go to prison typically constitute a select group, with lengthy histories of offending, strain-filled lives, low self-control, drug abuse and mental illness, residence in poverty-stricken areas, and more. We should, therefore, anticipate that the likelihood of reoffending would be high. In addition, within the prison population, a spectrum of individuals exists who lie at the right end of the bell curve distribution. Here, we find individuals who simply may have more exposure to a range of criminogenic factors or who have an accumulation of risk factors, including biological or genetic characteristics, that greatly increase the likelihood of offending. We can expect these individuals to be even more likely to offend.

In the end, we are left knowing that most people who enter prison come from and will return to lives at the margins of society. They face difficult times and have characteristics that make recidivism likely. Some of them are especially at risk of offending. We would like to identify these individuals accurately. We want especially to identify those at the most risk of committing more crime. Identifying such individuals entails, however, much error.

Before we proceed, we should distinguish between prediction and forecast. Many people, researchers included, use the two terms interchangeably. Others do not; in the latter case, there still may be definitional inconsistency among scholars or disciplines. Regardless of which word one uses, two distinct meanings can be identified. The first is the idea that we can make probabilistic statements about what *may* happen in the future. We might predict, for example, that a prisoner has a 60 percent chance of recidivating. He or she may or may not reoffend. However, if one were a betting person, the probability points to a better than random chance that the individual in fact will commit another crime. We term this type of statement a "prediction."

The second meaning captures the idea that we can identify what in fact *will* happen. Social scientists, and, for that matter, natural scientists, typically cannot know what will happen in the future and so eschew making statements about what in fact *will* happen.[5] We term this type of statement, where one states what *will* happen, a "forecast."

In recidivism studies, the distinction reduces to the difference between (a) saying that we anticipate that a person *might* recidivate (i.e., we make a prediction that there some probability exists that the person will recidivate) versus (b) saying that we predict that a given person *will* recidivate (i.e., we forecast that the person in fact will recidivate). Other meanings exist. For example, we might examine the past lives of a sample of individuals and use information about them to predict which ones likely committed crimes. Here, we are not attempting to predict the future. Rather, we are attempting to predict a past event. This backwards-looking prediction effort constitutes one way that researchers develop models that they use to create forward-looking predictions about what might happen in the future.

In discussing recidivism prediction (or risk-of-recidivating prediction), it will help if we have a concrete sense of some of the elements that go into a prediction. Figure 7.1 provides an illustration of what this endeavor entails. In the

---

Figure 7.1   Challenges in Predicting Who Will Reoffend

The reality: 66 inmates will reoffend (+) and 34 will not reoffend (–)

```
+  +  +  +  +  +  +  | −  −  −
+  +  +  +  +  +  +  | −  −  −
+  +  +  +  +  +  +  | −  −  −
+  +  +  +  +  +  +  | −  −  −
+  +  +  +  +  +  +  | −  −  −
+  +  +  +  +  +  + | −  −  −
+  +  +  +  +  + |   −  −  −  −
+  +  +  +  +  + |   −  −  −  −
+  +  +  +  +  + |   −  −  −  −
+  +  +  +  +  + |   −  −  −  −
```

The "+" signs in gray to the left of the thick bar identify all individuals who will reoffend. The "–" signs to the right of it identify all individuals who will not reoffend.

versus

The prediction of which inmates will reoffend (+) and which ones will not reoffend (–)

```
+  −  +  +  +  +  +  | −  −  −
+  +  +  +  +  −  −  | −  −  −
+  −  +  +  +  +  +  | −  −  −
+  +  −  +  +  +  +  | −  −  −
+  +  +  +  +  −  −  | −  +  +
−  +  +  +  +  +  + | −  +  −
+  +  −  −  +  + |   −  +  −  +
+  +  +  +  −  + |   −  −  −  +
+  −  −  +  +  − |   −  −  −  +
−  −  +  +  +  + |   −  +  −  +
```

The "+" signs indicate a prediction that an inmate will reoffend. When the sign is to the left of the thick bar, the prediction is accurate; otherwise, it is inaccurate. A "–" sign indicates a prediction that an inmate will not reoffend. When the sign is to the right of the thick bar, the prediction is accurate; otherwise, it is inaccurate.

Numbers that can be used to generate prediction accuracy statistics:

Total true "+"	= 66	Total true "–"	= 34
Predicted "+"	= 59	Predicted "–"	= 41
Correct "+"	= 50 (true positives)	Correct "–"	= 25 (true negatives)
Incorrect "+"	= 9 (false positives)	Incorrect "–"	= 16 (false negatives)

Statistics that can help with assessing prediction accuracy:

Overall accuracy	= 75%	= (50 + 25) / (66 + 34)	= (correct predicted positives + predicted negatives) / (total true positives + true negatives)
True positive rate (sensitivity) (hit rate among true "+")	= 76%	= 50 / 66	= correct predicted positives / total true positives
Positive predictive value (hit rate among predicted "+")	= 85%	= 50 / (50 + 9)	= correct predicted positives / (correct predicted positives + false positives)
False positive rate (false alarm / type I error)	= 26%	= 9 / 34	= false positives / total true negatives
True negative rate (specificity) (hit rate among true "–")	= 74%	= 25 / 34	= correct predicted negatives / total true negatives
Negative predictive value (hit rate among predicted "–")	= 61%	= 25 / (25 + 16)	= correct predicted negatives / (correct predicted negatives + false negatives)
False negative rate (false no alarm / type II error)	= 24%	= 16 / 66	= false negatives / total true positives

figure, we have used 66 percent as a recidivism rate because national studies have found that two-thirds of released prisoners will be rearrested within 3 years of release and because many recidivism studies use 3-year follow-up periods.[6] We can think of 66 as a percentage or as a rate (i.e., 66 per 100 individuals).

Figure 7.1 shows some of the complexity that goes into a prediction. In the top panel, we can see reality. On the left side of the panel, in shaded boxes with plus signs (+) signs, are the 66 individuals who *will* recidivate. (In this example, we are assuming that we know what actually will happen. In risk prediction efforts, we of course do not enjoy that omnipotent knowledge.) On the right side of the panel, in unshaded boxes with minus signs (-), are the 34 individuals who will *not* recidivate. Our goal? We want to predict accurately the 66 recidivists and, just as important, the 34 nonrecidivists.

Unfortunately, almost any prediction effort involves error. We can see that in the second panel. Here, we have predicted who will recidivate and who will not. The plus signs represent the individuals who we predicted would go on to commit crime; the minus signs represent the individuals who we predicted would not go on to commit crime. On the left side of the panel, in shaded boxes, are all the individuals who actually went on to commit crime; on the right side of the panel, in unshaded boxes, are all the individuals who did not commit crime.

We did pretty well. On the left side, in the shaded boxes, are many plus signs. These are individuals who we predicted (per the plus signs) would commit crime and, well, we were correct (per the shaded boxes). These are the true positives. Similarly, on the right side, in the unshaded boxes, there are many individuals who we predicted would not commit crime (indicated by minus signs) and who in fact did not commit crime. These are the true negatives.

Even though we seemed to do well, some mistakes occurred. On the right side of the panel, we can see some plus signs. These constitute individuals who we predicted would commit crime but in fact did not do so. They are false positives. Conversely, on the left side of the panel, we can see some minus signs. These are individuals who we predicted would not commit crime but in fact did so. They are false negatives.

All of this information can be combined in different ways to glean insight into the accuracy of our predictions. For example, we can compute the true positive rate, which consists of the percentage of all individuals who recidivated who we accurately identified as such. Here, that was 50 out of 66, for a true positive rate of 76 percent. This rate sometimes is referred to as the sensitivity of a given prediction effort. Alternatively, we can compute the true negative rate. It equals the percentage of individuals who did not recidivate who we accurately predicted would not recidivate. Here, the true negative rate is 25 out of 34, or 74 percent. This rate sometimes is referred to as specificity.

Two other related statistics can be computed—the positive predictive value and the negative predictive value. The first measures the accuracy of our prediction among only the cases where we predicted recidivism; here, positive predictive value is 50 out of 59, or 85 percent. The second measures the accuracy our prediction among only the cases where we predicted no recidivism; here, negative predictive value is 25 out of 41, or 61 percent.

Finally, a third set of statistics can be computed. One is the false positive rate. That consists of the percentage of true negatives for which we predicted recidivism. Here, nine of 34 true negatives were incorrectly predicted to recidivate, for a false positive rate of 26 percent. Another is the false negative rate. That consists of the percentage of true positives for which we predicted no recidivism would occur. Here, 16 of the 66 true positives were incorrectly predicted not to recidivate, for a false negative rate of 24 percent.

We also can compute a general measure of overall accuracy. In this case, it measures, on the one hand, the number of correct predicted recidivism cases (50) and the number of correct predicted nonrecidivism cases (25), and, on the other hand, the number of total true recidivism cases (66) and the total number of true nonrecidivism cases (34). The end result is a ratio, 75 out of 100, or 75 percent.

Why the complexity? We sometimes want more of one type of accuracy than another, or we want to avoid one type of error more than another. For example, if we want to identify almost every individual who recidivated, we will seek a true positive rate as close to 100 percent as possible. However, in this example, by identifying accurately *all* 66 such individuals we almost assuredly will risk having a high false positive rate. That is, many individuals will be labeled as future recidivists even though they in fact will not do so. If it were cancer, the situation could be likened to identifying all 66 individuals who had cancer. That sounds great, except for the fact that 34 individuals who do not have cancer will be told that they do.

There are no free lunches, and if we attempt to eliminate false positives, we typically will end up with less accuracy in identifying those who in fact will go on to recidivate. We want a high true positive rate (sensitivity), but we also want a low false positive rate, what sometimes is referred to as a type I error. If you are a judge at a sentencing hearing where you are deciding who to incarcerate, or if you are on a parole board making a decision about who to release, you want to avoid false negative (type II) errors as well. Predicting that someone will be a safe bet not to recidivate and then being proved wrong by a front-page story of a brutal murder or assault would make most of us uncomfortable. Worse, we would look inept. Why? Because we somehow should have known better. We should have known that the particular individual was going to commit a new and horrible crime.

So what do we do? We expand our risk prediction in such a way that almost anyone who appears to have any risk is classified as a positive—that is, as someone who likely will recidivate. In so doing, however, we create a high false positive rate. That is, we will identify many individuals as likely to recidivate who in fact will not go on to commit more crime. In so doing, we obligate considerable resources that might be used in better ways. We place people in pretrial detention who have little risk of reoffending. We place people in prison who will not reoffend. We release people from prison and place them on intensive supervision even though they in fact may be at minimal risk to reoffend. Mistakes are costly.

What thresholds do we use to inform our decisions? No statistics can answer that question. In the end, any such designations involve normative judgments. These judgments extend not only to the thresholds to use but also to determinations about which types of accuracy or error matter most in a particular context.

RISK PREDICTION APPROACHES

Risk can be assessed in many ways. In criminology and criminal justice, risk prediction has proceeded through four stages or generations.[7] First-generation approaches relied primarily on clinical judgment about whether an individual seemed likely to reoffend. These approaches suffered in part from inconsistency and error inherent to subjective assessments. They privilege clinical judgment and the insights that may derive from a lifetime of studying and working with criminals and from a deeper understanding of a particular individual, based on interviews and a review of case files.

Second-generation approaches focused primarily on statistical-based, or actuarial, risk prediction. These approaches avoided the problems associated with clinical judgment. However, they typically failed to incorporate insights from criminological theory. They also relied heavily upon static risk factors—that is, factors, such as age, that cannot be changed. Accordingly, their accuracy was limited and they shed little light on how to intervene with individuals to reduce their risk of reoffending.

Third-generation approaches emphasized both clinical judgment and statistical, or actuarial, methods and, concomitantly, inclusion of dynamic or criminogenic risk factors. The latter have sometimes been referred to as criminogenic "needs." According to the needs principle, effective interventions should focus on risk factors, such as antisocial attitudes, association with criminals, and poor self-control, that (a) are associated with offending (hence the term "criminogenic") and (b) that can be changed (hence the term "dynamic") in an individual to reduce criminal behavior.[8] These approaches constituted a significant advance over those that preceded them. The advance stemmed in part from building on evaluations of programs that effectively reduced recidivism. In that sense, they were empirically-based. For that same reason, they also were criticized for being atheoretical and not drawing on criminological theory. Proponents of third-generation approaches have identified ways in which the approaches in fact have built on theory.[9] The critique aside, this advance has generally been viewed as an improvement over earlier approaches. It also introduced complexity into prediction efforts and reintroduced the potential for inconsistency, error, and bias through reliance on clinical judgment.

Fourth-generation approaches have built on the prior approaches, especially third-generation efforts, to assess risk and, at the same time, to identify appropriate and effective intervention strategies. The latter emphasis is critical. The focus has turned not only to risk prediction but also to using risk and need assessment "[to guide and follow] service and supervision from intake through case closure."[10] Put differently, risk and need assessment can be used to guide service and supervision continuously. Doing so creates opportunities for achieving intermediate outcomes, such as the ability to interview successfully for a job. It also establishes a foundation for reducing recidivism. Frequently referred to as "structured clinical judgment," this approach necessarily requires a more systemic and dynamic view of risk prediction and intervention. As such, it stands in stark contrast to first- and second-generation approaches.

Included in third- and fourth-generation approaches is an emphasis on what have been termed human service principles of risk-need-responsivity (RNR).

Donald Andrews and colleagues have emphasized that in the development of these approaches,

> the corrections-based terms of *risk* and *need* were transformed into principles addressing the major clinical issues of who receives treatment (higher risk cases), what intermediate targets are set (reduce criminogenic needs), and what treatment strategies are employed (match strategies to the learning styles and motivation of cases: the principles of general and specific responsivity). General responsivity asserts the general power of behavioral, social learning, and cognitive-behavioral strategies. Specific responsivity suggests matching of service with personality, motivation, and ability and with demographics such as age, gender, and ethnicity.[11]

This combined emphasis on higher risk cases, reducing criminogenic needs, and responsivity constitutes a central feature of risk prediction and intervention efforts in corrections today.[12] That does not mean that third- and fourth-generation approaches are a mainstay in correctional systems. To the contrary, many risk prediction efforts today hew more to a first- or second-generation approach or an amalgam of unvalidated approaches.[13]

Development of the third- and fourth-generation approaches to risk prediction have led to an emphasis in some scholarly work on a parallel set of principles of effective service or intervention.[14] What are the principles? Francis Cullen and Paul Gendreau have provided one of the most concise accounts. The first is that "interventions should target the known predictors of crime and recidivism for change."[15] In focusing on such predictors, priority should be given to dynamic factors, such as "antisocial/procriminal attitudes, values, beliefs and cognitive-emotional states," "procriminal associates and isolation from anticriminal others," and "antisocial personality factors, such as impulsiveness, risk-taking, and low self-control."[16] The second is that "treatment services should be behavioral in nature" and entail both general responsivity and specific responsivity.[17] The third is that "treatment interventions should be used primarily with higher risk offenders, targeting their criminogenic needs (dynamic risk factors) for change."[18] The fourth principle is that an emphasis on a range of other considerations, such as quality program implementation and incorporation of specific responsivity into programming, can result in greater reductions in recidivism.[19]

The emphasis on principles of effective correctional intervention is useful for guiding program and intervention development. However, from a risk prediction perspective, they lead us to the critical insight that we need to include information about individual change into our prediction efforts. When, for example, individuals in prison change in one way or the other, or undergo certain experiences, the changes or experiences may provide useful information about whether an individual will be likely to recidivate.

Other lines of scholarship point to additional ways that risk prediction might be enhanced. For example, a considerable amount of emphasis has emerged in recent decades on the notion of protective factors. Here, it is simpler to think about a situation where a given factor is nonlinearly related to offending. It may be, for example, that individuals who have low to medium levels of strain are not especially likely to offend, and that, conversely, individuals who are high in strain are especially likely to offend. In this situation, one might view a situation of low or medium strain as protective against the likelihood of offending.[20]

We also can view protective factors as those forces that condition, or moderate, the effect of another. It may be, for example, that strain is a risk factor for recidivism, but more or primarily so for individuals low in self-control. Here, high levels of self-control could be viewed as protective against the influence of strain. Other personality characteristics, such as resiliency or ability to adapt, might be viewed in this sense as protective to the extent that they can buffer the influence of risk factors. This insight assumes importance, as we discuss below, because it underscores the potential need to create risk prediction models that incorporate the possibility of nonlinear relationships, such as threshold effects and interaction effects.

Most prediction efforts involve the use of risk prediction instruments. These require collection of data about the individuals. Then the information is scored in some way or another, added or combined in some manner, and eventually a final score results that identifies a person as at risk of offending. The process can be complicated, and the range of sources of information used by the instruments may be considerable. However, the core idea remains the same. This approach contrasts markedly with recent developments in risk prediction. These newer approaches still require good data—that is, information about an individual and, ideally, his or her background, prison experiences, family context, and more. However, they emphasize statistical analysis in developing predictions.

Not all risk prediction requires the use of instruments, but they do require data. One of the more prominent recent advances in prediction is the use of machine learning approaches.[21] This type of approach involves mining data—looking for linear, curvilinear, and interactive relationships—to identify patterns in individuals' pasts that may predict accurately future behavior. It is not a theoretical undertaking, one guided, for example, by an emphasis on one factor or another. And it is not an instrument undertaking; that is, decisions about how to score particular factors and, in turn, to combine the scores are not determined by a specific protocol. A benefit of machine learning approaches is that they allow for prediction of several categories of risk groups. A criticism of such approaches, however, is that they tend to be atheoretical and provide little consistent guidance about how to intervene with high-risk individuals. Even so, they provide another tool that correctional systems can use to improve their accuracy in identifying the most at-risk individuals. Such information in turn can be used to flag individuals for more attention. What types of attention? For that, traditional risk assessment approaches, including fourth-generation instruments and strategies, may be useful.

RISK PREDICTION SUCCESS

Risk prediction efforts sound ideal. We use some information, generate a model that helps us to predict who will be at risk of recidivating and who will not be, then rely on that model to generate actual predictions. Advances in risk assessment and modeling have yielded improvements over time in our ability to make better predictions. We now have, for example, many validated prediction instruments. Validation simply means that the instruments do better than chance at predicting who will recidivate.

Doing better than chance constitutes a low bar. It does not require, for example, that we are highly accurate with our predictions, just better than chance. What we really want is perfect prediction. "Everyone who will go on to offend can be identified through use of our prediction instrument. Conversely, everyone who will not go on to offend is also accurately identified." The reality? Our best prediction instruments involve significant error, resulting in either a large percentage of false positives (individuals who in fact will *not* go on to offend) or a large percentage of false negatives (individuals who in fact *will* go on to offend).

It remains difficult to provide a summary measure for comparing instruments, such that one could say, "This instrument is the best." Instead, researchers typically compare different statistical measures. Why? Some types of accuracy or error may matter more in certain contexts. That said, the area under the curve (AUC) of the receiver operating characteristic (ROC) is frequently used for comparing instruments with respect to their overall predictive accuracy; it has the added benefit of not being affected by base rates of outcomes.[22] As Seena Fazel and colleagues have observed, "the area under the curve is an index of sensitivity and specificity across score thresholds, and is currently considered the accuracy estimate of choice in violence risk assessment when measuring predictive accuracy."[23] ROC curves provide a graphical representation of the trade-off between sensitivity (i.e., the true positive rate) and specificity (i.e., the true negative rate) by plotting each relative to the other. One then can assess the trade-offs between the two when using varying cut-off scores, such as the cut-off to be used for assigning an individual to a "high risk of recidivism" category.[24]

The AUC statistic ranges from 0 to 1, where 0 is a perfect inability to predict (what might be characterized as perfect negative prediction); .5 is a prediction of a binary outcome, such as recidivism, that is no better than chance (50 percent sensitivity and 50 percent specificity); and 1.0 is a perfect ability to predict. In recidivism studies, the AUC "represents the probability that a randomly selected recidivist will obtain a higher score on the risk prediction instrument than a randomly selected nonrecidivist."[25] Although the AUC assesses the overall likelihood of recidivism, it does not assess the ability of an instrument to predict recidivism for a given cut-off value. Some accounts view a value of .70 as useful for an AUC threshold.[26] Others view this threshold as "too low for principled use in forensic settings."[27]

Many instruments aimed at predicting recidivism can achieve AUC values of .70 or higher and so may be viewed as good or accurate. Even so, many validated instruments have AUC values that are substantially lower.[28] They entail error and leave a considerable amount of variance in recidivism unexplained.[29] Many validated instruments, especially those focused on general offending as opposed to those focused on specific types of offending (e.g., violent or sex), have AUC values lower than the .70 threshold.[30] In addition, the AUC as a measure of predictive accuracy can be problematic. For example, it weights false positives and false negatives equally even though in some instances, as we discussed above, they may not be equal. In some cases, false negatives may entail more costs than false positives.

The point bears emphasis—many risk prediction instruments exist, yet few have been systematically compared with one another such that one could, on an empirical basis, confidently select one over another as being better.[31] The situation is further complicated because numerous instruments exist for specific groups, such as young sex offenders, older sex offenders, male offenders, female offenders, violent offenders, and so on. Some of the more commonly used actuarial instruments include the following: Level of Service Inventory–Revised (LSI-R); Psychopathy Checklist–Revised (PCL-R); Sex Offender Risk Appraisal Guide (SORAG); Static-99; and Violence Risk Appraisal Guide (VRAG). Some of the more commonly used structured clinical judgment instruments include the Historical, Clinical, Risk management-20 (HCR-20), Sexual Violence Risk-20 (SVR-20), Spousal Assault Risk Assessment (SARA), and Structured Assessment of Violence Risk in Youth (SAVRY).[32]

In each instance, a complicated array of measures can be used to make comparisons. And, in each instance, studies typically have been conducted that find that a given instrument may produce better-than-random-guess predictions.[33] Yet the studies may use different measures of recidivism, may have been developed with certain populations in mind, may not distinguish between types of crime, and so on. In addition, many risk instruments have not been validated at all or have not been subject to rigorous validation efforts.[34]

This situation has led to significant skepticism among scholars about the utility of risk assessment. For example, based on their systematic review and meta-analysis of recidivism prediction efforts, Fazel and colleagues concluded: "One implication of these findings is that, even after 30 years of development, the view that violence, sexual, or criminal risk can be predicted in most cases is not evidence-based. . . . Our review suggests that risk assessment tools in their current form can only be used to roughly classify individuals at the group level, and not to safely determine criminal prognosis in an individual case."[35]

Current scholarship highlights, however, that quantitative risk assessment constitutes a better approach than clinical judgment alone.[36] Among other things, risk instruments can provide more consistent predictions. In addition, the basis for the predictions is transparent, whereas clinicians can vary greatly in their assessment of risk and the basis for their assessment. The fact of significant error in prediction will not be solved statistically. Rather, as Fazel and colleagues concluded, normative judgments must be made about the trade-offs involved: "Ultimately . . . what constitutes an appropriate balance between the ethical implications of detaining people based on the predictive ability of these tools and the need for public protection will primarily be a political consideration."[37]

A pragmatic view consists of viewing any decision-making endeavor as one that carries the potential for mistakes. From this perspective, virtually any instrument or approach that provides a better-than-random-chance guess about who will likely reoffend merits use. However, an equally pragmatic view emphasizes the costs associated with generating predictions and mistakenly intervening when we should not, as well as mistakenly not intervening when we should. There exists, too, the problem of being able to identify a high-risk group but having no actionable information to guide us in effectively intervening with an individual.

In our view, the risks of recidivism prediction are more than sufficient to require considerable care in their use. We do not advocate eliminating risk prediction. In general, better-than-chance predictions provide a more credible foundation for informing critical correctional system decision-making than does an approach of flipping a coin or, worse yet, guessing incorrectly—worse than chance—in a patterned way. What we do advocate is the development of a more robust and credible scientific foundation for recidivism risk prediction and the use of uniform standards for assigning risk. To ground this argument, we discuss below some of the more prominent challenges associated with risk prediction in criminal justice.

THE CHALLENGES OF RISK PREDICTION

In highlighting challenges to risk prediction, we seek to highlight the complexity of risk assessment. At the same time, we seek to demonstrate that prediction entails more than simply identifying potential recidivists. It entails failing to identify them, failing to screen out nonrecidivists or those highly unlikely to recidivate, and failing to understand what contributes to recidivism. Much risk assessment leaves the causes of potential recidivism in the equivalent of a black box. That is, even if we accurately identify someone who likely will recidivate, we frequently know little about what exactly produces that risk or therefore what to do about it. Fourth-generation risk assessment approaches avoid some of these problems, but not entirely. Here, then, we proceed to identify a select set of challenges. Others exist, and discussions of them can be found in many sources.[38] Our focus, therefore, will zero in on some of the more critical challenges that will help illuminate the potential pitfalls and limits of risk prediction.

Challenge 1: Risk Assessment Is Costly

Few things in life are free, and the same goes for risk assessment. Typically, quality assessments require trained staff to administer instruments and code and interpret them. Reliance on untrained staff can create many problems and, of course, inaccurate predictions.[39] Sometimes multiple instruments may be required. Fees frequently must be paid to use certain instruments. Some may offer special insights primarily into such issues as drug abuse and mental illness. The assessment process can involve collecting information from multiple sources as well as interviews with the offender. Ideally, assessments occur regularly so that changes in potential risk can be identified. All of these steps entail substantial time and resources. Although new approaches to risk prediction, such as random forecast modeling, have emerged that can reduce expenses, the benefits still need to be sufficiently large to offset costs.[40]

Challenge 2: Risk Assessment Can Produce Implausible Predictions

As the earlier discussion highlighted, risk prediction almost invariably results in some amount of error. The only question is how much error a given prediction approach entails. One variant of this problem consists of extreme predictions, such as when an instrument assigns either a close to 0 percent chance of recidivism or a close to 100 percent chance of recidivism. Such predictions essentially imply that the instrument or those administering it can perfectly predict the future. That simply is not possible.[41] One might solve this problem by disallowing predictions that involve cut-offs near the 0 percent or 100 percent thresholds, but such an approach does not really change the situation. That is, prediction models still will generate implausible predictions. Even so, one might defensibly view extreme predictions as useful guides for the general propensity of an individual to reoffend. One still is left, however, with the questionable validity of a model that creates extreme predictions in the first place.

Challenge 3: Predictions Tend to Be Less Accurate for Specific Types of Crimes

A rich literature has emerged in criminology, one replete with theories of offending and empirical assessments of the factors that contribute to offending. Even so, no single correct conceptualization or measurement of offending exists. As a result, studies frequently may study a general measure of offending, certain categories of offending (e.g., violent, property, drug, sex) or specific offenses (e.g., murder, assault, burglary). From a policy perspective, a focus on particular categories of crimes or specific offenses may be warranted. From a theoretical perspective, however, there is little extant guidance about how best to aggregate or disaggregate crimes. Some scholars take the view that we should not disaggregate unless clear theoretical guidance exists to do so. Others observe that this approach amounts to combining acts that differ in critical ways, and that the act of combining them ignores these differences.

Viewed in this light, combining offenses amounts to the medical equivalent of combining a focus on hangnail, skin rashes, colds, heart disease, and more into one lumped-together category of illness. To do so seems patently illogical and would lead to a related logical problem—that of seeking to assess whether the causes of, say, a skin rash are the same as the causes of a heart attack or a particular type of cancer. Yet recidivism studies frequently combine crimes into one overarching offense category. At the same time, when they disaggregate by focusing on categories of crimes or specific offenses, they typically do so with no clear theoretical rationale.

Policy-focused emphases tend to side step the issue by leading researchers to focus on a particular type of recidivism. For example, in a given state or jurisdiction, there typically will be substantial concern about how to prevent convicted sex offenders from committing more sex crimes. Accordingly, a large body of work has emerged that aims to assess the risk of such recidivism among sex offenders.[42] This work highlights that more general risk assessment instruments produce less accurate predictions of sex crime recidivism than do the more specialized instruments. One problem, then, in criminal justice risk prediction involves the use of broad risk assessment instruments when specialized ones may be better.

Even so, we face the problem that there typically is little clear basis for knowing when to apply a more specialized instrument. And most offenders are generalists. That is, most offenders, even "specialists," commit a diverse array of crimes. Thus, a reliance on special instruments for seemingly unique groups presents a dilemma. These groups, for example, typically will be at risk of committing other types of crimes, not just specialist ones. In addition, other groups may be equally at risk of committing a particular type of crime. For example, many individuals sentenced to prison for assault may well, upon release, go on to commit sex crimes. Indeed, nationally, the bulk of new sex crimes will result from individuals who have not previously committed a sex crime.[43]

Risk prediction with rare events will entail even more error. When the base rate of a particular type of crime is low, prediction becomes more difficult and the likelihood of false positives increases.[44] The error increases, or becomes especially problematic, with small samples. Consider a crime like sexual assault. In a sample of 200 released prisoners, let us imagine that ten will go on to commit a sexual assault. Even the best prediction instruments will struggle to identify most of these individuals while simultaneously *not* creating a large number of false positives among the other 190 ex-prisoners.

Challenge 4: Recidivism Is Measured Inconsistently Across Studies

One of the barriers to efficient and effective risk prediction stems from the inconsistent conceptualization and measurement of recidivism. The broader problem centers on the construct of risk. An individual might be prone to commit crime for any number of reasons. This "prone-ness," or propensity, may be just that—a tendency, a likelihood, a probability of perhaps committing a crime. This propensity may stem from internal factors, such as a personality characteristic, but it may stem as well from external factors, such as how others respond to a given personality characteristic. For example, someone who is low in self-control may be more likely to offend. Yet this same person may be unlikely to offend in highly structured situations. Consider a low-self-control youth in a chaotic school environment and the same youth in a structured one. In the first instance, he or she may have a propensity to offend in one but not the other. The low self-control remains, but that characteristic in and of itself does not equate to a propensity unless it somehow can be activated or given room to express itself. Much the same can be said about other risk factors. Put differently, if we identify that a given person is at risk of offending, that risk is (a) just that, a risk, a probability, and (b) may say as much about the individual's environment as it does about the individual.

Measurement, too, is an issue. Ideally, we could compare instruments in their ability to predict offending as measured in different ways—any offending, type of offending, frequency of offending, timing of offending, and more. We might, for example, want to compare instruments with their ability to assess accurately the propensity to offend. Here, the focus is on accurately assessing a probability of recidivating; this latter approach essentially views the outcome, offending, not as a binary event but rather as a state of being that an individual has after release from prison. Accordingly, the focus centers on accurately measuring this state of being. Such an approach may result in greater predictive accuracy.[45] However, as emphasized above, there exists little agreement in the scholarly literature about how best to conceptualize or to measure offending or a propensity to offend.[46]

In any comparison of instruments or approaches, we would want consistent measurement of offending and the use of similar follow-up time periods (e.g., 1 year, 2 years, 3 years after release from prison). Unfortunately, risk prediction comparisons typically entail apples-to-oranges comparisons in that the studies being compared may use different data sources, measures of offending, and follow-up time periods. In addition, most of the time we want to know *how much* offending actually occurs. Typically, though, in recidivism studies, self-report data do not exist and researchers must rely on rearrest, reconviction, or reincarceration to measure recidivism. These measures underestimate true offending substantially, and the underestimates may vary by the age, sex, race, ethnicity, or other characteristics of the individual. They constitute far from ideal measures of offending.[47] Ultimately, all of these issues make it difficult to shop around for the best instrument.

Challenge 5: Predictions Frequently Do Not Capture Nonlinear Effects

Accurate prediction of the risk of offending requires, among other things, identifying the factors that contribute to offending. It requires, too, identifying how such factors may operate. Some may directly contribute to a risk of offending. As strain increases, so too may one's likelihood of offending. However, the effect may be nonlinear. It may be that, at some threshold or tipping point, strain dramatically increases the likelihood of offending. Alternatively, interactions may exist. For example, strain may be more likely to increase the risk of offending among individuals who are lower in self-control.[48]

Unfortunately, criminological theories typically provide little guidance about such issues as thresholds and interactions among a large set of risk factors.[49] Instrument developers may explore the use of different cut-offs for specific risk factors when creating at-risk groups and then assess whether certain cut-offs create more accurate predictions. This approach can improve accuracy, but it can be difficult to know exactly what cut-offs to use or which factors interact with one another. Machine learning approaches can address this problem better.[50] However, one is left with complicated interactional schemes that do not necessarily shed light on *why* an individual will likely commit more crime. We have the benefit of a more accurate risk prediction in this instance but lack a clear understanding about how to intervene.

The end result is a limited accuracy to predict offending and a limited ability to know how to intervene. One assessment of scholarship on sex offender recidivism aptly captures the problem: "The limitations of actuarial risk assessments are sufficient that experts have yet to reach consensus on the best methods for combining risk factors into an overall evaluation."[51]

Challenge 6: Predictions Do Not Include Many Factors Related to Recidivism

One of the central limitations of many risk assessment instruments consists of the fact that they do not include many of the factors that theory and research identify as criminogenic. Often, they rely only on a core set of static or dynamic risk factors and then include additional ones that duplicate these. In that case, they do not appreciably improve prediction. As Daryl Kroner and Jeremy Mills have noted, "developing independent sources of variance is likely key to increasing the predictive accuracy of risk assessment instruments."[52] Put differently, better risk prediction requires identifying a full set of factors that may cause offending and therefore collecting information on them and incorporating them into risk models.

Some of the gaps in risk prediction measures are startling. Consider, for example, that few risk prediction approaches incorporate information about the community context to which inmates return. That oversight is both telling and limiting. Implicitly, when we use only individual-level factors to generate risk prediction, we assume that the only important factors lie within the individual. However, many risk factors may lie outside of the person.[53] The focus on the individual is telling here because it suggests that the individual alone is responsible for his or her offending. That view has merit. However, all else equal, if we take two identical individuals and place them in different criminogenic conditions, we should not be surprised if one will be more likely than the other to recidivate. Research suggests, for example, that community conditions can and do influence this risk.[54]

Challenge 7: Predictions Do Not Include Changes That May Affect Recidivism

The failure to include individual change in risk prediction constitutes one of the more critical limitations in risk assessment approaches and practices to date. Consider, for example, that many risk assessment efforts ignore what happens inside prison, thus treating the prison experience as somehow irrelevant.[55] This approach runs counter to the emphasis in fourth-generation approaches to including dynamic measures or risk. When individuals spend a year or two in prison, they undergo many experiences that may change them. They may receive programming, be victimized, assault others, become more socially distant from family or friends, serve time in isolation, and more. All of these factors may help to predict recidivism. Other factors, too, may matter. Shawn Bushway and Robert Apel, for example, have argued that when individuals work to achieve certain goals, such as employment readiness certificates, they provide a signal that they may be at lower risk of offending.[56]

Risk assessment approaches that fail to include experiences and changes after release from prison also will limit prediction accuracy. When individuals leave prison, or while they serve time on probation or in some type of intermediate sanction, they undergo experiences and changes that may decrease or increase their probability of offending. To date, few risk assessment approaches monitor such changes, or more generally changes in the probability of recidivating, on a frequent basis (e.g., weekly or monthly). By extension, methodologies for knowing how to incorporate frequent assessment into risk monitoring efforts remain at a nascent stage of development. As Greg Ridgeway has noted, "although numerous prediction methods exist for static problems, the methodology for prediction from dynamic data streams is less developed."[57]

What would be ideal is risk prediction that can incorporate individual changes in real time to increase prediction accuracy.[58] When we fail to include such information, we miss important opportunities to make such improvements. Ridgeway has provided a useful illustration:

> Consider an example. A prediction model for a new probationer predicts a low risk of reoffense. However, within 1 week of beginning probation, the probationer fails to appear for the first substance abuse treatment session. In the second week, the probationer misses a curfew by 30 minutes. In week three, the probationer finds a part-time job. The assessed risk should adapt to the timing and nature of each of these events. However, this requires new methods of estimating and fielding prediction models.

In this example, the individual on probation arguably provides new information literally week by week. He or she issues a signal that tells us something about his or her risk of offending. For example, in week 1, the failure to appear for treatment might indicate a lack of motivation to change. It might also indicate that family or housing circumstances have changed in such a way as to preclude participation in treatment. Indeed, that possibility seems plausible given that in week 3, the probationer finds employment.

Incorporating real-time information in a meaningful, interpretable manner would challenge even the most theoretically informed and statistically savvy researcher. In everyday practice, practitioners have many responsibilities and face competing demands. They do not typically have the expertise, resources, or time to overcome this challenge. Even so, fourth-generation risk assessment approaches, as well as new statistical methodologies such as machine learning techniques, have provided paths toward improved, evidence-based risk prediction and intervention.

Challenge 8: A Lack of Theory Makes It Difficult to Interpret Predictions

Although exceptions exist, most extant risk prediction does not draw systematically on criminological theory.[59] Theory is not always helpful. It can impose blinders that lead us to focus only on a delimited set of factors. At the same time, it can provide a foundation for understanding why a given association exists and for identifying factors that should be included in risk prediction models, as well as how some of these factors should be combined. In some ways, the situation is tantamount to being told that one has a high likelihood of dying, yet the physician cannot tell you why. Hopefully, in this case, the physician is wrong. But even if he or she is correct, how can we use this information? Why exactly are we likely to die? What steps can we take to reduce this impending tragedy? Alas, probabilities do not typically provide us any information that is terribly useful. We know at most that some of the probability comes from factor A, some factor B, a small amount from factor C, and so on. The reality, however, may be that the bulk of the risk derives from a certain combination of A, D, and M factors that a given theory could help us both to know to identify and to interpret.

Machine learning approaches provide an example of the tension between those who would advocate for only theoretically informed prediction approaches and those who advocate for empiricist approaches that seek to increase our ability to predict, even if the increase occurs with little theoretical guidance. On the one hand, we should not be restricted by theory such that we ignore opportunities to develop models that improve our ability to predict offending. Richard Berk and Justin Bleich have emphasized that "one does not have to understand the future to forecast it with useful accuracy."[60] This claim echoes one found in the social sciences.[61] It boils down to common sense. Clearly, we do not necessarily need to know why an association exists for it to be useful. If we know that rainy weather the day before is correlated with rainy weather the next day, this information can serve as a useful, if imperfect, guide to how to dress.

On the other hand, correlations do not necessarily involve causation, as introductory statistical textbooks invariably emphasize. In addition, they tell us little about how to intervene. Without such information, we know at best which individuals who leave prison may be at risk of offending, which we of course want to know. But we do not necessarily know *why* they are more likely to offend or what to do to reduce that likelihood. For example, we might think that providing more supervision to a high-risk individual makes sense. Observe, however, that supervision will do little to nothing to address most causes of offending.[62] There is, then, nothing obvious about the usefulness of increased supervision. It is here that fourth-generation approaches to risk prediction *and* intervention can be more helpful because they provide guidance about how to adjust interventions in ways that address the risk factors specific to a given individual.[63] The approach is not perfect, but it is a step in the right direction.

Challenge 9: Science Cannot Determine the Cut-offs for Creating Risk Groups

Prediction instruments generate numbers. These then get translated into words. The words themselves are not scientific, yet they may be treated as reality. For example, no scientific consensus exists for determining what probability level constitutes a medium risk of reoffending versus a high risk of reoffending. Cut-off thresholds involve normative judgments about acceptable accuracy and error rates (true positives, true negatives, false positives, false negatives, etc.).

This issue compounds the problems associated with a lack of consistency across jurisdictions in the assessment instruments that they use to assess risk. The problem is not just that the assessment protocols and measures differ. They conceptualize and measure cut-offs for determining risk levels in different ways. This problem is further compounded by the fact that clinicians and criminal justice or correctional system practitioners typically do not understand the intricacies of risk prediction. Yet they may be the very ones who determine which cut-offs to use in determining whether a given individual is at risk of recidivism sufficient to warrant specialized supervision, intervention, or treatment.

Challenge 10: Science Cannot Determine the Level of Acceptable Error

This issue constitutes a variant of the cut-off issue. When we use different cut-offs for assigning risk, we implicitly make judgments about how much accuracy of a particular type and how much error of a particular type we can accept. The fact of error in prediction bears emphasis because it is central to prediction efforts and because some accounts treat prediction as a science, as if using this description means that we can rest and accept whatever estimates emerge from our modeling.[64]

No prediction science exists, or likely ever will, that can perfectly identify who will go on to offend. More relevant, no science can determine what constitutes acceptable error rates. That ultimately involves political and moral judgments about the relative weight to be given to identifying a problem, failing to identify a problem, treating people who do not need treatment, and failing to treat people who need it. In addition, even our best prediction approaches do not provide any scientific basis for knowing *how* we should intervene to reduce the likelihood of offending. They at best serve as the equivalent of a good weather forecast, telling us when a storm may happen. Sometimes they might suggest which interventions might be effective. However, the decision about which types of approaches—among those that are equally effective—to select entails reference to political and moral considerations that go beyond the purview of science. Indeed, such normative judgments are inescapable. For example, the commission of a serious offense may lead corrections officials to categorize an individual as high risk even though the individual may be at little risk of offending.[65] Such decisions may arise from normative judgments about tolerable risks and error rates; these judgments fall outside the realm of science and, at best, can be informed by it.

Challenge 11: Recidivism Prediction Says Little About Intervention and Responsivity

The emergence of fourth-generation risk assessment approaches has highlighted the central importance of understanding how to change an individual's risk of offending. Even so, as developers of these approaches have highlighted, we know little about what interventions work best with particular individuals and how offender characteristics influence the effectiveness, or potential effectiveness, of different types of interventions.[66] That situation opens the door to what Edward Latessa and colleagues have referred to as "correctional quackery."[67]

Science may help us to identify at-risk individuals, but then provides less solid evidence about what interventions reduce recidivism for which individuals under which circumstances, what sometimes is referred to as "needs assessment."[68] What happens then? Personal beliefs about what works rule the day. States or local jurisdictions invest in a diverse range of intermediate sanctions—such as intensive supervision, day reporting centers, home detention and electronic monitoring, shock incarceration—that do not effectively reduce recidivism or that rest on strong claims and assumptions about the conditions necessary to reduce it.[69] Or, alternatively, they invest in "correctional quackery," such as programs that largely ignore well-established correlates or causes of offending and focus on one factor, such as self-esteem or creativity, typically with little credible empirical evidence to back the investment.

Challenge 12: It Remains Unclear Which Instruments or Approaches Are Best

Although some risk prediction instruments, such as the LSI-R, have been well evaluated, their improvement over many other instruments—and their relative effectiveness for certain populations and certain types of crimes—remain largely unknown.[70] This situation is problematic. We want the best risk prediction that we can possibly have, we want it at the least cost, and we want to be confident our predictions are as valid as possible, with the least amount of error, for the population under our charge. It is a tall order.

Consider potential gender differences in offending. Many risk prediction efforts fail to take into account the possibility that the factors that contribute to female recidivism may differ from those that contribute to male recidivism and that gender-responsive sanctions and interventions may be more effective than those that are not.[71] Accordingly, they likely create substantially more error than we might view as acceptable.

The situation, however, is complicated. Consider a Venn diagram in which we contrast the causes of crime among males with the causes of crime among females. There likely will be considerable overlap, as research suggests.[72] Thus, it can be argued that focusing primarily on a core set of risk factors and needs may be more efficient than targeting risks and needs that may be unique to males or females, respectively. Even so, differences in the causes of male offending and female offending, respectively, or in responsiveness to specific types of treatment, may be of a sufficient magnitude in some instances or areas to make gender-specific interventions the more cost-efficient approach to take.

Accuracy, feasibility, and efficiency are all critical. We want accurate instruments. However, we also want instruments and approaches that a given jurisdiction can implement with the resources at its disposal. We want, too, instruments and approaches that are cost-efficient. Not least, we want instruments and approaches that provide evidence-based direction for the types of interventions that could feasibly be adopted or used in a given locale. Although considerable advances in risk assessment have occurred in recent decades, the need remains for identifying approaches that work best for different groups and under different conditions.

APPROACHES TO IMPROVE RISK PREDICTION

Can risk prediction be improved? Absolutely. A starting point is for scholars, federal and state agencies, and practitioners to work together to address some of the challenges and limitations discussed in the previous section. Here, we highlight some of directions that, in our view, merit particular attention by these groups.

First, incorporate theory into all aspects of risk prediction. Many approaches to developing theory exist, and many theories of offending and treatment exist. They typically are not right or wrong but rather more useful or less useful. Reliance on theory does not preclude exploratory empiricist approaches to improving prediction. Its main virtue lies in its ability to help guide selection of potentially important predictors of recidivism *and* to assist in making sense of why or how a given factor may influence offending. That information in turn can be critical for improving the assignment of individuals to various types of supervision, interventions, services, or treatment. How, then, to proceed? Drawing on one or another theory will not suffice because we will be hamstrung in our ability to predict accurately. A simple solution, therefore, is to draw on the insights from a diverse set of criminological theories and to turn to integrated theories of crime for assistance. Such theories can be complicated, confusing, and incoherent. Even so, they lead us to focus more holistically on the causes of offending among inmate and ex-prisoner populations.

As a field, criminology and criminal justice can only stand to benefit from seeking more powerful and complete accounts of recidivism. In recent decades, considerable attention has turned to understanding the onset of and desistance from offending. Correctional system populations offer a uniquely helpful group from which to learn about desistance. Efforts to integrate improved risk assessment with theory development present an ideal opportunity to achieve both greater predictive accuracy and greater knowledge about the causes of offending. From a life-course theoretical perspective alone, there exist many opportunities to explore and understand potentially critical turning points and how they affect desistance among ex-prisoners.[73] Consider, for example, the opportunities to refine mainstream criminological theories. A life-course perspective would lead us to investigate how strains or social bonds may vary by type or effect over the life course, how they may interact with each other, how responsive they are to interventions, how prison itself may provide a positive or negative turning point, and so on. Similar possibilities can be explored with other theories and would provide grounds for informing risk prediction and advancing theory.[74]

Second, use consistent measures of risk factors and recidivism. Without such consistency, it will remain difficult to develop and compare risk prediction instruments on a systematic, large-scale basis that takes advantage of the lessons that can be learned by the approaches used in different places and organizations.

Third, develop a more comprehensive set of potential risk factors for recidivism. Risk prediction instruments and modeling efforts typically rely on a core set of factors and omit other critical ones. Fourth-generation instruments and approaches have improved this situation considerably, but many jurisdictions do not use them. Even when they do, there remains substantial room for improvement. For example, inclusion of information about community contexts to which ex-prisoners return as well as in-prison and postprison experiences constitutes a rich avenue along which to improve risk prediction.[75] Here, again, more systematic reliance on criminological theory constitutes a primary avenue for improving this situation.

Fourth, systematically explore and test for nonlinear effects of risk factors. At the extreme, two factors may have no direct effect on recidivism and yet the interaction between the two may exert a profound effect. A match by itself will not start a fire, and fuel alone will not result in a fire. The two together, however, can do so. The nature of the interaction needs not be that extreme. For example, it may be that a given factor (e.g., strain) amplifies the effect of another (e.g., self-control) and does so to a greater or lesser extent depending on the level of the other factor (in this example, self-control). Nonlinear relationships need not involve interactions. For example, they instead may consist of thresholds, such that a given factor (e.g., strain) does not exert a strong or appreciable effect until a certain tipping point. Regardless, prediction accuracy may be greatly improved by investigating potential nonlinear relationships. As we discuss in the next chapter, most inmates and ex-prisoners do not have just one risk factor that increases their risk of recidivism but rather multiple risk factors. Some of these may add up to contribute to increased recidivism. They may also interact in ways that substantially increase the likelihood of future offending.

Fifth, identify how experiences and changes in circumstances or conditions affect the risk of offending. As a general rule, most individuals have core characteristics and backgrounds that may push them in certain directions, but they also typically undergo experiences or are exposed to new or different contexts that may affect them. Risk prediction that systematically assesses prison experiences and post-release contexts and conditions holds considerable potential for greatly improving our ability to identify accurately those who will most likely go on to offend. The predictions we make can be enhanced further if we include real-time information about significant events or changes in the lives of those on supervision.[76]

Sixth, identify the criminogenic factors that, if changed, may most reduce recidivism. Fourth-generation risk assessment approaches have highlighted the salience of this issue.[77] Once we know that an individual has a given risk of offending, we then logically want to know what to do to most reduce that risk.[78] For example, low self-control may contribute more than other risk factors to a propensity to offend. However, we may find that we can achieve a larger reduction in the risk of offending by focusing not on self-control, which may be difficult to address, but rather by focusing on helping the individual to improve their decisions about finding housing, selecting the friends or family members who will be most supportive, and so on. Research has clearly shown that cognitive and behavioral approaches work most effectively, in general, to reduce offending. This finding constitutes a core foundation from which to proceed. However, as Alese Wooditch and her colleagues have emphasized, "the question of which dynamic criminogenic needs are important to fostering positive outcomes remains unanswered."[79] What remains to be developed, then, is a more precise science that can guide, on empirical grounds, the selection of interventions. This science almost assuredly will lead in the direction of identifying the need to target multiple risk factors given that most offending likely stems from multiple causal forces, not just one or two.[80]

Seventh, develop an inventory of the best risk prediction instruments and approaches for particular populations, crimes, and contexts. No one instrument or approach works best for assessing risk and identifying appropriate interventions. What is best will vary depending on the population involved, the types of offending upon which we are focused, and the organizational and community contexts that set constraints on possible assessment and intervention approaches. There are aspects of risk assessment, too, that entail normative judgments about acceptable levels of accuracy and error. These mean that no one instrument or approach can be best in all places at all times. Regardless, we need a much more robust and credible body of scholarship for determining the instruments and approaches that will work best under different conditions and in different settings.

Eighth, systematically include practitioner insights about offender risk. Clinical judgment stands as a poor substitute for actuarially based risk assessments. The more effective approach, however, appears to involve a combination of actuarial assessment and clinical judgment. This approach creates room for inconsistency. Nonetheless, clinicians may offer unique insights that can help to improve prediction. Practitioners, too, can provide critical insights. Correctional system personnel have considerable experience with inmates and may have a great deal of information about them that would be relevant to identifying not only risk factors but also those that could be changed. Consider, for example, parole officers. They may be aware of criminogenic family or community contexts for some ex-prisoners and what might be done to change these contexts or reduce their influence.

Ninth, align risk prediction carefully with intervention assignment. This idea is central to the fourth-generation RNR model.[81] Risk prediction efforts themselves do not offer inherent policy implications or actable strategies. They result in individuals being assigned a relative risk score. What do you do with someone who is high risk? A typical response would be to place him or her on intensive supervision. However, this approach does not inherently address the factors that make the person at risk of offending. Far more preferable is to identify factors that contribute to the risk and then to employ interventions that address these factors. That sounds easier than it is. Risk factors themselves tell us little about the mechanisms through which they produce offending. The problem confronts social scientists in general, not just those who undertake risk assessment and intervention assignment. As Robert Sampson and colleagues have argued about causal analysis, even after we carefully determine empirically that a given association seems to be real, we may not know precisely how a given factor contributes to an outcome or how to influence it.[82] The challenge then consists of developing a body of research that provides clear guidance about the relative costs and benefits of different types and dosages of interventions for certain types of offenders and populations.

Tenth, prioritize high-risk offenders but do not ignore low-risk offenders. Research increasingly suggests that interventions can be more effective with high-risk offenders.[83] It also suggests that interventions with low-risk offenders may do little or even be harmful. However, the fact of being at risk of offending at all signals that an opportunity exists to avoid continued or escalated offending. We do not want to invest large amounts of resources for small gains, which is why the focus on high-risk individuals makes sense. Yet this type of thinking ignores the fact, as Nate Silver and others have highlighted, that risk prediction is inherently probabilistic—we estimate with some degree of confidence that an individual has between X and Y percent of reoffending.[84] As soon as we open the door to probability ranges, we realize that many individuals may reside in the moderate to high risk zone. We would not want to restrict our focus in these cases purely to the individuals with probabilities exclusively in whatever zone we viewed as high risk.

At the same time, a failure to intervene early with low-risk individuals means that we allow potentially avoidable crime to occur. That in fact constitutes the overriding logic of the juvenile justice system: intervene early and so avoid a situation where a youth becomes a chronic or serious offender.[85] The medical axiom "Do no harm" serves as a useful guide, whether in criminal justice, juvenile justice, or any other policy arena. That is, we should refrain from intervening unless we are confident that, at the least, we will not worsen the likelihood of offending. However, if we can intervene effectively, we should do so. A safe approach might be to emphasize low-cost interventions where little risk exists for worsening outcomes. Given that over three-fifths of individuals recidivate within 5 years of release from prison, we ideally would have individualized supervision and intervention plans for all ex-prisoners (and felons as well), an idea that we elaborate on in the next chapter. The effectiveness of such an approach, however, requires carefully calibrated, evidence-based risk assessment and assignment to appropriate sanctions and interventions.

Finally, develop guidelines that clearly explain risk prediction trade-offs—that is, the costs and benefits of using different thresholds for classifying individuals into different risk levels. Risk prediction is complicated, and it is not all science. Normative judgments must be made. Substantial error is involved. Room for confusion about which instruments to use and about instrument accuracy is great. Practitioners, as well as many scholars, can be prone to say an instrument is valid and that it accurately identifies recidivists. Such statements are wrong. Instruments always entail some level of accuracy and error. The same holds true of virtually any prediction or forecast and should be articulated.[86] A validated instrument may predict recidivism better than would occur by chance. That, however, does not mean the predictions it makes are highly accurate; and, again, even a high degree of accuracy still would entail significant error. Ultimately, for risk assessment to be helpful, those who use it should understand the strengths and limitations of the approaches that they use.

SHIFTING THE FOCUS OF RISK PREDICTION

Having discussed benefits and challenges associated with predicting which individuals are most likely to recidivate, we now shift gears to argue for broadening the notion of risk prediction in two ways. The first is to include a focus on outcomes other than recidivism. The second is more radical and consists of turning the focus of risk prediction to the organizational units that comprise the criminal justice system. Such a shift leads to a focus not on individuals and the relatively small gains that come from individual-focused interventions but rather on organizations and the larger gains that accrue from improving their decision making.[87]

Predicting Additional Outcomes Besides Recidivism

Consistent with the arguments that we have presented throughout the book and that we expand upon in the next two chapters, risk prediction ideally should involve a focus on more than recidivism narrowly defined. For example, it should include a focus on the likelihood of released prisoners—or convicted felons in general—obtaining housing and gainful employment and seeking or continuing mental health or drug treatment. Individuals who become homeless or unemployed or who live with untreated mental illness or drug addiction face and create many problems. Avoidable homelessness, unemployment, mental illness, or drug problems lead to more misery for the individuals and they simultaneously lead to more costs for society.

If we systematically assessed convicted felons or ex-prisoners for their risk of these different outcomes, we would be positioned to identify interventions that could lead to improvements in a broader array of outcomes. This more public health-focused approach comes with a significant downside of complicating the operations and costs of the criminal justice system. However, it carries with it the upside of potentially improving a wider array of outcomes, including crime and recidivism, at less cost.

Predicting System and Program Performance

The bulk of risk prediction efforts proceed from the premise that if we accurately identify the likelihood of offending and reduce it 10 or 20 percent, society will be substantially safer. If we could undertake such efforts systemwide, state by state, that in fact might be the end result. However, there exists no national system for monitoring how well entire state correctional systems or local courts and jails undertake risk assessment and intervention. Accordingly, we know only that some jurisdictions implement effective risk assessment instruments and approaches some of the time. The system gets a free pass.

One way to proceed, then, is not, in fact, to center our efforts on convicted felons and ex-prisoner risk assessment but rather to focus them on the performance of different parts of the criminal justice and correctional systems. The bulk of crime policy over the prior three decades has emphasized individual-focused responses to crime. Exceptions such as community-oriented policing exist. By and large, however, policy makers have focused on offenders, with a primary emphasis on incarcerating them. Risk prediction in criminal justice typically takes this logic the next step forward to identify individuals who may go on to commit crime. Practitioners then can use supervision and management strategies, treatment, assistance, or the like with these individuals. Such efforts make sense. They are good policy.

However, they lead us to focus on individuals and not on the organizations and systems that comprise the criminal justice and correctional systems or the many programs and interventions that they use to reduce recidivism. What if—in addition to typical risk prediction approaches—we applied risk prediction to these systems or organizations or programs that aim to reduce recidivism? The benefits of this approach would be considerable. For example, by identifying those programs with the highest likelihood of reducing recidivism among participants, we would know which programs to prioritize. By identifying parts of the correctional system that have the highest likelihood of contributing to reduced recidivism, we would know which parts merit support, change, or oversight.

Any such endeavor would carry with it substantial error. Ineffective programs might be classified as likely to be effective (false positives). Effective programs might be misclassified as likely to be ineffective (false negatives). Similarly, effective units within correctional systems might be classified as likely to be effective (more false positives) while others that are ineffective might be misclassified as effective (more false negatives). These errors, of course, constitute the very types of errors that can arise with predicting recidivism risk among individuals. In both cases, we seek to minimize such errors while seeking the higher good of allocating resources in ways that improve societal outcomes at the least cost.

How might risk prediction of criminal justice or correctional system organizations, systems, or programs occur? The large literature on performance monitoring provides guidance.[88] With individual-based risk prediction, we typically draw on theory and prior research to identify factors that may be associated with, or help us to predict, future offending. It is a combination of theory, logic, and empirical analysis that guides our efforts. A similar approach can be taken with organizations. We identify characteristics of, say, effective parole supervision units, we draw on empirical research on characteristics of effective units, we identify those that rely more on evidence-based practices, and we use this information to guide the development of a risk prediction model. We then collect data on these characteristics for parole units nationally or in a given state and we assess whether the characteristics indeed predict accurately those units with the lowest percentage of parolees recidivating. As with any evaluation effort, we want to adjust for differences in the types of individuals on parolee caseloads and other potential confounding factors. In the end, though, we should be able to identify units that perform well—that have low rates of parolee recidivism—and those that do not.

At that point, we would face the same dilemma that is faced with risk prediction involving ex-prisoners. That is, now that we have identified the units that seem likely to perform poorly, what do we do? With ex-prisoners, a weak response simply is to throw additional supervision and possibly a medley of services at them. A stronger response would be to identify specific factors that contribute to a particular individual's increased risk of recidivism.

In parallel fashion, we could do the same with organizations. We could simply penalize poor-performing units. That is a commonly used approach that one finds in many social policy arenas, such as education. Poorly performing schools, for example, might receive less funding. The logic involves an assumption that such schools then will be motivated to perform better in the future—the carrot of increased funding or support will engender better performance and the stick of withdrawn funding or support will deter worsening performance. A stronger response would be to identify what precisely causes poor performance at a particular parole unit and target interventions at these causal factors. Perhaps parole officer caseloads greatly exceed appropriate levels. Perhaps parole officer morale is poor. Perhaps the unit relies too heavily on inexperienced officers. These and many other possibilities exist, which is why an intervention that targets the unique causes of a unit's predicted performance would be more effective than a general strategy, such as reducing funding.

Such an approach may seem imminently sensible, yet it is not widely used. Consider, again, parole. An Urban Institute study by Jesse Jannetta and Aaron Horvath found that in most states, parole offices did not know if their agency monitored recidivism of current or former parolees.[89] The authors of the study concluded: "This suggests that recidivism is not a key outcome for assessing field office performance in many states."[90] In addition, they found that a central dimension of effective parole practice was not widely used: "Approaches to enhance parolee motivation and engage the parolee's pro-social supports are not common practice in many states." Specifically, "responses indicate that involving parolees in setting supervision goals, using motivational interviewing, and engaging significant others in the parolee's life were occurring less than half the time in the majority of states included in this analysis."[91]

Here, then, we can see one of the central, and odd, tensions in crime policy. On the one hand, we emphasize risk prediction for individual felons and ex-prisoners, and we do so in the belief that it will help us to intervene and reduce their recidivism. On the other hand, we ignore risk prediction of the organizations responsible for supervising and intervening with these same individuals. The disjuncture stands out because better risk prediction of which agencies likely will perform well and which will not would provide an opportunity to create larger reductions in recidivism. Improvements in just a handful of large parole agencies (or prisons or reentry programs) would produce aggregate gains in reduced recidivism that might easily exceed what would occur if we prioritized intensive supervision of a small number of individuals. In this example, we have focused on parole offices and agencies, but one might as easily focus on other dimensions of the correctional system, including prisons and various reentry programs. If we applied risk prediction approaches systemwide, the gains might well be substantially greater. If we applied them to communities, we might produce even more sizable gains.

CONCLUSION

The machinery of criminal justice begins with the commission of a crime. Not surprisingly, then, we expect this machinery ultimately to make society safer by reducing the recidivism of those who are convicted and sentenced. The concern about prisoner reentry in recent decades has led to increased attention to recidivism, both because of the dramatic increase in the numbers of people sent to prison and because of the high likelihood that they will commit more crime.

Fortunately, a robust body of research has developed that helps us to identify who is most likely to offend and what can be done to reduce it. We have a long way to go, however.[92] Current risk prediction practices nationwide are not well monitored, many jurisdictions rely on unvalidated risk assessment instruments, many that use validated instruments may not use the resulting information to determine which individuals receive various interventions, and even the best instruments and approaches result in considerable error.[93] They identify individuals as being at risk when the individuals in fact may be unlikely to recidivate, and they also identify individuals as not being at risk when the individuals in fact pose a very real threat to society. The benefits of risk assessment should not be understated, but neither should the limitations. Indeed, the challenges to effective risk assessment, as well as to the effective use of its results, underscore the need for considerable caution when undertaking risk prediction and, in turn, assigning individuals to risk groups and particular sanctions or interventions.

In media accounts, one sometimes reads about policy makers or corrections officials who embrace risk prediction. They utter statements such as, "We have the ability to identify with a high degree of accuracy those who will commit crime." We do not have that ability. No one does. Instead, we have the ability to make relatively accurate predictions that entail error. Whether the error is acceptable constitutes a judgment call, one that various jurisdictions will make differently. For risk prediction to be helpful, it is essential that those in positions of power fully understand the benefits and the limits of risk prediction. It is essential, too, that a number of steps be pursued to improve the accuracy and usefulness of risk prediction. Fortunately, again, cause for optimism exists given that these steps can be taken and, indeed, many jurisdictions and states have begun to do so.

One reason a focus on risk prediction can help improve the criminal justice system, and, no less, prisoner reentry, is that it can lead us to examine more carefully the logic of our crime responses. The best illustration of this perhaps can be seen in the use of intensive supervision for high-risk offenders. Little credible empirical research exists to suggest that intensive supervision itself does much to reduce recidivism. Indeed, why would it? Supervision alone does not address most of the major causes of offending. Yet it has tended to be the policy avenue of choice (when considering alternatives to prison) rather than widespread investment in the types of cognitive-behavioral programs that can more substantially reduce offending.[94] Indeed, this same policy thinking underlies the growth in incarceration—to reduce crime, we need only put people away in prison for long periods of time, even though incarceration itself does little to address the causes of crime that criminological theory and research have identified.[95] That is not to say that incarceration fails to serve retributive goals or possibly general deterrence goals. It might. But as a tool for reducing offending, it appears to do little.

A focus on risk prediction is useful for still another reason. It highlights that we can use recidivism—and other outcomes, such as housing, employment, mental illness, and substance abuse—to gauge how well different parts of the criminal justice and correctional system work. For example, if we turn our focus from individual offenders and to the systems that manage them, we can see that substantial improvements in recidivism might be had by monitoring the performance of these systems. Prisons and parole agencies or units could be graded on the percentages of their inmates or caseloads, respectively, who go on to recidivate. In turn, we could shift our focus from an exclusive emphasis on estimation of ex-prisoner recidivism and to the reasons why some prisons or parole agencies and units have lower recidivism rates. In short, we could undertake risk assessment of prisons and parole agencies, identify those at risk of creating more recidivism (or failing to reduce it), and intervene. This approach would accord with calls for greater government accountability and have the added benefit of producing larger aggregate reductions in recidivism than otherwise could occur.

Let us return, finally, to several of the book's goals and tie them to the focus on recidivism. First, we have argued that diverse perspectives can help us to understand and improve reentry. One such perspective is that reentry processes build on inmate backgrounds and in-prison experiences that may directly affect recidivism. The processes occur in family and community contexts that may influence recidivism. Improved risk prediction can come from incorporating such information. It can come, too, from modeling dynamic changes that occur in individuals during and after incarceration. In short, if we embrace the goal of improved recidivism prediction, we necessarily are led to more insight into the causes of and solutions to offending.

Second, we have argued that effective reentry policy requires addressing the broad range of factors that contribute to offending. Here, again, risk prediction leads us in that direction. Newer, so-called fourth-generation risk assessment approaches in particular do so. They emphasize consideration of static and dynamic factors and, just as importantly, assessment of treatment needs and identification of how best to match particular individuals to the interventions that will most effectively promote desistance.

Third, we have argued that better insight into reentry entails looking beyond prisoners. Here, again, risk prediction can lead us to appreciate that the return to society involves a return to family and community contexts that may increase offending. It also, in turn, can lead us to appreciate that recidivism occurs in context—it occurs among particular groups, in particular families, and in particular communities. Accordingly, we can see that the burden of recidivism falls more on certain groups, families, and communities. If we want to improve society, then we likely need to improve reentry outcomes for ex-prisoners and target resources toward the groups, families, and communities most affected by those who enter and leave prison. We also need to improve our risk prediction efforts for communities. If we can identify which communities will experience increased crime rates, and if we can identify the factors that contribute to them, we have the opportunity to intervene. We then can stem the tide of crime and reduce the need for imposing sanctions and dealing with the complicated question of how best to improve reentry.

Fourth, we have argued that scholarly and practitioner insights can be essential for advancing reentry policy and the understanding of reentry. Risk prediction efforts to date have been largely atheoretical and ignored large swaths of relevant criminological research. The tide is changing—newer instruments and assessment approaches build on extant theory and research. Even so, the room for improvement remains. In addition, there is considerable room for building on the experiences and insights of those who work in the correctional system. Risk assessment can seem to be the purview of trained clinicians and experts. Yet, those who work every day with inmate and parolee populations have significant insight into the lives of inmates and ex-prisoners. This insight could inform risk prediction substantially.

Finally, we have argued that many approaches can be used to improve reentry. Here, again, risk prediction is illustrative. If we increase the accuracy of our risk prediction efforts and tailor our sanctions and interventions accordingly, we have a greater chance of reducing recidivism. In turn, we have less of a need to resort to incarceration as a solution to crime.

DISCUSSION QUESTIONS

1. Why are recidivism rates of prisoners so high?

2. Which approaches to risk prediction likely best improve correctional system decision making about the risk that convicted felons present?

3. How do actuarial approaches to risk prediction improve over clinical (human) judgment?

4. What are some of the challenges associated with recidivism risk prediction?

5. What are productive ways to improve recidivism risk prediction?

6. How might criminological theory and risk prediction accuracy improve by incorporating theory more systematically into risk prediction efforts?

7. What benefits might come from expanding correctional system risk prediction to include a focus on noncrime outcomes (e.g., homelessness and unemployment)? Under what conditions would these benefits outweigh the costs?

8. What benefits might come from expanding risk prediction efforts to focus on correctional system agency performance? How might such a focus create potentially greater reductions in recidivism than efforts to focus risk prediction exclusively on felons and inmates?

CHAPTER 8

Diverse Inmate Populations and Reentry

In the media, criminals tend to be portrayed in similar ways, and the portrayals tend to be inaccurate.[1] Movies and television shows in particular depict hardened offenders who repeatedly engage in criminal activity. These offenders lack a moral compass. They brutally assault others with impunity and without remorse. More often than not, males—black males in particular—hold center stage. Frequently, too, they display remarkable intelligence and plan their crimes with care and diligence. In short, a highly distorted and typically incorrect picture emerges, one that likely fuels public concerns about crime.

It is, for example, one thing to be confronted with the image of a remorseless serial killer who repeatedly escapes capture. It is another to be confronted with someone who falls well below the national average on intelligence tests, is impulsive and so likely did not plan his or her crime or did not do so with much care, and engages in a wide variety of crimes, typically of low severity. The latter image accords much more with the reality of everyday crime.[2] The former might lead reasonable people to conclude that we can do nothing about crime except to lock up offenders for as long as humanly possible. From this perspective, no change can occur in individuals, and yet, at the same time, individuals should be held responsible for their conduct. From this perspective, too, no social forces or sociological conditions matter. Instead, incapacitation and retribution should carry the day. We should not bother investing in interventions because they will do little to nothing to change the criminal.

The problem with this approach? Its assumptions run counter to reality. It also contributes to inefficient, one-size-fits-all policy making that may result in more victimization and missed opportunities to improve public safety. Ironically and unfortunately, it also may do little to make the public feel that sufficient retribution occurs.

In fact, inmates vary greatly along many dimensions, as we discussed in Chapter 4. Some of these differences may be inconsequential for understanding the behavior of individuals during and after reentry. Others, however, may be quite consequential. They may contribute to misconduct and recidivism; they may adversely affect or be associated with inmate physical or psychological health; they may affect how inmates respond to the prison experience; they may affect programming needs; and they may adversely affect reentry outcomes as well as the families and communities to which ex-prisoners return. Some inmates, such as those placed in supermax confinement, do not just constitute a select group. They have experiences that distinguish them from many other inmates and that may have direct implications for their behavior during and after prison.

To advance the argument that a focus on inmate or ex-prisoner groups matters and the book's broader set of objectives, this chapter builds on the discussion in Chapter 4 of the inmate profile. In so doing, we highlight that inmates consist of diverse *groups*. Diversity aptly characterizes the ex-prisoner population. These individuals differ on many dimensions, much as the "typical" American citizen does. It may not be realistic to anticipate that prison systems and reentry approaches treat every inmate differently. Punishment, management, and assistance or treatment that varies for each and every individual is not possible, cost-efficient, or necessary. At the same time, failing to take account of critical differences among those who enter and leave prison constitutes a recipe for correctional system ineffectiveness and inefficiency. It also risks putting communities at risk of harm through increased crime and social disadvantage.

Below, we discuss why the diversity of the inmate and ex-prisoner population matters. We discuss, too, why the use of different perspectives to understand reentry can help shed light on the complexity and challenges of mass reentry. We then focus on three demographic groups in detail: the young, females, and minorities. The accounts of these groups is followed by a brief discussion of supermax security inmates, drug-abusers, the mentally ill or learning disabled, and other groups. To examine every divide along which to classify inmates would require an entire book or, really, several books.[3] Accordingly, we have a more modest goal: to underscore the importance of attending to group differences if we wish to understand reentry, improve it, and, ultimately, make society safer.

After presenting this argument, we turn it on its head. That is, we reverse course and present the more provocative idea that in fact individualized sanctioning and treatment ultimately may be the most effective and efficient approach to achieving justice and promoting public safety. This argument derives from the observation that most individuals who enter and leave prison have multiple problems and face multiple challenges. They may even be members of several of the different inmate groups that we highlight. Accordingly, any substantial improvement in reentry outcomes arguably requires a multifaceted approach, not one that emphasizes a particular characteristic or group. The scale of mass incarceration may largely preclude such an approach on a mass scale. That, however, reinforces a central point—as the country goes forward, it would do best to invest in an approach to sanctioning and intervention that most effectively and efficiently achieves correctional system goals. A first step in that direction consists of avoiding costly investments that have few demonstrable benefits and that lock us into more of the same.

THE DIVERSITY OF THE INMATE AND EX-PRISONER POPULATION AND WHY IT MATTERS

A Focus on Diverse Groups

In Chapter 4, we argued that inmate characteristics matter because they can be used by correctional systems to achieve several goals. In particular, the characteristics can be used (a) to assist with forecasting prison and parole capacity needs, (b) to identify and forecast prisoner treatment and service needs, (c) to identify and forecast prison management challenges, (d) to identify, monitor, and address inequality among inmates and ex-prisoners, and (e) to identify and forecast ex-prisoner supervision and reentry needs. Collectively, improvements on each of these fronts can enable correctional systems to operate more efficiently, to reduce recidivism, and to improve a range of reentry outcomes, including housing, employment, and mental health.

Here, we take a different tack and focus on inmate—and by extension, reentry—*groups*. Doing so reinforces the argument in Chapter 4. However, it does so not by considering a range of individual characteristics but rather by focusing on social groups and what makes them unique. Put differently, whereas Chapter 4 is more "characteristics" focused, this chapter is more "group" focused. The two approaches constitute complementary strategies for illuminating variation among the individuals who leave prison and the potential consequences of such variation. One key difference that a group-based focus highlights is the fact that we likely need to think about clusters of characteristics if we want to achieve correctional system goals more effectively and efficiently. When we consider groups, that idea more immediately surfaces. Groups share a number of characteristics. So, it makes sense that interventions should address the set of characteristics, not just one or another of them. This idea accords with what David Farrington and Brandon Welsh have referred to as the "blunderbuss approach."[4] Since we cannot know fully what contributes to an individual's behavior, and because many factors likely matter, we should consider targeting as many of them as we can.

We can think of any given inmate or ex-prisoner characteristic as a foundation for identifying a group. For example, age frequently is presented in studies as a demographic characteristic of individuals. Researchers may use it as a predictor of some outcome, such as misconduct or recidivism. When viewed as a characteristic, age simply constitutes but one of many other features of an individual that somehow together—without any clear theoretical rationale—tells us something about an individual's likelihood of engaging in some behavior. Consider, for example, that age negatively correlates with prison misconduct. Young people engage in more rule violations and violent behavior than do older people in prison. Why? We might speculate about a wealth of reasons, but in and of itself age reveals little.

By contrast, when we consider age as a basis for identifying a group, such as the young or old, we may be led to identify an array of factors that cluster together. For example, young people on average may have less education and a weak employment record, and may have less self-control or good judgment, than older individuals. We then have a more coherent foundation on which to understand how an individual may behave in prison or how well they will do when released back into communities. In addition, we are led to appreciate that interventions or supervision efforts likely need to focus on multiple dimensions, such as education, employment, and self-control or the development of better judgment.

Why a Focus on Groups Is Helpful

Against that backdrop, then, we use the book's five goals, or arguments—presented in Figure 8.1—to frame our discussion of several demographic groups. This approach allows us to highlight important differences among the groups and to ground our arguments in a way that complements and builds on the earlier discussions. To recapitulate, we argue that a variety of perspectives are needed to understand reentry better (goal 1), improving reentry requires insight into the diverse set of factors that cause offending and recidivism (goal 2), reentry has ripple effects on more than just the individuals released from prison (goal 3), insights from practitioners and scholars can greatly improve our understanding of reentry and how to improve punishment policies and public safety (goal 4), and diverse policy possibilities exist for improving reentry and, more broadly, criminal justice (goal 5).

Why does a focus on different inmate and ex-prisoner groups matter? First, it matters for the same reasons identified in Chapter 4—doing so can help correctional systems achieve their goals. For example, with a better understanding of rates of admission of young people into prison, corrections officials can better anticipate prison bed space need and parole capacity needs, treatment needs, prison management challenges, potential inequalities that may confront this group, and reentry supervision and reentry needs.

Second, it matters for legal or moral reasons. For example, juveniles must be provided educational opportunities, mentally ill inmates must be provided with treatment for their illness, prisons must abide by certain protocols to determine

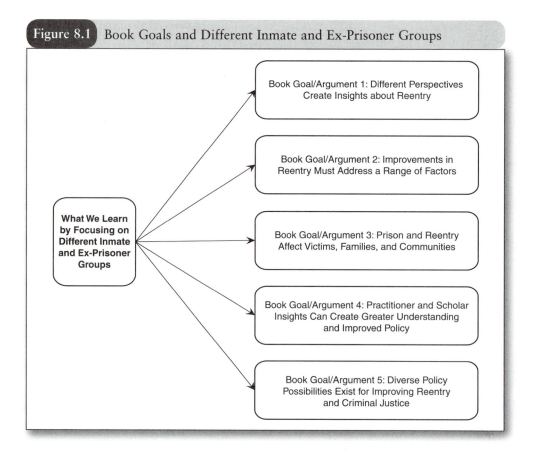

Figure 8.1   Book Goals and Different Inmate and Ex-Prisoner Groups

What We Learn by Focusing on Different Inmate and Ex-Prisoner Groups

Book Goal/Argument 1: Different Perspectives Create Insights about Reentry

Book Goal/Argument 2: Improvements in Reentry Must Address a Range of Factors

Book Goal/Argument 3: Prison and Reentry Affect Victims, Families, and Communities

Book Goal/Argument 4: Practitioner and Scholar Insights Can Create Greater Understanding and Improved Policy

Book Goal/Argument 5: Diverse Policy Possibilities Exist for Improving Reentry and Criminal Justice who can be placed and retained in supermax confinement, and so on. The law is, however, one thing, and moral considerations are another. Reasonably people may disagree about whether society has a moral obligation to address specific needs or challenges that some groups face. Younger prisoners, for example, typically face a greater risk of victimization.[5] Does that fact require morally that we take action? Arguably, yes. Similarly, what if, as some research suggests, supermax incarceration induces mental illness in some individuals?[6] Should supermax housing be terminated? Some would respond affirmatively, and others not. By focusing on different inmate groups, we draw attention to these questions and the importance of answering them.

Third, as emphasized above, a group-based approach enables us to highlight that any given individual does not consist of just one characteristic or another but rather clusters of them; policies that fail to take this fact into consideration are unlikely to succeed or are likely to be less effective than they otherwise could be. For example, mentally ill inmates may also have drug abuse problems and a limited network of social support. These factors together reduce the likelihood of a successful transition back into society and in turn point to the need for a reentry plan that considers all of these dimensions.

Fourth, and building on this last observation, a focus on groups of inmates and ex-prisoners allows us to zero in on a tension that confronts not only reentry but also punishment and criminal justice intervention policies more broadly. This tension centers on two needs. First, there is the need for generic policies or approaches that can be used efficiently with large numbers of individuals, such as those who are convicted of crimes, those who go to prison, and those who leave prison and return to society. Second, there is the need for and the importance of individualized or specialized policies or approaches that may be more effective with some groups.

The tension between generic and specialized approaches can be seen in many aspects of the criminal justice system. Punishment policies, for example, typically confront real-world case processing pressures that require courts to make processing and sanctioning decisions rapidly. Necessarily, generic, one-size-fits-all sanctioning has to occur to accommodate these pressures. This approach can be seen in sentencing guidelines, whereby the type of offense, prior record, presence of a gun, and other such factors dictate a particular sentence length for those sent to prison. As with mass production of any kind, efficiencies can flow from large-scale routinized operations. They enable the system to move so that cases are decided and moved off the court docket.

With this approach, however, we risk missing the mark with many individuals. A parallel issue can be found in education. Core curriculums have many virtues, which include the provision of a coherent education for many youth. However, they fall short with youth who lie far away from the mean. Gifted youth, for example, tend to be bored by assignments that fall well below their academic abilities, and youth who struggle in certain areas become frustrated when the assignments greatly exceed their abilities. Ideally, instruction is differentiated to ensure that academic challenges match a student's development, ability, and learning style.[7]

A similar scenario confronts us when we consider correctional interventions. Ideally, the interventions take into account the specific risks and needs and treatment responsivity of a given individual.[8] Such an approach creates the possibility of improved intervention effectiveness. But it can entail increased costs, including the need to develop the infrastructure to assess differences, to identify what works for specific individuals, and to ensure that an intervention is well implemented for each individual.

For these reasons and more, then, any individualized approach to sanctioning, managing inmates, or supervising and assisting individuals during reentry runs directly counter to system goals of efficiently processing, sanctioning, and managing large numbers of individuals. This tension cannot readily be resolved except through two approaches. First, reduce caseload pressures. Second, increase expenditures on staffing and the resources necessary to individualize the sanctioning, supervision, and treatment of those who enter our courts and are sanctioned.[9] A third possibility actually exists—generate information about when exactly the relative costs and benefits of individualized approaches to sanctioning individuals, or to managing and treating them during and after incarceration, yield greater returns than generic approaches to doing so. Here, then, empirically based evidence guides us in deciding how to proceed.

We do not pretend to have a solution to this tension, in part because it confronts almost any large organization. Our focus rather is to advance the objectives described above—these include highlighting how a focus on groups may be needed to help correctional systems achieve their goals and, at the same time, highlighting the existence of this tension and the need to address it. As we discuss in the conclusion, part of the challenge in creating more effective and efficient policy lies in developing the research infrastructure to determine empirically which approaches work best for which groups and do so most cost-efficiently. What is best does not have to be policies that most effectively produce intended outcomes. Rather, from this perspective, the best approach consists of one that produces the most improvement at the least cost. It may well be, for example, that generic reentry policies may be more cost-efficient in the long-run than more effective, but also more costly, individualized policies. Implicitly, the assumption underlying mass incarceration policies accords with that reasoning. It may be correct. However, as we discuss below, more than ample grounds exist to anticipate that generic may not always be best. In some cases, group-based approaches to achieving correctional system goals and helping the communities to which ex-prisoners return may be more effective and cost-efficient. Better yet may be approaches that individualize sanctioning and interventions for all people who enter our nation's criminal justice system.

THE YOUNGEST EX-PRISONERS

Nationally, approximately one-fourth of inmates are 25 years old or younger and 10–20 percent are 50 or older.[10] The precise percentages vary over time and among states. Regardless, by focusing on the two ends of the age spectrum, we can readily zero in on differences that may be relevant to understanding in-prison and post-release experiences and behavior. For example, a large body of scholarship highlights that youth continue developing along a range of dimensions—physically, psychologically, emotionally, cognitively, socially—well into their early 20s.[11] Their greater impulsivity and susceptibility to peer influence, as well as their lesser ability to delay gratification and hold a more future-focused orientation to completing tasks, do not automatically cease when they enter prison at a young age.[12] At the same time, we know that older inmates differ as well. They have more medical needs, are less likely to reoffend, and have a work history that may enhance their prospects for employment upon release relative to that of younger ex-prisoners.[13] Beyond these broad generalizations, why might we care about these or other age differences among inmates and ex-prisoners? To address that question, we examine age through the prism of the book's five main arguments and focus in particular on the youngest individuals who go to and leave prison.

Book Goal 1: The Argument That Diverse Perspectives Matter. We argue that diverse perspectives matter for understanding reentry and for identifying ways to improve outcomes among released prisoners. A focus on juveniles illustrates why. In the United States, as in many countries, a relatively arbitrary divide exists between the juvenile and adult justice systems. This divide in part stems from a belief that young people are less culpable for their behavior and deserve a second chance in life.[14] Juvenile justice tends to emphasize rehabilitation and reliance on a wide panoply of sanctions, interventions, and treatment, as well as diversion, whereas adult justice tends to emphasize punishment and reliance on probation and prison.

The divide is striking because it illuminates the fact that society structures its responses to crime in different ways that reflect cultural and philosophical views about adulthood. It is striking, too, because, as Travis Hirschi and Michael Gottfredson have argued, little evidence exists to support a fundamentally different approach to sanctioning the two groups.[15] Indeed, in 1993, they argued that the juvenile justice approach to sanctioning likely constitutes the most effective approach, one that would work equally well with adults. This argument held special salience because it surfaced at a time in which the juvenile justice system became more criminal-like in orientation.[16] They reasoned that scholarship pointed to the importance of structuring criminal justice responses to criminal behavior in ways that more nearly mirror that of juvenile justice, not the other way around. Drawing on theory and research on the causes of offending as well as studies on the effectiveness of various interventions among juveniles and adults, they arrived at the conclusion that adult offenders are as likely to benefit from rehabilitation as are juveniles. They argued that adults are as amenable and responsive to change as well.

If we accept this argument, then the approach to reentry should be modified to accord more with how the juvenile justice system operates. Doing so would be costly, of course, but such costs might be offset by following the juvenile court's emphasis on non-incarcerative sanctions. If we do not accept this argument, then a more modest adjustment would be to create the equivalent of a third justice system for young adults. This system would serve those who are not quite juveniles but not quite adults either. The approach would not require creating an entire separate system of laws or agencies, though it could. Instead, it could involve incorporating more of a juvenile justice philosophy within the correctional system, especially for younger inmates and ex-prisoners. For example, 20-year-olds might be targeted more so than older inmates for rehabilitative interventions and support services upon release.

Here, then, we can see that a historical perspective on the punishment and treatment of juveniles versus young adults leads to a different way of thinking about reentry. It is not just that the approach to preparing young adults for incarceration and how to manage the pains of imprisonment likely should differ. It is that we are led to think differently about our entire approach to punishment and treatment of those who violate the law. Other perspectives, such as those that follow, may lead us as well to question whether current approaches constitute the best ones for improving inmate and ex-prisoner behavior.

Book Goal 2: The Argument That Diverse Causes of Offending Matter. Few studies provide clear evidence that the causes of offending vary systematically across groups. Even so, many studies indicate that some causes may be more prevalent in some groups. For example, individuals in their late teenage years and early 20s tend to be more impulsive than adults. In addition, younger people tend to rely on their parents more. In this sense, the social support or bonds that parents provide (or fail to provide) may constitute a unique cause of offending for younger inmates and ex-prisoners. That said, it may not be clear which causes of offending apply to a given inmate or may be the most important.

When we think about young adults, such as those in the 18–25 year-old range, what seems likely? First, as Rolf Loeber and David Farrington and colleagues have observed, we lack sufficient empirical research to state with confidence how individuals in this age range differ.[17] A large body of scholarship on the causes of offending has focused primarily on adolescents. By contrast, scholarship on prisons and recidivism tends to focus either on the juvenile justice system or the adult justice system. We know that younger adults in prison rely more than older inmates on their parents and family, their psychosocial development lags behind that of older inmates, their experience in the workforce is limited, and they have less familiarity with how to live independently.[18] We know, too, that younger inmates tend to experience more victimization than do older inmates.[19] Those with prior juvenile justice system involvement tend to perceive the adult system as considerably more unfair and uncaring than what they experienced in the juvenile justice system.[20] We know that upon release, younger people may be more likely to rely on parents, to be susceptible to peer influence, and to be impulsive. Collectively, such considerations suggest that younger inmates may be led to offending through different causal mechanisms than those that hold for older inmates. They suggest, too, that they experience prison and reentry differently from that of older inmates and return to different social contexts.

Book Goal 3: The Argument That Diverse Impacts on Groups and Others Matter. Discussions of reentry frequently center primarily on ex-prisoners and recidivism. However, reentry arguably affects other groups and has a broader range of effects than this emphasis indicates. Most inmates have family members and friends who may be affected by their incarceration. That is not difficult to appreciate, but it perhaps is easier to do so when we focus on the very young in prison. For example, an 18-year-old in prison may have been living with his or her parents. Incarceration largely precludes much if any contact with family. The emotional effect of incarceration on the 18-year-old may be greater than for older inmates. It also may be greater, too, for his or her parents compared to that of what older inmates' parents experience.

Scholarship establishes that the characteristics of victims typically mirror that of offenders. From a community perspective, then, we might well be more concerned about older juveniles and younger adults in the community and the effects of ex-prisoners on them. Younger ex-prisoners will be more likely to recidivate, as compared to older ex-prisoners. They also will be more likely to rely on and embed themselves with a group of peers. Put differently, prisons nationally release a group of individuals, young adults, who may exert an especially harmful effect on the communities to which they return. Despite the potential for such adverse effects, young people have not been prioritized in reentry efforts.

Book Goal 4: The Argument That Practitioner and Scholar Insights Matter. One of the central arguments that we have sought to make is that practitioners' and scholars' insights should be better integrated into policy making and implementation. How might this idea be evident in a focus on young people? A point of departure is to consider, again, the juvenile justice system. One of us (Daniel) worked in a residential center typical of many that exist to confine juvenile offenders. The young people at the center had a constellation of risk factors that interacted with one another, including a history of abuse and neglect, violence, limited education, mental illness, and limited life skills. This insight affected how staff worked with each youth and it led to a multifaceted approach to helping them.

If a study of the center had been undertaken, it certainly is conceivable that the center might not have been found to be effective or that the benefits failed to outweigh the costs. Regardless, the approach routinized into juvenile justice system practices—which can include oversight of youth confined as juveniles and held in youth facilities until age 21 or 22—consists of a multifaceted approach. Why? Juvenile justice interventions proceed from the assumption that doing so constitutes a more effective way of reducing recidivism and improving a youth's life chances. That approach stems from the insights and beliefs of those who work in the juvenile justice system, and it accords with scholarly reviews that emphasize the greater effectiveness of interventions that address a myriad of risk factors.[21] Yet it stands in marked contrast to the approach taken with both adult and young adult offenders in the criminal justice system.

A roundtable on youth reentry conducted by the Urban Institute highlighted this point. Scholars provided reviews of different topics and offered assessments about factors that might affect youth reentry and about other topics as well. Practitioners, too, with direct experience working with young people offered their views and highlighted issues that otherwise might be missed. They emphasized, for example, the fact that many of the youth with whom they worked had minimal experience in how to recreate in a "normal" way or to have an intimate relationship. A young person incarcerated at age 16 or 17, for example, and not released until age 21 or 22, essentially misses out on critical socialization experiences that other youth have.[22] Does that matter? People may disagree about whether it does so on normative grounds. As a pragmatic matter, however, yes, it does. Individuals who do not know how to have fun in a law-abiding manner essentially will be, per social learning theory, more likely to engage in deviance. Similarly, those who do not have intimate relationships may be, per social bond theory, less constrained to engage in deviance.

This type of observation may well be more likely to emerge from the individuals who work directly with youth and see first-hand how they fare upon release. That does not mean that their views necessarily are correct or should dictate policy. It means simply that they may shed light on how incarceration affects individuals and how reentry experiences and outcomes may be improved.

Book Goal 5: The Argument That Diverse Policy Possibilities Exist. In an era of silver-bullet approaches to crime—with mass incarceration constituting the most obvious example—what can be learned from a focus on younger inmates and ex-prisoners about the possibilities for improving reentry? As the discussion above highlights, once we view inmates as individuals with constellations of risk factors and unique life experiences and as individuals returning to varied social contexts, we are led to consider a much wider array of policies, programs, and interventions for reducing their recidivism and improving their life chances.

The juvenile justice system provides many examples of how to proceed. Sanctions tend to follow a continuum, from less severe to more severe as youth come into repeated contact with the court. Diversion is employed more—the court seeks to intervene even in minor delinquency cases. It seeks to refer youth for services and treatment to help the youth and to reduce the likelihood of additional offending. Probation frequently is coupled with treatment and services. Custodial facilities vary greatly and tend to be smaller and offer a broader array of mechanisms for holding youth accountable and for addressing their different risks and needs. The juvenile justice system is not perfect, and much of what occurs within it can be of poor quality and questionable expense.[23] Even so, it provides a model to the criminal justice system of how a more comprehensive and nuanced set of sanctions, services, and treatment might be created.[24]

FEMALE EX-PRISONERS

Although women constitute a relatively small proportion—less than 10 percent—of all inmates, their presence in jails and prisons has increased.[25] Nationally, more than 100,000 women are housed in state and federal institutions, and in recent decades their rate of incarceration has increased more rapidly than that of men.[26] As we discussed in Chapter 4, female ex-prisoners differ from males across a range of dimensions. Females are more likely to be incarcerated for drug crimes and substantially less likely to be incarcerated for violent crimes.[27] They are also more likely to have experienced different types of victimizations and to be addicted to drugs and alcohol.[28] Perhaps most notably, female inmates are substantially more likely than males to have children and to be the primary caretakers of them. [29] The culture in women's prisons differs from that of men's.

In women's prisons, for example, inmates may take on different family roles with one another. In addition, officer-inmate relationships may differ and so, too, may the types of programming.[30] Not least, the mental health of female inmates differs from that of male inmates. For example, approximately 73 percent of females in prison report symptoms of a mental disorder, compared with 55 percent of males.[31] Female inmates also report higher rates of victimization, especially sexual victimization, during incarceration.[32]

These differences can have important implications for female inmates' experiences in prison and during reentry. For example, because of the increased likelihood of separation from children, the strain of severed social ties and the anxiety of trying to rebuild intimate social networks upon release may be greater than what males experience. In addition, any differences in the needs and deficits experienced by female inmates are amplified by the fact that American prisons still tend to be largely male-dominated institutions—they primarily house men, they are staffed by men for the most part, and programming and treatment efforts typically have been designed with men in mind. As a result, many correctional systems find themselves ill equipped to address the unique needs presented by female inmates.[33] Here again, we use the book's overarching goals as a framework both to advance several arguments about reentry and to highlight dimensions that make reentry a potentially different experience for women.

Book Goal 1: The Argument That Diverse Perspectives Matter. Consideration of females as a specific, unique group of the inmate population directly illustrates the argument that diverse perspectives matter for understanding and improving prisoner reentry. Current approaches to incarceration and prisoner reentry represent a largely male-oriented perspective towards punishment.[34] Prison systems traditionally have been organized around the need for, and challenges related to, maintaining order and safety in institutions for male inmates. Females historically have been accorded a second-class status within the prison system. They have received less treatment and reside in facilities that lie farther away from their families and home communities, in part because fewer female institutions exist to allow for more proximate placements.[35] These different experiences in turn may affect reentry. Visitation, for example, may reduce recidivism, but this benefit may be less likely to occur among women if they reside farther away from home; distant placements in general will reduce the likelihood of visitation.[36]

A gender-specific perspective of imprisonment and prisoner reentry sheds light on unique challenges that female inmates may face prior to and during incarceration. For example, prior to incarceration, females typically are the primary caretaker of one or more children and serve as the head of the household.[37] This role may lead female inmates to feel more isolated and, at the same time, more anxious about their children and family members who previously depended on them. Females also are more likely to have been victimized and to have been addicted to drugs prior to entering prison, which increases the need for psychological and substance abuse treatment and counseling. Female inmates, too, have higher rates of serious mental illness. Research indicates that female inmates mistrust officers, potentially more so than do male inmates, and experience higher rates of officer victimization.[38]

A corollary to the above observations is that the reentry experiences of women differ. If they have more serious mental health problems and if these have gone unaddressed, then they face more challenges in successfully returning to society. Similarly, if they served as the primary caretaker of their children, the interruption created by going to prison may make it difficult for them to resume that role and so create additional strains during reentry.

Such possibilities highlight that reentry is complicated and may vary across groups, in turn highlighting the need for interventions that take into account the complexity. For example, compelling arguments can be and have been made that gender-responsive interventions can more effectively facilitate improved inmate behavior and postrelease outcomes.[39]

Book Goal 2: The Argument That Diverse Causes of Offending Matter.
Scholarship highlights both commonalities and differences in the causes of offending among males and females, respectively.[40] As a general matter, it appears that some of the identified correlates of crime identified by theory—such as lower self-control, weak social bonds, high levels of strain, association with criminals—contribute to offending for both groups. However, there can be variation in the way in which some factors operate. For example, the influence of criminal associates may be greater among males than among females.[41] In addition, as we have emphasized, females are more likely than males to have experienced abuse and sexual victimization and to be addicted to drugs and alcohol.[42] The loss of contact with children may be especially debilitating or frustrating, and may contribute to recidivism and poor reentry outcomes more so than for male ex-prisoners. Similarly, female inmates are less likely than men to have learned a trade or marketable skill during prison, which reduces their likelihood of finding employment and having resources that would enable them to avoid becoming enmeshed in further criminal activity.[43]

Consideration of these differences holds more than academic interest. To the extent that unique criminogenic experiences or characteristics exist among women, it makes sense to develop in-prison and postrelease reentry policies that take them into account. For example, correctional systems could provide vocational training that better equips women for the job markets that they will face.[44] They also could create more opportunities for female inmates to maintain contact with their children and families during incarceration and then provide referrals to community-based agencies that could help released female inmates to reunite with their families.

Book Goal 3: The Argument That Diverse Impacts on Groups and Others Matter. A focus on female inmates illustrates that any discussion of reentry implicates many groups, not just inmates. When caregivers go to prison, their children and families may be affected.[45] Children may end up in foster care, they may be less likely to go to school and more likely to drop out, they may be more likely to be victimized, and so on. That is not to say that in some cases children may be better off, especially if their mother abused them. However, maternal absence can create a range of harms for children as well as other dependents. The breakdown of families creates concerns broadly about the well-being of communities and their ability to exercise informal social control. Todd Clear and other scholars have identified the adverse effects that mass incarceration has had on communities. One of the avenues consists of adversely affecting family structure.[46] For example, prior to the punitive turn in American corrections, a sentence to probation may have been more likely than a sentence to prison for certain crimes. During the punitive turn, however, lengthy prison sentences became more likely and created the potential for adversely affecting children, families, and communities.

Book Goal 4: The Argument That Practitioner and Scholar Insights Matter. Historically, women's unique needs and experiences in prison and during reentry have gone unaddressed because the size of the female inmate population was perceived to be negligible. Also, scholarship and commentary on prison experiences stemmed from male-dominated disciplines, including the social sciences. Patricia Van Voorhis and others have drawn attention to this problem. Drawing on the insights of officers and inmates and a range of empirical studies, they have shown that gender differences not only exist but also have consequences for how women fare in prison and after release.[47] The observations of inmates, prison staff, corrections officials, probation officers, and social workers continue to shed light on how the prison and prisoner reentry experiences differ between males and females. Their insights hold the potential for identifying ways to avoid harmful effects of incarceration on inmates and their families.[48]

Book Goal 5: The Argument That Diverse Policy Possibilities Exist. The emerging literature on gender differences in offending and gender differences in the effectiveness of various sanctions and interventions highlights that a one-size-fits-all approach likely does not work. Indeed, it may be counterproductive. At the same time, the gender literature raises an interesting and previously neglected dimension of reentry—the family. The reality is that many men in prison have children and families who depend upon them. Historically, however, this fact attracted relatively little scholarly attention. That has changed and with it attention to gender differences and gender-responsive programming. In turn, these changes highlight that prisons can be operated differently. Perhaps the most obvious example consists of an emphasis on family ties. As soon as we shift from a focus on retribution and turn toward a focus on the salience of family for the inmate and his or her children, spouse, partner, and extended kin, a range of opportunities arise. For example, prisons can create visitation hours and areas that encourage rather than discourage family contact. Similarly, release planning can include an emphasis on family reunification in cases where it is appropriate, safe, and possible.

RACIAL AND ETHNIC MINORITY EX-PRISONERS

The disproportionate representation of racial and ethnic minorities in the prison population has garnered significant attention from scholars and policy makers. America incarcerates minorities, especially blacks, at substantially higher rates than it does whites. By extension, minorities experience substantially higher risks of exposure to potential harms that may result from incarceration. Among all state inmates in 2011, there were 465,180 white inmates (34 percent), 509,677 black inmates (38 percent), and 282,353 Hispanic inmates (23 percent) (see Table 4.2).[49] The differences become even more pronounced for minority males. For example, black males have an incarceration rate that is roughly seven times greater than that for white males; for black females, the incarceration rate is roughly three times greater than that for white females. Similar differences emerge for Hispanics, although they are more muted—incarceration rates are roughly three times greater for Hispanic males than for white males and roughly two times greater for Hispanic females than for white females.[50] Lifetime prevalence estimates indicate that incarceration constitutes a statistically normative experience for minorities. Forecasts from the Bureau of Justice Statistics, for example, indicate that one in 17 white males will have spent time in prison at some point in their lives. By contrast, one in three black males and one in six Hispanic males will have been incarcerated throughout their lives.[51]

Racial and ethnic differences in incarceration might be caused by different factors. The differences might stem from racial and ethnic differences in offending. In that case, the incarceration differences might make sense. Even then, however, we face the question of how much the differences in offending stem from exposure to more adverse social conditions. If more crime results, we face the peculiar situation of allowing these conditions to persist, resulting in more crime, and then using incarceration to respond to it. If the goal were to reduce crime, a more effective approach might be to ameliorate the social conditions. That likely would be more effective than leaning on a tool that at best might reduce crime at great cost and at worst might worsen crime (at great cost) and, simultaneously, create greater social inequality.

Perhaps, though, the differences stem more from institutionalized bias in law enforcement practices or court decision making. Perhaps, in turn, these differences become more pronounced because of a unique set of disparate experiences that minorities undergo, including greater rates of incarceration, fewer opportunities to participate in prison-based rehabilitative programming, more mistreatment while incarcerated, tougher enforcement of postrelease supervision conditions, a return to areas characterized by more social disadvantage, and increased use of incarceration as a consequence of violating conditions of parole.[52] Such a possibility is plausible if not probable, especially since, as compared with whites, minorities typically will have lower levels of educational attainment, limited financial resources, and more anemic employment histories. All of these factors may make successful desistance more difficult and rehabilitative intervention potentially all the more important.[53]

The history of tense racial and ethnic relations in the United States as well as continued racial and ethnic inequality underscore the importance of viewing mass incarceration and reentry through the prism of race and ethnicity.[54] The factors discussed above—such as potential differences in offending, differences in the factors that give rise to offending, and differences in criminal justice and correctional system processing and experiences—reinforce the importance of such an approach. Here, then, we revisit the book's goals, as we did with the focus on young ex-prisoners and female ex-prisoners. We use them as a guide to develop arguments about reentry and to illustrate that reentry can entail different experiences, sometimes dramatically different ones, for diverse social groups, including racial and ethnic minorities. If we wish to understand and improve reentry outcomes, we need an appreciation of such differences.

Book Goal 1: The Argument That Diverse Perspectives Matter. We have argued that the use of different perspectives can shed light on important ways in which reentry unfolds and how policies may need to be designed to improve reentry outcomes. If we turn to a focus on minorities, this idea can be readily appreciated. For example, a large body of scholarship establishes that minorities, more so than whites, reside in areas characterized by substantial social and economic disadvantage and in some cases higher crime rates.[55] Such conditions can give rise to higher levels of offending. Upon release from prison, those who return to disadvantaged communities may have higher recidivism rates. For racial and ethnic minorities, this possibility carries important implications for their reentry prospects. Minority populations are more likely to live in impoverished, crime-ridden communities, to have been exposed to crime as youth, to have parents or family members who have been incarcerated, and to be raised in single-parent households or dysfunctional families.[56] Accordingly, their risk of recidivism may be higher, but not necessarily because of their individual-level characteristics. Rather, they may be higher because of the social contexts to which they return.

Alongside of this issue is that of disparities in treatment and sanctioning of convicted felons. For example, research has found that minorities, young black males in particular, may be viewed as less amenable to treatment, less willing to reform, and more deserving of punishment, in part because they may be perceived as a potential threat to social order in mainstream society.[57] The end result can be an emphasis on less treatment and more incarceration for minorities. A return to impoverished communities in turn may increase the likelihood of recidivism and a return to prison, thereby fueling a vicious cycle of evermore incarceration among minorities, with the attendant impacts that such removal and reentry can have on families and communities.

Viewed in this light, we can see that arguably as much attention should be given to identifying and understanding racial and ethnic divides in offending, law enforcement practices, and punishment as to what can be done to improve reentry outcomes for minorities. Indeed, the risk otherwise is that of perpetuating a vicious cycle that results in evermore greater racial and ethnic disparities in incarceration at increased social and financial cost. At the same time, we can see, too, that consideration of these divides points directly to the salience of developing reentry plans, supervision, and assistance that take into account the social and economic realities that confront minorities. Although all ex-prisoners face challenges to successful reentry, many of these challenges, including potential employer discrimination, are amplified for minorities.[58]

Book Goal 2: The Argument That Diverse Causes of Offending Matter. The causes of offending are likely similar across racial and ethnic groups.

However, the exposure of minority groups to criminogenic factors—including increased economic strain, social stigmatization, and worsened perceptions of legitimacy of the justice system—is substantially higher. Inequalities in the social contexts to which different groups are exposed likely contributes to a greater risk of offending.[59] This situation does not reduce the personal responsibility of individuals who offend. Few victims of a violent crime would countenance the idea that an offender's background or social context should relieve him or her of responsibility for their behavior. Even in juvenile court, where we typically presume that youth are less culpable for their actions, we set the bar higher for serious crimes.[60] At the same time, the social context of many minorities clearly elevates their risk of offending and recidivism.

A failure to address that inequality amounts to an acceptance that punishment policies necessarily will be allocated more to minorities without creating more public safety. Indeed, less safety might result if incarceration creates criminogenic effects for those who go to and leave prison or if reentry barriers impede their ability to become productive members of society.[61] This observation underscores the usefulness of considering community characteristics as risk factors that may affect desistance.[62]

Two observations highlight the importance of examining the diverse circumstances that some inmate groups face. One is the fact that minority inmates are more likely to be incarcerated for drug crimes.[63] The difference may stem from greater law enforcement attention to this group, to the greater likelihood that in some communities minority groups may be more likely to abuse illegal substances, or to some combination of the two.[64] While incarcerated, their drug problems may be poorly addressed, if at all.[65] After prison, drug relapse is likely, especially in areas characterized by marked disadvantage and limited access to social services. In this example, we can see that minority status, as a marker, constitutes a proxy for a range of different experiences, social contexts, and challenges that may directly affect reentry success.

A second is the fact that minority ex-prisoners face disproportionately worse employment prospects compared with white ex-prisoners. Employment can be critical to successful transitions back into society and helping individuals to desist from future crime.[66] Differences in employment histories and labor market opportunities for any given group thus can contribute to differences in reentry success. Although all inmates leave prison with considerably reduced chances of gainful employment, scholarship suggests that minority citizens may be especially disadvantaged in labor markets as a result of their felony convictions and incarceration[67] and their lower levels of educational attainment.[68] From theoretical and policy perspectives, attention to social context, such as community disadvantage and employability, thus constitute important potential causes of offending, the targeting of which might help to reduce recidivism.

Book Goal 3: The Argument That Diverse Impacts on Groups and Others Matter. The disproportionate incarceration of minorities clearly implicates not only those who commit crime but also their families and communities. Bruce Western and Christopher Muller, as well as other scholars, have highlighted the ways in which mass incarceration has affected these groups.[69] In many minority communities, incarceration itself is normative. Joan Petersilia has observed that "serving a prison term is becoming almost a normal experience in some poor, minority communities. In fact some communities are so severely affected by crime and imprisonment that they no longer recognize it as a problem."[70] In some of these communities, one-fifth or more of the adult male population may be in prison; incarceration directly affects the social structure of these communities.[71] For many children and families, the idea that a brother, father, or uncle might be incarcerated barely warrants a raised eyebrow.[72] This familiarity with incarceration does not mitigate the harms that occur for families. To the contrary, an array of harms arises from this situation. Children lack parents, marriages either do not occur or dissolve, families lose income that could pay for housing and food, drug abuse increases, delinquency and crime increase, in part because informal social control networks and institutions weaken, and community disadvantage becomes further entrenched.[73]

The extant and growing literature on reentry reinforces the concern that these impacts exist and thus constitute an important part of policy deliberations aimed at reducing crime. We want punishment to help, not harm. When it fails to reduce crime, a red flag should go up. Even if incarceration reduces crime, the emergence of social harms for children, families, and communities should be a red flag. More flags should go up if punishment actually increases crime and cause these harms. The potential for all of these problems can readily be seen when we focus on the effects of mass incarceration on minorities. Doing so underscores that if we want to understand and improve reentry, we necessarily must examine how it occurs and what its impacts are for different groups. It also underscores that reentry discussions almost ineluctably lead us back to a focus on what we want from punishment.

Book Goal 4: The Argument That Practitioner and Scholar Insights Matter. A considerable prod to reentry research and policy deliberations has come from practitioners. Jeremy Travis, Joan Petersilia, and others have highlighted the numerous efforts made by those in the corrections field to understand better what could be done to improve outcomes among those released from prison.[74] The foot soldiers in criminal justice and corrections understand directly the challenges associated with the increased processing demands that occurred in recent decades. Prosecutors and courts, as well as prison and community supervision systems, have had to improvise to handle increased caseloads.[75] Typically, these different groups themselves have highlighted the importance of race and ethnicity in discussions about how to reduce crime and to improve sentencing and reentry practices.[76]

Community advocates, too, have drawn attention to the consequences of mass incarceration and the challenges of reentry. Social service agencies have struggled to devise new ways of improving reentry and have done so on shoestring budgets. Some support has occurred nationally through such efforts as the Serious and Violent Offender Initiative (SVORI) in 2002 and the Second Chance Act in 2007. Yet much of the work on reentry has emanated from locally based efforts that have stemmed from direct knowledge of or experiences with the consequences of mass incarceration and reentry.[77]

Scholars, too, have played a central role. Over the past decade, a voluminous body of research has illuminated a diverse array of dimensions involving reentry. Investigation of the racial and ethnic dimension of mass incarceration has constituted one prominent strand of this research. Studies have identified the challenges discussed above and investigated many other ways in which minorities, incarceration, and reentry are intertwined. For example, some research has identified that minority inmates may experience more discrimination and victimization while in prison. It has found that these experiences may reduce their perceptions of the legitimacy of the criminal justice system and increase their likelihood of offending.[78] It has identified, too, the persistence of racial and ethnic segregation in prisons, driven in part by efforts to separate gangs that may be divided along racial or ethnic lines, despite Supreme Court decisions banning segregation.[79] Moral arguments may undergird these decisions. However, at a pragmatic level, one of the reasons for concern stems from studies that indicate that segregation may reinforce group stereotypes, harm inmate and staff relations, and contribute to victimization.[80]

In short, practitioners and scholars together have been central to highlighting the complex nature of reentry. In addition, they have underscored the critical importance of examining how race and ethnicity play a role in crime, sentencing, corrections, and reentry. Put differently, reentry constitutes a policy domain in which it is difficult to sustain the assertion that the views of those on the ground have had little effect on policy or that the work of scholars has had no effect. Quantifying the effects is no easy task and may not be possible. Still, some basis for optimism exists and is reflected in ongoing efforts nationally to understand and improve reentry.

Book Goal 5: The Argument That Diverse Policy Possibilities Exist. As for young inmates and female inmates, no one-size-fits-all approach will work for racial and ethnic minorities. The focus on race and ethnicity, more so than the focus on these two other groups, highlights that reentry outcomes ultimately may be improved most by attending to racial and ethnic inequality in the social conditions of minorities in America and in developing non-incarcerative sanctions that may pose fewer risks to families and communities. Failure to do so means that we may need to sink ever greater amounts of resources into incarceration without appreciably altering the "demand" for it. Indeed, the vicious cycle consists of investing more in incarceration, and then even more, because of high recidivism rates and the tendency of policies to turn punitive when a particular crime receives prominent media attention.

If we turn our focus to those who go to and come out of prison, we can see that increasing their chances of success may require investment in housing, employment, and drug treatment services. It may require efforts to maintain ties between inmates and the families and communities from which they come. Such efforts may help to reduce recidivism—and thus one of the central conduits into the correctional system and one of the central causes of its expansion—and to improve outcomes for children, families, and communities.

OTHER GROUPS OF EX-PRISONERS

No one correct way exists to classify those who go to prison or leave it. Rather, classification efforts are more useful, or less useful, for achieving particular goals. Our argument in this chapter is that a wide range of groups exist that can lead us to think differently about prison and reentry and, ultimately, how to improve outcomes for ex-prisoners and society. When we focus on young people or females or minorities, for example, we can see that each group may come from different backgrounds and social contexts. They may have unique needs, deficits, and strengths, and they may experience prison differently. The causes of offending for these groups may vary as well. In addition, their reentry experiences may affect others in different ways. Accordingly, as many practitioners and scholars suggest, we likely need group-specific policies, programs, and practices to improve their life chances and to help (rather than harm) communities.

To this point, we have discussed three demographic groups—the young, females, and minorities. There are, however, many other social groups that could be used to illustrate the argument. Here, we briefly touch on several such groups and then identify others that warrant careful consideration in crafting correctional system and reentry policies. No one group merits more attention than others, if only because prison systems vary in how many inmates fit one group or another. In addition, the discussion here is far from comprehensive. We seek only to underscore the argument that inmate and ex-prisoner groups exist and that group differences may lead us to understand better the complexity of reentry and to identify ways to improve reentry outcomes for ex-prisoners and the families and communities to which they return.

SUPER-MAXIMUM SECURITY EX-PRISONERS

As we have discussed in earlier chapters, federal and state prison systems embraced super-maximum security ("supermax") incarceration in the 1980s and thereafter. Little is known about who goes into supermax housing or for how long or how frequently.[81] Accounts suggest that the most violent and disruptive individuals reside in such housing and that blacks are disproportionately represented in it.[82] In reality, though, supermax housing operates largely as a black box phenomenon, one that requires much more illumination if we are to fully understand what happens in them and how they affect inmates. As the case study highlights, research suggests that supermax facilities not only house a unique population, they also create an atmosphere and experience that harm them. In turn, the individuals who leave such facilities may be more likely to recidivate, suffer from mental illness, and have considerable difficulty finding stable employment and housing.

Chapter 8 Case Study: Supermax Inmates and Reentry

The prison population contains diverse inmate groups. Many of them do not have any one characteristic that sets them apart. Instead, they share a constellation of characteristics and life experiences that set them apart. These groups present unique challenges to prison systems and may face dim prospects during reentry.

Supermax inmates constitute one such group. These individuals tend to have violent criminal histories that place them well above the typical violent offender. Many of them suffer from mental illness. They likely have substantially lower self-control than other inmates. In addition, the isolation that they experience largely precludes participating in rehabilitative programming. It also makes it difficult to maintain social ties to family and friends and may adversely affect mental health. Many inmates exhibit heightened fear, paranoia, hallucinations, and suicidal thoughts while confined in isolation (Harrington 1997; Haney 2003; Rhodes 2004; King 2005; Smith 2006; Goode 2012; Cohen 2013).

Accounts of supermax confinement describe it as a dehumanizing experience (Rhodes 2004; Tietz 2012; Cohen 2013). Inmates typically have limited to no normative social interaction, leave their cells only if handcuffed, receive food through a narrow door opening, and in many instances never see daylight. They hear rather than see other supermax inmates. A visit to a supermax can sound like a cacophony of echoing yells, taunts, and screams (Rhodes 2004). Some inmates respond through persistent defiance and create urine-and-feces cocktails that they throw at officers (Pizarro and Stenius 2004; Rhodes 2004; Kluger 2007; Tapley 2010).

By most accounts, supermax inmates return to society in worse condition than when they left. The extended isolation can mean that they are ill-equipped to negotiate normal everyday interactions with others. Such interactions may be highly stressful. In addition, the lack of program participation may limit their opportunities for any type of gainful employment upon release. They may have difficulty finding housing where they can stay for an extended period of time. Mental illness presents additional challenges for many of these inmates as well. Despite such barriers to a successful return to society, supermax inmates sometimes are released directly from prison back into their home communities, and many of them receive little to no special transitional assistance (Harrington 1997; Lowen and Isaacs 2012).

Little credible empirical evidence about the reentry experience of supermax inmates exists (Mears 2008b, 2013). Most of what is known to date comes from qualitative studies or anecdotal accounts provided in news stories. However, several studies suggest that supermax incarceration may worsen recidivism upon release (Lovell et al. 2007; Mears and Bales 2009). These studies have only begun to scratch the surface. For example, research by Daniel Mears and William Bales (2010) indicates that some individuals may be incarcerated in supermax confinement for a few months, but others may spend years in it. A large body of studies indicates that many different types of individuals go into supermax

(Continued)

(see, for example, Lovell et al. 2000). Some, for example, fit the profile of nuisance inmates, while others fit more the profile of a gang leaders (Riveland 1999b). We can anticipate that such dimensions, as well as having a mental illness, might well alter the effect of supermax incarceration on reentry outcomes.

DRUG-ABUSING EX-PRISONERS

Drug abuse and addiction among those who go to prison is widespread. As we discussed in Chapter 4, over one-third of inmates have a history of drug abuse and dependence problems. Do such problems warrant attention? Many scholars and practitioners would say yes because reducing drug abuse and addiction amounts to treating a health problem, which amounts to a good unto itself. At the same time, addressing this problem may reduce offending and homelessness and improve the likelihood of obtaining and maintaining a job as well as becoming a help rather than hindrance to family.

However, the connection between drug abuse or addiction and criminal behavior is tricky.[83] Sometimes, for example, involvement in crime may contribute to a drug problem. Sometimes, too, drug problems and offending may stem from similar causes, such as poverty, difficult life circumstances, low self-control, or the like. In addition, when, as can be the case with some interventions, a program reduces drug abuse and recidivism, it may be due to improving a causal factor related both to drug abuse and to offending.

This complexity underscores the point that a focus on groups may be helpful, especially if we focus on the clusters of characteristics that may apply to them. With drug abuse, for example, many factors are implicated. Drug abuse and addiction typically are greater among men, whites, the young, and single people (e.g., never married or divorced).[84] Disabilities and co-occurring mental health problems are correlated as well with drug abuse and addiction.[85] Other factors, too, such as poverty, stress, and level of self-control may be involved. When we focus on drug problems, then, we are led—or should be led—to consider much more than drugs. If we do not, then our interventions likely will achieve, at best, short-term gains.

MENTALLY ILL OR LEARNING DISABLED EX-PRISONERS

The individuals who go to and leave prison constitute a disadvantaged population. That can be seen in the prevalence of mental illness and learning disabilities among inmates. The prevalence of mental illness is five to 24 times greater among inmates compared with members of the general public.[86] One of the significant policy shifts in the 1960s and 1970s involved the deinstitutionalization of mentally ill individuals, which, according to some scholars, contributed to increased incarceration.[87] The argument, supported by some research, reduced to the following: These individuals remained incarcerated, and what changed was the place of incarceration. Regardless, studies find that the prevalence of mental illness in prisons broadly mirrors what one finds among individuals who come from areas characterized by high levels of social and economic disadvantage.[88] Accordingly, even without deinstitutionalization, we would expect that mental illness would be greater among the inmate and ex-prisoner population given the social and economic characteristics of this group. Disabilities, too, feature more prominently among inmates and ex-prisoners in part because many of these individuals come from disadvantaged areas where disabilities are less likely to be identified, treated, or addressed.

For these individuals, incarceration may constitute an especially stressful and difficult experience to negotiate. Among individuals who do *not* enter prison with a mental illness, the conditions in prisons may induce the onset of one or more mental disorders. Accounts of long-term inmates point to this problem. For example, they find that these individuals increasingly, throughout their time in prison, become introverted, withdrawn, and suicidal.[89] The challenges for learning disabled inmates parallel those for those with mental illness. Learning disabilities can lead to difficulty with writing, math, or communication, including understanding verbal or nonverbal cues or expressing themselves. The end result can be considerable frustration at not being understood and not understanding others. This latter situation of course can be especially problematic in prison settings.

As with the other groups that we have discussed, those with mental illness and learning disabilities do not have only one condition that primarily affects their prison and reentry experiences but typically a cluster. They may, for example, have limited education, suffered childhood abuse or victimization, and come from poverty-stricken families or communities. None of these challenges or conditions need justify any criminal behavior or prison misconduct. Collectively, though, they highlight that assisting this group toward a trajectory of successful reentry would require more than addressing mental illness or learning disabilities alone.

STILL OTHER GROUPS OF EX-PRISONERS

Many other groups of ex-prisoners can be identified and warrant attention in their own right.[90] Indeed, entire books exist that focus on certain groups. Gay, lesbian, and transgendered individuals face innumerable challenges in prison, including a greater likelihood of sexual victimization, and recidivism upon release.[91] Sexual dynamics in prison are complicated and can include coerced sex, including rape. Such acts do not occur with the frequency that early scholarship suggested; estimates indicate that 1–3 percent of inmates experience sexual victimization.[92] Such victimization, however, occurs more frequently among homosexual, bisexual, transsexual, or transgendered individuals.[93]

Pregnant women who commit crime, or mothers who recently have given birth to a child and commit a crime, also present special challenges. States vary in whether they provide nurseries where pregnant women can stay during and after delivery of a child. Most states have relied on them less in recent decades due to concerns about security and fiscal costs.[94] Many pregnant incarcerated women have already experienced high-risk pregnancies because of poverty, a history of abuse, drug addiction, and sexually transmitted diseases.[95] Specialized health care thus must be provided throughout the pregnancy. In addition, whether a nursery exists or not in a given prison, mothers and infants alike undergo significant stress because of the limited contact, or lack of contact, that they have with each other. Infants may be placed in the foster care system. Then, upon release, parents encounter substantial barriers to assuming custody of their children. They typically will find that reuniting with children can be difficult, especially when the children have little familiarity with or attachment to them.

Still other groups can be identified, including chronically ill inmates, individuals who need or are placed in protective custody, sex offenders, veterans, gang members, and older or geriatric inmates. Each of these groups has specific conditions or characteristics that may influence their prison stay and reentry. They also may have unique experiences in prison and during reentry that stem from how prison officials or others treat them.

In each instance—as well as with the groups discussed above—we can see why group-based approaches to supervising, managing, and assisting inmates and ex-prisoners might be necessary to improve in-prison and post-release behavior and outcomes. However, we can see, too, that correctional systems and efforts to improve reentry experiences and outcomes run directly into cost considerations. Financial constraints alone may preclude doing much more than warehousing individuals in prison and offering perfunctory supervision upon release. Legal requirements may require additional services or treatment. But beyond that, any effort to provide supervision, management, or assistance on a large scale almost necessarily requires some type of more generic approach with most inmates. In short, we confront the tension identified earlier in this chapter—namely, that of trying to strike a balance between (a) employing generic approaches to supervising, managing, and assisting all ex-prisoners and (b) employing individualized, or group-based, approaches to doing so.

REVISITING SANCTIONING AND REENTRY

Problems With Focusing on
Inmate or Ex-Prisoner Characteristics or Groups

We have argued that a characteristics-based approach to understanding inmate behavior and reentry may be highly limited and that a group-based approach may be better. Among other things, it enables us to see more clearly that any given characteristic may not tell us much about the constellation of factors that affect an individual's likelihood of behaving in prison and faring well upon release. By contrast, when we focus on groups, we can see clearly that an individual who is a member of a given group may well have many characteristics that in isolation or in interaction with one another contribute to behavior.

However, as this chapter has highlighted, an abundance of groups exist. Ironically, that returns us back to the problem that we can see with focusing on any one particular characteristic. Specifically, we lack a clear theoretical or empirical foundation on which to know how to proceed. For example, which groups most merit attention and in what ways?

Answers to this question are challenging for many reasons. Many of us typically belong to multiple groups, as do prisoners. Which classifications best help us to improve prison and reentry outcomes? Of course, some classifications derive from a heavy dose of common sense—if a woman is pregnant, that seems relatively straightforward. She is pregnant, and legal and medical considerations come into play. However, this same woman could be drug dependent, suffer from a mental illness, and have little in the way of family support.

Although a group-focused approach may be better than an approach driven by focusing on one particular characteristic, it raises problems. One way to see how even a group-based approach to managing, supervising, and intervening with inmates and ex-prisoners can present challenges is to focus on drug courts. These ascended into prominence in the 1990s and remain highly popular. A large part of prison growth nationally has stemmed from increased and tougher sentencing of drug offenders. That growth fueled interest in developing ways to reduce drug offending. One obvious target was treatment. How, though, could a focus on treatment garner widespread support in a context in which the country still was highly concerned about crime and disenchanted with rehabilitation? Drug courts emerged as a vehicle for engendering such support. Beginning in 1989, drug courts rapidly proliferated throughout the United States, in part because they emphasized accountability and drug treatment, not rehabilitation in broad terms, which might have reduced support for them.[96]

Drug court proponents tend to emphasize the benefits of such courts in reducing substance abuse relapse and offending and possibly in improving educational and employment outcomes. Courts that have more predictable sanctions, adhere to best-practice treatment approaches, employ drug testing and high-quality case management, and provide more intensive treatment and supervision appear to be more effective than those that fall short along one or more of these dimensions.[97] But many drug courts do not have high-quality implementation, often because of cost considerations, and so do not appreciably improve outcomes.[98]

What we know, then, is that drug courts can work if implemented well and if they carefully monitor and treat individuals. The more holistic drug courts—that consider an individual's array of needs and problems—appear to be most effective.[99] But drug courts that enjoy less funding or support may have to give primary attention to drug treatment and so reduce their effectiveness. Beyond drug courts, there exists a wide range of drug abuse and addiction interventions. Although some of them may take a holistic approach, many do not. These courts and interventions then come to emphasize one problematic offender characteristic over others.

The problem lies in the fact that individuals in the criminal justice system typically have many problems that warrant attention. Focusing on one over all the others then likely achieves at best a short-term gain. This approach can be highly effective when only one problem exists. But it can be ineffective and even harmful when multiple problems exist.

A Big Solution: Reinventing Criminal Justice and Corrections

As we can see, a focus on specific inmate or ex-prisoner characteristics can be risky. It can lead us to miss the potential for an individual to have multiple risks and needs that warrant intervention to reduce their likelihood of offending. A focus on groups can serve as a corrective to that problem. Yet it also can lead us down the road of prioritizing some groups over others, treating individuals as if they belong more to one group than another, and failing to intervene effectively with a larger swath of the inmate and ex-prisoner population.

One solution to this problem exists and it comes from focusing on the cause of the problem. We might point to many causes. However, a central cause stems from delimiting the focus of criminal justice to reducing crime and recidivism. In one fell swoop, this focus necessarily restricts our attention to punishment and public safety. Criminal justice system and correctional system officials then emphasize steps to achieve these goals. That is, of course, understandable. From their perspective, it would be unreasonable to take steps to achieve other societal goals because doing so would exceed the scope of their charge.

However, if we view crime from a public health perspective, we can see that many of the individuals in the criminal justice system constitute a high-risk population. Taking this observation a step further, we can see prisons as a perfect type of catchment area for identifying some of the most at-risk groups in society. They are individuals with markedly higher levels of health problems and many of the correlates of such problems.[100] They come from and return to areas of marked disadvantage, where health problems and other social problems, such as poor education and high poverty, exist. The individuals who leave prison help us to identify these areas, but they also may contribute to problems in them.[101]

A social welfare or social service perspective leads to much the same insight. If our charge were to improve social welfare in society and to identify groups or areas most in need of services, an efficient way to guide our efforts would be to focus on high-crime groups and areas. Lacking that, we could focus on those who go to prison and monitor them upon release. Where else might one find such a concentrated population of unhealthy and at-risk individuals?

The perspectives are useful in creating other insights. For example, if we use them to look at mass incarceration, we can see that mass incarceration is largely focused on retribution. Certainly, some crime reduction has occurred, perhaps through a mix of incapacitation, general deterrence, and specific deterrence.[102] However, little emphasis can be seen on using sanctions or interventions that might create greater public safety and, at the same time, greater public health and improvements in the social welfare of offenders and their families and communities.

What if the criminal justice and correctional systems were reinvented as public health and social service agencies?[103] Their charge would not be simply to punish or improve public safety but to provide comprehensive individual case management and area-based services that might provide greater gains in public safety and simultaneously improve health and social welfare outcomes.

That may never happen. It is, indeed, a bit Pollyannaish to think that a single system could achieve so many societal goals—more satisfactory levels of retribution, more humane punishment, improved public health, stronger communities, including better schools and stronger families, and so on. Worse than that, for those who hew to a more vengeful tendency, the notion of using criminal activity to identify individuals, groups, and areas especially in need of public health and social service interventions would seem repugnant.

Why, then, do we mention this idea? First, it highlights that in reality, the nation's investment in mass incarceration constitutes a missed opportunity to invest in strategies that might more effectively drive down crime (and thus reduce calls for vengeful responses). Second, it highlights how limited the effectiveness of a prison-as-punishment likely is in reducing overall crime rates. Why? It does nothing to address the family and community conditions from which prisoners come and to which they will return. Indeed, as we have discussed, it may worsen them. Third, it underscores the argument that we have made throughout this chapter—sanctions and interventions that do not systematically address the range of deficits and problems of most inmates and ex-prisoners likely will never do much to reduce crime, much less improve community conditions that give rise to crime and other social problems. Consider, again, drug courts. They illustrate that comprehensive approaches to supervising, managing, and treating individuals can reduce recidivism and improve other outcomes. Yet they also illustrate that without adequate funding and without an emphasis on the range of problems that offenders have, no such benefits accrue.

Drug courts illustrate, too, that programmatic efforts focusing on select groups likely exert little effect on crime or social welfare broadly given that they serve a relatively small number of individuals. Indeed, large-scale reduction in crime through drug courts and other smaller-scale efforts that focus on small numbers of individuals is unlikely.[104]

Even so, drug courts illustrate that a comprehensive approach to intervening with offenders ultimately may be the most cost-beneficial avenue to take. That leads us to the insight that specialized courts—and, more broadly, specialized correctional system practices—may be needed for *all* offenders, not just select groups. Logically, this approach would mean turning all aspects of court and correctional systems into the ideals envisioned for specialized court efforts. These include attention to the range of risks and needs that individuals have, the contexts from which they come, quality supervision and treatment, and an emphasis on case management guided by the goals of improved life outcomes, not just reduced recidivism. Such an approach makes imminent sense from a public health or social welfare perspective. Indeed, it makes sense, as we discuss below, from the perspective of juvenile justice.

A Smaller Solution: Infusing Criminal Justice with Health and Welfare Perspectives

Reinventing the criminal justice and correctional systems in the above manner may not be feasible or even ideal. A more modest solution would be to invest in low-cost case management approaches that facilitate linkages to public health and social service agencies and organizations. The correctional system would continue to impose probation and prison terms on individuals. However, the system would be infused with a public health and social service mission. This mission would not require directly providing health or social services. Instead, legislatures could provide correctional systems with funds for agency units that would facilitate access to, but not pay for, services.

In many respects, the solution amounts to returning parole to its historically dual emphasis on supervision and on social work. However, this dual emphasis would not be restricted purely to parole. It would apply to all aspects of criminal justice processing and sanctioning. Indeed, in juvenile justice, this approach constitutes the ideal that was articulated by the juvenile court's founders.[105] One might simply extend it to the adult justice system.[106]

One might, too, emphasize communities as "clients" of the criminal justice and correctional systems. From a public health perspective, the notion of communities as clients seems obvious. It is less obvious when viewed through the prism of the correctional system as it operates today. For example, correctional systems hire individuals whose main focus consists of supervising offenders. No distinct agency, unit, or organization within correctional systems exists to promote public safety or well-being generally in particular communities.

This more modest solution then includes funding individuals within correctional systems who would be charged with helping individuals released to particular communities to access public health or social services. These individuals, however, would seek to improve the availability and quality of these services in those areas where it might most be needed. They might do so by serving in an official capacity as individuals charged with identifying where such needs exist and bringing them to the attention of correctional system officials and lawmakers.

CONCLUSION

To the extent that individuals who go to prison have multiple deficits or face multiple challenges, a focus on groups can help us recognize that there likely is no appreciable benefit to addressing just one problem, such as drug abuse. Similarly, there is little advantage to be gained by focusing on certain characteristics, such as age. Such characteristics at most point to a risk factor for misconduct or recidivism. They tell us little about which groups may be most likely to recidivate or why. Multiple problems and challenges constitute the statistical norm rather than the exception among ex-prisoners. Accordingly, supervision and interventions likely need to be multifaceted to achieve substantial improvements in recidivism and reentry outcomes.

This idea helps illuminate why interventions that primarily emphasize one problem area may be unlikely to reduce recidivism much or improve reentry outcomes. For example, the record of success for employment programs is poor.[107] Why? It may have to do with the emphasis given to just one problem area rather than the multiple problems that ex-prisoners have or face. It helps explain, too, why recidivism improvements may be greater in interventions that offer more comprehensive supervision, treatment, and services. Drug courts illustrate this idea—many of them emphasize this type of comprehensive approach and appear to be more effective than those that give primary if not exclusive priority to drug treatment.

To the extent that we focus on inmate and ex-prisoner groups and that doing so provides us with a more accurate understanding of their risks and needs, then we have an ability to improve the achievement of correctional system goals.

We can monitor the entry and prevalence of certain groups into the prison system and their release back into communities. More important, we can use this information to estimate prison and parole supervision capacity needs as well as the types and amounts of supervision, services, and treatment needed. Risk prediction, too, likely can be improved. Instead of trying to estimate risk based on adding up a number of risk factors, we likely should be focused on identifying the clusters of factors that, when present together, disproportionately elevate the likelihood of recidivism. Practitioners in the field may not necessarily understand statistical risk prediction models (though many do). However, they can readily appreciate, and indeed typically can easily highlight, how clusters of personal, family, and community factors can interact with each other to produce a very high probability of recidivism, homelessness, unemployment, and more.

A focus on groups helps us see that there can be no silver-bullet solution to managing inmates better or to improving their reentry experiences and outcomes. Rather, we need a range of approaches that address the complicated and intensive cluster of problems that inmates bring to the table and the challenges that they will face.

Because of this fact, mass incarceration and get-tough efforts likely worsen rather than improve public safety and other dimensions of social life. For example, when drug-abusing inmates receive no treatment or when inmates who have never held a job for more than a few months receive no employment training, they likely will be worse off after prison than before they entered it. They have a felony record. Their drug problem may have continued unabated. And they have a lengthier period of unemployment. Any taxpayer might reasonably balk at spending money on programs to help individuals who have harmed others and seem hell-bent on not changing, but almost all inmates eventually return home.[108] In this case, they return home after a long stay in what frequently may be a criminogenic prison setting and face the likelihood of continued drug abuse and unemployment. No one wins in this scenario.

Much the same can be said for other inmate groups. For example, the victimization of young inmates may exert a greater adverse effect on their behavior during and after incarceration. In addition, to the extent that they are continuing to develop—morally, educationally, psychologically, emotionally, and in other ways—the failure to intervene in a timely manner constitutes a twofold problem. On the one hand, we miss an opportunity to create considerably larger improvements in behavior, given that younger ex-prisoners are more likely to recidivate. On the other hand, we allow criminogenic forces to exert a greater influence given that younger inmates likely are more susceptible to them.

A more effective correctional system would be one that relied less on incarceration and that provided individualized sanctioning and intervention. That approach constitutes the ideal in juvenile justice and springs from the observation that youthful offenders frequently have many problems, not just one. Addressing a youth in his or her totality may provide the most effective avenue to promoting desistance *and* to improving other life outcomes. Indeed, instead of prioritizing specific groups, we perhaps should recognize that almost *all* inmates belong to multiple groups and have a wide variety of problems. Our best hope for effective and cost-efficient criminal justice may lie with highly individualized sanctions, incarceration experiences, and reentry supervision and assistance.

Doing so would be costly, yes. However, we otherwise are left trying to piece-meal different efforts that privilege one characteristic or group over another. For example, we end up investing more in drug treatment than in assisting inmates with learning disabilities or weak employment histories. We instead could take stock of a given inmate's and ex-prisoner's characteristics, the groups to which he or she belongs, and the family and community from which he or she comes and then devise interventions that may work best for that individual.

We recognize that this approach currently lacks much in the way of empirical evidence. Correctional systems do not generally take a systemic approach to managing, treating, supervising, and assisting all inmates and ex-prisoners. Rather, they invest more heavily in some groups (e.g., drug offenders, supermax inmates) than in others.

Still, a focus on individual characteristics and group characteristics might be far less effective and efficient than an approach that considers each individual in their totality. From this perspective, no warrant exists in using age, sex, race, ethnicity, type of offense, mental illness, or the like to identify a "master" status for any given inmate or ex-prisoner. An individual may be all of these things and more. Consider, for example, a young adult male with learning disabilities who has been physically abused as a child, is drug-addicted, has never worked, no longer has ties to his foster family, and will return to a community where crime, homelessness, and unemployment constitute the norm. If we focus on only one dimension (e.g., drug abuse), we are throwing money down a well. We will get little to nothing in return.

Alternatively, we can attempt to devise prison management and programming strategies and reentry approaches that attempt to take into account this person in his entirety. The goal would be to use such approaches to facilitate desistance, increase employment, and reduce homelessness and other adverse outcomes. Such strategies and approaches would be expensive and complicated, though less so if we reduced investment in lengthy prison terms and invested more in shorter prison stays and alternative sanctions. They would be difficult to blue-print for others to use. And they would be difficult to evaluate for those very reasons. However, no canned program likely can achieve that goal. Rather, at best, it will help to improve a particular outcome in a marginal way for a temporary period of time, without in any appreciable way altering the likelihood of longer-term desistance or improved social outcomes.

A shift in correctional system philosophy and practice would be necessary to achieve a more coherent and multifaceted approach to sanctioning and intervention. This shift would require infusing correctional system efforts with a public health and social welfare orientation. This approach would entail seeking to improve outcomes not only for those who offend but also the families and communities to which they return. One need not adopt a liberal or conservative orientation to embrace this idea. Instead, we can proceed in response to a simple question: Which approach best reduces recidivism, crime, homelessness, unemployment, and delinquency among families and communities? Mass incarceration, with its clear potential for producing adverse effects on crime and on families and communities? Or an approach that seeks to address multiple problems among offenders and that targets efforts to improve conditions in the areas where most offenders reside? As we discuss in the next chapter, a wide range of strategies in fact exist to achieve the broader goal not just of improving public safety but also of improving public health and well-being. There is no question that prison must constitute a central pillar of an effective correctional system. But it is just that—one pillar.

DISCUSSION QUESTIONS

1. What inmate groups—for example, the young, females, minorities, drug abusers, mentally ill, learning disabled, supermax prisoners—merit specialized attention during and after incarceration? Why?

2. How should reentry planning take into account the fact that inmates typically fit into multiple groups? For example, an inmate might be young, male, and black and have a drug problem and co-occurring mental disorder; and he may also have a learning disability and have spent time in supermax confinement.

3. What are the risks of using generic approaches—instead of individualized approaches—to inmate and reentry management, supervision, and assistance?

4. What are the risks of attempting to individualize all such efforts?

5. How can correctional systems balance the tension—what ultimately are the relative costs and benefits—between (a) providing generic management, supervision, and assistance for all inmates and ex-prisoners and (b) individualizing such efforts for specific groups?

6. The groups who go to prison share many of the characteristics of those who are served by public health and social service agencies. Historically, however, these agencies have operated largely independent from one another. How might public health, social service, and correctional system agencies be configured to achieve their respective goals more effectively?

CHAPTER 9

*Reentry Policy and What
Works to Improve
Reentry Outcomes*

In the 1990s, a report funded by the National Institute of Justice identified that many criminal justice interventions are ineffective, some are promising, and some are effective. The analysis, and subsequent work, led to substantial concern that many policies in criminal justice lack a solid research base.[1] That concern holds today and it holds true for efforts to reduce recidivism among prisoners.[2] There are, however, signs of and causes for optimism. What are they? We answer this question in this chapter, but before doing so discuss the background that highlights the critical need to shift America's crime policies in a more cost-effective direction.

This chapter is organized as follows. First, we argue that incarceration, as a crime-reducing and recidivism-reducing policy, rests on weak empirical grounds. Evidence of beneficial effects in achieving satisfactory levels of retribution or justice appears to be minimal. Second, we then amplify this argument by highlighting that incarceration may generate collateral consequences that produce harms potentially sufficient to offset any putative gains that may arise from it. Third, extending this argument further, we draw attention to the problem of correctional system programming, including reentry efforts, that rest on little to no coherent or credible theoretical foundation. In so doing, and as a prelude to shifting gears and waxing more optimistic, we discuss the problem of what Edward Latessa and colleagues have referred to as "correctional quackery"—that is, investment in approaches that either are unlikely to be effective or have been shown to be ineffective.[3] Fourth, we point to a related problem—the lack of systematic, institutionalized research on the bulk of correctional system policies, programs, and practices.

The subsequent sections turn more optimistic and prescriptive and include recommendations for improving prisoner reentry and public safety. In the fifth section, we argue that there exist numerous opportunities to improve prisoner reentry experiences and outcomes and, more broadly, to improve sanctioning practices and the correctional systems. Specifically, there are pre-prison, in-prison, and postrelease opportunities to improve reentry. In each instance, they include a focus on supervision, assistance, and preparation; education and employment; housing; inmate health; planning, decision making, and life skills; and social support. In the sixth section, we identify general guidelines and strategies that states and local jurisdictions can take to improve reentry. Seventh, we emphasize the importance of identifying not only sanctions and interventions that work (e.g., reduce crime) but also that do so cost-efficiently.

The final chapter sections argue for changes that go well beyond prisoners. Specifically, in section eight, we call for the creation of victim justice and community justice systems. Such a focus is necessary if our responses to crime are to be more effective and if they are to address the collateral consequences of incarceration. Ninth, we argue that many of the arguments that we present apply not only to the reentry population but also to convicted felons in general. Many felons do not go to prison. Yet these individuals face many of the same issues that ex-prisoners do, such as the potential for collateral consequences and invisible punishments. Finally, we argue that any serious attempt to create more government accountability, as policy makers have advocated, requires a substantial investment in improving research. Without it, the government will remain largely unable to document that policies, programs, and practices that they support are needed, effective, or cost-efficient.

THE INEFFECTIVENESS OF INCARCERATION IN IMPROVING PUBLIC SAFETY OR OTHER OUTCOMES

In Chapters 3 and 5, we discussed the limited evidence for incarceration achieving any of a range of effects, including achieving satisfactory levels of retribution, reducing recidivism, reducing crime rates, or creating satisfactory levels of justice for victims, communities, and society at large. It might be claimed that mass incarceration—that is, the rapid and increased investment in prisons during the 1980s and 1990s—contributed to upwards of 25 percent or so of the reduction in crime that occurred in the subsequent decade.[4] Few credible estimates of this effect exist, however, and those that do exist rest heavily on unproven assumptions.[5] At the same time, these estimates typically do not account for different counterfactual scenarios. What if, for example, $10 billion had been invested in schools and communities rather than prisons from 1990 to 1995? Or in different portfolios of sanctions? Would crime have gone down even more? Less? Or would there have been no difference? By and large, we simply do not know.

In considering the effects of incarceration, we should be cognizant of the fact that states vary in their sentencing laws and their use of prison, including who gets imprisoned and what alternatives they otherwise might have received. They vary in why they increased their use of incarceration, the duration and timing of the increase, and the timing in the de-escalation in the use of incarceration.[6] They vary as well in their investment in crime prevention efforts and in policies to alleviate poverty, improve employment rates, and so on. This variation across states and over time makes it difficult to show that mass incarceration in a direct or obvious way reduced crime rates relative to what would have happened if it had not occurred.[7]

Recidivism reduction seems to be an obvious benefit of prison, too. Yet empirical research has produced few credible estimates of incarceration effects. Among extant studies, evidence points to incarceration exerting criminogenic effects—that is, it worsens recidivism. Fewer studies have found that incarceration reduces recidivism. Still others have found that there appears to be no effect.[8] The situation is worse than that, however. For example, we know little about the extent to which lengthier sentences reduce recidivism (and for whom such an effect might occur). We know, too, almost nothing about whether incarceration is effective at reducing recidivism among individuals who previously have been incarcerated. Also, we know little about the precise conditions under which incarceration may reduce recidivism. In some communities, local interventions and probation practices may be highly ineffective. In these cases, incarceration might well produce a better outcome. In other communities, available interventions and probation practices could be of a high quality. We can anticipate that in these cases incarceration may not be effective and, indeed, might contribute to more rather than less recidivism as compared to what would have occurred if the local interventions were used.[9]

Here, we should take heed of the seemingly self-evident logic that imprisonment should deter offenders. Perhaps it does. However, the effect might well be overwhelmed by off-setting influences, a classic case of the cure being worse than the disease because of the harms that it creates. Consider, again, that prison does little to address an individual's life circumstances. An individual might feel a great deal of pain because of imprisonment, and their fear of ever again experiencing that pain may diminish their likelihood offending. Yet they leave prison and still may have a drug problem and be homeless and unable to find gainful employment. Notably, the prison experience itself may have a criminogenic effect that occurs alongside of the specific deterrent effect. For example, incarceration may result in a severing of social ties to family and community. As Raymond Paternoster has observed:

> While prison, and more rather than less prison, may send a deterrent message to would-be offenders that punishment is credible and severe, it may, in the longer-term, make it much more difficult for those who have been imprisoned to desist when they leave the penitentiary. There is an abundant literature that vividly describes the many and onerous obstacles to employment, housing, and full civic participation that ex-offenders face upon release from prison. . . . These obstacles have the effect of decreasing the utility of non-offending. Confronted by the fact that employment is substantially impaired because of their criminal record, public housing is restricted, and other penalties to citizenship exist, crime subsequent to imprisonment may be the more rational alternative for some past offenders.[10]

It might be anticipated that incarceration when coupled with postrelease supervision will reduce recidivism. However, empirical studies provide little support for that idea. For example, a national study undertaken by Amy Solomon and colleagues found that mandatory parole supervision appeared to exert no beneficial effect in reducing recidivism.[11] A review by Anne Piehl and Stefan

LoBuglio of supervision efforts reinforces that assessment.[12] Under certain conditions, and perhaps if coupled with treatment and services, supervision may reduce recidivism; on its own, however, supervision appears to achieve little.

Does incarceration contribute effectively to society feeling that satisfactory retribution has occurred? Not all of us are retributivist in orientation, but enough of us are that punishment for punishment's sake remains a central goal of punishment policy. The question thus is highly relevant. Unfortunately, too little evidence exists to answer it with confidence. As discussed in Chapter 3, we have no science of retribution, one that would identify which types of sanctions in which contexts achieve maximum levels of ideal retribution. "Ideal" here ultimately refers to a community-based view of the type and amount of punishment deemed to be appropriate. It does not have to mean lots of punishment nor does it have to mean incarceration.

So, how well does incarceration, much less a dramatic increase in it, achieve retribution? We simply do not know. All that we do know is that even in the face of historically unprecedented prison growth, the public has tended to feel that punishments are too lenient. Citizens, however, do not know much about crime rates or the use of various punishments, much less how many individuals go to prison or how long their prison terms will be. In addition, the perceived leniency does not mean that the public wants more prison. Rather, we at most can conclude that they want more punishment. What they really seem to want is an assurance that, in response to crime, government is taking effective steps to ensure that retribution, deterrence, and crime prevention occur. In general, though, the public appears to be skeptical about government effectiveness along all of these dimensions.

Not least, does incarceration or an increase in it lead to more justice? Do those charged with crimes, victims, communities, or society at large feel that conviction and sentencing decisions are fair and equitable? Do they feel that their particular needs and circumstances have been listened to and addressed? Here, again, research is largely silent, and so we are left with a logical inference. Specifically, given that the criminal justice system is overwhelmingly geared toward criminals, it seems unlikely to do much to make victims or communities feel that their voices are heard and that legitimate or effective justice has occurred. Consider that victim rights in many cases have taken a back seat to retribution. For example, prosecutors in some jurisdictions have sought aggressive sentences for domestic violence abusers, even when doing so goes against victim preferences and potentially may run against the victim's best interests. The result? Lengthier processing times and victims who feel doubly victimized.[13] There is, too, the considerable evidence that criminal justice policies and practices can be discriminatory in their use or effects and that minorities may view law enforcement and the courts as less than credible because of their perceived lack of legitimacy.[14] The result here can be greater mistrust of the criminal justice system and a perception that this system produces more injustice than justice.

THE INEFFECTIVENESS OF INCARCERATION DUE TO COLLATERAL CONSEQUENCES

As we discussed in earlier chapters, mass incarceration occurred alongside of a punitive turn in American criminal justice policy. This shift in policy brought with it a host of invisible punishments that punished individuals in ways that went beyond mere incarceration and created barriers to successful reentry. Employment, housing, voting, and welfare restrictions, limited access to educational loans, difficulty obtaining driver's licenses—these and more have been targeted by policy makers. However, the result appears not to be improved public safety but rather to have marginalized a population that already is likely to be unemployed and homeless, disinclined to vote or obtain further education, and so on.

In the final analysis, then, we have a situation in which those who go to prison may return to society more likely to recidivate, wind up homeless, be unemployed, have drug and mental health problems that have worsened, and hold weaker ties to family and community. It is not just crime, then, that may worsen due to criminogenic effects of incarceration. It is these other harms that communities may experience—more homelessness, unemployment, and social and economic disadvantage, disenchantment with and mistrust of the criminal justice system, a youth population that grows up viewing such conditions as normative, broken homes, and more.[15]

Here, again, ideally we would have an empirical study that could establish how incarceration causes potential benefits and harms.[16] No such studies exist. Accordingly, we are left having to cobble together what the most likely scenario appears to be given available theory and evidence. We recognize that empirical studies might one day counter our assessment. And we recognize, too, that others may disagree with the assessment. We recognize these possibilities and yet, based on our review, arrive at the view that mass incarceration not only has been extremely costly from a financial and social perspective but also has provided few obvious gains. The best-case scenario appears to be some potential reduction in crime rates. That is cause for cheering. But that best-case scenario involves substantial financial cost and the likely co-occurrence of increased recidivism and a multitude of potential harms to children, families, and communities.

There is, too, the final kicker—when we invest in emergency responses, we do so to address an emergency. Perhaps a dramatic increase in incarceration was warranted to impede increased crime and then to drive it down. However, we are left, then, with incarceration rates at emergency levels without any clear evidence that they can or will appreciably reduce crime in a non-emergency situation. Even with the stabilization of prison populations in recent years and the slight decline more recently, the country as a whole has invested in a level of incarceration that still is three to four times greater than what would have occurred if prison expansion had occurred in a more linear manner during the 1980s and subsequently. In short, the country for the foreseeable future is stuck investing in an emergency response that almost inescapably precludes large-scale investment in alternative approaches to crime prevention.[17]

Before proceeding, we should emphasize that a science of unintended effects and of collateral consequences is sorely needed. Few studies of crime policies or programs, including research on correctional system interventions, systematically evaluate the types and magnitudes of harms that occur.[18] An exception is a study by Brandon Welsh and Michael Rocque. Their study found that relatively few crime prevention programs (4 percent) have harmful effects.[19] The study did not per se focus on reentry programs. Rather, it focused on such programs as drug courts and mentoring interventions. Even so, the study is instructive and reassuring—it would appear that many noncustodial sanctions produce few harms. Would the same hold true, however, for incarceration and the wide range of invisible punishments that collectively constitute the punitive turn in American corrections? We do not know.

What we can say is that the estimate almost assuredly underestimates the true base rate or prevalence of harm created by many correctional interventions, sanctions, mass incarceration, and various invisible punishments. Why? Several reasons can be identified. First, selection effects likely are involved. For example, studies may find harmful effects but the authors do not seek to publish the results, or journals do not accept them, because they mistrust the results.

Second, many interventions, sanctions, and policies go unevaluated that may be likely to produce harms. A benefit of program evaluation is that practitioners may attend more carefully to full, high-quality implementation, in part because they know that their efforts are being monitored. Interventions that go unevaluated may have more implementation problems. These in turn may contribute to a failure to achieve intended effects and, at the same time, potential harms. For example, if program staff harass participants, that may engender ill will among the participants and a greater disrespect for authority. From a defiance theory perspective, such changes in turn may contribute to a greater level of offending upon release.[20]

A third reason is theory failure.[21] Put simply, a policy or program design may be flawed, such that the intervention, by design (even if unintentionally), actually may cause more of a problem rather than less of it. The plethora of interventions that constitute "correctional quackery" give credence to this concern.[22] Scared Straight programs are illustrative. Welsh and Rocque have observed that there is no clear theoretical foundation for anticipating beneficial program effects.[23] If anything, a stronger theoretical basis appears to exist for anticipating harmful effects. For example, young people, the target of Scared Straight programs, may be especially responsive to challenges to prove themselves. Accordingly, and, again, per defiance theory, they may act out in ways that show that they can meet or exceed the challenge.[24]

Fourth, not all harms are quantified in evaluation studies. We only see what we measure. If a study examines recidivism, it will present results on recidivism, and not, typically, homelessness, unemployment, mental illness, family dysfunction, and the like. The flip side of this concern, however, is that studies may understate potential benefits. For example, a drug court evaluation that fails to examine the effects of the court on reducing drug addiction would provide a distorted assessment of the court's benefits.

The broader issue? Careful empirical assessment of unintended effects has not been undertaken for mass incarceration. An assessment of collateral consequences ideally would involve systematic identification of potential harms throughout a state or given jurisdiction. It would involve, too, identification and quantification of opportunity costs. For example, when a state builds a prison it misses an opportunity to invest in some other type of policy intervention. What costs and harms arise from this missed opportunity? What missed benefits occur? Ultimately, we want empirically based answers to such questions to provide balanced assessments of the impact of mass incarceration. Absent such assessments we are left with the cumulative weight of theoretical and empirical work on specific types of collateral consequences and harms. These suggest, as we have argued above, that mass incarceration may well have produced more harm than good.

CORRECTIONS EFFORTS FREQUENTLY REST ON WEAK THEORETICAL AND EMPIRICAL GROUNDS

A car design based on incorrect assumptions about physics, chemistry, and more will not run. Few of us, for example, would buy a vehicle made of paper and glue, at least not one that we intended to use for transportation to and from work. Similarly, a drug that targets a factor unrelated to cancer will not reduce, eliminate, or cure cancer. Other examples could be provided, but the point would be the same—to reduce a problem, we need to target the cause of the problem. We may do so directly or indirectly. For example, if X needs Y to be present to cause Z, we can directly target X. Alternatively, we can minimize its ability to affect Z through an indirect means—specifically, we can remove Y and, in so doing, render X harmless.

When devising a solution to a problem, it can be helpful to build on knowledge about the problem. Yes, paradigm shifts can occur and result in new insights that prior paradigms would be unable to identify.[25] In addition, practitioners and others with on-the-ground perspectives can be uniquely situated to provide insights. The rest of the time, however, we would be well served if we took heed of the insights to be found in theory and research. Indeed, it would be unusual not to do so.

Oddly, though, American criminal justice and correctional policy is replete with sanctions, interventions, programs, practices, and the like that seemingly ignore science. They build on personal views about what somehow must work. And they frequently appear to have no overlap with theory or research on the causes of offending. As we noted at the beginning of the chapter, Latessa and colleagues have termed such efforts "correctional quackery" and have catalogued a large number of them.[26]

One example is in-prison interventions like art therapy and self-esteem programs. Such efforts might advance an offender's artistic abilities, allow them to express their views, or enhance their self-esteem, and such improvements conceivably might reduce recidivism. There is little credible empirical evidence to support such claims. Regardless, one might readily allow that the effects could happen. Are they, however, plausible? Consider that neither approach in any direct way builds on extant theory or research on the causes of crime or desistance. As investors, we at the least would want interventions to target known causes of crime, especially those that exert the strongest effects on offending. Interventions that fail to do so start out behind the eight ball, all the more so if there is no compelling theoretical or empirically based argument to support an exclusive focus on a single factor, such as self-esteem.

Another prominent example involves boot camps. The military-like structure of boot camps can be appealing to some policy makers and members of the public. Somehow we can feel confident that offenders will be held accountable.

Indeed, in a military-like setting, how could offenders not be kept in line? Notably, however, empirical research consistently has reported null effects of boot camps.[27] On theoretical grounds, we can anticipate why—they do little to nothing to address known causes of offending. They do not, for example, in any obvious way undertake activities designed to improve an individual's social bond, reduce strain, increase self-control, alter labeling processes, and so on.[28]

The boot camp theme unfortunately can be found to underlie many of the get-tough policy reforms that surfaced in recent decades. Although exceptions can easily be identified, the overarching pattern consists of investing in control-oriented, retributivist responses that simultaneously fail to target in a systematic manner the diverse causes of criminal behavior. Mass incarceration—including the emphasis both on more incarceration and lengthier terms of incarceration—constitutes the most obvious and prominent example.[29]

Is punishment satisfying? Presumably, yes, at some basic level it can help us to feel that at least some type of action was taken. Is it sufficient? No, not even on retributivist grounds. Those who have been victims of crime, for example, may want as much punishment as is possible for offenders. Putting retribution aside, though, punitive sanctions do not in any obvious way reduce recidivism or crime rates. Why? They do little to address known causes of crime.

It is not, however, just punitive interventions that have received considerable attention. As we discussed above, states and local jurisdictions also have invested substantially in "correctional quackery." They also have invested in a wide range of efforts for which little credible supporting empirical evidence exists. Latessa and colleagues have catalogued many of these efforts, as have many others.[30] One such unsupported intervention is the faith-based programs that states under both Republican and Democratic administrations have invested in. There is, however, little evidence—from studies that use strong research designs to address selection effects—that they reduce recidivism.[31] What makes these types of efforts stand out is that rely on the notion that offending stems primarily from a moral or personal failing. Correct that failing and all will be well. This view is not necessarily wrong, but it neglects the role that contextual factors play in offending. Put differently, faith-based programs in part exemplify a way of thinking that locates the causes of crime, and thus its cure, almost exclusively within the individual. Ultimately, the correctional system deals with individuals and so focusing on changing these individuals makes logical sense.[32] Yet changing individuals without changing their circumstances or the settings to which they return likely will do little to appreciably reduce recidivism or to make society safer.

MINIMAL EVALUATION OF MOST REENTRY POLICIES, PROGRAMS, AND PRACTICES

In an era in which increasing calls have been made to create more government accountability and to operate government more efficiently, the lack of investment in criminal justice and correctional system research stands out. Companies typically invest large sums of money in research and development and in monitoring their operations. Without such an investment, companies risk inefficiency and miss opportunities to improve efficiency. Oddly, though, the United States—both at federal and state levels—has embarked on large-scale growth in criminal justice and corrections with little corresponding investment in research.

Consider that in recent years, annual expenditures for criminal justice—including funding for law enforcement, the judiciary, and corrections—have exceeded $200 billion.[33] This estimate does not reflect any assumptions about the costs of crime itself, which some scholars have pegged at $1 trillion to $3 trillion annually.[34] These costs come in many forms and include pain and suffering; money spent by individuals and companies on crime protection measures; time spent by individuals, various agencies, and government attempting to repair victimization harms; effects on perceived or actual quality of life; and more.

Yet the combined budget for the two federal agencies responsible for criminal justice research nationally—the National Institute of Justice and the Bureau of Justice Statistics—is only an estimated $100 million.[35] That amounts to considerably less than 1 percent of annual expenditures on criminal justice. More precisely, it represents 5 percent of 1 percent of such expenditures. As Alfred Blumstein has observed, this budget pales in comparison to what the United States spends to conduct research in other areas: "For medical matters, the National Institutes of Health has a total annual budget of about $30 billion and the Bureau of Labor Statistics has a budget of about $600 million just for measuring labor markets."[36]

The discrepancy is striking. Nationally, the federal government invests "more than 2 percent of its gross domestic product (GDP) for research and development."[37] Private industry not infrequently invests even more on research and development, with some large companies investing 5 to 10 percent or more of revenues on it.[38] However, a pittance is spent on crime and justice research. The shortfall stands out all the more because states and foundations do not compensate through large-scale investment in research. It stands out as well because federal criminal justice research funds support studies, data collection, and analyses that cover virtually every aspect of crime, criminal justice, and corrections. The limited funds and the breadth of coverage together impede creation of systematic, in-depth knowledge about the many topics that fall under these broad umbrellas.

In short, if the federal government prioritized crime and justice research as it does research on other social problems or in a manner that paralleled a business approach, investment in crime, criminal justice, and corrections would be substantially greater. A thought experiment puts the situation in stark relief—nationally, we spend as much on research as it might cost to build one high-technology prison. Yet an investment in research might well identify that building a prison is unnecessary. It also might identify approaches to reducing crime that would reduce the need for incarceration. Here, one need only consider supermax prisons—in 1980, states did not have supermax housing and yet, over the next 30 years, all but a handful of states created it—and did so with minimal empirical assessment of whether the housing was needed. To date, it still remains largely unknown whether the housing effectively improves prison order; we do know that it worsens inmate mental health and recidivism.[39]

A legitimate counter to the concerns about funding is that exceptions exist. For example, in 2010, Congress appropriated several million dollars, augmented by funding from the Pew Charitable Trusts, to create the Justice Reinvestment Initiative, which in turn sought to promote research-based correctional reforms.[40] In 2007, Congress enacted the Second Chance Act, which provided $165 million in grants to support efforts to improve reentry.[41]

Also, in 2002, the U.S. Department of Justice awarded over $100 million in grants to states under the Serious and Violent Offender Reentry Initiative (SVORI).[42] This effort aimed to increase insights into ways in which strategically administered services and supervision might improve reentry outcomes. It provided some important insights, including the observation that implementation challenges plagued many of the reentry programs. To illustrate, many of the programs experienced considerable challenges in fully providing various services, treatments, and types of supervision. Participant profiles, such as their specific risks and needs, did not always accord with what was intended for the programs. In addition, the amount and quality of intervention frequently was not sufficient to achieve appreciable improvements in intermediate outcomes (e.g., obtaining housing or employment) or in longer-term outcomes (e.g., recidivism). Some of the specific SVORI programs demonstrated improvements in recidivism, but on the whole the improvements were modest.[43] From a research perspective, the evaluation of SVORI highlighted a longstanding concern in criminal justice research—namely, insufficient funding for studies leads to underpowered assessments of programs and policies, thus making it difficult to generate credible estimates of program effects (or the lack of effects).[44]

We do not want to suggest that there are not bright spots on the horizon. Indeed, the Justice Reinvestment Initiative, the Second Chance Act, and SVORI testify to the interest in and support for improving public safety. Even so, funding constraints impede the ability to generate a strong research foundation on which to improve reentry and other punishment policies on a large scale. The situation is akin to using a laser pointer to explore a large underground cavern. Progress can be made here and there, but the full contours of the cavern and diversity of life in it will remain largely unknown.

PRE-PRISON, IN-PRISON, AND POSTRELEASE APPROACHES TO SUCCESSFUL REENTRY

Given the problems that plague criminal justice and correctional system research and policy, is there any cause for optimism? Absolutely. In the following pages, we identify a wide range of approaches that can be taken to improve reentry as well as criminal justice and correctional system policy. In this section, we focus on three different stages where reentry efforts can be targeted: (a) pre-prison (i.e., the period just before individuals go to jail or prison); (b) in-prison (i.e., the period of time during which individuals are incarcerated); and (c) postrelease (i.e., the period after individuals are released from prison). Each stage offers unique opportunities for improving the likelihood that those who leave prison have the best chance possible for desisting from crime and obtaining housing, employment, treatment, and services. At each stage, there are policies, programs, and practices that can serve as the vehicle for improving reentry. In addition, at each stage, there exist six areas that reentry efforts can target to facilitate a successful return to society. These include (a) supervision, assistance, and preparation; (b) education and employment; (c) housing; (d) inmate health; (e) planning, decision making, and life skills; and (f) social support. These three stages, the emphasis on policies, programs, and practices, and the six target areas are depicted graphically in Figure 9.1.

The figure's logic warrants elaboration. All too often, policy makers and practitioners endorse support of a *program*. That makes sense. A program is tangible. We might be able to visualize it even if we have never seen the program. However, programs at best offer a piecemeal approach to improving reentry. In addition, they constitute but one of several ways that we can improve reentry. At least two others stand out: policies and practices. *Policies* consist of state laws or administrative decisions, whether formally or informally articulated, for how different parts of the correctional system should operate. *Practices* consist of the innumerable decisions that those who work in criminal justice and corrections make every day. For example, one parole officer might take a hands-off approach

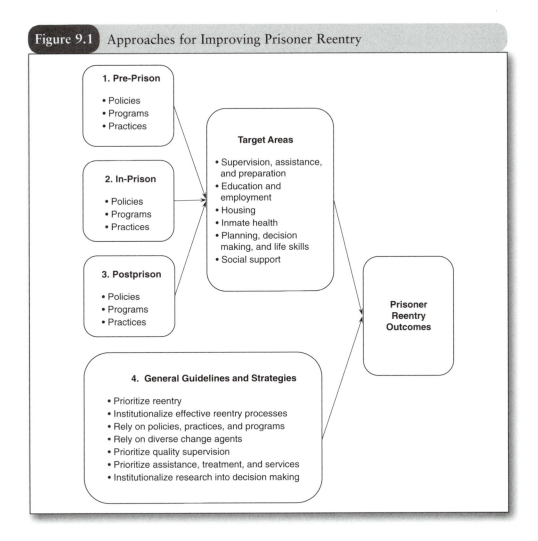

Figure 9.1   Approaches for Improving Prisoner Reentry

1. Pre-Prison
• Policies
• Programs
• Practices

2. In-Prison
• Policies
• Programs
• Practices

3. Postprison
• Policies
• Programs
• Practices

Target Areas
• Supervision, assistance, and preparation
• Education and employment
• Housing
• Inmate health
• Planning, decision making, and life skills
• Social support

Prisoner Reentry Outcomes

4. General Guidelines and Strategies
• Prioritize reentry
• Institutionalize effective reentry processes
• Rely on policies, practices, and programs
• Rely on diverse change agents
• Prioritize quality supervision
• Prioritize assistance, treatment, and services
• Institutionalize research into decision making

to supervising a parolee while another might seek to intervene and help in whatever way he or she can. The different practices do not constitute programs or policies and yet might affect greatly parolee outcomes. As the figure indicates, policies, programs, and practices prior to, during, and after reentry can be undertaken to improve recidivism, housing, employment, health, and other outcomes. The figures indicate, too, that these outcomes can come from focusing on one or more target areas. Given that most individuals who enter and leave prison have a multitude of deficits and face many barriers to reentry, it can make sense to employ multipronged strategies. Indeed, many reentry efforts do just that.[45]

In the bottom half of the figure, we identify general guidelines and strategies that can be taken to improve prisoner reentry. We discuss these in the subsequent section, after discussing pre-prison, in-prison, and postrelease reentry efforts and approaches. Our reasoning here is simple: It can be easy to get lost in the forest when looking at the trees. In this instance, we can get mired down in focusing on the many different specific aspects of reentry policy, programming, and practice. Accordingly, we use the general guidelines and strategies section to describe the "forest"—that is, the many different approaches that states and local jurisdictions can take to improve more systematically and comprehensively reentry outcomes.

Several tables describe ways that reentry experiences and outcomes can be improved. Table 9.1 presents pre-prison possibilities, Table 9.2 presents in-prison possibilities, Table 9.3 presents postrelease possibilities, and Table 9.4 presents general guidelines and strategies. We culled the different ideas from a large number of sources and introduced new ones that we identified through consideration of prior theory and research and its implications for different aspects of reentry.[46] Scholarship on mass incarceration and reentry has burgeoned. The result is a large number of meta-analyses, comprehensive reviews, journal articles, books, reports, briefs, and more that highlight effective or promising reentry efforts. They all tend to cover similar territory, though some of course touch on some areas more than others.

Our primary emphasis here ultimately is to convey the forest for the trees. In so doing, we seek to underscore that no silver-bullet solutions exist for improving reentry and public safety in America or anywhere else for that matter. Rather, what is needed are comprehensive, research-based approaches that involve constant assessment, monitoring, and evaluation to ensure that taxpayer dollars are used to their greatest effect. The Bureau of Justice Assistance, the Bureau of Justice Statistics, the Office of Juvenile Justice and Delinquency Prevention, and the National Institute of Justice, as well as many other organizations, provide rich repositories of information about programs and efforts that can be undertaken to improve reentry. (A list of such organizations is provided in Table 9.5.) Here, again, we want to emphasize the need for a systematic approach that tackles reentry from diverse vantage points and that is tailored to specific populations and contexts.

Pre-Prison Approaches to Improving Reentry

"An ounce of prevention is worth a pound of cure." This aphorism from Benjamin Franklin is directly relevant for criminal justice—if we have less crime, then we have less need of punishment or various interventions. Similarly, if someone already has committed a crime, then early intervention can reduce future offending that they otherwise might undertake and thus reduce the attendant need for sanctions. In some cases, that intervention may be prison. In others, it might not be prison and yet we still might incarcerate an individual. Why? Calls for retribution alone might dictate a term of incarceration. Regardless, we also want prison to reduce recidivism. We know, though, that it might worsen recidivism and other outcomes, and we know some of the reasons, including negative experiences while incarcerated, a weakening of family ties, difficulty finding housing and work upon release, and so on.

Typically, reentry policy discussions zero in on the postrelease period as a time to intervene. Sometimes there are calls to begin taking steps to improve postrelease outcomes by intervening while a person is incarcerated. However, in all likelihood, some of the most effective steps that we can take to reduce recidivism and improve other reentry outcomes may occur before a convicted felon actually gets sent to prison. An ounce of effort at this stage may well reduce the need for a pound of intervention at a later stage. It is similar to the work that the military ideally would do to help ensure that individuals are prepared not only for life as a soldier but also life upon return back to civilian society. Table 9.1 reveals that, in fact, many possible avenues exist to lay the groundwork for successful reentry.

Table 9.1   Pre-Prison: Improving Reentry Through Policies, Programs, and Practices

a. Supervision, Assistance, and Preparation

- Create groundwork to prepare inmates for reentry.
- Identify the risks and criminogenic needs of each convicted offender.

b. Education and Employment

- Identify educational needs and educational program enrollment.
- Identify professional strengths and weaknesses for future employment opportunities.
- Engage employment assistance services prior to an individual being transferred to prison.

c. Housing

- Create a housing plan for inmates.
- Encourage families of inmates to assist inmates with housing upon release.

d. Inmate Health

- Screen and assess convicted offenders for physical and mental health issues.

e. Planning, Decision Making, and Life Skills

- Identify and teach appropriate planning, coping, and decision-making skills.
- Educate inmates on the realities of the prison experience.
- Create a financial plan.

f. Social Support

- House inmates near their social support network.
- Educate families about coping with a loved one who is imprisoned.
- Educate family members and friends about supporting or visiting an inmate.
- Institute pre-prison ceremonies in communities.
- Offer family support prior to incarceration.

a. Supervision, Assistance, and Preparation. Consider that reentry success may depend on adequate supervision and access to social services that can facilitate access to housing and treatment. It also may depend on an inmate feeling and being prepared for life as a prisoner. The latter may be especially critical to ensuring that individuals are not adversely affected by prison and, conversely, that they may benefit from it. This observation highlights the potentially critical importance of working with parole and local social service agencies to discuss an offender's impending transfer and plans for how to support him or her during and after incarceration.

How such preparation could occur might vary. One possibility is to conduct risk and needs assessments that could be used to inform decisions about how best to work with the inmate prior to, during, and after transfer to prison. Many individuals serve no more than 2 years in prison, and up to 9 or 12 months of that term may be spent in a local jail. Accordingly, risk and needs assessments can be critical to arriving at more effective decisions about managing and assisting an individual during the interim period in jail and the follow-up period in prison. This assessment could be used as well to begin devising plans for the individual's eventual release back into the community. Reentry planning may be irrelevant for individuals serving 5 or 10 years, but even in these cases, any steps that can be taken to ensure a smooth transition to prison could yield benefits in the form of reduced misconduct in prison and possibly reduced recidivism.

b. Education and Employment. The educational and employment backgrounds for most individuals who go to prison look anemic. By and large, this background does not change during a prison term. Given that situation, it makes sense to begin laying the groundwork for identifying educational and employment opportunities that may exist when an individual leaves prison. Doing so may help the individual feel more optimistic about their chances and so improve their behavior during and after incarceration. (It also may serve as a corrective against an individual feeling overly optimistic about the chances of success upon release.[47]) In addition, it may contribute to a greater likelihood of participating in an educational program or securing a job. The court, correctional system, and local social service providers all could be enjoined to collaborate in supporting an individual and his or her family in advancing educational and employment opportunities for a convicted felon. Potential employers, for example, might be identified who would commit to considering an individual for employment if he or she can emerge from prison with a largely spotless record of behavior. Here, again, given that many inmates may serve relatively short terms of incarceration, this groundwork can be easier to undertake prior to the individual being transferred to a state prison.

c. Housing. Homelessness in the weeks and months after release from prison is likely for many individuals. Even when housing can be obtained, it may place an ex-prisoner's family at risk or put the ex-prisoner in a criminogenic setting or context. The convicted felon and his or her family may be largely unaware of these issues, and yet they are inescapable. Upon release from prison, housing will be needed, and families and friends may be the first place to which ex-prisoners turn. Unfortunately, they may not always be able to help or, again, may be put at risk by housing the ex-prisoner. For these reasons, creating a housing plan prior to transfer to prison can constitute one cornerstone of a successful strategy for reentry. Families and friends could be part of any such planning, but the courts, correctional system, and local social service agencies could focus more broadly on all available options in the community.

d. Inmate Health. The physical or mental health of many individuals who go to prison is poor. That does not magically change during incarceration and, indeed, inmate health may worsen. Here, the Benjamin Franklin dictum is directly on point: Early detection and treatment of illness translates into less illness, a lower likelihood of illness progressing into a more severe stage or condition, and less cost. Jails, no less than prisons, can be conduits for communicable diseases. Accordingly, thorough screening and assessment while individuals are in jail can be critical for improving health outcomes at this stage as well as when individuals subsequently are transferred to prison. Although many jails conduct screening and assessment, all-too-frequently these efforts rely on instruments and approaches that have not been validated and are given short shrift. A public health perspective on incarceration highlights that investment in a validated, well-implemented screening and assessment, as well as treatment, might well avoid greater costs down the line.

e. Planning, Decision Making, and Life Skills. Numerous accounts point to the many deficits that inmates have and the considerable disadvantage that characterizes the settings from which they come. Deficits and disadvantage do not excuse offending or constitute grounds for sympathizing with offenders. They do, however, underscore the fact that the typical offender makes poor decisions and likely will continue to do so during and after incarceration.[48] The causes of the poor decision making may vary, but the end result remains the same—more offending and other adverse outcomes. Accordingly, educational efforts ideally would begin prior to transfer to prison. These efforts would not necessarily be traditional ones, such as those oriented towards helping individuals obtain a high school degree or vocational training. Rather, they would be focused on helping inmates to understand how they make decisions and how they can make better ones. Any such effort, however, should not consist of simply explaining. It should focus as well on practicing making better decisions. Knowing what to do and developing habits that involve doing the right thing are not the same, as a large body of scholarship on correctional programming highlights.[49]

This emphasis on better decision making holds special relevance for the transition to prison. While incarcerated, inmates face many challenges, including the potential for victimization, abuse, loss of hope, and more. The opportunities for making poor decisions are ubiquitous. By the same token, individuals have room to determine how they will respond to prison conditions. Many inmate accounts identify abuses that would challenge any of us. In the end, however, the inmate must choose how to respond. Advance preparation therefore can be essential, just as it would be for soldiers who enter combat situations that fall outside their prior life experiences.

Just as clearly, better decision making may facilitate creation of more viable and effective plans for reentry. Consider inmate finances. Most prisoners have limited financial resources and will leave prison with even less. One strategy consists of hoping that this situation will change. Such magical thinking will do little to help them when, 1 or 2 or 3 years later, they leave prison. Developing a plan for how they will pay for housing, food, education, supporting their children or family, and so on constitutes an area where improved decision-making skills is critical.

f. Social Support. Social support is a dimension that many different theories of crime implicate, albeit in different ways. For example, for strain theory, families may constitute a potential source of strain or a resource for coping with strain. By contrast, for social bond theory, families may constitute a vehicle through which individuals feel more bound to conform with social norms and laws. Families and communities, too, can constitute resources that enable individuals to negotiate life circumstances in ways that enable or encourage prosocial behavior and make recourse to criminal behavior unnecessary or unproductive.[50] Regardless of the mechanism, it remains clear that strong social support networks can be instrumental for individuals in maintaining a pro-social life and having a successful reentry.

What efforts can be undertaken prior to incarceration to foster such support? Many possibilities exist. For example, one approach that prison systems take is to place individuals in facilities near to the communities from which they come. Doing so can facilitate more visitation and linkages to locally available social services that could be accessed upon release.

Another approach is to educate families about the realities of incarceration and to support their efforts to visit and assist incarcerated family members. Such efforts should emphasize the challenges that the families themselves will face during the period of incarceration and during reentry. These challenges include difficulties with finances, transportation, child care, housing, and more. When families struggle to meet these challenges, they provide a weaker foundation of support for inmates and ex-prisoners. This foundation is weakened further when, as frequently occurs, inmates create additional burdens for families.

Still another approach is to initiate welcoming-back ceremonies prior to incarceration. When individuals leave prison, there typically is no one to welcome them back. In addition, they face barriers that create a sense of social exclusion. Scholars have advocated approaches that take a different line. It involves the use of ceremonies, perhaps undertaken by criminal courts, that signal to individuals that they no longer are felons or prisoners but rather citizens who, if they conform to societal norms and laws, are welcome back.[51] This approach has not been well evaluated, but the premise rests on a sound theoretical logic that emphasizes the salience of communities, and informal social control mechanisms, as a means of promoting public order. Encouraging communities to participate in a welcoming-back process implicitly recognizes and encourages the value of informal social control. In addition, it avoids criminogenic labeling of offenders and conveys to ex-prisoners several messages—they are being watched (deterrence) and they will be supported. A simple way to initiate this process prior to incarceration consists of apprising the convicted felon of the reentry ceremony that awaits him or her.

In-Prison Approaches to Improving Reentry

In addition to undertaking reentry preparation prior to incarceration, we can use the in-prison period as a time to further prepare offenders for reentry. Here, again, we can identify six dimensions to target our efforts. Of course, we could wait until the last minute, just before inmates leave prison. In so doing, however, we miss innumerable opportunities to create successful desistance trajectories. Indeed, we likely cement a negative reentry experience, one that includes more offending, homelessness, unemployment, illness, and more. Put differently, the imprisonment period constitutes a perfect time to take steps to improve reentry.

Table 9.2   In-Prison: Improving Reentry Through Policies, Programs, and Practices

a. Supervision, Assistance, and Preparation
- Prioritize reentry planning.
- Train prison staff to adopt a pro-social role with inmates.
- Enhance staff training for in-prison and reentry-focused programs and services.
- Base early-release decisions on program participation while in prison.
- Institute a system of discretionary parole release.
- Implement ways for inmates and officers to provide suggestions for improving order.

b. Education and Employment
- Institute education and academic skills training programs.
- Institute work and vocational skills programs.
- Emphasize skilled work programs that are tailored to inmates' communities.

c. Housing
- Create a housing plan for inmates as they near release.

d. Inmate Health
- Undertake health screening at intake and throughout an inmate's term of incarceration.
- Provide medical programming, services, and treatment.
- Create prison environments that are conducive to physical and mental health.
- Arrange community drug treatment and relapse prevention for inmates near release.
- Establish health care treatment plans prior to release.

e. Planning, Decision Making, and Life Skills
- Educate inmates nearing release about the challenging realities of the reentry process.
- Provide interpersonal, financial, and life skills training.
- Implement cognitive-behavioral rehabilitative programming.
- Allow inmates autonomy to the extent possible to promote responsibility.

f. Social Support
- Promote family and friend visitation and communication.
- Include community-based organizations and families in inmate reentry planning.
- Create community support groups for families of inmates.

a. Supervision, Assistance, and Preparation. Pre-prison reentry preparation can and should continue when individuals go to prison. Corrections personnel can be assigned to work with inmates to develop reentry plans. Reentry courts conceivably could participate in this work. The plans would include details about what the inmate can do while incarcerated to adjust to prison life and to obtain experiences, such as educational or vocational training, that might help them upon release. Such planning would serve indirectly to convey to inmates the importance of creating goals and developing viable strategies for achieving these goals.

This planning would serve, too, to signal to corrections personnel that prison should serve not only to punish but also to prepare inmates in ways that promote public safety and well-being. Cultural change in institutional settings can be challenging. Yet it may constitute one of the most powerful ways that prison systems can achieve greater social order and simultaneously improve ex-prisoner reentry outcomes.[52] A focus on reentry preparation might help create such change. A related approach is to undertake staff training about ways to work with and supervise inmates effectively. Working in prisons can be difficult. Yet some approaches to managing inmates will bring out the worst in them and other approaches will create more compliance. Officers do not magically acquire knowledge of these skills. Education and training as well as a culture of professionalism that supports humane and effective intervention are needed.

Under many sentencing laws, individuals who go to prison have little incentive to behave. Implementing early-release options, whether through discretionary parole board decision making or use of behavioral performance measures, constitutes a critical carrot that states can use to motivate individuals to behave while in prison. The behavioral criteria that parole boards use can vary but should be viable. Requiring good conduct alone would not likely be sufficient. Rather the bar should include full compliance with prison rules and expectations and active participation in available programs and services. Inmates should have to work to signal that they warrant early release.[53] Avoiding misconduct alone, which can be difficult in prison, would not suffice.

Other approaches to supervising, assisting, and preparing inmates for release exist. Indeed, the possibilities are endless, though not all necessarily will be effective.[54] In addition, some may work better in some contexts than others. A classic tension in prison management consists of dramatic swings from one approach to another. One prison warden employs a militaristic approach, then the next one employs a decentralized, officer- or inmate-empowering approach.[55] Such swings almost invariably risk inefficiency and long-term ineffectiveness. When one approach has been used for many years, there likely needs to be a gradual progression to a new way of operating prisons. Ultimately, the possibilities that will be effective in a given prison or correctional system likely vary and depend on the creativity of officers and administrators. One idea would be to regularly solicit ideas from officers and inmates about how to improve prison operations and then to show that at least some of the time these ideas are implemented.

b. Education and Employment. Evidence that education and employment programs improve inmate behavior and reentry outcomes is mixed. Yet, with a prison population, almost any effort that focuses primarily on one dimension likely will do little to affect appreciably offending or other outcomes given that inmates typically have multiple deficits and both come from and will return to disadvantage. Accordingly, it would seem to make sense to prioritize education and employment programming for inmates. Doing so highlights that successful reentry constitutes a priority and conveys that the prison system is committed to facilitating success. Although funding for such programming declined in recent decades, numerous opportunities exist to promote more of it. One option, of course, is to increase funding for these types of programmatic efforts. Another is to create ties with local universities and colleges to provide instruction.

Providing meaningful work training and opportunities in prison can be difficult. Even under the best circumstances, it will be difficult to ensure that job readiness training results in a greater ability for an ex-prisoner to secure employment. Prisons, for example, can do little to affect the employment conditions in the communities to which ex-prisoners return. Nonetheless, if we want inmates to have jobs, some preparation is critical. In addition, if employment-related programming was coupled with efforts to work with communities, it might be possible to increase the chances that some employers will hire released prisoners.

c. Housing. Inmates make many incorrect assumptions about what life will entail upon release, and that can include assumptions about housing.[56] Compounding this problem is the likelihood that they will leave prison with little to no money and encounter a world in which family and friends may not embrace them. Accordingly, the pre-prison planning for living arrangements should continue, and inmates should be provided lists of specific housing opportunities in the communities to which they return. It is not sufficient simply to have designated reentry housing; specific backup plans should be identified. In addition, inmates should be counseled about the housing challenges that they will face upon release. Not least, families and community organizations in the areas to which inmates will be returned should be included in developing inmate plans for housing.

d. Inmate Health. Untreated physical illness, including communicable diseases, and mental illness create many problems for inmates, correctional systems, families, and communities. Many possibilities exist for improving inmate health. The simplest, though costly, approach involves undertaking health screening and assessment of all individuals at intake. Communicable diseases constitute a significant problem in prisons, and so periodic health screenings should occur. Treatment of diagnosed illness should be implemented promptly, with special attention to ensuring continuity of care from the community to the prison setting. Health care plans should be developed that help inmates continue needed treatment upon release.

A general strategy involves creating prison environments that foster health. Prisons do not frequently pursue this strategy. Nutrition may be poor, opportunities to exercise may be limited, little programming may be available to assist inmates in pursuing meaningful educational or vocational training, inmate-to-inmate and inmate-officer relationships may be strained, and so on. All of these factors conspire against physical or mental health. Efforts to create healthier prison settings thus may be critical for improving inmate health and likely officer health as well.

e. Planning, Decision Making, and Life Skills. Pre-prison efforts to improve inmate planning, decision making, and life skills should continue in prison. As inmates near the end of their prison term, special emphasis should be given to developing specific plans for all facets of the release process, including challenges related to housing, employment, resuming relationships with family members and friends, health care, and drug treatment. The typical inmate has poor planning skills and likely underestimates considerably the challenges that he or she will face.

Most inmates have multiple deficits. Research consistently has found that cognitive-behavioral programming can be especially effective in improving inmate behavior and reducing recidivism. Such programming should be prioritized, as should processes for ensuring accurate matching of inmates, and their various needs, with appropriate interventions. Numerous programs with a foundation in cognitive-behavioral intervention exist; the challenge thus lies in funding such programs, implementing them well, and ensuring appropriate placements.[57]

Bizarre though it may seem when discussing prisoners, more rather than less inmate autonomy should occur. Imposed structure can ensure greater order in prisons, but it leaves inmates with little ability to develop the ability to make better decisions on their own. This general problem holds across a range of social situations. During medical school, for example, students may learn how to diagnose and treat patients in a group setting where they consult with other students and their teacher and where they are allowed considerable time to arrive at their diagnoses. Such training does little to facilitate accurate decision making in the real-world context that the students will face, one where they typically must make diagnoses on their own with little time for deliberate contemplation of the many diagnostic possibilities.[58] So, too, inmates who receive few opportunities to make decisions about their day-to-day lives will not be well-prepared to make pro-social, healthy decisions upon release. Can inmates be given such possibilities? Yes. Many prison wardens find ways to maintain order and yet challenge inmates to develop better decision-making skills.[59]

f. Social Support. The pre-prison efforts to increase social support of inmates should continue during imprisonment. Prison officials should take steps to increase visitation and communication with family, friends, and other visitors, such as volunteers from faith-based and community-based organizations. Simple steps can be taken, including expanded visiting hours, creating more welcoming visitation facilities, reducing the costs of phone calls, and using video visitation. For some inmates, a critical turning point in their lives that contributes to desistance can be the support of others, including volunteers or members of the community to which they return.[60] Visitation and these other forms of social support require little cost and yet may promote a turn away from criminal behavior.

As inmates near release, they or prison system personnel should be in communication with community service providers, family members, and friends. These groups and individuals ideally would be involved with the inmate's reentry plan to help ensure that he or she has a social support network for addressing reentry challenges and ensuring continuity of care.

While inmates are incarcerated, attention to their families and communities may improve both in-prison and postrelease behavioral outcomes. Families may experience considerable strain when a loved one is incarcerated. Such strain may preclude visitation; it also may inhibit a successful transition back to the family upon release. Similarly, communities that send large numbers of individuals to prison or receive them may be ill equipped to support these individuals. A vicious cycle thus ensues—inmates may engage in more misconduct and fare more poorly in prison, and they may be more likely to offend upon release. Accordingly, reentry efforts ideally would target families and communities for services and support.

Postprison Approaches to Improving Reentry

Finally, in addition to taking steps prior to and during incarceration to improve reentry outcomes, we can employ a variety of approaches after inmates have been released to improve these outcomes. As with the discussions above,

Table 9.3   Postprison: Improving Reentry Through Policies, Programs, and Practices

a. Supervision, Assistance, and Preparation
- Use static and criminogenic risk factors to assess the likelihood of recidivism.
- Create and use research-based parole supervision classification systems.
- Educate ex-prisoners and those who live or work with them about reentry challenges.
- Notify law enforcement when an inmate is to be released and sent home.
- Establish requirements for parole board membership.
- Minimize the parole supervision period.
- Imbue parole with a dual emphasis on supervision and social work assistance.
- Limit invisible punishments and seal criminal records.
- Identify volunteer opportunities for ex-prisoners to demonstrate a pro-social identity.

b. Education and Employment
- Identify education or employment mentors.
- Provide employment assistance.
- Offer certificates of employment readiness.

c. Housing
- Monitor housing arrangements to ensure that ex-prisoners do not become homeless.
- Allow ex-prisoners access to subsidized housing.

d. Inmate Health
- Refer ex-prisoners for needed health services.
- Refer individuals with a history of addiction to outpatient treatment facilities.

e. Planning, Decision Making, and Life Skills
- Offer cognitive-behavioral interventions.
- Offer training on basic life skills, including negotiating interpersonal conflict.

f. Social Support
- Encourage participation in support groups for ex-prisoners.
- Institute welcome-back community ceremonies.
- Promote family reunification efforts that provide guidance and mentoring.
- Foster community involvement in the reentry process.

we focus here on six dimensions that various policies, programs, and practices could target. In many ways, the initial transition matters most—the likelihood of recidivism is greatest in the first months after release. As with most experiences in life, a good start can be the difference between a good or bad outcome.

a. Supervision, Assistance, and Preparation. Correctional systems operate with insufficient resources to provide ideal types and levels of supervision, support, and services. Thus, they have to triage based on assessed risk for recidivism and need for services. Validated fourth-generation risk and needs assessment should be undertaken prior to release and ideally these would be updated periodically during the postrelease period to capture potential changes in criminogenic factors. This information should be used to assign parolees to specific types and levels of supervision, support, and services. It can be used as well to help inmates understand what they need to do to prepare for life on the outside. Such assessments should occur for all inmates as they leave prison to ensure that those released to no supervision still are identified as needing services that, if provided, might improve their desistance chances.

Reentry is all too often poorly understood by offenders and those who work or associate with them. One critical element of a reentry plan is to ensure that offenders, their families and communities, employers, and those who supervise or treat them understand the reentry experience and challenges associated with it. A related element is to ensure that law enforcement agencies are apprised of when inmates are released to their jurisdiction. They then can provide potentially more attention to certain areas.

Requirements for parole board membership should be established. Currently, most states require few if any qualifications for parole board membership. Governors typically appoint members. Requirements for parole board membership might help to alleviate political pressures that board members may experience and ensure that they are properly qualified to assess risk and to make determinations about which inmates warrant release.

Supervision periods should be restricted and coupled with a social work emphasis. There is little evidence that supervision reduces recidivism or improves other outcomes. Can intensive supervision alone reduce recidivism? The results of studies to date are inconsistent, which may reflect the fact that supervision alone does nothing to address many of the prominent factors, such as poor self-control, strain, and weak social bonds, that give rise to offending. This idea underscores the importance of a parole approach that operates in a more traditional manner, one in which supervision is coupled with a social work function aimed at assisting ex-prisoners to adjust and find housing, employment, and treatment.

Limiting invisible punishments and sealing criminal records should also be considered. No robust body of empirical research supports these approaches to reducing recidivism. At the same time, many accounts highlight the potential for them to increase it and adversely affect other reentry outcomes. Restricted access to public housing, employment, education, and more, and limits on voting and holding office—these and more may satisfy retributive impulses, yet likely do more harm than good. Are there some cases where certain restrictions may make sense? Sure. On the whole, however, it likely is more effective and cost-efficient to minimize invisible punishments.

Create opportunities for ex-prisoners to show that they have changed and would like to contribute to the community. By and large, sentencing and corrections in America focuses on punishment, but a more effective approach may be introducing opportunities, such as coordinated volunteer efforts to provide services to communities, for ex-prisoners to demonstrate that they can be pro-social and are committed to desistance. Reentry courts embody this type of idea.

b. Education and Employment. In-prison education and job preparation will do little to help ex-prisoners secure employment if they face substantial barriers to employment upon release. One strategy, then, for improving reentry involves relying on education or employment mentors, who could be volunteers from the community and who would assist the ex-prisoner. The focus could be on identifying educational opportunities in the local community that might create avenues to employment or identifying employment opportunities.

A related strategy is to implement employment assistance programs. Evidence of their success remains to be established, yet some efforts have been found to be successful in helping released prisoners to find jobs and desist from crime. These programs can include assistance with job placement, provision of transitional employment, and employment readiness training. Employers may be more willing to hire ex-offenders who demonstrate successful rehabilitation by completing programs that emphasize employment readiness. Participation in and completion of such programs may signal to potential employers that an ex-offender constitutes a safe bet and is unlikely to reoffend.[61]

c. Housing. Inmate housing should be monitored in the days, weeks, and months after release. Homelessness or residence with criminal associates should be avoided and yet may be difficult to avoid. For these reasons, parole officers or social workers should monitor ex-prisoner housing. When necessary, they should seek to assist inmates in accessing subsidized housing or a series of temporary living arrangements until permanent housing can be secured.

d. Inmate Health. Continuity of care should be prioritized. Individuals who received treatment while incarcerated should continue to receive it upon release. Corrections personnel should work with local service providers to arrange for such care and to work with the individual to help him or her take responsibility for participating in treatment. Inmates with continuing drug treatment problems or who relapse into drug abuse should be referred for services and treatment. Correctional system personnel or an assigned social worker should monitor compliance and work with the individual to help them avoid relapse.

e. Planning, Decision Making, and Life Skills. A mainstay of any effort to improve reentry outcomes is an emphasis on assisting ex-prisoners to make better plans and decisions and to develop basic life skills. Poor planning and decision making can be improved through a variety of interventions, not least cognitive-behavioral programs. Typically, we seek to address the causes of a problem to solve it, but the contributing factors to poor planning and decision making defy enumeration and may stem from early childhood social contexts and upbringing. Therefore, the focus here should be on strategies, such as cognitive-behavioral counseling, that can change criminogenic thinking and improve decision making. As part of individualized programming, ex-prisoners ideally would be required to participate in life skills training, with special emphasis on strategies to find work and manage conflict.

f. Social Support. Another mainstay of successful desistance involves social support, which can come from many different individuals and groups. Other ex-prisoners could be encouraged to form support groups. Families and friends can be encouraged to support ex-prisoners. Reentry ceremonies with these individuals and groups, as well as members of the community, can be undertaken and so provide ex-prisoners with a sense of possibility. At the same time, such ceremonies can highlight to ex-prisoners that others care about them and also, in essence, will be watching them. Such support and informal control may promote desistance.

Many families of ex-prisoners reside in areas of disadvantage. When inmates return home, they can create burdens on these families. Accordingly, support to these families may strengthen them and, in turn, promote desistance. Such support can take many forms, including linkages to social service agencies, assistance in finding more suitable housing, family counseling, and more.

Similarly, many communities carry a disproportionate reentry burden.[62] Including communities in reentry planning would provide one platform for highlighting this issue and identifying ways to assist the communities. No one-size-fits-all approach would work. However, one approach would be for parole officers to meet regularly with community residents to update them on the progress of different parolees, to identify assistance that they may need or want, and to brainstorm ideas for how ex-prisoners in the community could be supported in ways that would strengthen the community.

GENERAL GUIDELINES AND STRATEGIES FOR IMPROVING REENTRY

To this point, we have discussed three different stages—pre-prison, in-prison, and postprison—at which reentry policies might be targeted. In so doing, we seek to emphasize that reentry outcomes will not likely be appreciably improved by any one effort. Rather, large-scale improvements likely require a comprehensive approach that consists of a diverse range of efforts. Here, we extend this argument by identifying what we have termed general guidelines and strategies for improving reentry outcomes. These are presented in Table 9.4.

The very fact that so many opportunities exist to improve these outcomes underscores that a silver-bullet approach will do little to make society safer. By extension, no laundry list of evidence-based interventions will do much to help in and of themselves. It may be that in a given set of studies, a particular prison-based intervention has been found to reduce recidivism. That does not mean the intervention should be implemented in any given state. A far more effective approach to reducing recidivism, for example, might be to employ probation more frequently and use incarceration less.[63] In this instance, the more effective approach, probation, would preclude the need for the in-prison program. Do lists of evidence-based policies and programs have a place? Yes, but, in our view,

Table 9.4   General Guidelines and Strategies for Improving Prisoner Reentry Outcomes

---

1. Make Successful Reentry a Policy Priority

- Support crime prevention policies and efforts broadly.
- Embrace a public health and social welfare mission and assess diverse reentry outcomes.
- Invest in a diverse portfolio of sanctioning options.
- Educate the public about effective strategies for achieving criminal justice goals.
- Prioritize principles of effective intervention over specific programs.
- Plan for decreased use of incarceration when appropriate.

2. Institutionalize Effective Reentry Processes

- Prioritize reentry processes that accord with principles of effective intervention.
- Promote social support throughout incarceration and during reentry.
- Address the barriers to successful reentry that ex-prisoners face.
- Involve communities in punishment and reentry.

3. Rely on Policies, Programs, and Practices as Well as Diverse Change Agents

- Use policies, programs, and practices to improve reentry outcomes.
- Draw on diverse change agents to improve reentry.

4. Prioritize Quality Supervision, Assistance, Treatment, and Services

- Prepare for reentry at the moment of conviction.
- Rely on supervision with "teeth."
- Individualize interventions and, at the same time, address group-specific risks and needs.
- Target high-risk individuals and multiple criminogenic factors.
- Make reentry supervision, assistance, treatment, and services dynamic in nature.

5. Institutionalize Research into Policy, Program, and Practice Decisions

- Create a science of punishment.
- Prioritize more and better criminal justice evaluation research.
- Establish a clear definition and measure of successful reentry.
- Monitor the experiences of individuals as they progress through the correctional system.
- Develop a knowledge bank of effective and ineffective policies, programs, and practices.
- Collect information from individuals with on-the-ground experience and insight.
- Identify insights and lessons from related fields, such as the study of soldier reentry.

---

they should be pursued only as part of a more general empirically based assessment about the causes of crime and recidivism in a specific jurisdiction and about the range of possible changes that might be introduced to reduce both.[64] Fortunately, many organizations, such as those listed in Table 9.5, have provided useful summaries of research on effective interventions. These organizations can be consulted when states and local jurisdictions develop comprehensive plans for improving reentry and reducing crime.

Table 9.5   Organizations Providing Information on Prisoner Reentry

Bureau of Justice Assistance	http://www.bja.gov
Bureau of Justice Statistics	http://www.bjs.gov
Center for Employment Opportunities	http://ceoworks.org
Council of State Governments Justice Center	http://csgjusticecenter.org
National Criminal Justice Reference Service	https://www.ncjrs.gov
National HIRE Network	http://www.hirenetwork.org
National Institute of Corrections	http://nicic.gov
National Institute of Justice	http://www.nij.gov
National Resource Center, Children and Families of the Incarcerated	http://fcnetwork.org
Office of Justice Programs—Crime Solutions	http://www.crimesolutions.gov
Office of Juvenile Justice and Delinquency Prevention	http://www.ojjdp.gov
The Osborne Association	http://www.osborneny.org
RAND	http://www.rand.org
Reentry Central: The National Website on Reentry	http://www.reentrycentral.org
Reentry.net	http://www.reentry.net
Service Network for Children of Inmates	http://www.childrenofinmates.org
United States Department of Justice	http://www.justice.gov
Urban Institute	http://www.urban.org

Before proceeding, the logic of focusing on general guidelines and strategies bears further discussion. A central limitation of an intervention-focused approach—one where we look for a specific program that we can implement in prison—to improving reentry is that we miss the forest for the trees. Programs are great: They tend to be small-scale and so we can conduct more rigorous evaluations of them. Accordingly, we can generate more empirical evidence about their potential effectiveness. At the same time, they bias us in the direction of smaller-scale change. In addition, we indirectly are led away from emphasizing "forest" changes, such as revising our use of incarceration, changing the culture of a prison system, and customizing in-prison and postrelease efforts to be maximally effective. These changes may be more difficult to assess empirically, but they hold the potential to create much more public safety than ever could arise through implementation of hundreds of evidence-based programs. To use another analogy—if a river threatens to flood a town, we can put all our energy into adding sandbags along the river walls (the sandbags amount to various programs) or we can undertake that work alongside of efforts to divert the river further upstream.

We argue that policy makers and correctional systems should be focused on systems-level assessments of the need for various policies, programs, and practices. And they should revise these efforts continuously to achieve maximum gains in public safety at the least cost. Similar arguments have been leveled by others. Jeremy Travis, for example, has argued for the use of principles of effective reentry that, when pursued collectively, hold the potential to improve reentry outcomes. These principles include (a) preparing inmates for reentry; (b) building bridges between prisons and communities; (c) seizing the moment of release as a special moment for leveraging large improvements in reentry outcomes; (d) strengthening concentric circles of support for inmates and ex-prisoners; and (e) promoting, broadly, successful reintegration.[65] Similarly, Joan Petersilia has advocated reforming four major areas of reintegration practices, including (a) altering the prison experience; (b) changing prison release and revocation practices; (c) revising postprison services and supervision; and (d) fostering "collaborations with the community and enhancing mechanisms of informal social control."[66]

Latessa and his colleagues have promoted still another approach—the use of "core correctional practices (CCPs)," which in turn build on the Correctional Program Assessment Inventory (CPAI) that Paul Gendreau and Donald Andrews developed.[67] CCPs include a focus on such dimensions as (a) anticriminal modeling, (b) effective reinforcement, (c) effective disapproval, (d) effective use of authority, (e) problem solving, (f) relationship skills, (g) cognitive restructuring, (h) skill building, and (i) motivational enhancement.[68] Building on these dimensions, the researchers have promoted the Evidence-Based Correctional Program Checklist (CPC).[69] It can be used to identify how well a program accords with research on the known predictors of recidivism and effective intervention. It also provides information about how a program might be strengthened to improve outcomes. In so doing, it illustrates the salience of research to program development and accountability.

Other sets of principles, areas of reintegration practice, and correctional practices could be identified. What unites the best ones, in our view, is a reliance on credible theory and research. They are united, too, by the advocacy of a more comprehensive approach to thinking about how best to improve reentry. The CPC approach, for example, implicitly highlights that we should care less about any one specific intervention, or a "brand name" intervention, than that the host of correctional interventions in everyday use accord broadly with dimensions that characterize effective interventions.

The five sets of guidelines and strategies that we present consist of the following: (a) make successful reentry a policy priority; (b) institutionalize effective reentry processes; (c) rely on diverse policies, programs, and practices as well as diverse change agents; (d) prioritize quality supervision, assistance, treatment, and services; and (e) institutionalize research into policy, program, and practice decisions. These recommendations build on prior scholarship. At the same time, they emphasize more explicitly the need to approach reentry from a macro perspective *and* a micro perspective. Better sentencing policies, for example, can avoid the need for unnecessary correctional interventions. Yet, for any given correctional population, we need interventions that can effectively reduce their recidivism and improve other outcomes. In addition, the guidelines and strategies include an emphasis on systemic approaches to reentry, such as relying on diverse policies, programs, and practices as well as diverse change agents. Not least, they include a strong emphasis on research as the basis for guiding policy decisions. Below, we discuss each of the sets of guidelines and strategies.

1. *Make Successful Reentry a Policy Priority*

If we do not prioritize a goal, we are unlikely to achieve it. Reentry has not constituted a priority in America. That can be seen in a largely knee-jerk reaction to crime: build more prisons to have less crime. A more effective approach to reentry involves making reentry outcomes a top policy priority. That involves planning. If we send someone to jail or prison, there should be a solid empirical basis for it. We should know when either jail or prison constitutes the most effective or best option. In some cases, retribution may dictate incarceration, but even then we should have an empirical foundation for making this determination. Several pathways exist for making successful reentry a policy priority and, in turn, for improving reentry outcomes and public safety and using taxpayer dollars more wisely. Jail reentry, too, requires attention. The experiences and consequences of jail stays, even when they occur not as a punishment but as a temporary confinement pending trial, can have adverse effects that parallel those that can occur for inmates and ex-prisoners as well as for their families and communities.[70]

One approach is to emphasize crime prevention. If we reduce crime, we reduce punishment, including incarceration. In turn, we have less need of reentry interventions. How do we reduce crime? Lots of ways exist—we can strengthen families, support child nutrition and health, improve education, promote stronger communities and the informal social controls that they can exert, develop more strategic law enforcement efforts that target hot spots of crime and that work with communities, and fund a broad array of noncustodial sanctions. We can use prisons, too. But we should not expect them to achieve much on their own. Which combinations of interventions should we use? What precise portfolio should exist? That depends on the causes of crime in a given area and available resources. As we emphasize below, research provides a critical foundation for devising a meaningful and cost-efficient portfolio for reducing crime.

A second approach is to have criminal justice and correctional systems embrace a public health and social welfare mission and to emphasize rehabilitation. This recommendation may seem daft. Yet a punishment system that ignores the many deficits of offenders is unlikely to do much to reduce recidivism. The typical inmate is a poster child for intervention—they have physical and mental health problems alone that would lead public health officials, if crime were not involved, to clamor for taking action. In many cases, these same individuals already may be involved with or served by social service agencies, yet these agencies may be largely ignored or uninvolved once the machinery of criminal justice begins. A public health and social service mission appears, on the face of it, more likely to achieve not only recidivism reductions but also improved public health, more employment, less unemployment, and more.

If we can reduce recidivism and, at the same time, improve health, housing, and employment outcomes, society is better off. A focus on prison-as-retribution and prison-as-deterrent does almost nothing, by design, to achieve such outcomes. By contrast, a focus on public health and social welfare could do so. Can such a shift occur? Certainly. One might, for example, grade prisons and parole offices on a variety of measures, including recidivism, homelessness, and health outcomes. One might grade them, too, on how well they coordinate their efforts with public health and social service agencies. Indirect evidence of the ability of correctional systems to include a public health and social service mission can be seen in the fact that many of these systems vary in their emphasis on rehabilitation and professionalism.[71] In addition, many examples exist of efforts to support successful "jail reentry" by taking advantage of the opportunity to intervene proactively with an at-risk population. Those who go to jail may not end up receiving sanctions, or may be given noncustodial sanctions, yet they may have criminogenic risks and needs that, if addressed, could improve recidivism, employment, family, education, and health outcomes.[72] Of course, a criminal justice system that embraces public health and social welfare would be more effective if the juvenile justice system itself did so as well.[73]

A third approach to making reentry a policy priority entails the creation of a diverse range of sanctioning options. This emphasis returns us again to the idea that less incarceration reduces the need for addressing the potential criminogenic effects of prison and the challenges of reentry. According to some estimates, correctional systems spend ten times more on an inmate's last day in prison as they do on the inmate's first day after release.[74] Without a range of options, policy makers and the courts are more likely to resort to incarceration. Ideally, jurisdictions would have many sanctions that could achieve better a reduction in offending and still achieve a desired level of retribution. The bar that incarceration sets is high. It can be financially costly, the bulk of empirical evidence suggests that it worsens recidivism, and, worse yet, incarceration can harm communities. In some instances, it may be absolutely necessary. However, retribution and reduced offending can be obtained through rehabilitative interventions and a large array of intermediate sanctions at far less cost. Are such interventions always effective? No. However, they cost less and likely engender fewer collateral consequences for offenders and their families and communities. Are such interventions less punitive? No. By and large, rehabilitation-oriented sanctions still can be retributive and carry with them the added bonus that they typically will reduce recidivism more so than will incarceration. Restorative justice approaches to sanction illustrate this idea, as do many other noncustodial sanctioning options, including fines.[75]

Fourth, in a related vein, policy makers and the correctional system can seek to educate the public through different media about the relative costs and benefits of different sentencing options. Public understanding of crime, the criminal justice system, and the costs and benefits of prison relative to other sanctions is limited. That situation creates the potential for the public to make incorrect assumptions about crime and the effectiveness of available sanctions and, in turn, to call for more incarceration even when alternative sanctions may be more effective. Policy makers then feel compelled to resort to silver-bullet solutions such as incarceration.

Fifth, prioritize principles of effective intervention over specific programs. Individuals who are incarcerated will not improve on their own, generally. And deterrence appears unlikely to occur or to exert an appreciable effect across most inmates.[76] Perforce, then, we need policies, programs, and practices that address inmate deficits and facilitate successful returns to society. Policy makers and correctional systems administrators sometimes tend to embrace specific programs, especially if these programs appear to be novel and at least a few studies highlight their (potential) effectiveness. Such an approach leads to specialized intervention for the few and ignores the large amount of programming and practices that occur within correctional systems. A more effective approach to improving reentry outcomes lies in ensuring that *all* correctional system activities—policies, programs, interventions, practices, and decisions—accord with principles of effective intervention.[77] Should we invest in specific programs? Yes, when the need exists, when a credible body of research shows that it can be effective and identifies the conditions necessary for it to be successful, when other more critical needs do not need to be addressed, and when more cost-efficient approaches do not exist for improving reentry.

The focus on effective intervention provides an added benefit—it provides a foothold for informing debates about prison privatization. Advocates of privatization point to the potential for more cost-efficient incarceration and improved recidivism outcomes; opponents argue that privatization can lead to abuses of inmates and creates a profit incentive that undermines correctional system goals. Research to date provides little empirical evidence that prison privatization creates an all-else-equal experience for inmates or that it reduces recidivism more so than occurs among inmates released from government-run prisons.[78] In the end, resolution of the debate about privatization will require a considerably more robust body of research. We submit that any resolution requires assessment of the extent to which privatization results in correctional system experiences grounded in the principles of effective intervention. Any private prison can provide lower-cost custodial housing. The real challenge, and the real benefit to society, lies in providing an experience that improves public safety and does so at lower cost than otherwise would occur. Cheaper housing that results in worse recidivism outcomes, or missed opportunities to improve them, does not help society. Ultimately, the standard for publicly run or privately run efforts should be demonstrable evidence of adherence to principles of effective correctional intervention at the least necessary cost.

A final approach to prioritizing prisoner reentry involves the flip side of focusing on crime reduction (and thus the need for incarceration)—specifically, it entails planning for downsizing prison systems.[79] Politically, it has been far easier to call for building prisons than to call for their decreased use. It remains the case, and likely will for the foreseeable future, that calling for prison closures will be political death for policy makers. However, that creates a conundrum. What we want is for policy makers to support incarceration when we need it and decrease its use when we do not need it (or as much of it). As when a country goes to war, a precondition of engagement should be a clear description of engagement and cessation. This idea, when applied to prison growth, entails describing exactly how much incarceration we need, determining the period of time for which any increase or decrease will occur, and building in a predetermined resumption of prior levels of incarceration unless an empirically based, nonpartisan process is followed for not doing so. Any such effort means substantially improving the forecasting abilities of state criminal justice and correctional system agencies. It also likely requires the creation of nonpartisan research agencies that must provide forecasts and the assumptions on which the forecasts relay. It requires, too, built-in constraints that preclude large-scale increases in incarceration and that demand strong policy analysis, coupled with credible research, for allowing increases to occur. The goal ultimately is not less punishment but rather more effective punishment, using diverse approaches that achieve retribution, justice, public safety, and other outcomes at less cost.

2. Institutionalize Effective Reentry Processes

A focus on reentry processes is a critical part of efforts to improve reentry outcomes. When we focus only on a program, we may neglect the fact that reentry constitutes but one phase within a larger set of phases and that reentry success can be impeded or facilitated in diverse ways. When we focus on improved reentry processes throughout the correctional system, we are led to consider how all the actions, interventions, and decisions of this system may influence the success of individuals as they move from prison back into society.

One strategy for achieving this goal consists of prioritizing reentry efforts that accord with the principles of effective intervention. These efforts include reentry preparation, classification and assessment, supervision, assistance, and treatment. They also include parole offices and their missions, as well as the sufficiency of staffing to provide adequate supervision and assistance. If, for example, parole offices focus exclusively on supervision, we miss a critical opportunity to identify problems in ex-prisoners lives that, if unaddressed, may well contribute to adverse outcomes. Failing to intervene in such circumstances is tantamount to allowing ourselves to be harmed. If we know it will rain and take no umbrella with us, we should hardly be surprised when we get wet. Similarly, we know that most inmates will fail upon release and do so for a multitude of reasons. Using parole as a vehicle for implementing principles of effective intervention thus is an investment that has substantial potential in improving reentry outcomes. More broadly, infusing correctional systems with effective, evidence-based practices provides a more comprehensive, systemic foundation for improving reentry. Such change can be facilitated through the use of the CPAI or CPC.

A second strategy consists of promoting strong social support networks. Inmates' number one concern while incarcerated tends to be the isolation they feel from family, friends, and community. The concern is warranted. When they leave prison, inmates frequently will find that their social support network, such as it may have been, has eroded. If we want individuals to refrain from crime, find housing, secure employment, and more, then social support has to feature prominently in any comprehensive effort to improve reentry outcomes. Placing inmates closer to their home communities can help. However, a more systematic effort is needed, especially if an inmate's social ties consist primarily of criminals. For example, prisons and parole offices could develop community partnerships with universities, faith institutions, social service agencies, and others to create a web of support that could help ensure that released prisoners receive assistance and, indirectly, a form of informal supervision.

Third, correctional systems should address the many barriers to successful reentry—including finding housing and gainful employment, securing appropriate treatment for physical illness or mental illness, obtaining social services, reintegrating with family, and more—that ex-prisoners face. Here, as with military soldiers who return home, empirical research clearly establishes that reentry is fraught with difficulty. A simple step consists of eliminating the many invisible punishments that legislatures have enacted. Punishment that never stops accords well with a retributive stance. If these punishments serve to enhance retribution, and if such enhancements reflect the public will, then perhaps they may be justified. However, if the goal is to reduce recidivism, little evidence to date suggests that they help. Might there be general deterrent effects to justify them? Yes, but few studies have identified such effects. And the benefits may be offset by increased recidivism or a failure to reduce it through a combination of supervision and assistance efforts that themselves reflect the principles of effective correctional intervention.

Not least, effective reentry depends on strong communities. Releasing individuals to environments that may be criminogenic will do little to help them. At the same time, these individuals create a burden on communities, which in turn engenders a vicious cycle. Can communities, especially those mired in entrenched poverty, be changed? Yes, but for it to be sustainable, the change typically must come from within the community. Community policing efforts provide a testament to the fact that community-focused interventions can be extraordinarily difficult and require on-the-ground support from residents and leaders. At the same time, such efforts hold considerable potential for reducing crime and improving the quality of life of residents.[80] In turn, they create a foundation for helping communities address reentry productively, in ways that help the community and ex-prisoners alike.

3. Rely on Policies, Programs, and Practices as Well as Diverse Change Agents

To improve virtually any social problem, it can help to attack it through different approaches and by relying on different organizations and groups. No less holds true for crime and reentry. A central limitation of efforts to reduce crime and to punish lies in a reliance on silver-bullet solutions. Tougher sentencing laws provide the most obvious example. Within the prison system, we can see it in supermax housing. We can see it, too, in efforts that at first blush appear to be multifaceted. For example, many community policing efforts stumble because they employ a top-down approach that ignores community residents.

The solution is at once simple and yet complex—seek to improve reentry through a wide range of policies, programs, and practices. Doing so provides the foundation for a more systematic, comprehensive, and effective approach to crime prevention and punishment. The complex part? Identify the specific policies, programs, and practices that collectively will provide the most cost-efficient approach to crime prevention and punishment, including reentry. Here, our silver-bullet solution involves substantially funding research that can provide the information necessary for identifying an approach portfolio of policies, programs, and practices. We see no possible shortcut. With relevant information, states and local jurisdictions can identify the scope of the crime problem, its causes, and the potential solutions to it. With a strong research infrastructure, they can assess the effectiveness of diverse sanctions and interventions, and they can adjust policies, programs, and practices as needed.[81] The importance of monitoring and improving the everyday decision making and practices of the correctional system cannot be understated. Although policies and programs seem more tangible, the everyday decisions and practices collectively affect far more individuals.[82] For example, when prosecutors and the courts rely on prison when intermediate sanctions might be more effective, they in one fell swoop obligate the system to expend far more resources than otherwise would be necessary.

Diverse change agents, too, are a critical part of the solution. Criminal justice and corrections tend to adopt a top-down approach, one that privileges the agency of court and system actors. However, other groups—offenders themselves, victims, families, communities, and community organizations—likely have more influence on crime reduction and ex-prisoner success. Many courts and correctional systems rely on other groups in a largely piecemeal manner. Law enforcement agencies do so as well. Policy makers typically must listen to different constituents, yet many crime policies appear largely divorced from the realities of communities where most crime occurs. An effective approach to reducing crime and recidivism entails more than piecemeal involvement. It requires that criminal justice and correctional systems involve these different groups on a regular basis. Doing so creates more accountability and the potential for preventing crime and identifying effective punishments and interventions. It would be challenging. And it would require a revised image of the mission of criminal justice and corrections. Yet without a greater reliance on diverse change agents, we are left with an approach to crime and punishment that remains primarily reactive and ineffective.

4. Prioritize Quality Supervision, Assistance, Treatment, and Services

Reentry outcomes can be affected by many factors, including an individual's background, in-prison experiences, and family and community context. The most direct avenue to reducing recidivism and improving other reentry outcomes involves changing individuals during or after their term of incarceration. How best can such change be achieved?

One approach involves preparing for reentry at the moment of conviction.[83] This idea was suggested above when identifying ways that reentry might be improved through pre-prison approaches (Table 9.1) and in-prison approaches (Table 9.2). Starting early provides an efficient way to begin planning for housing, employment, treatment, and service needs upon release. It can inform as well efforts to develop social support and assistance during incarceration.

A second consists of relying on targeted supervision with "teeth."[84] Excessive supervision caseloads essentially preclude any real monitoring. They encourage, too, a more bureaucratic approach that prioritizes violation recordkeeping as opposed to substantively meaningful oversight and assistance. The end result is law enforcement net widening that increases costs and yet may do nothing to reduce recidivism.[85] Reliance on validated risk assessment approaches to classify inmates can help to ensure that supervision occurs where it is most needed. At the same time, lowering caseloads can help to ensure that ex-prisoners are deterred or have fewer opportunities to engage in crime. Such an approach alone will not likely reduce recidivism much. However, if coupled with a social service mission, it holds considerable potential to do so. This approach, for example, can reduce the likelihood that we adopt a knee-jerk response to parole violators and return them to prison. As Piehl and LoBuglio have emphasized, "failure to abide by the terms of conditional release is inevitable."[86] It also can increase the likelihood that criminogenic risk and need factors are addressed.

Third, individualize interventions and, at the same time, address group-specific risks and needs. This approach ensures that supervision, assistance, treatment, and services can be configured to achieve maximum reductions in recidivism. The group focus stems from the fact that individual-level characteristics alone will not determine outcomes. For example, cultural variation alone may dictate that we approach intervention with one group differently than we do with another. The individual focus stems from the fact that our interventions ideally target, to the extent possible, the specific factors that give rise to offending for a particular individual.

Fourth, systems should target high-risk individuals and multiple criminogenic factors. This strategy is grounded in the risk-needs-responsivity (RNR) model, which itself is grounded in multiple criminological theories, such as learning theory and social bond theory. Why focus on multiple criminogenic factors rather than one that appears to be the most important? Put differently, why, as David Farrington and Brandon Welsh have advocated, pursue a "blunderbuss" approach? The simple reason is that we rarely know which causal factors merit the most attention. Also, most human behavior, including crime, stems from multiple causes, not just one. Another reason for targeting multiple risk factors is that it frequently may not be clear which risk factors and criminogenic needs may be most amenable to change or whether, if we change them, the end result will be reduced offending. For example, criminogenic attitudes and beliefs might contribute to offending, but reducing them may do little to reduce recidivism if an ex-prisoner returns to a context in which all of his or her friends and family members engage in crime or where strong economic incentives to offend exist. Sometimes, too, we do not need to target a causal factor directly. Instead, we might target a factor that moderates the causal factor or an intervening variable through which the causal factor operates. For example, self-control might contribute to offending, but it might be more effective to focus on reducing opportunities for an individual to offend than to reduce his or her self-control. The larger point? In the face of causal complexity and uncertainty, an omnibus approach to targeting multiple criminogenic factors may be the most effective and cost-efficient way to reduce recidivism.

Fifth, as individuals change during reentry, so, too, should supervision and interventions.[87] That is, we should make reentry efforts dynamic in nature. When an individual maintains employment for several months, it provides an indication that perhaps less supervision may be needed. By the same token, when a parolee stops showing up to work, it should raise a flag and spark investigation into what has happened. How should supervision and assistance change? It depends entirely on the changes in the individual's life and context.

Machine learning approaches to risk prediction illustrate one way that change can be monitored and used to adjust risk estimates and identify potential areas in need of more or less intervention.[88]

5. Institutionalize Research into Policy, Program, and Practice Decisions

Effective social policy, program, and practice ultimately depends on accurate information about social problems, including their scope, distribution, causes, potential solutions, and the costs of such solutions.[89] Yet criminal justice and correctional system efforts proceed daily with relatively little relevant or accurate information about such dimensions.[90] We can see that reflected in the nominal investment that the federal government and states typically have provided in measuring and monitoring criminal justice and correctional system activities. How, then, can this situation be improved?

A critical first step consists of creating a science of punishment. Policy makers ideally should have solid empirical information about the complexity of public views about crime and punishment, the types and amount of crime, the causes of crime, the range of sanctioning options available, and the relative costs and benefits of these different approaches. Any such science will require a substantial commitment to and funding for research. It is, however, necessary. Too often, for example, policy discussions appear to give too little or too much weight to retribution without considering the other goals of punishment. Retribution dictates punishment, but we do not want punishment to simultaneously create more social harm. How exactly, though, do we achieve retribution? Which punishment approaches produce more retribution than others? How do we ensure proportionality in punishment? Fairness in sanctioning? Which sanctions provide the most specific deterrence? General deterrence? Which sanctions provide the best combination of these different goals and do so for the least cost while producing the fewest unintended effects?

These questions and more warrant research-based answers. Relying on blunt and largely inaccurate assumptions about the retributive or deterrent effect of incarceration constitutes a needlessly expensive approach to punishment in an era in which so many advances in theory and research have occurred. It also almost assuredly gives rise to what Brian Forst has termed "errors of justice"—decision-making errors that result in wrongful convictions, delegitimization of the criminal justice system, and socially suboptimal sanctioning.[91] A science-based approach to punishment would focus systematically on reducing these errors. In addition, it would rely on forecasts, regularly updated, that explicitly model assumptions. Doing so can help sensitize legislators, corrections officials, and the public to how extreme some assumptions must be to justify certain policies.[92] It can lead, too, not only to more accurate predictions but also to greater understanding about the relative confidence that we can have in any of a range of policy options. In such a situation, we are far better situated to make informed decisions about the relative trade-offs of competing policy options.

A second is to prioritize more and better evaluation research. Current correctional system efforts should be empirically monitored and evaluated so that we may create, identify, or implement effective and efficient policies, programs, and practices. Such research should be aimed at systematically documenting the need for various policies, programs, or practices, the theory and science underlying proposed efforts, and the quality of their implementation. The foundation for undertaking such work exists already in many places. The development of improved database systems bodes well for improving the ability of criminal justice and correctional systems to undertake research.

The quality of decision making throughout criminal justice and correctional systems should be monitored and assessed. As with the medical system, many decisions contribute to the management of "clients"—in this case, offenders— and yet few systems know how well they undertake decision making.[93] The room, for example, for confirmation bias to influence all aspects of criminal justice processing is considerable. Prosecutors, judges, prison officers, and others may be inclined to view certain individuals as risky and confirm that assessment based on the assumption that these individuals in fact must be prone to offending. In any business, success or failure can rest heavily on the accumulation of smart or bad decisions. For the business of justice and corrections to be a success, decision-making monitoring is essential.

Notably, the mere act of undertaking studies can help administrators, officials, and practitioners to make adjustments that improve outcomes. As Cheryl Maxson has observed, clear evidence of this benefit can be seen in the evaluation of the Gang Resistance Education and Training (G.R.E.A.T.) program.[94] When program administrators and staff first were presented with results of the evaluation, they turned their attention to identifying ways to improve the program so that it could be more effective. Undertaking empirical research can serve to keep these same groups focused on full and quality implementation. Not least, it can motivate them by highlighting that their efforts are recognized and that improved outcomes, not just going through the motions, constitute the ultimate goal.

The Justice Reinvestment Initiative provides one model for institutionalizing research in policy development.[95] It helps states to identify factors, such as probation and parole revocations, specific sentence policies and practices, insufficient community supervision and support, and parole processing delays, that can contribute to excessive use of incarceration. It also uses research to identify strategies that might reduce the need for incarceration, such as a greater reliance on intermediate sanctions and community-based treatment.

The institutionalization of research can occur through many mechanisms. Funding is a necessity, as is more and better data. An institutionalized approach to research could involve regular collection of data from inmates, officers, wardens, and corrections officials through computerized survey protocols. The resulting information could be used to identify prison facilities that may be experiencing problems that might bode ill for reentry success.

Collection of insights from staff constitutes an especially important avenue for improving insight into the correctional system, including prison and parole operations and experiences. The officers who work in corrections arguably have the most relevant insight about inmates and ex-prisoners. They have unique insight, too, into correctional system management and how more efficient and effective approaches may exist for achieving system goals.

As part of enhancing the research foundation for criminal justice and corrections, there is a need for expertise in creating and analyzing data. Simple steps to ensure that such expertise informs data and analysis include expanding the research infrastructure of correctional systems, creating independent justice system research agencies, and forging stronger ties between correctional systems and universities and research organizations.

A third step is to develop a clear definition of success. For example, we need consistent measures of recidivism that use consistent time frames and, ideally, that rely on self-report data. Without such consistency, we lack a strong foundation for comparing the results of different sanctions and interventions. And without self-report data, we encounter difficulty in drawing inferences about policy or program success. Many interventions, for example, entail more supervision of ex-prisoners, whether by parole officers, service providers, law enforcement officers, or others. The end result can be reduced offending. Yet analysis of arrest data might make it appear that the intervention failed because of higher arrest rates due to the increased supervision. In addition to consistent measures of recidivism, we need consistent measures of other reentry outcomes, including housing, employment, substance abuse, mental health, and family functioning.[96] Without such measures, policy evaluations that focus purely on recidivism risk understating or overstating the overall costs or benefits of a given effort.

A fourth step is to monitor the experiences of individuals as they progress through the correctional system. As individuals proceed from jail to prison and then return to the community, they accumulate many experiences. They may change. These experiences and changes may provide critical information about how well they will fare back in society. Monitoring systems should be implemented and should merge in information from official records data (e.g., prison administrative data) and surveys (e.g., inmate and officer questionnaires). This monitoring could be used to track and predict inmate misconduct and recidivism using information about an individual's background and prison experiences. Tracking and prediction efforts could be enhanced further by incorporating information about family and community contexts and how these may influence desistance.

Much of what occurs in corrections goes unmeasured and thus unseen. That is problematic because it creates room for abuse. It also constitutes a missed opportunity to hold prison systems accountable and to collect data that might inform recidivism prediction and intervention efforts. Monitoring the experiences of inmates and what occurs in prisons and while individuals are on parole thus can serve multiple purposes.

A fifth step is to develop a knowledge bank of effective and ineffective policies, programs, and practices. State and local criminal justice and correctional system agencies should not have to reinvent the wheel. A knowledge bank developed by credible, nonpartisan organizations can prevent this problem. Any such repository should include information about how to prevent crime (and thus obviate the need for more punishment and incarceration) and the diverse range of intermediate sanctions that courts can use as alternatives to incarceration. As discussed above, Table 9.5 lists organizations that provide information about effective interventions. A knowledge bank, or repository, should privilege research from a diverse set of fields (e.g., biology, criminology, psychology, public policy, sociology, social work). Biosocial approaches, for example, have been neglected in crime policy discussion and yet they identify factors that may contribute to offending and to potential pathways for intervention.[97] The reality is that a considerable amount of scholarly work, including policy analysis, occurs in "silos," with relatively little cumulative knowledge across disciplines. Cross-disciplinary work can provide a more comprehensive platform for advancing scholarship and policy.

A sixth step is to collect information from individuals with on-the-ground experience and insight about the operations of criminal justice, corrections, and reentry.[98] Decision making about how best to improve system operations and reentry without insights from those who work within it or who are affected by it almost assuredly creates inefficiency. At the same time, listening to the voices of just one group will provide a distorted assessment that leads to the same outcome. Similarly, one-time assessments provide little ability to obtain accurate assessments, make adjustments, evaluate the changes, and thus improve continuously. Computerized survey methodologies can be undertaken inexpensively and could be used to undertake regular data collection of the views, experiences, insights, and recommendations of law enforcement officers, corrections personnel, and, no less, inmates and ex-prisoners and those who work with them. Surveys of the public could be used as well to develop measures of satisfaction with the justice system. These in turn would allow policy makers to employ a critical performance benchmark for comparing criminal justice system performance over time and across areas. Such an approach in fact could be used to evaluate different components of the correctional system as well.[99] Not least, regular collection of data from criminal justice and correctional system personnel could be used to improve policy design and implementation. Community corrections officers, for example, "serve as experts at the crucial nexus where prisons and the community meet," and so are uniquely positioned to identify how public safety and community well-being can be improved.[100]

A final step is to seek insights from other relevant fields. One example—we can learn much from efforts to assist soldiers when they return home from service. These individuals face parallel challenges to those faced by individuals who leave prison. They also present similar challenges to their families and communities.[101] Seeking insights from soldier reentry may help shed light on how prisoner reentry outcomes might be improved. Because the focus would not be on criminals alone, it also might lead policy makers, practitioners, researchers, and the public to understand better the importance of interventions that address diverse individual risks, needs, and contexts, and that do not assume that, somehow, reentry will be unproblematic.

THE IMPORTANCE OF EVIDENCE OF COST-EFFICIENCY, NOT JUST IMPACTS

Cost-efficiency refers to achieving the most amount of gain for the least amount of cost. It is a common-sense idea that policy makers frequently tout and one that most of us in our day-to-day lives follow, if imperfectly. Unfortunately, despite substantial advances in criminal justice cost-efficiency assessments, such assessments remain the exception rather than the rule.[102]

The emphasis on evidence-based policy and practice obscures this situation. Why? Policy makers and researchers alike frequently equate "evidence-based" with "effective." When an intervention improves outcomes, that should be cause for celebration. Yet some interventions require large sums of money and produce only small gains. Consider incarceration. It may reduce recidivism, but the cost it entails should give us pause. If we can reduce recidivism equally well, or approximately as well, and at substantially less cost, that would be the more rational approach.

We highlight this point because a system of justice guided by cost-efficiency considerations would likely result in a correctional system that looks considerably different from what exists in America. It would not eliminate retribution or the need for prisons. It would, however, lead us to attend to the relative benefits and costs of diverse sanctions and to be exquisitely clear about what exactly we purchase with a given sanction. When viewed in this light, the emergence of mass incarceration appears all the more remarkable. The United States embarked on an unprecedented level of prison growth that will continue for the indefinite future to impose financial constraints on the country. Perhaps a cost-efficiency analysis would find that the benefits in retribution and through incapacitation effects outweighed the costs and did so appreciably better than any other investment strategy. But that seems unlikely. Public opinion studies consistently find the public to be disenchanted with criminal justice and correctional systems, research documents that incarceration may well worsen recidivism, studies consistently have identified harmful effects of imprisonment on families and communities, and many effective and less costly sanctions exist.

One solution to improving reentry, then, entails requiring cost-efficiency evaluations to be a core feature of criminal justice policy making and correctional system decision making. To be useful, such evaluations will need to include assessments of policy effects on crime and recidivism as well as other outcomes—such as housing, employment, and health—for ex-prisoners and the communities to which they return. They also will need to consider the relative costs and benefits of investing in crime prevention efforts. For example, a policy that seeks to reduce opportunities for offending might well create more net benefits than a policy that seeks to enhance prison sentences for drug dealers.

THE NEED FOR AN OFFENDER, VICTIM, AND COMMUNITY JUSTICE SYSTEM

Although our focus has been on prisoner reentry, we have emphasized throughout that crime has effects on victims, families, and communities and that sanctions—as well as the sanctioning process—can have effects on them as well. The point bears emphasis: We have a *criminal* justice system in America. It is focused primarily on criminals and not these other groups. There is, for example, no victim justice system and no "families of those who go to prison" justice system. The result? We have a system of punishment that does little to help victims, families, or communities. Worse, this system in many instances worsens outcomes for these groups.[103]

Consider the situation of a mother who commits a crime and who has several children. The court sentences her to prison for one year and the children go to foster homes. In some cases, the crime may dictate this outcome, but in many cases reasonable people may disagree about what to do. In some cases, the children may be better off apart from the mother and in others not. Currently, however, the criminal justice system, with its singular focus on punishment, is not required to balance the trade-offs involved in this situation.

Consider, too, studies that have found that incarceration increases rather than decreases recidivism. Credible assessments remain in short supply, so such assessments should be viewed with caution. Even so, the implications are profound—we may be spending money and creating more, not less, crime. Perhaps such effects are offset by general deterrence effects that lower crime rates. Possibly. Such a possibility remains speculative.

A system of justice that was forced to consider cost-efficiency and how best to help victims and communities would be unlikely, in our view, to invest primarily in incarceration. Instead, it likely would be led to a diversified portfolio of approaches. These might well include calls by communities for more crime prevention efforts and by victims for more satisfactory approaches to retribution, justice, and assistance, treatment, or services. Susan Herman, for example, has advocated the development of a system of "parallel justice" that would help to ensure that victims' views and experiences are understood and their needs addressed.[104] The end result might well be improvements in outcomes beyond just crime and that result in more justice for all who are affected by crime and punishment.

Another way to arrive at this idea is to consider a public health perspective. Imagine a situation where one is charged with the public health of citizens in a given state. Prevention efforts likely would constitute a primary activity. In thinking about how to address crime, one might well leave it to the courts to identify a just response. At the same time, however, one might weigh in heavily against any response that adversely affected communities. It is precisely this type of check that is needed to avoid costly and ineffective sanctioning and simultaneously to create insights about how best to punish and promote community well-being.

REENTRY LESSONS AND CONVICTED FELONS WHO DON'T GO TO PRISON

Our focus has been on prisoner reentry, although we have detoured considerably. For example, we have emphasized the importance of crime prevention to reduce the need for prison and thus for reentry interventions. Another detour warrants emphasis—convicted felons who do not go to prison. Unless previously incarcerated, these individuals are unaffected by prison. That makes them different: They have no prison experience that might affect their lives or families and they experience no reentry.

In other respects, however, non-incarcerated felons are similar to those who go to prison. Their social and demographic characteristics are similar, they come from disadvantaged backgrounds, they have levels of physical and mental illness that are higher than what one finds in the general population, and so on.[105] They also face many of the invisible punishments that ex-prisoners encounter upon release, such as restrictions on voting, housing, employment, holding public office, and more. They also face many of the collateral consequences of a felon label, such as difficulty in being hired and in maintaining a residence with family. Such parallels should give pause for thought given that individuals on probation greatly outnumber those in prison.

What lessons can we glean from a focus on reentry when thinking about this population? In all likelihood, most of the insights, especially those enumerated in Table 9.4, apply equally well. The obvious exception is that we have no need to document the in-prison experience for this group. Even so, there remains the need to document the experiences that convicted felons have while on probation or while serving a sentence to some type of intermediate sanction and how these may affect recidivism and other outcomes, such as housing and employment.

THE IMPORTANCE OF GOVERNMENT ACCOUNTABILITY AND EVIDENCE-BASED PRACTICE

Calling for greater accountability and creating the foundation for it are two different things. Policy makers increasingly have called for government accountability. In so doing, they sometimes equate accountability with evidence-based practice. And in the latter instance, they tend to equate "evidence-based" with research that establishes that a given policy intervention may produce desired effects. Such a conceptualization is needlessly narrow.

Accountability might more productively be viewed as a situation where government relies on an evaluation research framework for enacting and funding policy.[106] First, is there credible research that shows that a problem exists that needs addressing? Second, is there solid theory and logic, supported by empirical research, that a given policy can be effective? For example, does it clearly change the causes of that problem to an appreciable degree? Third, is the policy well implemented? Fourth, in cases where the policy is well implemented, how large are the benefits? Fifth, how cost-efficient is the policy relative to other policies? Viewed in this light, we can see that when government funds a program that has been shown to reduce recidivism, that does not necessarily demonstrate accountability, especially if the funds might have been spent elsewhere to greater gain. Rather, accountability occurs when government demonstrates that it funds policies based on credible answers to all five of these questions.

Too much criminal justice and correctional policy fails the accountability test.[107] Perhaps the simplest illustration of this claim can be seen by the lack of correctional system transparency. Prisons operate largely in the equivalent of a black box. Few of us, researchers included, know much about what goes inside prisons.[108] How well do they comply with their own rules and procedures? To what extent do they implement effective management strategies? How frequently are inmates abused, and how much does abuse vary across facilities? In most instances, we have few or no systematic, empirically based answers. There may be an intensive study of one prison. There may be, too, an audit, one that a prison system passes. Neither sources, however, document the extent to which a correctional system implements well any of a range of policies, procedures, programs, and practices. Much the same can be said for parole practices.

In short, if we want more accountability—and ideally more effective and efficient policy—then a commitment to research is critical. That commitment creates the foundation for more effectively and efficiently reducing crime. In turn, it creates the basis for ensuring that incarceration only occurs when it is necessary and the most efficient sanctioning option. Not least, it creates the groundwork for improving prisoner reentry experiences and outcomes.

CONCLUSION

In this chapter, we presented the glass-half-empty perspective on corrections and reentry and then the glass-half-full perspective. The glass-half-empty perspective unfortunately has much to support it. We have a great deal of crime policy, including reentry efforts, that rest on weak theoretical and empirical grounds. Much of this policy appears to increase rather than decrease crime and to create harmful collateral consequences. In particular, weakly justified investments in prisons have imposed substantial costs on America. Such an approach has been facilitated by anemic investment in research that could inform policy development, implementation, and assessment, and that could serve as a check against ideologically based claims and assumptions.

Fortunately, there is much support for the optimistic, glass-half-full perspective too. Many policy makers have called for "smart justice" to help orient discussion around what works rather than politicized debates about conservative or liberal positions.[109] Such discussion will be critical. At the same time, opportunities abound for placing criminal justice and correctional policy on a more evidence-based foundation and, in particular, for improving reentry efforts. These opportunities exist prior to individuals going to prison, while they are incarcerated, and after they are released. The larger returns will come from implementing evidence-based principles that can guide policy development and implementation systemwide. Such an approach holds the potential for improving the effectiveness and efficiency of the entire justice system.

More optimistically, if less pragmatically, we have argued that improvements in prisoner reentry can come from creating a justice system centered not only on offenders but also victims and the communities from which they come. This system, if infused with a public health and social service mission, could undertake sanctions and interventions that consider their broad impacts. It could serve, too, as a check against investments that may provide short-term benefits along one dimension (e.g., a sense that some requisite level of retribution has been achieved) but few benefits for victims and communities. The potential for unintended harms, too, might be more readily appreciated and identified. Such benefits would be even more likely if government funded research sufficient to provide the accountability that policy makers and the public want.

1. What conditions would be necessary for incarceration to produce dramatic reductions in crime or recidivism? How likely is it that these conditions have been or could be met?

2. How might incarceration and a primary reliance on get-tough sanctioning produce more harm than good?

3. What are the consequences of investing in reentry policies, programs, or practices that rest on weak theoretical or research foundations?

4. How can a lack of investment in research not only undermine the identification of effective sanctioning and reentry policies but potentially contribute to a greater investment in effective interventions?

5. What types of pre-prison, in-prison, and postrelease reentry policies, programs, and practices seem most likely to be ineffective? Which ones seem most likely to be effective? Which merit the most investment and why?

6. What general guidelines or strategies exist for most effectively sanctioning all who commit crime, for reducing crime and recidivism, and for improving justice?

7. How can cost-efficiency analyses be incorporated into decisions about proposed or existing approaches to improving reentry?

8. How might a victim justice system or a community justice system best be configured? How might such systems contribute to more justice and public safety?

9. In what ways do convicted felons who do not go to prison—such as those who are sentenced to probation—differ from those who are incarcerated? What kind of reentry do they experience?

10. How can government accountability be improved through investment in research? What steps can be taken to ensure that we develop a stronger scientific foundation on what policies, programs, and practices produce the largest improvements in public safety at the least cost?

CHAPTER 10

Conclusion

This book is about prisoner reentry and something more—how reentry itself reflects a central problem in American criminal justice and what can be done to address it. The large-scale release of individuals from prisons back into homes and communities has not occurred of its own accord. Mass incarceration, and, by extension, mass reentry, reflects a failure to implement effective crime prevention efforts and to employ a diverse range of evidence-based sanctions. It reflects an emphasis on silver-bullet policy making.

This emphasis itself derives from wishful thinking that views crime as due to simple causes that somehow inhere in individuals. The reality? Crime results from a complicated mix of individual characteristics, social contexts, community conditions, other social problems, political and economic dynamics, and, not least, local, state, and federal policy making and the exercise of formal social control. Crime, of course, drives criminal justice and correctional system interventions that directly affect millions of convicted felons each year; and it indirectly affects all those with whom they come into contact. Yet crime alone does not dictate criminal justice in America. How exactly we respond to crime says as much about prevailing public views about crime and justice, societal changes, political forces, and more as it does about crime.

This problem can be likened to what happens in a magic show. The magician holds in one hand an object that attracts our attention and then deftly uses the other hand to undertake a manipulation that enables "magic" to occur. We fail to see the trick and so believe that magic created the rabbit in the hat.

How does this situation relate to mass incarceration and reentry? Crime does indeed drive our criminal justice system. Ultimately it is individuals, not social conditions, who commit crime. Accordingly, we should focus on punishing those who commit crime. We should put people in prison. That makes sense. But focusing on this issue, which we hold in our left hand, unfortunately leads to an intensive reliance on incarceration to achieve public safety.

Such observations distract us from what lies in the right hand—to wit, the diverse set of forces that create variation among individuals in their likelihood of offending and variation across areas in crime rates. In fact, variation in the causes of offending and crime constitute but one part of a constellation of factors that highlight the need for more than just incarceration if we are to reduce crime effectively and efficiently. In short, if we focused on the right hand, we would not likely focus the bulk of our attention on prisons. We would focus on addressing this diverse constellation of factors.

Consider an example that we have emphasized in the book: Mass incarceration and reentry reflect a forced separation of justice responses to crime from public health and social service responses to it. Retribution, justice, a focus on public safety—these all understandably drive the development of a system geared toward convicting and punishing criminals. Yet these individuals are more than "criminals." They consist of individuals who typically carry with them a host of deficits and who typically reside in families and communities characterized by marked disadvantage. That does not excuse criminal behavior. It underscores, however, that we should not expect their offending to stop simply because they have been sent to prison. Retribution can be likened to pain medication—it may help us to feel a bit better, but it does nothing to resolve the cause of the pain and, indeed, may distract us from taking effective steps to reduce or eliminate it. Should we punish in such a way as to achieve a sense of retribution? Absolutely. But punishment that causes more crime or that leads us to miss opportunities to prevent more crime is perverse. Public health and social service perspectives highlight this problem and identify that the problem goes deeper. By failing to address social disadvantage among children, families, and communities, we allow crime to occur. Indeed, we enable adverse health outcomes, unemployment, homelessness, and poor education to cement certain individuals, groups, and communities into a cycle of further disadvantage.

Other factors swirl around prisoner reentry and, in turn, shed light on the need for more nuanced approaches to crime, criminal justice, corrections, and, yes, reentry. For example, get-tough responses to crime, especially in the 1980s and 1990s, occurred alongside of policy shifts that placed more of the locus of responsibility for adverse conditions on individuals. Do individuals have volition and choose to engage in crime? Yes. Do individuals commit crimes? Yes. Should we punish them? Yes. And yet we know that social conditions affect individuals and so contribute to their offending and to crime rates. Focusing our efforts on individuals who commit crimes makes sense—they chose to commit crimes and should be held accountable. By the same token, it makes sense to address factors that give rise to crime. That means that we should hold families, schools, and communities accountable and target them for intervention as well. We should hold state government and policy makers accountable, too, especially when they fail to take steps to prevent crime or to punish more effectively, including creating more effective retribution and justice.

In short, successful reentry depends on improving our criminal justice and correctional systems and, more broadly, policy making. It depends on systemic approaches that rely on credible information and research rather than piecemeal fixes. Funding highly effective programs that reduce the recidivism of one hundred or so individuals each year may feel good. It cannot, however, compete with more comprehensive approaches to policy making. The latter hold the potential to reduce crime far more effectively. The simplest example is incarceration. What else could we buy with the money devoted to building, staffing, and operating a new facility that expands prison capacity statewide and that will remain operating for years to come? We know that the prison investment will not in any clear way reduce recidivism. It might worsen it. We can hope that it will achieve some incapacitation and general deterrent effect. It might. It might not. Set against these possibilities is the question of what else we could do with the millions of dollars used for the new facility. For the cost of building and operating it, we could purchase many different punishments, treatment, services, and the like. We could purchase crime prevention programs.

At a minimum, we could specify how we want to carve up our investments in crime prevention and punishment. We could have a business plan grounded in state-of-the-art empirical research. At present, the lion's share of funds goes into law enforcement, jails and prisons, and the supervision of individuals on probation and parole. Little is available to support crime prevention or rehabilitation on a systematic large-scale basis or to punish in a more equitable manner that simultaneously achieves justice and improves public safety. Put differently, we have a criminal "punishment" system and an administrative apparatus geared toward just that—punishment. This apparatus includes the imposition of barriers that make reintegration difficult if not impossible for many offenders. It does not prioritize crime prevention, rehabilitation, or attending to the families of offenders, victims, or communities. Rather, it relentlessly focuses on a punitive response to crime. At least one of the authors of this book has strong retributivist leanings, but even the most ardent retributivist can recognize that public safety efforts require that we focus on the causes of crime. How does large-scale investment in prisons achieve this outcome? A business plan that places public safety and well-being squarely at the center of attention would not in any obvious way lead to a near-exclusive emphasis on punishment and incapacitation as a means of achieving these goals.

These observations and the arguments that we have presented throughout the book contributed to our recommendations in Chapter 9. They include our central recommendation—infusing criminal justice and corrections with a public health and social welfare mission, one that prioritizes the health, safety, and well-being of citizens. Such a mission would provide a touchstone for evaluating punishment policies. Incarcerate for lengthier periods of time? Yes, but only if that constitutes the most cost-efficient and effective way to achieve justice and make offenders and victims, including communities, healthier. Such a mission would, among other things, force policy makers and criminal justice officials to consider the adverse effects of their efforts. Consider, for example, that correctional systems do not need to worry about the effect of in-prison experiences on inmates or their families. By and large, they do not get graded on recidivism outcomes, much less adverse effects on inmates' families, victims, or communities. A public health–focused system of justice, by contrast, would require our criminal justice and corrections systems to demonstrate not just recidivism improvements but also evidence that they helped victims, families, and communities.

A second central recommendation that we have emphasized is the critical importance of relying on research to inform policy making and policy monitoring. Crime results from many factors, and these factors may vary by community or over time. Only with identification of these factors can we effectively reduce crime. Otherwise, we are left like the proverbial dog chasing its tail, allowing crime to occur and then punishing the (few) offenders who get caught. It is, as we have emphasized, worse than that. When we catch the offenders, we typically only punish. We do not address the criminogenic factors that contributed to their behavior or that of individuals in the high-crime communities from which they typically come. There is no mystery, then, that almost all ex-prisoners recidivate.

Are these pie-in-the-sky recommendations? No, we do not think so. As discussed in Chapter 9, policy makers and practitioners can select from a broad range of approaches to improve criminal justice, corrections, and, not least, prisoner reentry. Examples of these approaches abound. Too often, they exist in piecemeal fashion—a bright spot here and there. Yet they provide evidence that thoughtful, empirically based, balanced approaches to public safety exist.

What is needed is for policy makers and states to tackle criminal justice, corrections, and reentry in a coherent, comprehensive manner. No one way exists to make that happen. Certainly, locking more people up or setting more prisoners free will do little.[1] Necessary ingredients, in our view, include creation of a nonpartisan agency responsible for creating and updating state (or local) strategic plans and for undertaking empirical research. This agency would be responsible for creating and updating the plan and showing how research informs it. Plans, as with research or any other undertaking, have limited utility if they rest on weak foundations. Such an agency therefore would require a considerable infusion of funds. We make no apology about this cost. Law enforcement, criminal justice, corrections, reentry—much of it occurs in the equivalent of a black box. If we, as a society, want a responsive, efficient, and effective criminal justice system, then better information must be prioritized. That information includes documenting the good and the bad. Many local jurisdictions and states undertake phenomenal work that goes unappreciated. Many others waste taxpayer dollars. In an era in which data are more readily available, generated, and analyzed, that should not happen.

We have arrived at this overarching assessment, as well as the recommendations in Chapter 9, through a series of arguments. First, perspectives matter. When we view reentry, or most criminal justice policy, through a too-narrow lens, we end up with piecemeal understanding and interventions. Reentry can be viewed through many prisms, including historical context, the nature of in-prison and postprison contexts and experiences, the sanctioning and life experiences of different groups of individuals who go to prison, the practice and pitfalls of recidivism prediction, and the diverse outcomes relevant for assessing reentry policy. Such perspectives lead us to consider crime causation and recidivism as well as the mission of the criminal justice and correctional system differently. Our hope is that it leads policy makers, practitioners, researchers, and the public away from silver-bullet thinking about how to understand and improve reentry and criminal justice in America.

Second, improved public safety is most likely to occur if we target the causes of crime and recidivism. That includes a focus on individuals and the many factors that give rise to their offending. Such factors may include characteristics specific to them, but it also may include characteristics of the families and communities where they reside. If we want to reduce offending, a good starting place is to address these different factors, not to ignore them or to focus only on one or two problems that an individual may have. If we want to reduce crime appreciably, our best investments will lie with a focus on families and communities. For scholars, opportunities abound for advancing theory by studying sentencing and philosophical and cultural shifts in sanctioning as well as analysis of desistance processes, causal effects of in-prison and postprison experiences, family and community contextual influences on offending and other reentry outcomes, variable effects of different sanctions and interventions on desistance, assessment of the mechanisms through which these effects arise, and more.

Third, how we understand reentry—and crime, criminal justice, and corrections more broadly—varies greatly if we focus on victims, families, and communities. This understanding is, we submit, essential for devising more effective justice system efforts. It highlights, for example, that the bulk of criminal justice and correctional system decisions are offender focused and require little attention to how victims, families, and communities may be affected. Here, again, if we want to improve reentry, then, ironically, we may well want to look away from offenders and toward others. If we created a justice system that truly responded to the needs of victims, families, and communities, we almost assuredly would see improvements in public safety, both through reduced recidivism and through lower crime rates.

Fourth, the theory and practice of criminal justice, corrections, and reentry would be enhanced if the insights of practitioners and scholars were better integrated. The people who patrol communities, who work with inmates, probationers, and parolees and who provide services and treatment to offenders, victims, and their families—all of these individuals possess unique insight into how we might best help reduce crime and strengthen families and communities. Few jurisdictions or states tap this insight on a regular basis. This missed opportunity is paralleled by the lack of robust, ongoing interaction of researchers with policymakers and practitioners. Many exceptions to this situation exist. If, however, we want to see systemic improvements to policy and practice, mechanisms must be instituted that enable the views of scholars and on-the-ground practitioners to be heard. Such improvements can occur through many avenues, such as surveying these different groups on a regular basis and presenting the resulting information to policy makers. It is not that difficult to create solutions when so many voices exist. The challenge lies in funding and supporting research that organizes and empirically assesses the insights from these voices and in instituting a policy-making process that builds directly on insights gleaned from such research. Improving this process is essential. Jeremy Travis has referred to a "jurisprudence of reintegration" to capture the idea that legislatures need to weigh in heavily in creating improved reentry policy.[2] Here, we echo this idea, but emphasize that this jurisprudence should be far-reaching, focused on diverse actors (e.g., federal and state legislatures, executive agencies, the courts) and on crime and justice policy in general and anchored by empirical research.[3]

Fifth, substantial improvements in reentry outcomes ultimately require improved criminal justice and correctional system policy and practice. These in turn require improved law making and a reliance on a systematic, empirically based strategic plan for enhancing public safety. What will not work, as we have argued throughout this book, is a reliance on piecemeal investment in programs.

If the house is falling apart, investing in top-of-the-line marble countertops makes little sense. The same can be said of criminal justice, corrections, and reentry. No amount of deluxe programming will offset the inefficient and ineffectiveness that comes from relying on expensive investments, such as incarceration, when cheaper alternatives, such as probation, might be more effective. Similarly, investing in deluxe programs will do little if inmates return to impoverished communities with minimal employment opportunities. Improved public safety ultimately will require states and local communities to develop coherent strategic plans. These plans must be grounded in research on the distribution and causes of crime and the most efficient and effective policy portfolios that these states and communities can afford to improve public safety. Reentry investments constitute but one part of such a portfolio. Fortunately, as Chapter 9 attests, whether our attention turns broadly to criminal justice and corrections or more specifically to reentry, a large number of options exist. We need only the political and public will to transition from the era of mass incarceration to an era of effective crime and justice policy. The hallmark of such an era will be a system of justice that is truly grounded in evidence about what works and that truly creates justice and improves public safety and well-being.

Notes

Chapter 1

1 Stolz (2002).
2 Feeley and Simon (1992).
3 Martinson (1974).
4 Skogan (1995).
5 Garland (2013).
6 The figure presents thirty-five countries from a list of 222 reported in Walmsley (2013); these were selected to illustrate variation in world incarceration rates. For all 222 countries, the United States still has the highest incarceration rate. Estimates for each country typically spanned the 2011 through 2013 period. Countries report incarceration figures for varying time periods, necessarily creating some imprecision in making comparisons for any given year. In general, the rank ordering of countries by rate of incarceration does not change greatly from one year to the next. Updated estimates can be found at the International Centre for Prison Studies' website (http:// www.prisonstudies.org/world-prison-brief).
7 Walmsley (2013:1).
8 Glaze and Parks (2012).
9 Mears (2010:14).
10 Petersilia (2003); Travis (2005).
11 Kyckelhahn (2012).
12 Clear (2007); Mears (2010).
13 Langan and Levin (2002); Durose et al. (2014).
14 Durose et al. (2014:8, 15). The 5-year rearrest rates by type of offense were: any (77 percent), violent (71 percent), property (82 percent), drug (77 percent), and public order (74 percent) (Durose et al. 2014:8).
15 Durose et al. (2014:15).
16 Nagin et al. (2009).
17 Mears (2013).
18 Petersilia (2003); Travis (2005); Villettaz et al. (2006); Western (2006); Clear (2007); Nagin et al. (2009); Mears (2007, 2010); Gottschalk (2006, 2011); Cullen et al. (2011); Durlauf and Nagin (2011); Bales and Piquero (2012); Garland (2013); Cochran, Mears, and Bales (2014); Travis et al. (2014).
19 Mears (2010); Mears and Barnes (2010).
20 Laub and Sampson (2003); Laub (2004); Piquero et al. (2007).

21 See, for example, Garland (2001); Greenberg and West (2001); Tonry (2004); Gottschalk (2006); Spelman (2006, 2008, 2009).
22 Garland (2013).
23 See, generally, Mears (2010).
24 See, for example, Maruna (2001); Petersilia (2003); Tonry (2004); Travis (2005); Travis and Visher (2005); Gottschalk (2006); Western (2006); Bushway et al. (2007); Clear (2007); Ross and Richards (2009); Alexander (2012); Latessa et al. (2014); Crow and Smykla (2014).
25 Mears (2008a).
26 Travis (2005: xxiii).
27 Nagin et al. (2009).
28 Petersilia (1991).
29 Petersilia (1991); Kraska (2006); Mears (2010).
30 Mears (2010).
31 The ASC's complete award description is available online at http://www.asc41.com/awards/SutherlandAward.html.
32 Garland (2013).
33 Cullen (2011).
34 See, generally, Rossi (1980); Mears (2010).
35 Mears and Stafford (2002).
36 Kraska (2006:167).
37 Kraska (2006:169).
38 Mears and Bacon (2009).
39 See, for example, Lynch and Sabol (2001); Travis (2005).
40 Travis (2005).

Chapter 2

1 Travis (2005:70); see also Barker (2009); Green (2013).
2 See, for example, Cullen and Gendreau (2000); MacKenzie (2006); Lipsey and Cullen (2007); Cullen and Jonson (2012); Craig et al. (2013).
3 Siennick (2014).
4 Useem and Piehl (2008).
5 Mears (2010).
6 Garland (2013:478).
7 Petersilia (2003).
8 Welsh and Pfeffer (2013).
9 Travis (2005:70).
10 Ewald and Uggen (2012:85).
11 Ewald and Uggen (2012:85).
12 Petersilia (2003:105).
13 Travis (2005:69). The reference to invisible punishment can be found in Michel Foucault's work (see, e.g., Foucault 1978; see also Hamilton 1996 and Hutchings 1999).
14 Wilkins et al. (1991); Travis (2005).
15 Stuntz (2011).
16 Travis (2005:43).
17 Raphael and Stoll (2009).
18 Cullen and Jonson (2012).
19 Gibbs (1975); Paternoster (2010).
20 Blumstein and Beck (1999).

21 Blumstein and Beck (1999:54).
22 Carson and Sabol (2012:10).
23 Nadelmann (2004); Sevigny and Caulkins (2004).
24 Mears (2010).
25 Forer (1994).
26 Forer (1994:3).
27 Wilson et al. (2006).
28 Mancini and Mears (2013).
29 Mancini et al. (2013); Mancini (2014).
30 Blomberg (1980).
31 Mears (2012a).
32 Mears (2012a).
33 Mears (2010:17).
34 Garland (2013:478); see also Travis and Lawrence (2002).
35 Petersilia (2003); Travis (2005).
36 Travis (2005:42).
37 Travis (2005:49).
38 Lynch and Sabol (2001:11); see also Lawrence et al. (2002).
39 Phelps (2011:56).
40 Gaes et al. (1999); Farabee (2005); Rhine et al. (2006); Mears (2010).
41 MacKenzie (2006); Lipsey and Cullen (2007); Mears (2008a, 2010).
42 Chesney-Lind and Mauer (2003); Ewald and Uggen (2012); LeBel and Maruna (2012).
43 Travis (2005:69), citing 42 U.S. Code sec. 13662(c).
44 Petersilia (2003:120).
45 Petersilia (2003); Travis (2005); Harding et al. (2013).
46 Metraux and Culhane (2004); Geller and Curtis (2011).
47 Harding et al. (2013).
48 Petersilia (2003); Harding et al. (2013).
49 Lageson and Uggen (2013).
50 See, for example, Bushway et al. (2007); Visher et al. (2011); Bushway and Apel (2012); Lageson and Uggen (2013).
51 Mears and Mestre (2012).
52 Holzer et al. (2007); Petersilia (2003); Wang et al. (2010); Mears, Wang, and Bales (2013); Stahler et al. (2013).
53 Lageson and Uggen (2013:208).
54 Petersilia (2003:113); see also Travis (2005); Bushway et al. (2007); Holzer et al. (2007).
55 Petersilia (2003:114); see also Chesney-Lind and Mauer (2003).
56 Petersilia (2003:115).
57 Bushway et al. (2007); Ewald and Uggen (2012); LeBel and Maruna (2012).
58 Mears, Cochran, and Siennick (2013).
59 Travis (2005:69).
60 Travis (2005:69).
61 Petersilia (2005:124).
62 Petersilia (2005:125).
63 Sugie (2012).
64 Miller and Spillane (2012).
65 Manza and Uggen (2006).
66 Uggen et al. (2012:1).
67 Travis (2005:69).

  68　Travis (2005:69).
  69　Pryor and Thompkins (2013:459).
  70　Petersilia (2003:105); see, generally, Chesney-Lind and Mauer (2003).
  71　Mears (2010).
  72　Mancini et al. (2013); Mancini and Mears (2013).
  73　Rossi and Berk (1997).
  74　Rossi and Berk (1997:10).
  75　Miller and Spillane (2012); LeBel and Maruna (2012).
  76　Tonry (2004); Phelps (2011); Garland (2013).
  77　Paternoster (2010).
  78　Paternoster (2010:785).
  79　Stafford and Warr (1993); Jacobs (2010).
  80　Paternoster (2010:803); see also Nagin (2013).
  81　Paternoster (2010:803).
  82　Paternoster (2010:804–805).
  83　Paternoster (2010:815).
  84　Petersilia (2003); Travis (2005); Mears (2010).
  85　Mears (2010).
  86　Nagin et al. (2009).
  87　Travis (2005:70).
  88　Mears (2013).
  89　Mears and Bacon (2009).
  90　Roberts et al. (2003); Roberts and Hough (2005a-b); Lee et al. (2014).
  91　Rossi and Berk (1997).
  92　Nagin et al. (2009); Spelman (2006, 2008, 2009); Paternoster (2010); Wermink et al. (2013); Travis et al. (2014).
  93　MacKenzie (2006); Mears (2010); Cullen and Jonson (2012).
  94　Alongside of large-scale trends such as mass incarceration lie many micro-level and meso-level changes that occurred among state and local criminal justice jurisdictions. Understanding such variation is of interest in its own right (Garland 2013). However, it is important work, too, for identifying specific areas where the most gains in effective and efficient processing and sanctioning can be obtained.
  95　Mears and Bacon (2009).
  96　Mears and Bacon (2009).
  97　Travis (2005); Vitiello (2013).
  98　Roman and DeStefano (2004); Sevigny et al. (2013).
  99　Sampson (2013).
  100　Mears, Wang, and Bales (2013).
  101　Mears (2008a).
  102　Hawken and Kleiman (2009).
  103　Mears and Bacon (2009).

Chapter 3

  1　See, for example, Gottschalk (2006); Barker (2009); Tonry (2009a); Blomberg and Lucken (2010); Stuntz (2011); Simon (2012); Garland (2013).
  2　Gawande (2007, 2009).
  3　See, generally, Travis et al. (2014).
  4　Simon (2012); Garland (2013).
  5　Blumstein and Beck (1999:54).

6 That insight is one that flows from system analytic perspectives (Meadows 2008).

7 Heilbroner (1990) has provided a compelling account of ways in which law enforcement behavior is affected in part by their understanding of how the courts will respond to arrests for certain types of illegal behavior.

8 Tonry (2009a).

9 Rand and Catalano (2007).

10 Spelman (2006, 2008, 2009).

11 Baumer (2011).

12 See, however, Simon (2007).

13 Burstein (1998, 2003, 2014).

14 See, generally, Stolz (2002).

15 Kahneman (2011).

16 Groopman (2007).

17 Forst (2004); Mears and Bacon (2009).

18 Tonry (2009a).

19 Cullen et al. (2000); Mears (2010).

20 Roberts et al. (2003); Roberts and Hough (2005a-b); Ramirez (2013).

21 Tonry (2004); Unnever and Cullen (2010).

22 Roberts and Stalans (1998:32); see also Ramirez (2013).

23 Roberts (1992); Roberts and Stalans (1998); Cullen et al. (2000); Roberts et al. (2003); Roberts and Hough (2005a-b); Unnever and Cullen (2010).

24 Roberts and Stalans (1998:48).

25 Unnever (2014).

26 Nagin et al. (2006); Mears, Hay, et al. (2007).

27 See, for example, Unnever and Cullen (2010).

28 Unnever and Cullen (2010).

29 See, however, Ramirez (2013).

30 Unnever (2014).

31 Ramirez (2013:357).

32 Cullen et al. (2000); Nagin et al. (2006); Unnever and Cullen (2010).

33 Pew Charitable Trusts (2012a).

34 Cullen et al. (2000); Mears (2010).

35 Stolz (2002); Marion and Oliver (2006, 2009); Simon (2007); Oliver and Marion (2008).

36 Caplow and Simon (1999:65).

37 See, generally, Useem and Piehl (2008).

38 Skogan (1995:60).

39 Braden (1996).

40 Finckenauer (1978:17).

41 Finckenauer (1978:24).

42 Finckenauer (1978:23).

43 Merlo et al. (1997:150).

44 Feld (1999).

45 Mauer (1999:13).

46 Republican National Committee (2012:37).

47 Roberts et al. (2003:3).

48 Garland (2013:480–481). See also Tonry (2009a).

49 Simon (2007, 2012).

50 Alexander (2012).

51 Western (2006); Wacquant (2009).

52 Unnever and Cullen (2010).

53 Beckett and Sasson (2000); Peffley and Hurwitz (2002); Chiricos et al. (2004); Peterson et al. (2006).
54 Mears (2010).
55 Sparks et al. (1996); Bottoms (1999).
56 Mears and Reisig (2006); Mears and Watson (2006).
57 Mears (2012a).
58 Hogan et al. (2005); Costelloe et al. (2009); Vieno et al. (2013).
59 Cullen et al. (2000).
60 Cullen and Jonson (2012).
61 Mears (2010).
62 See, for example, Hutchings (1999); Gottschalk (2006); Simon (2007); Oliver and Marion (2008); Welsh and Harris (2008); Mears (2010); Lerman (2013).
63 Spelman (2006, 2008, 2009). See also Durlauf and Nagin (2011).
64 Nagin et al. (2009); Paternoster (2010); Cullen et al. (2011); Lerman (2013); Mears, Cochran, and Cullen (2014).
65 Nagin et al. (2009); Cochran, Mears, and Bales (2014).
66 Meade et al. (2013).
67 Mears (2010); Durlauf and Nagin (2011).
68 Rossi and Berk (1997); Cullen et al. (2000).
69 Roberts and Stalans (1998:39).
70 Roberts and Stalans (1998:39).
71 Cullen et al. (2000); Roberts et al. (2003); Roberts and Hough (2005a-b).
72 Roberts and Stalans (1998:50).
73 Rossi and Berk (1997:7).
74 Rossi and Berk (1997:8).
75 Roberts and Stalans (1998:43).
76 Pew Charitable Trust (2012a:2).
77 Martinson (1974); Cullen and Jonson (2012).
78 Tonry (1997); Cullen and Gendreau (2000); Petersilia (2003); Mears, Cochran, et al. (2011).
79 Mears, Cochran, and Cullen (2014).
80 Crouch (1993); Petersilia and Turner (1993); Deschenes et al. (1995); Spelman (1995); Petersilia (1997); May et al. (2005); Taxman (2012).
81 See, generally, Petersilia and Turner (1993); Petersilia (1997); Tonry (1997); Piehl and LoBuglio (2005); MacKenzie (2006); Lipsey and Cullen (2007); Mears and Barnes (2010); MacKenzie (2012); Taxman (2012).
82 Cochran, Mears, and Bales (2014).
83 Roberts and Stalans (1998:49).
84 Roberts and Stalans (1998:49).
85 Pew Charitable Trusts (2012a).
86 Phelps (2013).
87 Mears (2010).
88 See, however, Mears and Stafford (2002). Some causes are asymmetric. In such cases, an increase in a cause may produce more of a problem, but a decrease in the cause will have no effect on the problem. For example, if we increase our tooth brushing, we reduce the number of cavities that we will get. However, once a cavity exists due to a lack of tooth brushing, no amount of increased tooth brushing will cause the cavity to go away.

89   Cochran, Mears, and Bales (2014).
90   See, generally, Kahneman (2011).
91   Blumstein (1997, 2008); Sherman (2004); Mears (2010).
92   See, for example, Baumer (2011).
93   Baumer (2011).
94   Riveland (1999a); Lynch and Sabol (2001).
95   Brown (2013); Phelps (2013).
96   Weiman et al. (2007:30).
97   Weiman et al. (2007:30).
98   Garland (2001); Lynch (2007); Wacquant (2009).
99   Caplow and Simon (1999); Weiman et al. (2007); Zimring (2007); Garland (2013).
100   See, for example, Pew Charitable Trusts (2013).
101   Meadows (2008).
102   Blumstein and Beck (1999).
103   Garland (2013:484).
104   Blumstein and Beck (1999).
105   See also Sabol (1999).
106   Mears and Bacon (2009).
107   Durkheim (1985); this compilation consists of essays Durkheim wrote in the late 1800s and early 1900s.
108   Durkheim (1985:100).
109   Zimring (2005, 2007); Simon (2012).
110   See, for example, Harmon (2013).
111   See, for example, Gottschalk (2006); Barker (2009); Alexander (2012); Simon (2012); Garland (2013).
112   Mears and Stafford (2002).
113   Stolz (2002).
114   Mears (2010).
115   Garland (2013:487).
116   Alexander (2012); see also Wacquant (2009).
117   The account involves arguments that can be found in many scholarly analyses of mass incarceration, including those by Blumstein (1997), Cullen and Gendreau (2000), Garland (2001), Gottschalk (2006), Simon (2007, 2012), Oliver and Marion (2008), Welsh and Harris (2008), Blomberg and Lucken (2010), Mears (2010), and others.
118   Mears (2010).
119   Barker (2009).
120   Garland (2013:483); see, generally, Barker (2009) and Simon (2012).
121   Garland (2013:482).
122   See, generally, Garland (2013).
123   Clear (2007).
124   Gottschalk (2013).
125   Karmen (1992).
126   Davis et al. (2003); Hickman and Simpson (2003); Felson and Pare (2008).
127   Stolz (2002).
128   Mears and Bacon (2009).
129   Mears (2013).

Chapter 4

1 Here we draw in part on Mears and Cochran (2014), a chapter entitled "Who Goes to Prison?" In that chapter, as in other works (e.g., Lynch and Sabol 2001; Travis et al. 2001; Petersilia 2003, 2005; Western 2006; Useem and Piehl 2008; Gottschalk 2006, 2011; Raphael 2011; Carson and Sabol 2012; Mears and Cochran 2012; Visher and Travis 2012), the focus centers on the profile of the "typical" inmate. In the current chapter, our focus is less on providing a complete description of prisoner characteristics. These other accounts, including Mears and Cochran (2014), provide such information in comprehensive detail. Instead, we attend more to identifying *why* inmate characteristics are relevant to a discussion of reentry.

2 See, for example, Travis et al. (2001); Petersilia (2003, 2005); Raphael (2011); Carson and Sabol (2012); Visher and Travis (2012); Mears and Cochran (2014).

3 Mears (2010).

4 Beck and Greenfeld (1995); Mears (2010).

5 Mears (2010).

6 Wolf et al. (2007).

7 Mushlin (2002); Easton (2011).

8 Steiner and Meade (2014).

9 Steiner and Meade (2014:143).

10 Wolf et al. (2007).

11 Mears and Travis (2004).

12 Such changes are entirely possible—see, for example, Liska et al. (1999).

13 Irwin and Cressey (1962).

14 Adams (1992); Mears, Stewart, et al. (2013).

15 Mears (2008a).

16 See, generally, Pettit and Western (2004); Travis (2005); Warren et al. (2006); Western (2006); Wang and Mears (2010); Tonry (1995, 2008, 2011, 2012); Spohn (2014).

17 Spohn (2014).

18 See, for example, Doerner and Demuth (2014).

19 Blowers and Doerner (2013).

20 Mears, Stewart, et al. (2013); Hemmens and Stohr (2014).

21 See, generally, Hemmens and Stohr (2014).

22 Fleisher and Decker (2001).

23 Hemmens and Stohr (2014).

24 Mears and Bales (2009); Hemmens and Stohr (2014).

25 Tonry (2012:55).

26 Arbach-Lucioni et al. (2012).

27 Steiner and Wooldredge (2014).

28 Wang et al. (2010); Mears, Wang, and Bales (2013).

29 Hemmens and Stohr (2014:122).

30 Carson and Sabol (2012:10).

31 Blumstein and Beck (1999).

32 Blumstein and Beck (1999); Mears (2010).

33 Gendreau et al. (1997); Steiner (2009); Cunningham et al. (2011); Arbach-Lucioni et al. (2012).

34 Beck and Johnson (2012).

35 Blumstein et al. (1986).

36 Harlow (2003).

37 Durose et al. (2014:6).
38 Durose et al. (2014:7).
39 Nagin et al. (2009); Cullen et al. (2011); Cochran, Mears, and Bales (2014).
40 Adams (1992); Liebling (1999).
41 Pew Charitable Trusts (2012b).
42 Pew Charitable Trusts (2012b).
43 Garland (2013); Cochran, Mears, and Bales (2014).
44 Uggen et al. (2005); Cochran and Mears (2013); Meade et al. (2013).
45 Gendreau et al. (1997); Wooldredge et al. (2001); Sorensen and Cunningham (2010).
46 Rose and Clear (2003); Uggen and Wakefield (2005).
47 Beck and Mumola (1999); Carson and Sabol (2012).
48 Chiu (2010); Stal (2012).
49 Tonry (2011); Alexander (2012).
50 Western (2006:3).
51 Petersilia (2005); Clear (2007); Mears, Wang, et al. (2008); Tonry (2011, 2012).
52 Carson and Sabol (2012).
53 Harrison and Beck (2005).
54 Chesney-Lind and Pasko (2013).
55 Blevins et al. (2010); Solinger et al. (2010); Wolff and Shi (2011); Cobbina et al. (2012).
56 Carson and Sabol (2012).
57 Matthews and Hubbard (2008); Wright et al. (2012).
58 James and Glaze (2006); Guthrie (2011); Wright et al. (2012).
59 Harlow (2003).
60 Hayes (2002); Herrington (2009); McKenzie et al. (2012).
61 Visher et al. (2011).
62 Harlow (2003); Petersilia (2005); see also Ramakers et al. (2014).
63 Uggen et al. (2005); Bushway et al. (2007); Bushway and Apel (2012).
64 Mears and Mestre (2012).
65 Wang et al. (2010).
66 Mears and Cochran (2012).
67 Petersilia (2003:36–37).
68 James and Glaze (2006); Mumola and Karberg (2006).
69 Mears (2001, 2004b).
70 Guy et al. (2005); Felson et al. (2012); Houser et al. (2012).
71 Kubrin and Stewart (2006).
72 See, generally, Bushway et al. (2007); Clear (2007); Mears, Wang, et al. (2008); Sampson (2009); Wang et al. (2010); Mears, Wang, and Bales (2013).
73 Christian (2005); Cochran and Mears (2013); Hemmens and Stohr (2014).
74 Durose et al. (2014).
75 Pratt and Cullen (2000).
76 Mears, Cochran, and Siennick (2013).
77 Mumola (2000).
78 Cochran and Mears (2013).
79 Bottoms (1999).
80 See, generally, Agnew (2005); see also Mears and Cochran (2013); Mears, Cochran, and Beaver (2013).
81 Farrington and Welsh (2007:96).

82   Stafford and Mears (2014).
83   Gawande (2007); Groopman (2007); see, generally, Mears and Bacon (2009).
84   Brown et al. (1996); Carson and Sabol (2012).
85   See, generally, Petersilia (2003), Travis (2005), Blumstein and Wallman (2006), Mears (2010), Spelman (2006, 2008, 2009), Garland (2013), and Gottschalk (2013).
86   Garland (2013).
87   Baumer and Lauritsen (2010).
88   Mears (2010).
89   Mears (2010).
90   Cullen and Jonson (2012).
91   See, for example, Blumstein and Beck (1999), Nadelmann (2004), and Mauer (2009).
92   Provine (2007).
93   Reaves (2010).
94   Marvell and Moody (2006).
95   Mears (2010:17).
96   Pettit and Western (2004); Warren et al. (2006); Clear (2007).
97   Travis (2005); Gottschalk (2006, 2011); Tonry (2011, 2012).
98   Mauer (2009); Tonry (2009a); Mears (2010).
99   Mears (2010).
100 Mears (2010).
101 Petersilia (2003, 2005).
102 Maruna (2001); Nagin et al. (2009).
103 See, generally, Forer (1994).

Chapter 5

1   Visher and Travis (2003, 2011).
2   See, generally, Cullen and Jonson (2012).
3   Rothman (1971).
4   Durose et al. (2014).
5   Cullen et al. (2011).
6   Vermink et al. (2013).
7   Nagin et al. (2009).
8   Ekland-Olson et al. (1983).
9   Cochran, Mears, Bales, and Stewart (2014).
10   Mears (2001, 2004b).
11   Lipsey and Cullen (2007).
12   Cochran and Mears (2013).
13   Mears and Barnes (2010).
14   Tyler (1990); Franke et al. (2010); Steiner and Meade (2014).
15   Steiner and Meade (2014).
16   DeLisi (2003); Mears and Mestre (2012); Cochran, Mears, Bales, and Stewart (2014).
17   Steiner and Meade (2014:132).
18   Steiner and Meade (2014:133); see also Rand (2009) and Beck and Johnson (2012).
19   DeLisi (2003); Steiner and Wooldredge (2013).
20   Petersilia (2003); Travis (2005); see, however, Makarios and Latessa (2013).
21   Clemmer (1940).
22   Irwin and Cressey (1962); Johnson (1976); Harer and Steffensmeier (1996); DeLisi (2003).

23 DeLisi (2003); Steiner and Meade (2014).

24 See, for example, Harer and Langan (2001); Drury and DeLisi (2010); Makarios and Latessa (2013).

25 Lahm (2008); Mears, Stewart, Siennick, and Simons (2013).

26 Clemmer (1940); Sykes (1958).

27 Sykes (1958).

28 Tyler (1990); Bottoms (1999); Steiner and Meade (2014).

29 Bottoms (1999).

30 See, for example, Blevins et al. (2010); Felson et al. (2012).

31 Hochstetler and DeLisi (2005); Blevins et al. (2010); Mears, Stewart, et al. (2013).

32 See, for example, Trulson et al. (2011); Cochran, Mears, Bales, and Stewart (2014).

33 Akers and Sellers (2012).

34 Agnew (2005); Cochran (2012, 2014).

35 Akers and Sellers (2012).

36 Bushway and Apel (2012); Mears and Mestre (2012).

37 See, for example, Clemmer (1940); Sykes (1958); Conover (2000); Rhodes (2004); Comfort (2008); Hassine (2009); Ross and Richards (2009).

38 Lynch and Sabol (2001); Lawrence et al. (2002).

39 Cullen and Jonson (2011).

40 Mears, Roman, et al. (2006).

41 Mears, Winterfield, et al. (2003).

42 See, for example, Sherman et al. (2002); Petersilia (2003); Travis (2005); Lipsey and Cullen (2007); MacKenzie (2006, 2012); Mears (2010); Welsh and Pfeffer (2013); Latessa et al. (2014).

43 Mears (2010).

44 Lipsey and Cullen (2007).

45 Cullen and Jonson (2011).

46 Clemmer (1940).

47 See, for example, Wilson et al. (2003).

48 Bushway and Apel (2012).

49 Mears, Winterfield, et al. (2003); Cullen and Jonson (2011).

50 Mears (2010).

51 Mitchell et al. (2007); Cullen and Jonson (2011).

52 Farabee (2005); Mears (2008a).

53 Hairston (1991); Adams (1992).

54 Adams (1992); Liebling (1999); Petersilia (2003); Bales and Mears (2008); Cochran (2012); Mears, Cochran, Siennick, and Bales (2012); Cochran and Mears (2013); Listwan et al. (2013).

55 Sykes (1958).

56 See Maruna (2001); see, conversely, Rhodes (2004).

57 Holt and Miller (1972); Hairston (1991); Cochran and Mears (2013).

58 Berg and Huebner (2011).

59 Cochran and Mears (2013).

60 Mears, Cochran, et al. (2012); Duwe and Clark (2013).

61 Monahan et al. (2011).

62 Hagan and Dinovitzer (1999).

63 Bales and Mears (2008); Cochran (2012, 2014); Duwe and Clark (2013); Mears, Cochran, Siennick, and Bales (2012); cf. Siennick et al. (2013).

64 Cochran and Mears (2013).

65 Cochran (2014).

66 Liebling (1999); Jiang and Winfree (2006); Ross and Richards (2009); Cochran (2012, 2014); Listwan et al. (2013); Siennick et al. (2013).

67 Hairston (1991); Christian (2005); Comfort (2008).

68 See, however, Mears, Cochran, Siennick, and Bales (2012).

69 Mumola (2000); Christian (2005); Christian et al. (2006); Comfort (2008).

70 Steiner and Meade (2014:133).

71 Listwan et al. (2010, 2013, 2014).

72 Steiner and Meade (2014).

73 Beck and Johnson (2012); Steiner and Meade (2014).

74 Listwan et al. (2012).

75 Burnam et al. (1988); Listwan et al. (2010, 2013).

76 Listwan et al. (2013).

77 Gibbons and Katzenbach (2006).

78 Riveland (1999a); Gibbons and Katzenbach (2006); Shalev (2009); Mears (2013).

79 See, generally, Shalev (2009); Mears (2013); Ross (2013).

80 Haney (2003, 2008); Smith (2006).

81 Haney (2003); Rhodes (2004); Mears and Reisig (2006); Mears and Watson (2006); Mears and Bales (2009, 2010); Ross (2013); cf. O'Keefe et al. (2013).

82 Mears (2013).

83 Lovell et al. (2007); Mears and Bales (2009).

84 See, generally, Akers and Sellers (2012) and Cullen and Jonson (2012).

85 Maruna (2001).

86 LeBel and Maruna (2012); LeBel (2012); see, generally Braithwaite (1989).

87 Maruna (2001); Rose and Clear (2003); Burnett and Maruna (2004); Uggen et al. (2004); LeBel et al. (2008); Visher and O'Connell (2012).

88 Giordano et al. (2007); Visher and O'Connell (2012).

89 LeBel et al. (2008); Mears (2010); LeBel (2012); Visher and O'Connell (2012).

90 Travis (2005); see also Maruna (2011).

91 Visher and O'Connell (2012).

92 See, generally, Farabee (2005).

93 See, generally, Lipsey and Cullen (2007).

94 See, generally, Braithwaite (1989).

95 See, for example, Gottschalk (2006, 2011, 2013); Spelman (2006, 2009); Nagin et al. (2009); Mears (2010); Cullen et al. (2011); Garland (2013); Nagin (2013); Cochran, Mears, and Bales (2014).

96 See, for example, Western (2006:176–188).

97 Travis et al. (2014).

98 See, example, Vermink et al. (2013).

99 See Gendreau et al. (2000); Smith et al. (2002); Villettaz et al. (2006); Nagin et al. (2009); Mears and Mestre (2012).

100 Nagin et al. (2009).

101 For example, Windzio (2006); Nagin et al. (2009); Mears and Barnes (2010); Cullen et al. (2011); Cobbina et al. (2012); Mears (2012b); Wolff et al. (2012); Cochran, Mears, and Bales (2014).

102 See, for example, Bhati and Piquero (2008); Cullen et al. (2011); Durlauf and Nagin (2011).

103 See, generally, Baird and Rosenbaum (1988); von Hirsch and Ashworth (1992); Rossi and Berk (1997).

104 Morris and Rothman (1995).

105 Golden (2006).
106 See, generally, Cullen et al. (2014).
107 Rossi and Berk (1997).
108 See, for example, Nagin et al. (2006).
109 Welsh and Harris (2008).
110 Mears (2008a, 2010); Mears and Bacon (2009); Mears and Barnes (2010); Mears and Butts (2008).
111 Tonry (1997); Petersilia (2003); Piehl and LoBuglio (2005).
112 Mears and Bacon (2009).
113 Mears (2010); Welsh and Pfeffer (2013).
114 Mears, Stewart, Siennick, and Simons (2013).
115 Nagin et al. (2009); Cullen and Jonson (2012).
116 See, generally, Akers and Sellers (2012).
117 See, for example, Sherman (1993).
118 Bottoms (1999).
119 Fagan (2010); Nagin et al. (2009); Vermink et al. (2013); Cochran, Mears, and Bales (2014).
120 Mears (2010); Spelman (2006, 2009); Nagin and Snodgrass (2013); Cochran, Mears, and Bales (2014).
121 Mears (2010).
122 Mears (2008a).
123 See, generally, Mears (2008a, 2010).

Chapter 6

1 Mears (2010).
2 See, for example, Doyle and Peterson (2005), Riviere et al. (2011), White et al. (2012), Danish and Antonides (2013).
3 Travis (2005).
4 Maruna (2001).
5 See, generally, Sampson (2009, 2013).
6 Travis (2005: xxi).
7 LeBel and Maruna (2012); Visher and O'Connell (2012).
8 LeBel and Maruna (2012:660).
9 Chesney-Lind and Mauer (2003); Petersilia (2003); Travis (2005); Ewald and Uggen (2012); LeBel and Maruna (2012); Visher and Travis (2012).
10 See, generally, Roberts and Hough (2005a-b).
11 Garland (2013).
12 Mears and Bacon (2009).
13 See, for example, Petersilia (2003); Travis (2005); Paternoster (2010); Visher and Travis (2012).
14 Blumstein (1997).
15 LeBel and Maruna (2012:660).
16 Manza and Uggen (2006).
17 Uggen et al. (2012:1).
18 Petersilia (2003:105); Travis (2005:69); Pryor and Thompkins (2013:459); see, generally, Chesney-Lind and Mauer (2003) and LeBel and Maruna (2012).
19 LeBel and Maruna (2012).
20 LeBel and Maruna (2012).

21 Laub and Sampson (2003); LeBel and Maruna (2012); see also Visher and O'Connell (2012).
22 Adams (1992).
23 La Vigne et al. (2007).
24 LeBel and Maruna (2012).
25 Travis et al. (2001).
26 Travis et al. (2001); Metraux and Culhane (2004); Geller and Curtis (2011); Austin and Irwin (2012).
27 Petersilia (2003:120).
28 See, generally, LeBel and Maruna (2012).
29 See, for example, Kubrin and Stewart (2006) and Wang et al. (2010).
30 Yahner and Visher (2008); Kirk (2009).
31 Irwin (2005); La Vigne et al. (2007); LeBel and Maruna (2012).
32 Hattery and Smith (2010:93); emphasis in original.
33 See, generally, Pager (2007).
34 Petersilia (2003:113); see also Travis (2005); Bushway et al. (2007); Holzer et al. (2007).
35 Bushway and Reuter (2002); Bushway (2011); Bushway and Apel (2012).
36 LeBel and Maruna (2012:662).
37 Adams (1992).
38 Bales and Mears (2008).
39 Mears, Cochran et al. (2012); Cochran and Mears (2013); Cochran (2014).
40 Visher and O'Connell (2012).
41 Hattery and Smith (2010:79).
42 Petersilia (2003:246).
43 Bales and Mears (2008); Yahner and Visher (2008); Visher and Travis (2012); Cochran (2014).
44 Kubrin and Stewart (2006); LeBel and Maruna (2012).
45 Cochran and Mears (2013).
46 Petersilia (2003:36–37); Mumola and Karberg (2006); see, generally, Mears (2001, 2004b).
47 LeBel and Maruna (2012).
48 MacKenzie (2006); LeBel and Maruna (2012).
49 Winterfield and Castro (2005).
50 Mears (2001, 2004b); one example of an attempt to quantify the shortfall among juvenile offenders in Texas can be found in Kelly et al. (2005).
51 Visher and Travis (2012).
52 Petersilia (2005:125).
53 Travis (2005).
54 See, for example, Piehl and LoBuglio (2005); LeBel and Maruna (2012).
55 As cited in LeBel and Maruna (2012:672); emphasis in original.
56 Travis (2005).
57 Petersilia (2003); Travis (2005); Western (2006); Bushway et al. (2007); Mears and Barnes (2010); Visher and Travis (2011); Ewald and Uggen (2012).
58 Ewald and Uggen (2012); see, generally, Western (2006) and Bushway et al. (2007).
59 Schnittker and John (2007); Massoglia (2008); Wakefield and Uggen (2010).
60 Mears and Cochran (2012).
61 Nagin et al. (2009); Cochran, Mears, and Bales (2014).
62 Weiser (2011).

63 Glaze and Maruschak (2008).
64 Petersilia (2003); Travis (2005).
65 Ewald and Uggen (2012).
66 Wildeman (2014).
67 Turanovic et al. (2012).
68 See, generally, Johnson and Easterling (2012).
69 Clear (2007); Nagin et al. (2009); Cochran, Mears, and Bales (2014).
70 Ewald and Uggen (2012).
71 Sampson (2009, 2012).
72 DeFina and Hannon (2010).
73 See, for example, discussions in Travis (2005), Clear (2007), and Sampson (2012).
74 Rose and Clear (1998); DeFina and Hannon 2013).
75 Western and Wildeman (2009:234); see also Wilson (1987); Western (2006); Western and Muller (2013).
76 Ewald and Uggen (2012).
77 Petersilia (2003); Unnever (2008); Western and Muller (2013); Lee et al. (2014).
78 Abramsky (2006).
79 Manza and Uggen (2006).
80 Ewald and Uggen (2012:94).
81 Spelman (2006, 2009).
82 Clear (2007); Nagin et al. (2009); Cochran, Mears, and Bales (2014).
83 Ridgeway (2013).

Chapter 7

1 Nagin et al. (2009) and Cullen and Jonson (2012) have offered useful accounts of the ways that criminological theories offer competing predictions about the effects of prison.
2 Durose et al. (2014).
3 See, for example, Travis (2005:33).
4 Piquero et al. (2007); LeBel and Maruna (2012).
5 Nate Silver (2012:149) has provided a useful and discussion of the distinctions.
6 Langan and Levin (2002).
7 Andrews et al. (2006); Slobogin (2012); Rhodes (2013).
8 Latessa et al. (2014).
9 See, for example, Andrews et al. (2006).
10 Andrews et al. (2006:8).
11 Andrews et al. (2006:7); emphases in original.
12 Latessa et al. (2014).
13 Berk and Bleich (2013); see also Mears (2004b).
14 Clements (1996); Cullen and Gendreau (2000); Bonta (2002); Andrews et al. (2006); Latessa et al. (2014).
15 Cullen and Gendreau (2000:145).
16 Cullen and Gendreau (2000:145), citing Andrews (1995:37).
17 Cullen and Gendreau (2000:145).
18 Cullen and Gendreau (2000:147).
19 Cullen and Gendreau (2000:147–148).
20 Farrington and Welsh (2007:22).
21 Berk (2012); Berk and Bleich (2013).

22 According to Streiner and Cairney (2013:304), the ROC analysis "dates back to World War II and the merging of signal detection theory with the development of radar." They have provided a useful historical example of the issue of trade-offs with prediction:

When the gain of the radar set (comparable to the volume control on a radio) is at zero, no signal (in this case representing an enemy plane) is detected. Increasing the gain lets more signals in, but it also increases the amount of noise that is picked up and possibly misinterpreted as a true signal. At low levels of gain, the noise is very weak and unlikely to be falsely labelled, but at the same time, only very strong signals (very large or close planes, to continue the example) are detected and many true signals are missed. As the gain is turned up even further, weaker signals are picked up, but so is more noise (things that can seem like aircraft but are not, such as rain clouds or a flock of birds). At some point, further increases become counterproductive, in that the noise (false positives) begins to outweigh the signals (true positives). (Pp. 304–305.)

23 Fazel et al. (2012:3).

24 Dolan and Doyle (2000:305).

25 Stockdale et al. (2014:121), citing Rice and Harris (1995).

26 Rice and Harris (1995); Dolan and Doyle (2000); Stockdale et al. (2014).

27 Vrieze and Grove (2010:20); see also Fazel et al. (2012).

28 Kroner and Mills (2010).

29 Kroner and Mills (2001).

30 Fazel et al. (2012).

31 See, for example, Kroner and Mills (2001).

32 See Fazel et al. (2012) for discussion and review of both sets of instruments.

33 See, for example, Kroner and Mills (2001); see, generally, Latessa et al. (2014).

34 Gendreau et al. (1996); Mears (2004a); Latessa et al. (2014).

35 Fazel et al. (2012:5); see also Gottfredson and Moriarty (2006) and Slobogin (2012).

36 Andrews and Bonta (2010); Latessa et al. (2014).

37 Fazel et al. (2012:5).

38 One of the most comprehensive and widely cited books is Andrews and Bonta (2010). Gendreau et al.'s (1996) assessment of predictors of recidivism also has been widely cited in the risk prediction literature. See, generally, Bonta (2002); Andrews et al. (2006); Gottfredson and Moriarty (2006); Bushway and Apel (2012); Slobogin (2012); Makarios and Latessa (2013); Rhodes (2013); Ridgeway (2013).

39 Latessa et al. (2014:39).

40 Ritter (2013).

41 Vrieze and Grove (2010).

42 Mancini (2014).

43 Mancini (2014).

44 Hanson et al. (2003).

45 Vrieze and Grove (2010:6).

46 Sweeten (2012).

47 Vrieze and Grove (2010).

48 Berk and Bleich (2013).

49 Mears and Cochran (2013); Mears, Cochran, and Beaver (2013).

50 Berk (2012).

51 Hanson et al. (2003:154).

52 Kroner and Mills (2001:485); see also Mears and Mestre (2012).

53 Wright and Cesar (2013).

54 Kubrin and Stewart (2006); Mears, Wang, et al. (2008).

55 Bushway and Apel (2012); Mears and Mestre (2012).

56 Bushway and Apel (2012).

57 Ridgeway (2013:546).

58 Mears and Mestre (2012); Ridgeway (2013).

59 Andrews et al. (2006).

60 Berk and Bleich (2013:516).

61 See, for example, the discussion in Gibbs (1989).

62 Latessa et al. (2014).

63 Andrews et al. (2006).

64 Cf. Pew Charitable Trusts (2011).

65 Gottfredson and Moriarty (2006:193).

66 Andrews et al. (2006:23).

67 Latessa et al. (2014:85).

68 Gottfredson and Moriarty (2006:192).

69 Latessa et al. (2014:85–101).

70 Kroner and Mills (2001); Vrieze and Grove (2010); cf. Latessa et al. (2014).

71 Pelissier et al. (2003); Van Voorhis et al. (2010); Cobbina et al. (2012); Mears, Cochran, and Bales (2012); Van Voorhis (2012); Chesney-Lind and Pasko (2013).

72 See, for example, Zahn et al. (2010).

73 Mears, Cochran, and Siennick (2013).

74 Mears and Cochran (2013); Mears, Cochran, and Beaver (2013).

75 See, generally, Wright and Cesar (2013).

76 Ridgeway (2013).

77 Latessa et al. (2014).

78 Gottfredson and Moriarty (2006).

79 Wooditch et al. (2014:278).

80 Stafford and Mears (2014).

81 Latessa et al. (2014:103–122).

82 Sampson et al. (2013).

83 Listwan et al. (2014).

84 Silver (2012:61).

85 Mears, Cochran, et al. (2011).

86 Silver (2012:177).

87 Forst (2004); Mears and Bacon (2009).

88 Mears (2010).

89 Jannetta and Horvath (2011).

90 Jannetta and Horvath (2011:2).

91 Jannetta and Horvath (2011:2).

92 Gottfredson and Moriarty (2006); Rhodes (2011, 2013); Slobogin (2012); Latessa et al. (2014).

93 Latessa et al. (2014).

94 Cullen and Jonson (2012); Latessa et al. (2014).

95 Nagin et al. (2009).

Chapter 8

1 Roberts (1992); Roberts and Stalans (1998); Cullen et al. (2000); Roberts et al. (2003); Gilliam and Iyengar (2000, 2005); Roberts and Hough (2005a-b); Unnever and Cullen (2010); Unnever (2014).
2 Gottfredson and Hirschi (1990).
3 See, for example, Tonry (2009b) and Gideon (2013).
4 Farrington and Welsh (2007:96).
5 Mears and Travis (2004).
6 Mears (2013).
7 Pfeiffer (2013).
8 Cullen and Gendreau (2000); Cullen and Jonson (2012).
9 Mears and Bacon (2009).
10 Beck and Mumola (1999); Mears and Travis (2004); Carson and Sabol (2012).
11 Loeber and Farrington (2012); Woolard (2012); Emeka and Walters (2013).
12 See, generally, Loeber and Farrington (2012).
13 Mears and Cochran (2012); Aday and Krabill (2013); Mears, Cochran, and Siennick (2013).
14 Feld and Bishop (2012).
15 Hirschi and Gottfredson (1993).
16 Mears (2002); Fagan (2010).
17 Loeber and Farrington (2012).
18 Mears and Travis (2004).
19 Adams (1992).
20 See, for example, Bishop and Frazier (2000).
21 See, for example, Farrington and Welsh (2005, 2007); MacKenzie (2006); Welsh and Farrington (2006); Lipsey and Cullen (2007); Loeber and Farrington (2012); cf. Mears, Cochran, et al. (2011).
22 See Mears and Travis (2004) and other articles in the 2004 special issue of the journal *Youth Violence and Juvenile Justice*.
23 Mears, Cochran, et al. (2011).
24 See, for example, Greenwood and Turner (2011, 2012); Krisberg (2012); MacKenzie and Freeland (2012).
25 Carson and Sabol (2012).
26 Harrison and Beck (2005).
27 Carson and Sabol (2012).
28 Mumola and Karberg (2006); McDaniels-Wilson and Belknap (2008); Blackburn, Mullings, and Marquart (2008).
29 Mumola (2000); Holsinger (2014).
30 Holsinger (2014).
31 James and Glaze (2006); Holsinger (2014).
32 Wolff and Shi (2011).
33 Belknap (1996).
34 Van Voorhis et al. (2010).
35 Coughenour (1995); Belknap (1996); Langan and Pelissier (2001); Celinska and Siegel (2010).
36 Mears, Cochran, Siennick, and Bales (2012).
37 Belknap (1996).
38 Belknap (1996); Holsinger (2014).

39 See, generally, Van Voorhis (2012) and Holsinger (2014).

40 See, for example, Mears, Ploeger, and Warr (1998), Steffensmeier and Allan (1996), Belknap (2006).

41 Mears, Ploeger, and Warr (1998).

42 Salisbury and Van Voorhis (2009).

43 Morash, Haarr, and Rucker (1994); Belknap (1996); Holsinger (2014).

44 Salisbury and Van Voorhis (2009).

45 See, for example, Geller et al. (2011) and Chung (2012).

46 Clear (2007); see also Western (2006); Western and Muller (2013).

47 Van Voorhis (2012).

48 See, for example, Cobbina (2010); George (2010); Johnson (2012).

49 Carson and Sabol (2012).

50 Guerino et al. (2012); Hemmens and Stohr (2014).

51 Bonczar (2003).

52 See, generally, Curtin (2000); Tonry (2011, 2012); Berg and DeLisi (2006); Kubrin and Stewart (2006); Clear (2007); Washington (2008); Hipp et al. (2010); Alexander (2012); Boessen and Cauffman (2013); Mears, Stewart, et al. (2013); Stahler et al. (2013); Hemmens and Stohr (2014).

53 Petersilia (2003); Western (2006); Bushway et al. (2007); Pettit (2012).

54 Western (2006); Tonry (2011, 2012).

55 McPherson et al. (2001); Mauer and Chesney-Lind (2002); Kubrin and Stewart (2006); Peterson et al. (2006); Western (2006); Sampson (2009); Peffley and Hurwitz (2010); Tonry (2011, 2012).

56 Alba et al. (1994); Clear (2007); Western and Wildeman (2009); Western and Muller (2013).

57 The literature is vast. See, for example, Chiricos et al. (2004); Peterson et al. (2006); Pager (2007); Wang and Mears (2010); Pettit (2012); Mears, Pickett, et al. (2013).

58 Petersilia (2003); Travis (2005); Western (2006); Clear (2007).

59 Tonry (2011).

60 Butts and Mears (2001).

61 See, for example, Kubrin and Stewart (2006); Mears, Wang, et al. (2008); Mears, Wang, and Bales (2013).

62 Mears, Cochran, and Siennick (2013).

63 Guerino et al. (2012).

64 Tonry (2011).

65 Mears, Winterfield, et al. (2003); Petersilia (2003); Travis (2005); Huebner et al. (2007).

66 Travis (2005); Wang et al. (2010); Berg and Huebner (2011).

67 Pager (2003); Holzer et al. (2007).

68 Petersilia (2003).

69 Western and Muller (2013); see also Western (2006); Clear (2007); Sampson (2009); Western and Wildeman (2009); Pettit (2012); Wildeman (2014).

70 Petersilia (2003:28).

71 Lynch and Sabol (2004); see also Clear (2007).

72 Clear (2007).

73 Lynch and Sabol (2004); Western (2006); Clear (2007); Sampson (2009); Pettit (2012).

74 Petersilia (2003); Travis (2005).

75 Heilbroner (1990); Riveland (1999a); Mears and Bacon (2009).

76 See, for example, Forer (1994).

77   Numerous accounts of such efforts can be found in publications at the Urban Institute (www.urban.org), the National Institute of Justice (www.nij.gov), the What Works in Reentry Clearinghouse (whatworks.csgjusticecenter.org), and other organizations.

78   See, generally, Hemmens and Stohr (2014); Listwan et al. (2014).

79   Spiegel (2007); Hemmens and Stohr (2014).

80   Trulson et al. (2008); Hemmens and Stohr (2014).

81   Lovell et al. (2000); Mears and Bales (2010).

82   Mears and Bales (2010); Mears (2013).

83   White and Gorman (2000); Wooditch et al. (2014).

84   Compton et al. (2007).

85   Compton et al. (2007).

86   Mears (2001, 2004b); Mears and Aron (2003); Petersilia (2003); Lorie and Bryant (2013).

87   Liska et al. (1999).

88   Mears (2004b).

89   Adams (1992); Liebling (1999); Lorie and Bryant (2013).

90   See, generally, Gideon (2013).

91   Hensley et al. (2013).

92   Hensley et al. (2013).

93   Hensley et al. (2013).

94   Henriques et al. (2013).

95   Henriques et al. (2013).

96   Mears (2010).

97   Rossman et al. (2011:5).

98   Goldkamp (2003).

99   Rossman et al. (2011).

100 Mears and Cochran (2012).

101 Clear (2007).

102 Spelman (2006, 2008, 2009); Mears (2010).

103 Some officials have called for just such an approach—see, for example, Forer (1994).

104 Pollack et al. (2013).

105 Butts and Mears (2001).

106 Hirschi and Gottfredson (1993).

107 Bushway and Apel (2012).

108 Travis (2005).

Chapter 9

1   Sherman et al. (1997).

2   Mears (2010).

3   Latessa et al. (2014:93).

4   Spelman (2006, 2008, 2009).

5   Travis et al. (2014).

6   Garland (2013:505).

7   Nagin et al. (2009); Mears (2010); Cochran, Mears, and Bales (2014).

8   Nagin et al. (2009).

9   Cochran, Mears, and Bales (2014); Mears, Cochran, and Cullen (2014).

10 Paternoster (2010:820).

11 Solomon et al. (2005).

12 Piehl and LoBuglio (2005).

13 See, for example, Davis et al. (2003).

14 Tonry (2004, 2008, 2011, 2012).

15 Hagan and Dinovitzer (1999); Petersilia (2003); Travis (2005); Sugie (2012).

16 Mears and Barnes (2010).

17 Petersilia and Cullen (2014).

18 Mears (2010).

19 Welsh and Rocque (2014).

20 Sherman (1993).

21 Mears (2010); Welsh and Rocque (2014).

22 Latessa et al. (2014).

23 Welsh and Rocque (2014).

24 See the discussions in Finckenauer (1982) and Welsh and Rocque (2014). See also Sherman (1993).

25 Mears and Stafford (2002).

26 Latessa et al. (2014).

27 Wilson et al. (2005).

28 Latessa et al. (2014).

29 Pew Charitable Trusts (2012b); Cochran, Mears, and Bales (2014).

30 See, for example, Sherman et al. (1997); Mears (2010).

31 Mears, Roman, et al. (2006).

32 Farabee (2005).

33 Mears (2010).

34 See, for example, Anderson (1999) and Cohen (2005).

35 Blumstein (2013).

36 Blumstein (2013:723).

37 Congressional Budget Office (2007:3).

38 See, for example, Jaruzelski et al. (2013:5). Precise estimates of investment in research and development, and in efforts to monitor and improve operations, can vary because of differences in how companies treat, for tax and other purposes, research expenditures (Chan et al. 2002).

39 Mears (2013).

40 La Vigne et al. (2014).

41 Bureau of Justice Assistance (2013).

42 Lattimore et al. (2010).

43 Lattimore et al. (2010:262).

44 Lattimore et al. (2010:262); see, generally, Lipsey (1998) and Weisburd et al. (2003).

45 Lattimore et al. (2010).

46 Many sources provide information about ways to improve prisoner reentry. Some of the ones used to create the tables for this chapter include the following: Adams (1992); Gendreau et al. (1996); Cullen and Gendreau (2000); Maruna (2001); Lawrence et al. (2002); Petersilia (2003); Farabee (2005); Travis (2005); Clear (2007); Tonry (2009b); Andrews and Bonta (2010); Lattimore et al. (2010); Mears (2010); Mears and Barnes (2010); Bushway and Apel (2012); MacKenzie (2006, 2012); Austin and Irwin (2012); Cullen and Jonson (2012); Taxman (2012); Craig et al. (2013); Gideon (2013); Green (2013); Lerman (2013); Pew Charitable Trusts (2013); Samuels et al. (2013); Schlager (2013); Welsh and Pfeffer (2013); Wright and

Cesar (2013); Crow and Smykla (2014); Cullen et al. (2014); Latessa et al. (2014); Steiner and Meade (2014); Travis et al. (2014); Mays and Ruddell (2015). In reality, this list only scratches the surface. Numerous special issues of journals, such as volume 47 of *Crime and Delinquency* (2001), volume 139 of *Daedalus,* and volume 651 of the *Annals* (2014), focus on reentry as well and what can be done to improve it.

47 Visher and O'Connell (2012).

48 Farabee (2005).

49 Latessa et al. (2014).

50 Cullen (1994).

51 See, for example, Travis (2005) and Maruna (2001, 2011).

52 Bottoms (1999).

53 Bushway and Apel (2012) have described a similar idea in discussing how to identify which inmates are unlikely to recidivate. A good "signal" is one that requires an individual to work hard to show (consciously or not) a change in his or her likelihood of offending.

54 See, generally, Sparks et al. (1996) and Bottoms (1999).

55 Morris (2002) has provided a wonderful illustration of this problem.

56 Ross and Richards (2009); Visher and O'Connell (2012).

57 Latessa et al. (2014).

58 Groopman (2007).

59 See, for example, DiIulio (1987), Sparks et al. (1996), Bottoms (1999), Morris (2002), and Cullen et al. (2014).

60 Maruna (2001).

61 Bushway and Apel (2012).

62 Clear (2007).

63 See, for example, Cochran, Mears, and Bales (2014).

64 Mears (2010).

65 Travis (2005:323–340).

66 Petersilia (2003:171).

67 Gendreau and Andrews (1989); Latessa et al. (2014).

68 Latessa et al. (2014:64).

69 Latessa et al. (2014:229).

70 Parsons (2014).

71 Bottoms (1999).

72 Parsons (2014).

73 Butts and Mears (2001); Mears and Travis (2004); Farrington and Welsh (2007).

74 Travis (2005:334).

75 Cullen and Jonson (2012:212).

76 Meade et al. (2013); Cochran, Mears, and Bales (2014); Mears, Cochran, and Cullen (2014).

77 MacKenzie (2006); Cullen and Jonson (2012); Latessa et al. (2014).

78 Mears (2010).

79 Petersilia and Cullen (2014).

80 Skogan (2003); Innes et al. (2009); Reisig (2010).

81 Mears (2010).

82 Mears and Bacon (2009).

83 Travis (2005).

84 Petersilia (2003).

85 Piehl and LoBuglio (2005).
86 Piehl and LoBuglio (2005:131).
87 Ridgeway (2013).
88 Berk (2012).
89 Mears (2010).
90 Travis et al. (2014).
91 Forst (2004).
92 Silver (2012).
93 Groopman (2007); Mears and Bacon (2009).
94 Maxson (2013).
95 La Vigne et al. (2014).
96 Mears and Barnes (2010).
97 Rocque et al. (2012).
98 Kraska (2006); Wright and Cesar (2013).
99 Ridgeway and MacDonald (2014).
100 Lutze (2014:257).
101 Doyle and Peterson (2005).
102 Roman et al. (2010).
103 Karmen (1992); Clear (2007); Felson and Pare (2008).
104 Herman (2010).
105 Mears (2004a, b); Cochran, Mears, and Bales (2014).
106 Mears (2010).
107 Mears (2010).
108 Mears (2008a).
109 Pew Charitable Trusts (2013).

Chapter 10

1 Stuntz (2011:14).
2 Travis (2005); see also Travis et al. (2014).
3 Stolz (2002); Travis (2005).

References

Abramsky, Sasha. 2006. *Conned: How Millions Went to Prison, Lost the Vote, and Helped Send George W. Bush to the White House.* New York: The New Press.

Adams, Kenneth. 1992. "Adjusting to Prison Life." Pp. 275–359 in *Crime and Justice,* edited by Michael H. Tonry. Chicago: University of Chicago Press.

Aday, Ronald H., and Jennifer Krabill. 2013. "Older and Geriatric Offenders: Critical Issues for the 21st Century." Pp. 203–232 in *Special Needs Offenders in Correctional Institutions,* edited by Lior Gideon. Thousand Oaks, CA: Sage.

Agnew, Robert. 2005. *Why Do Criminals Offend? A General Theory of Crime and Delinquency.* Los Angeles: Roxbury.

Akers, Ronald L., and Christine S. Sellers. 2012. *Criminological Theories: Introduction, Evaluation, and Application.* 6th ed. New York: Oxford University Press.

Alba, Richard D., John R. Logan, and Paul E. Bellair. 1994. "Living With Crime: The Implications of Racial/Ethnic Differences in Suburban Location." *Social Forces* 73:395–434.

Alexander, Michelle. 2012. *The New Jim Crow: Mass Incarceration in the Age of Colorblindedness.* New York: The New Press.

Anderson, David A. 2012. "The Cost of Crime." *Foundations and Trends in Microeconomics* 7:209–265.

———. 1999. "The Aggregate Burden of Crime." *Journal of Law and Economics* 42:611–642.

Andrews, Donald A. 1995. "The Psychology of Criminal Conduct and Effective Treatment." Pp. 35–62 in *What Works: Reducing Offending,* edited by James McGuire. West Sussex, England: John Wiley and Sons.

Andrews, Donald A., and James Bonta. 2010. *The Psychology of Criminal Conduct.* 5th ed. New Providence, NJ: Mathew Bender and Company.

Andrews, Donald A., James Bonta, and J. Stephen Wormith. 2006. "The Recent Past and Near Future of Risk and/or Need Assessment." *Crime and Delinquency* 52:7–27.

Arbach-Lucioni, Karin, Marian Martinez-Garcia, and Antonio Andres-Pueyo. 2012. "Risk Factors for Violent Behavior in Prison Inmates: A Cross-Cultural Contribution." *Criminal Justice and Behavior* 39:1219–1239.

Armistead-Jehle, Patrick, Scott L. Johnston, Nathaniel G. Wade, and Christofer J. Ecklund. 2011. "Posttraumatic Stress in U.S. Marines: The Role of Unit Cohesion and Combat Exposure." *Journal of Counseling and Development* 89:81–89.

Austin, James, and John Irwin. 2012. *It's About Time: America's Imprisonment Binge.* 4th ed. Belmont, CA: Wadsworth.

Baird, Robert M., and Stuart E. Rosenbaum, eds. 1988. *Philosophy of Punishment*. Buffalo, NY: Prometheus Books.

Bales, William D., and Daniel P. Mears. 2008. "Inmate Social Ties and the Transition to Society: Does Visitation Reduce Recidivism?" *Journal of Research in Crime and Delinquency* 45:287–321.

Bales, William D., and Alex R. Piquero. 2012. "Assessing the Impact of Imprisonment on Recidivism." *Journal of Experimental Criminology* 8:71–101.

Barker, Vanessa. 2009. *The Politics of Imprisonment: How the Democratic Process Shapes the Way America Punishes Offenders*. New York: Oxford University Press.

Baumer, Eric P. 2011. "Crime Trends." Pp. 26–59 in *The Oxford Handbook of Crime and Criminal Justice,* edited by Michael H. Tonry. New York: Oxford University Press.

Baumer, Eric P., and Janet Lauritsen. 2010. "Reporting Crime to the Police, 1973–2005: A Multivariate Analysis of Long-Term Trends in the NCS and NCVS." *Criminology* 48:131–185.

Beck, Allen J., and Lawrence A. Greenfeld. 1995. *Violent Offenders in State Prison: Sentences and Time Served*. Washington, DC: Bureau of Justice Statistics.

Beck, Allen J., and Candace Johnson. 2012. *Sexual Victimization Reported by Former State Prisoners, 2008*. Washington, DC: Bureau of Justice Statistics.

Beck, Allen J., and Christopher J. Mumola. 1999. *Prisoners in 1998*. Washington, DC: Bureau of Justice Statistics.

Beckett, Katherine, and Theodore Sasson. 2000. *The Politics of Injustice: Crime and Punishment in America*. Thousand Oaks, CA: Pine Forge Press.

Belknap, Joanne. 2006. *The Invisible Woman: Gender, Crime, and Justice*. 3rd ed. Cincinnati, OH: Wadsworth.

———. 1996, "Access to Programs and Health Care for Incarcerated Women." *Federal Probation* 60:34.

Berg, Mark T., and Matt DeLisi. 2006. "The Correctional Melting Pot: Race, Ethnicity, Citizenship, and Prison Violence." *Journal of Criminal Justice* 34:631–642.

Berg, Mark T., and Beth Huebner. 2011. "Reentry and the Ties That Bind: An Examination of Social Ties, Employment, and Recidivism." *Justice Quarterly* 28:382–410.

Berk, Richard A. 2012. *Criminal Justice Forecasts of Risk: A Machine Learning Approach*. New York: Springer.

Berk, Richard A., and Justin Bleich. 2013. "Statistical Procedures for Forecasting Criminal Behavior: A Comparative Assessment." *Criminology and Public Policy* 12:513–544.

Bhati, Avinash S., and Alex R. Piquero. 2008. "Estimating the Impact of Incarceration on Subsequent Offending Trajectories: Deterrent, Criminogenic, or Null Effect?" *Journal of Criminal Law and Criminology* 98:207–253.

Bishop, Donna M., and Charles E. Frazier. 2000. "Consequences of Transfer." Pp. 227–276 in *The Changing Boundaries of Juvenile Justice: Transfer of Adolescents to the Criminal Court,* edited by Jeffrey Fagan and Franklin E. Zimring. Chicago: University of Chicago Press.

Blackburn, Ashley G., Janet L. Mullings, and James W. Marquart. 2008. "Sexual Assault in Prison and Beyond: Toward an Understanding of Lifetime Sexual Assault Among Incarcerated Women." *The Prison Journal* 88:351–377.

Blevins, Kristie R., Shelley J. Listwan, Francis T. Cullen, and Cheryl L. Jonson. 2010. "A General Strain Theory of Prison Violence and Misconduct: An Integrated Model of Inmate Behavior." *Journal of Contemporary Criminal Justice* 26:148–166.

Blomberg, Thomas G. 1980. "Widening the Net: An Anomaly in the Evaluation of Diversion Programs." Pp. 572–592 in *Handbook of Criminal Justice Evaluation,* edited by Malcolm W. Klein and Katherine S. Teilmann. Beverly Hills, CA: Sage.

Blomberg, Thomas G., and Karol Lucken. 2010. *American Penology: A History of Control.* 2nd ed. New Brunswick, NJ: Transaction Publishers.

Blowers, Anita N., and Jill K. Doerner. 2013. "Sentencing Outcomes of the Older Prison Population: An Exploration of the Age Leniency Argument." *Journal of Crime and Justice* (forthcoming).

Blumstein, Alfred. 2013. "Linking Evidence and Criminal Justice Policy." *Criminology and Public Policy* 12:721–730.

———. 2008. "Federal Support of Local Criminal Justice." *Criminology and Public Policy* 7:351–358.

———. 1997. "Interaction of Criminological Research and Public Policy." *Journal of Quantitative Criminology* 12:349–362.

Blumstein, Alfred, and Allen J. Beck. 1999. "Population Growth in U.S. Prisons, 1980–1996." Pp. 17–61 in *Prisons,* edited by Michael H. Tonry and Joan Petersilia. Chicago: University of Chicago Press.

Blumstein, Alfred, Jacqueline Cohen, Jeffrey A. Roth, and Christy Visher. 1986. *Criminal Careers and "Career Criminals."* Vol. 1. Washington, DC: National Academy Press.

Blumstein, Alfred, and Joel Wallman, eds. 2006. *The Crime Drop in America.* New York: Cambridge University Press.

Boessen, Adam, and Elizabeth Cauffman. 2013. "Moving From the Neighborhood to the Cellblock: The Impact of Youth's Neighborhoods on Prison Misconduct." *Crime and Delinquency* (forthcoming).

Bonczar, Thomas P. 2011. *National Corrections Reporting Program: Time Served in State Prison, By Offense, Release Type, Sex, and Race.* Washington, DC: U.S. Department of Justice. Available online at http://www.bjs.gov/index.cfm?ty=pbdetail&iid=2045 (accessed April 10, 2014).

———. 2003. *Prevalence of Imprisonment in the U.S. Population, 1974–2001.* Washington, DC: Bureau of Justice Statistics.

Bonta, James. 2002. "Offender Risk Assessment: Guidelines for Selection and Use." *Criminal Justice and Behavior* 29:355–379.

Bottoms, Anthony E. 1999. "Interpersonal Violence and Social Order in Prisons." Pp. 205–282 in *Prisons,* edited by Michael H. Tonry and Joan Petersilia. Chicago: University of Chicago Press.

Braden, Maria. 1996. *Women Politicians and the Media.* Lexington: University Press of Kentucky.

Braithwaite, John. 1989. *Crime, Shame, and Reintegration.* Cambridge, UK: Cambridge University Press.

Brown v. *Plata.* 2011. Case 09-1233. U.S. Supreme Court. May 23.

Brown, Elizabeth K. 2013. "Foreclosing on Incarceration? State Correctional Policy Enactments and the Great Recession." *Criminal Justice Policy Review* 24:317–337.

Brown, Jodi M., Darrell K. Gilliard, Tracy L. Snell, James J. Stephan, and Doris James Wilson. 1996. *Correctional Populations in the United States, 1994.* Washington, DC: Bureau of Justice Statistics.

Bureau of Justice Assistance. 2013. *Fact Sheet on Second Chance Act Grant Program Accomplishments.* Washington, DC: U.S. Department of Justice.

Bureau of Justice Statistics. 2000. *Correctional Populations in the United States, 1997.* Washington, DC: U.S. Department of Justice.

Burnam, Audrey M, Judith A. Stein, Jacqueline M. Golding, Judith M. Siegel, Susan B. Sorenson, Alan B. Forsythe, and Cynthia A. Telles. 1988. "Sexual Assault and Mental Disorders in a Community Population." *Journal of Consulting and Clinical Psychology* 56:843–850.

Burnett, Ros, and Shadd Maruna. 2004. "So 'Prison Works' Does It?: The Criminal Careers of 130 Men Released From Prison." *The Howard Journal* 43:390–404.

Burstein, Paul. 2014. *American Public Opinion, Advocacy, and Policy in Congress: What the Public Wants and What It Gets.* New York: Cambridge University Press.

———. 2003. "The Impact of Public Opinion on Public Policy: A Review and an Agenda." *Political Research Quarterly* 56:29–40.

———. 1998. "Bringing the Public Back In: Should Sociologists Consider the Impact of Public Opinion on Public Policy?" *Social Forces* 77:27–62.

Burt, Martha R. 1981. *Measuring Prison Results: Ways to Monitor and Evaluate Corrections Performance.* Washington, DC: National Institute of Justice.

Bushway, Shawn D. 2011. "Labor Markets and Crime." Pp. 183–209 in *Crime and Public Policy,* edited by James Q. Wilson and Joan Petersilia. New York: Oxford University Press.

Bushway, Shawn D., and Robert Apel. 2012. "A Signaling Perspective on Employment-Based Reentry Programming." *Criminology and Public Policy* 11:21–50.

Bushway, Shawn D., and Peter Reuter. 2002. "Labor Markets and Crime." Pp. 191–224 in *Crime: Public Policies for Crime Control,* edited by James Q. Wilson and Joan Petersilia. Oakland, CA: Institute for Contemporary Studies.

Bushway, Shawn D., Michael Stoll, and David Weiman, eds. 2007. *Barriers to Reentry? The Labor Market for Released Prisoners in Post-Industrial America.* New York: Russell Sage.

Butts, Jeffrey A., and Daniel P. Mears. 2001. "Reviving Juvenile Justice in a Get-Tough Era." *Youth and Society* 33:169–198.

Caplow, Theodore, and Jonathan Simon. 1999. "Understanding Prison Policy and Population Trends." Pp. 63–120 in *Prisons,* edited by Michael H. Tonry and Joan Petersilia. Chicago: University of Chicago Press.

Carlson, Bonnie E., Layne K. Stromwall, and Cynthia A. Lietz. 2013. "Mental Health Issues in Recently Returning Women Veterans: Implications for Practice." *Social Work* 58:105–114.

Carson, E. Ann, and Daniela Golinelli. 2013a. *Prisoners in 2012: Advance Counts.* Washington, DC: Bureau of Justice Statistics.

———. 2013b. *Prisoners in 2012: Trends in Admissions and Releases, 1991–2012.* Washington, DC: Bureau of Justice Statistics.

Carson, E. Ann, and Joseph Mulako-Wangota. 2014. *National Prisoner Statistics Program.* Corrections Statistical Analysis Tool. Washington, DC: U.S. Department of Justice. Available at http://www.bjs.gov (accessed May 15, 2014).

Carson, E. Ann, and William J. Sabol. 2012. *Prisoners in 2011.* Washington, DC: Bureau of Justice Statistics.

Celinska, Katarzyna, and Jane A. Siegel. 2010. "Mothers in Trouble: Coping With Actual or Pending Separation From Children Due to Incarceration." *The Prison Journal* 90:447–474.

Chan, Louis K. C., Josef Lakonishok, and Theodore Sougiannis. 2002. "The Stock Market Valuation of Research and Development Expenditures." *The Journal of Finance* 56:2431–2456.

Chesney-Lind, Meda, and Marc Mauer, eds. 2003. *Invisible Punishment: The Collateral Consequences of Mass Imprisonment.* New York: The New Press.

Chesney-Lind, Meda, and Lisa Pasko, eds. 2013. *The Female Offender: Girls, Women, and Crime.* Thousand Oaks, CA: Sage.

Chiricos, Ted, Kelly Welch, and Marc Gertz. 2004. "Racial Typification of Crime and Support for Punitive Measures." *Criminology* 42:359–389.

Chiu, Tina. 2010. *It's About Time: Aging Prisoners, Increasing Costs, and Geriatric Release.* New York: Vera Institute of Justice.

Christian, Johnna. 2005. "Riding the Bus: Barriers to Prison Visitation and Family Management Strategies." *Journal of Contemporary Criminal Justice* 21:31–48.

Christian, Johnna, Jeff Mellow, and Shenique Thomas. 2006. "Social and Economic Implications of Family Connections to Prisoners." *Journal of Criminal Justice* 34:443–452.

Chung, Yiyoon. 2012. "The Effects of Paternal Imprisonment on Children's Economic Well-Being." *Social Service Review* 86:455–486.

Clear, Todd R. 2007. *Imprisoning Communities: How Mass Incarceration Makes Disadvantaged Neighborhoods Worse.* New York: Oxford University Press.

Clements, Carl B. 1996. "Offender Classification: Two Decades of Progress." *Criminal Justice and Behavior* 23:121–143.

Clemmer, Donald. 1940. *The Prison Community.* New York: Holt, Rinehart, and Winston.

Cobbina, Jennifer E. 2010. "Reintegration Success and Failure: Factors Impacting Reintegration Among Incarcerated and Formerly Incarcerated Women." *Journal of Offender Rehabilitation* 49:210–232.

Cobbina, Jennifer E., Beth M. Huebner, and Mark T. Berg. 2012. "Men, Women, and Postrelease Offending: An Examination of the Nature of the Link Between Relational Ties and Recidivism." *Crime and Delinquency* 58:331–361.

Cochran, Joshua C. 2014. "Breaches in the Wall: Imprisonment, Social Support, and Recidivism." *Journal of Research in Crime and Delinquency* 51:200–229.

———. 2012. "The Ties That Bind or the Ties That Break: Examining the Relationship Between Visitation and Prisoner Misconduct." *Journal of Criminal Justice* 40: 433–440.

Cochran, Joshua C., and Daniel P. Mears. 2013. "Social Isolation and Inmate Behavior: A Conceptual Framework for Theorizing Prison Visitation and Guiding and Assessing Research." *Journal of Criminal Justice* 41:252–261.

Cochran, Joshua C., Daniel P. Mears, and William D. Bales. 2014. "Assessing the Effectiveness of Correctional Sanctions." *Journal of Quantitative Criminology* 30:317–347.

Cochran, Joshua C., Daniel P. Mears, William D. Bales, and Eric A. Stewart. 2014. "Does Inmate Behavior Affect Post-Release Offending? Investigating the Misconduct-Recidivism Relationship Among Youth and Adults." *Justice Quarterly* 31:1044–1073.

Cohen, Andrew. 2013. "An American Gulag: The Mentally Ill at Supermax." *The Atlantic Monthly,* online article series. Available at http://www.theatlantic.com/personal/archive/2012/06/an-american-gulag-0151-the-mentally-ill-at-supermax/258818.

Cohen, Mark A. 2005. *The Costs of Crime and Justice.* New York: Routledge.

Comfort, Megan L. 2008. *Doing Time Together: Love and Family in the Shadow of the Prison.* Chicago: University of Chicago Press.

Compton, Wilson M., Yonette F. Thomas, Frederick S. Stinson, and Bridget F. Grant. 2007. "Prevalence, Correlates, Disability, and Comorbidity of DSM-IV Drug Abuse and Dependence in the United States: Results From the National Epidemiologic Survey on Alcohol and Related Conditions." *Archives of General Psychiatry* 64:566–576.

Congressional Budget Office. 2007. *Federal Support for Research and Development.* Washington, DC: Congressional Budget Office.

Conover, Ted. 2000. *Newjack: Guarding Sing Sing.* New York: Random House.

Costelloe, Michael T., Ted Chiricos, and Marc Gertz. 2009. "Punitive Attitudes Towards Criminals: Exploring the Relevance of Crime Salience and Economic Insecurity." *Punishment and Society* 11:25–49.

Coughenour, John C. 1995. "Separate and Unequal: Women in the Federal Criminal Justice System." *Federal Sentencing Reporter* 8:142–144.

Craig, Leam A., Louise Dixon, and Theresa A. Gannon, eds. 2013. *What Works in Offender Rehabilitation: An Evidence-Based Approach to Assessment and Treatment.* Malden, MA: Wiley-Blackwell.

Crouch, Ben M. 1993. "Is Incarceration Really Worse? Analysis of Offenders' Preferences for Prison over Probation." *Justice Quarterly* 10:67–88.

Crow, Matthew S., and John O. Smykla. 2014. *Offender Reentry: Rethinking Criminology and Criminal Justice.* Burlington, MA: Jones and Bartlett.

Cullen, Francis T. 2011. "Beyond Adolescence-Limited Criminology: Choosing Our Future—the American Society of Criminology 2010 Sutherland Address." *Criminology* 49:287–330.

———. 1994. "Social Support as an Organizing Concept for Criminology." *Justice Quarterly* 11:527–560.

Cullen, Francis T., Bonnie S. Fisher, and Brandon K. Applegate. 2000. "Public Opinion About Punishment and Corrections." *Crime and Justice* 27:1–79.

Cullen, Francis T., and Paul Gendreau. 2000. "Assessing Correctional Rehabilitation: Policy, Practice, and Prospects." Pp. 109–175 in *Policies, Processes, and Decisions of the Criminal Justice System,* edited by Julie Horney. Washington, DC: National Institute of Justice.

Cullen, Francis T., and Cheryl L. Jonson. 2012. *Correctional Theory: Context and Consequences.* Thousand Oaks, CA: Sage.

———. 2011. "Rehabilitation and Treatment Programs." Pp. 293–344 in *Crime and Public Policy,* edited by James Q. Wilson and Joan Petersilia. New York: Oxford University Press.

Cullen, Francis T., Cheryl L. Jonson, and Daniel S. Nagin. 2011. "Prisons Do Not Reduce Recidivism: The High Cost of Ignoring Science." *The Prison Journal* 91:48S–65S.

Cullen, Francis T., Cheryl L. Jonson, and Mary K. Stohr. 2014. *The American Prison: Imagining a Different Future.* Thousand Oaks, CA: Sage.

Cunningham, Mark D., Jon R. Sorensen, and Mark P. Vigen. 2011. "Correlates and Actuarial Models of Assaultive Prison Misconduct Among Violence-Predicted Capital Offenders." *Criminal Justice and Behavior* 38:5–25.

Curtin, Mary E. 2000. *Black Prisoners and Their World, Alabama, 1865–1900.* Charlottesville: University Press of Virginia.

Danish, Steven J., and Bradley J. Antonides. 2013. "The Challenges of Reintegration for Service Members and Their Families." *American Journal of Orthopsychiatry* 83:550–558.

Davis, Robert C., Barbara E. Smith, and Bruce Taylor. 2003. "Increasing the Proportion of Domestic Violence Arrests That Are Prosecuted: A Natural Experiment in Milwaukee." *Criminology and Public Policy* 2:263–282.

DeFina, Robert, and Lance Hannon. 2013. "The Impact of Mass Incarceration on Poverty." *Crime and Delinquency* 59:562–586.

———. 2010. "For Incapacitation, There Is No Time Like the Present: The Lagged Effects of Prisoner Reentry on Property and Violent Crime Rates." *Social Science Research* 39:1004–1014.

DeLisi, Matt. 2003. "Special Report: Criminal Careers Behind Bars." *Behavioral Sciences and the Law* 21:653–669.

Deschenes, Elizabeth Piper, Susan Turner, and Joan Petersilia. 1995. *Intensive Community Supervision in Minnesota: A Dual Experiment in Prison Diversion and Enhanced Supervised Release*. Santa Monica, CA: RAND.

DiIulio, John J., Jr. 1987. *Governing Prisons*. New York: Free Press.

Doerner, Jill K., and Stephen Demuth. 2014. "Gender and Sentencing in the Federal Courts: Are Women Treated More Leniently?" *Criminal Justice Policy Review* 25:242–269.

Dolan, Mairead, and Michael Doyle. 2000. "Violence Risk Prediction: Clinical and Actuarial Measures and the Role of the Psychopathy Checklist." *British Journal of Psychology* 177:303–311.

Doyle, Michael E., and Kris A. Peterson. 2005. "Re-Entry and Reintegration: Returning Home after Combat." *Psychiatric Quarterly* 76:361–370.

Drury, Alan J., and Matt DeLisi. 2010. "The Past Is Prologue: Prior Adjustment to Prison and Institutional Misconduct." *The Prison Journal* 90:331–352.

Durkheim, Emile. 1985. *The Rules of Sociological Method*. Translated by Steven Lukes. New York: The Free Press.

Durlauf, Steven N., and Daniel S. Nagin. 2011. "Imprisonment and Crime: Can Both Be Reduced?" *Criminology and Public Policy* 10:13–54.

Durose, Matthew R., Alexia D. Cooper, and Howard N. Snyder. 2014. *Recidivism of Prisoners Released in 30 States in 2005: Patterns From 2005 to 2010*. Washington, DC: Bureau of Justice Statistics.

Duwe, Grant, and Valerie Clark. 2013. "Blessed Be the Social Tie That Binds: The Effects of Prison Visitation on Offender Recidivism." *Criminal Justice Policy Review* 24:271–296.

Easton, Susan. 2011. *Prisoners' Rights: Principles and Practice*. Devon, UK: Willan.

Ekland-Olson, Sheldon, William R. Kelly, and Michael Supancic. 1983. "Sanction Severity, Feedback, and Deterrence." Pp. 129–165 in *From Evaluating Performance of Criminal Justice Agencies*, edited by Gordon P. Whitaker and Charles D. Phillips. Thousand Oaks, CA: Sage.

Emeka, Traqina Q., and Nelseta Walters. 2013. "Juveniles Behind Bars." Pp. 21–50 in *Special Needs Offenders in Correctional Institutions*, edited by Lior Gideon. Thousand Oaks, CA: Sage.

Ewald, Alex, and Christopher Uggen. 2012. "The Collateral Effect of Imprisonment on Prisoners, Their Families, and Communities." Pp. 83–103 in *The Oxford Handbook of Sentencing and Corrections*, edited by Joan Petersilia and Kevin R. Reitz. New York: Oxford University Press.

Fagan, Abigail A. 2013. "Family-Focused Interventions to Prevent Juvenile Delinquency: A Case Where Science and Policy Can Find Common Ground." *Criminology and Public Policy* 12:617–650.

Fagan, Jeffrey. 2010. "The Contradictions of Juvenile Crime and Punishment." *Daedalus* 139:43–61.

Farabee, David. 2005. *Rethinking Rehabilitation: Why Can't We Reform Our Criminals?* Washington, DC: The AEI Press.

Farrington, David P., and Brandon C. Welsh. 2007. *Saving Children From a Life of Crime: Early Risk Factors and Effective Interventions.* New York: Oxford University Press.

———. 2005. "Randomized Experiments in Criminology: What Have We Learned in the Last Two Decades?" *Journal of Experimental Criminology* 1:9–38.

Fazel, Seena, Jay P. Singh, Helen Doll, and Martin Grann. 2012. "Use of Risk Assessment Instruments to Predict Violence and Antisocial Behaviour in 73 Samples Involving 24,827 People: Systematic Review and Meta-Analysis." *British Medical Journal* 345:e4692.

Feeley, Malcolm M., and Jonathan Simon. 1992. "The New Penology: Notes on the Emerging Strategy of Corrections and Its Implications." *Criminology* 30:449–474.

Feld, Barry C. 1999. *Bad Kids: Race and the Transformation of the Juvenile Court.* New York: Oxford University Press.

Feld, Barry C., and Donna M. Bishop, eds. 2012. *The Oxford Handbook of Juvenile Crime and Juvenile Justice.* New York: Oxford University Press.

Felson, Richard B., and Paul-Phillipe Pare. 2008. "Gender and the Victim's Experience With the Criminal Justice System." *Social Science Research* 37:202–219.

Felson, Richard B., Eric Silver, and Brianna Remster. 2012. "Mental Disorder and Offending in Prison." *Criminal Justice and Behavior* 39:125–143.

Finckenauer, James O. 1982. *Scared Straight and the Panacea Phenomenon.* Englewood Cliffs, NJ: Prentice-Hall.

———. 1978. "Crime as a National Political Issue: 1964–76: From Law and Order to Domestic Tranquility." *Crime and Delinquency* 24:13–27.

Fleisher, Mark S., and Scott H. Decker. 2001. "An Overview of the Challenge of Prison Gangs." *Corrections Management Quarterly* 5:1–9.

Forer, Lois G. 1994. *A Rage to Punish: The Unintended Consequences of Mandatory Sentencing.* New York: Norton.

Forst, Brian. 2004. *Errors of Justice: Nature, Sources, and Remedies.* New York: Cambridge University Press.

Foucault, Michel. 1978. *Discipline and Punish: The Birth of the Prison.* New York: Random House.

Franke, Derrick, David Brierie, and Doris Layton Mackenzie. 2010. "Legitimacy in Corrections: A Randomized Experiment Comparing a Boot Camp With a Prison." *Criminology and Public Policy* 9:89–118.

Gaes, Gerald G., Timothy J. Flanagan, Laurence L. Motiuk, and Lynn Stewart. 1999. "Adult Correctional Treatment." Pp. 361–426 in *Prisons,* edited by Michael H. Tonry and Joan Petersilia. Chicago: University of Chicago Press.

Garland, David. 2013. "The 2012 Sutherland Address: Penality and the Penal State." *Criminology* 51:475–517.

———. 2001. *The Culture of Control: Crime and Social Order in Contemporary Society.* Chicago: University of Chicago Press.

Gawande, Atul. 2009. *The Checklist Manifesto: How to Get Things Right.* New York: Metropolitan Books.

———. 2007. *Better: A Surgeon's Notes on Performance.* New York: Metropolitan Books.

Geller, Amanda, and Marah A. Curtis. 2011. "A Sort of Homecoming: Incarceration and the Housing Security of Urban Men." *Social Science Research* 40:1196–1213.

Geller, Amanda, Irwin Garfinkel, and Bruce Western. 2011. "Paternal Incarceration and Support for Children in Fragile Families." *Demography* 48:25–47.

Gendreau, Paul, and Donald A. Andrews. 1989. *The Correctional Program Assessment Inventory.* St. Johns, Canada: University of New Brunswick.

Gendreau, Paul, Claire Goggin, Francis T. Cullen, and Donald A. Andrews. 2000. "The Effects of Community Sanctions and Incarceration on Recidivism." *Forum on Corrections Research.* 12:10–13.

Gendreau, Paul, Claire E. Goggin, and Moira A. Law. 1997. "Predicting Prison Misconduct." *Criminal Justice and Behavior* 24:414–431.

Gendreau, Paul, Tracy Little, and Claire Goggin. 1996. "A Meta-Analysis of the Predictors of Adult Offender Recidivism: What Works!" *Criminology* 34:575–608.

George, Erin. 2010. *A Woman Doing Life: Notes From a Prison for Women.* New York: Oxford University Press.

Gibbons, John J., and Nicholas de B. Katzenbach. 2006. *Confronting Confinement: A Report of the Commission on Safety and Abuse in America's Prisons.* New York: Vera Institute of Justice.

Gibbs, Jack P. 1989. "Three Perennial Issues in the Sociology of Deviance." Pp. 179–198 in *Theoretical Integration in the Study of Deviance and Crime: Problems and Prospects,* edited by Steven F. Messner, Marvin D. Krohn, and Allen E. Liska. Albany: State University of New York Press.

———. 1975. *Crime, Punishment, and Deterrence.* New York: Elsevier.

Gideon, Lior, ed. 2013. *Special Needs Offenders in Correctional Institutions.* Thousand Oaks, CA: Sage.

Gilliam, Franklin D., Jr., and Shanto Iyengar. 2005. "Super-Predators or Victims of Societal Neglect? Framing Effects in Juvenile Crime Coverage." Pp. 148–166 in *The Framing of American Politics,* edited by Karen Callaghan and Frauke Schnell. Pittsburgh, PA: University of Pittsburgh Press.

———. 2000. "Prime Suspects: The Influence of Local Television News on the Viewing Public." *American Journal of Political Science* 44:560–573.

Giordano, Peggy C., Ryan D. Schroeder, and Stephen A. Cernkovich. 2007. "Emotions and Crime over the Life Course: A Neo-Meadian Perspective on Criminal Continuity and Change." *American Journal of Sociology* 112:1603–1661.

Glaze, Lauren E. 2011. *Correctional Populations in the United States, 2010.* Washington, DC: Bureau of Justice Statistics.

Glaze, Lauren E., and Erinn J. Herberman. 2013. *Correctional Populations in the United States, 2012.* Washington, DC: Bureau of Justice Statistics.

Glaze, Lauren E., and Laura M. Maruschak. 2008. *Parents in Prison and Their Minor Children.* Washington, DC: Bureau of Justice Statistics.

Glaze, Lauren E., and Erika Parks. 2012. *Correctional Populations in the United States, 2011.* Washington, DC: Bureau of Justice Statistics.

Golden, Tim. 2006. "The Battle for Guantánamo." *New York Times Magazine,* September 17, pp. 60–71, 140–145.

Goldkamp, John S. 2003. "The Impact of Drug Courts." *Criminology and Public Policy* 2:197–206.

Goode, Erica. 2012. "Prisons Rethink Isolation, Saving Money, Lives and Sanity." *New York Times.* March 11, p. A1.

Gorman, Steve. 2013. "U.S. High Court Backs Order on California Prison Crowding." *Reuters,* August 2. Available at http://www.reuters.com/article/2013/08/02/us-usa-california-prisons-idUSBRE97113J20130802.

Gottfredson, Michael R., and Travis Hirschi. 1990. *A General Theory of Crime.* Stanford, CA: Stanford University Press.

Gottfredson, Stephen D., and Laura J. Moriarty. 2006. "Statistical Risk Assessment: Old Problems and New Applications." *Crime and Delinquency* 52:178–200.

Gottschalk, Marie. 2013. "The Carceral State and the Politics of Punishment." Pp. 205–241 in *The Sage Handbook of Punishment and Society,* edited by Jonathan Simon and Richard Sparks. Thousand Oaks, CA: Sage.

———. 2011. "The Past, Present, and Future of Mass Incarceration in the United States." *Criminology and Public Policy* 10:483–504.

———. 2006. *The Prison and the Gallows: The Politics of Mass Incarceration in America.* New York: Cambridge University Press.

Grattet, Ryken, Joan Petersilia, Jeffrey Lin, and Marlene Beckman. 2009. "Parole Violations and Revocations in California: Analysis and Suggestions for Action." *Federal Probation* 73:2–11.

Green, David A. 2013. "Penal Optimism and Second Chances: The Legacies of American Protestantism and the Prospects for Penal Reform." *Punishment and Society* 15:123–146.

Greenberg, David F., and Valerie West. 2001. "State Prison Populations and Their Growth, 1971–1991." *Criminology* 39:615–653.

Greenwood, Peter W., and Susan Turner. 2012. "Probation and Other Noninstitutional Treatment." Pp. 723–747 in *The Oxford Handbook of Juvenile Crime and Juvenile Justice,* edited by Barry C. Feld and Donna M. Bishop. New York: Oxford University Press.

———. 2011. "Juvenile Crime and Juvenile Justice." Pp. 88–129 in *Crime and Public Policy,* edited by James Q. Wilson and Joan Petersilia. New York: Oxford University Press.

Groopman, Jerome. 2007. *How Doctors Think.* Boston: Houghton Mifflin.

Guerino, Paul, Paige M. Harrison, and William J. Sabol. 2012. *Prisoners in 2010.* Washington, DC: Bureau of Justice Statistics.

Guthrie, Barbara. 2011. "Toward a Gender-Responsive Restorative Correctional Health Care Model." *Journal of Obstetric, Gynecologic, and Neonatal Nursing* 40:497–505.

Guy, Laura S., John F. Edens, Christine Anthony, and Kevin S. Douglas. 2005. "Does Psychopathy Predict Institutional Misconduct Among Adults? A Meta-Analytic Investigation." *Journal of Consulting and Clinical Psychology* 73:1056–1064.

Hagan, John, and Ronit Dinovitzer. 1999. "Collateral Consequences of Imprisonment for Children, Communities, and Prisoners." Pp. 121–162 in *Prisons,* edited by Michael H. Tonry and Joan Petersilia. Chicago: University of Chicago Press.

Hairston, Creasie F. 1991. "Family Ties During Imprisonment: Important for Whom and for What?" *Journal of Sociology and Social Welfare* 18:87–104.

Hamilton, Robert F. 1996. *The Social Construction of Reality.* New Haven, CT: Yale University Press.

Haney, Craig. 2008. "A Culture of Harm: Taming the Dynamics of Cruelty in Supermax Prisons." *Criminal Justice and Behavior* 35:956–984.

———. 2003. "Mental Health Issues in Long-Term Solitary and 'Supermax' Confinement. *Crime and Delinquency* 49:124–156.

Hanson, R. Karl, Kelly E. Morton, and Andrew J. R. Harris. 2003. "Sexual Offender Recidivism Risk: What We Know and What We Need to Know." *Annals of New York Academy of Sciences* 989:154–166.

Harding, David J., Jeffrey D. Morenoff, and Claire W. Herbert. 2013. "Home Is Hard to Find: Neighborhoods, Institutions, and the Residential Trajectories of Returning

Prisoners." *Annals of the American Academy of Political and Social Science* 647:214–236.

Harding, Richard W. 2012. "Regulating Prison Conditions: Some International Comparisons." Pp. 432–460 in *The Oxford Handbook of Sentencing and Corrections,* edited by Joan Petersilia and Kevin R. Reitz. New York: Oxford University Press.

Harer, Miles D., and Neal P. Langan. 2001. "Gender Differences in Predictors of Prison Violence: Assessing the Predictive Validity of a Risk Classification System." *Crime and Delinquency* 47:513–536.

Harer, Miles D., and Darrell J. Steffensmeier. 1996. "Race and Prison Violence." *Criminology* 34:325–355.

Harlow, Caroline W. 2003. *Education and Correctional Populations.* Washington, DC: Bureau of Justice Statistics.

Harmon, Mark G. 2013. "'Fixed' Sentencing: The Effect on Imprisonment Rates Over Time." *Journal of Quantitative Criminology* 29:369–397.

Harrington, Spencer P. M. 1997. "Caging the Crazy: 'Supermax' Confinement Under Attack." *The Humanist* 57:14–19.

Harrison, Paige M., and Allen J. Beck. 2006. *Prisoners in 2005.* Washington, DC: Bureau of Justice Statistics.

———. 2005. *Prison and Jail Inmates at Midyear 2004.* Washington, DC: Bureau of Justice Statistics.

Hassine, Victor. 2009. *Life Without Parole: Living in Prison Today.* New York: Oxford University Press.

Hattery, Angela J., and Earl Smith. 2010. *Prisoner Reentry and Social Capital: The Long Road to Reintegration.* Lanham, MD: Lexington Books.

Hawken, Angela, and Mark Kleiman. 2009. *Managing Drug-Involved Probationers With Swift and Certain Sanctions: Evaluating Hawaii's HOPE.* Washington, DC: National Institute of Justice.

Hayes, Susan C. 2002. "Early Intervention or Early Incarceration? Using a Screening Test for Intellectual Disability in the Criminal Justice System." *Journal of Applied Research in Intellectual Disabilities* 15:120–128.

Heilbroner, David. 1990. *Rough Justice: Days and Nights of a Young D.A.* New York: Random House.

Hemmens, Craig, and Mary K. Stohr. 2014. "The Racially Just Prison." Pp. 111–126 in *The American Prison: Imagining a Different Future,* edited by Francis T. Cullen, Cheryl L. Jonson, and Mary K. Stohr. Thousand Oaks, CA: Sage.

Henriques, Zelma W., and Bridget P. Gladwin. 2013. "Pregnancy and Motherhood Behind Bars." Pp. 83–116 in *Special Needs Offenders in Correctional Institutions,* edited by Lior Gideon. 2013. Thousand Oaks, CA: Sage.

Hensley, Christopher, Helen Eigenberg, and Lauren Gibson. 2013. "Gay and Lesbian Inmates: Sexuality and Sexual Correction Behind Bars." Pp. 233–258 in *Special Needs Offenders in Correctional Institutions,* edited by Lior Gideon. 2013. Thousand Oaks, CA: Sage.

Herman, Susan. 2010. *Parallel Justice for Victims of Crime.* Washington, DC: National Center for Victims of Crime.

Herrington, V. 2009. "Assessing the Prevalence of Intellectual Disability Among Young Male Prisoners." *Journal of Intellectual Disability Research* 53:397–410.

Hickman, Laura, and Sally S. Simpson. 2003. "Fair Treatment or Preferred Outcome: The Impact of Police Behavior on Victim Reports of Domestic Violence Incidents." *Law and Society Review* 37:649–676.

Hipp, John R., Joan Petersilia, and Susan Turner. 2010. "Parolee Recidivism in California: The Effect of Neighborhood Context and Social Service Agency Characteristics." *Criminology* 48:947–979.

Hirschi, Travis, and Michael H. Gottfredson. 1993. "Rethinking the Juvenile Justice System." *Crime and Delinquency* 39:262–271.

Hochstetler, Andy, and Matt DeLisi. 2005. "Importation, Deprivation, and Varieties of Serving Time: An Integrated Lifestyle-Exposure Model of Prison Offending." *Journal of Criminal Justice* 33:257–266.

Hogan, Michael J., Ted Chiricos, and Marc Gertz. 2005. "Economic Insecurity, Blame, and Punitive Attitudes." *Justice Quarterly* 22:392–412.

Holsinger, Kristi. 2014. "The Feminist Prison." Pp. 87–110 in *The American Prison: Imagining a Different Future*, edited by Francis T. Cullen, Cheryl L. Jonson, and Mary K. Stohr. Thousand Oaks, CA: Sage.

Holt, Norman, and Daniel Miller. 1972. *Explorations in Inmate-Family Relationships*. Research Report No. 4. Sacramento, CA: California Department of Corrections.

Holzer, Harry J., Steven Raphael, and Michael A. Stoll. 2007. "The Effect of an Applicant's Criminal History on Employer Hiring Decisions and Screening Practices: Evidence From Los Angeles." Pp. 117–150 in *Barriers to Reentry? The Labor Market for Released Prisoners in Post-Industrial America*, edited by Shawn D. Bushway, Michael Stoll, and David Weiman. New York: Russell Sage.

Houser, Kimberly A., Steven Belenko, and Pauline K. Brennan. 2012. "The Effects of Mental Health and Substance Abuse Disorder on Institutional Misconduct Among Female Inmates." *Justice Quarterly* 29:799–828.

Huebner, Beth M., Sean P. Varano, and Timothy S. Bynum. 2007. "Gangs, Guns, and Drugs: Recidivism Among Serious, Young Offenders." *Criminology and Public Policy* 6:187–221.

Hutchings, Peter J. 1999. "Spectacularizing Crime: Ghostwriting the Law." *Law and Critique* 10:27–48.

Innes, Martin, Laurence Abbott, Trudy Lowe, and Colin Roberts. 2009. "Seeing Like a Citizen: Field Experiments in 'Community Intelligence–Led Policing.'" *Police Practice and Research* 10:99–114.

Irwin, John. 2005. *The Warehouse Prison: Disposal of the New Dangerous Class*. Los Angeles: Roxbury.

Irwin, John, and Donald R. Cressey. 1962. "Thieves, Convicts, and the Inmate Culture." *Social Problems* 10:142–155.

Jacobs, Bruce A. "Deterrence and Deterrability." *Criminology* 48:417–411.

James, Doris J., and Lauren E. Glaze. 2006. *Mental Health Problems of Prison and Jail Inmates*. Washington, DC: Bureau of Justice Statistics.

Jannetta, Jesse, and Aaron Horvath. 2011. *Surveying the Field: State-Level Findings From the 2008 Parole Practices Survey*. Washington, DC: The Urban Institute.

Jaruzelski, Barry, John Loehr, and Richard Holman. 2013. *The Global Innovation 1000: Navigating the Digital Future*. New York: Booz and Company.

Jiang, Shanhe and L. Thomas Winfree. 2006. "Social Support, Gender, and Inmate Adjustment to Prison Life: Insights From a National Sample. *The Prison Journal* 86:32–55.

Johnson, Elizabeth I., and Beth Easterling. 2012. "Understanding Unique Effects of Parental Incarceration on Children: Challenges, Progress, and Recommendations." *Journal of Marriage and Family* 74:342–356.

Johnson, Lee M. 2012. *Experiencing Corrections: From Practitioner to Professor*. Los Angeles: Sage.

Johnson, Robert. 1976. *Culture and Crisis in Confinement*. Lexington, MA: DC Heath.

Kahneman, Daniel. 2011. *Thinking, Fast and Slow*. New York: Farrar, Straus and Giroux.

Karmen, Andrew J. 1992. "Who's Against Victims' Rights? The Nature of the Opposition to Pro-Victim Initiatives in Criminal Justice." *Journal of Civil Rights and Economic Development* 8:157–175.

Kelly, William R., Tammy S. Macy, and Daniel P. Mears. 2005. "Juvenile Court Referrals in Texas: An Assessment of Criminogenic Needs and the Gap Between Needs and Services." *The Prison Journal* 85:467–489.

King, Roy D. 2005. "Effects of Supermax Custody." Pp. 118–145 in *The Effects of Imprisonment*, edited by Alison Liebling and Shadd Maruna. Portland, OR: Willan Publishing.

Kirk, David S. 2009. "A Natural Experiment on Residential Change and Recidivism: Lessons From Hurricane Katrina." *American Sociological Review* 74:484–505.

Kluger, Jeffery. 2007. "The Paradox of Supermax." *Time Magazine*, March, pp. 52–53.

Kraska, Peter B. 2006. "Criminal Justice Theory: Toward Legitimacy and an Infrastructure." *Justice Quarterly* 23:167–185.

Krisberg, Barry. 2012. "Juvenile Corrections." Pp. 748–770 *The Oxford Handbook of Juvenile Crime and Juvenile Justice*, edited by Barry C. Feld and Donna M. Bishop. New York: Oxford University Press.

Kroner, Daryl G., and Jeremy F. Mills. 2001. "The Accuracy of Five Risk Appraisal Instruments in Predicting Institutional Misconduct and New Convictions." *Criminal Justice and Behavior* 28:471–489.

Kubrin, Charis E., and Eric A. Stewart. 2006. "Predicting Who Reoffends: The Neglected Role of Neighborhood Context in Recidivism Studies." *Criminology* 44:165–198.

Kyckelhahn, Tracey. 2012. *State Corrections Expenditures, FY 1982–2010*. Washington, DC: Bureau of Justice Statistics.

Lageson, Sarah, and Christopher Uggen. 2013. "How Work Affects Crime—And Crime Affects Work—Over the Life Course." Pp. 201–212 in *Handbook of Life-Course Criminology*, edited by Chris L. Gibson and Marvin D. Krohn. New York: Springer.

Lahm, Karen F. 2008. "Inmate-on-Inmate Assault: A Multilevel Examination of Prison Violence." *Criminal Justice and Behavior* 35:120–137.

Langan, Neal P., and Bernadette M. M. Pelissier. 2001. "Gender Differences Among Prisoners in Drug Treatment." *Journal of Substance Abuse* 13:291–301.

Langan, Patrick A., and David J. Levin. 2002. *Recidivism of Prisoners Released in 1994*. Washington, DC: Bureau of Justice Statistics.

Latessa, Edward J., Shelley J. Listwan, and Deborah Koetzle. 2014. *What Works (and Doesn't) in Reducing Recidivism*. Waltham, MA: Anderson Publishing.

Lattimore, Pamela K., Christy A. Visher, and Danielle M. Steffey. 2010. "Prisoner Reentry in the First Decade of the 21st Century." *Journal of Victims and Offenders* 5:253–267.

Laub, John H. 2004. "The Life Course of Criminology in the United States: The American Society of Criminology 2003 Presidential Address." *Criminology* 42:1–26.

Laub, John H., and Robert J. Sampson. 2003. *Shared Beginnings, Divergent Lives: Delinquent Boys to Age 70*. Boston: Harvard University Press.

Lauritsen, Janet L., and Maribeth L. Rezey. 2013. *Measuring the Prevalence of Crime With the National Crime Victimization Survey*. Washington, DC: Bureau of Justice Statistics.

Lauritsen, Janet L., Jennifer G. Owens, Michael Planty, Michael R. Rand, and Jennifer L. Truman. 2012. *Methods for Counting High-Frequency Repeat Victimizations in the National Crime Victimization Survey*. Washington, DC: Bureau of Justice Statistics.

La Vigne, Nancy, Samuel Bieler, Lindsey Cramer, Helen Ho, Cybele Kotonias, Deborah Mayer, . . . Julie Samuels. 2014. *Justice Reinvestment Initiative State Assessment Report*. Washington, DC: The Urban Institute.

La Vigne, Nancy, Lisa E. Brooks, and Tracey L. Shollenberger. 2007. *Returning Home: Exploring the Challenges and Successes of Recently Released Texas Prisoners*. Washington, DC: The Urban Institute.

Lawrence, Sarah, Daniel P. Mears, Glenn Dubin, and Jeremy Travis. 2002. *The Practice and Promise of Prison Programming*. Washington, DC: The Urban Institute.

LeBel, Thomas P. 2012. "Invisible Stripes? Formerly Incarcerated Persons' Perceptions of Stigma." *Deviant Behavior* 33:89–107.

LeBel, Thomas P., Ros Burnett, Shadd Maruna, and Shawn Bushway. 2008. "The 'Chicken and Egg' of Subjective and Social Factors in Desistance From Crime." *European Journal of Criminology* 5:130–158.

LeBel, Thomas, and Shadd Maruna. 2012. "Life on the Outside: Transitioning From Prison to the Community." Pp. 657–683 in *The Oxford Handbook of Sentencing and Corrections,* edited by Joan Petersilia and Kevin R. Reitz. New York: Oxford University Press.

Lee, Hedwig, Lauren C. Porter, and Megan Comfort. 2014. "Consequences of Family Member Incarceration: Impacts on Civic Participation and Perceptions of the Legitimacy and Fairness of Government." *Annals of the American Academy of Political and Social Science* 651:44–73.

Lerman, Amy E. 2013. *The Modern Prison Paradox: Politics, Punishment, and Social Community*. New York: Cambridge University Press.

Liebling, Alison. 1999. "Prison Suicide and Prisoner Coping." *Crime and Justice* 26: 283–359.

Lipsey, Mark W. 1998. "Design Sensitivity: Statistical Power for Applied Experimental Research." Pp. 39–68 in *Handbook of Applied Social Research Methods,* edited by Leonard Bickman and Debra J. Rog. Thousand Oaks, CA: Sage.

Lipsey, Mark W., and Francis T. Cullen. 2007. "The Effectiveness of Correctional Rehabilitation: A Review of Systematic Reviews." *Annual Review of Law and Social Science* 3:297–320.

Liska, Allen E., Fred E. Markowitz, Rachel Bridges-Whaley, and Paul E. Bellair. 1999. "Modeling the Relationships Between the Criminal Justice and Mental Health Systems." *American Journal of Sociology* 104:1742–1773.

Listwan, Shelley J., Mark Colvin, Dena Hanley, and Daniel Flannery. 2010. "Victimization, Social Support, and Psychological Well-Being." *Criminal Justice and Behavior* 37:1140–1159.

Listwan, Shelley J., Leah E. Daigle, Jennifer L. Hartman, and Wendy P. Guastaferro. 2014. "Poly-Victimization Risk in Prison: The Influence of Individual and Institutional Factors." *Journal of Interpersonal Violence* 29:2458–2481.

Listwan, Shelley J., Dena Hanley, and Mark Colvin. 2012. *The Prison Experience and Reentry: Examining the Impact of Victimization on Coming Home*. Washington, DC: Report Submitted to the National Institute of Justice. Doc. No. 238083.

Listwan, Shelley J., Christopher J. Sullivan, Robert Agnew, Francis T. Cullen, and Mark Colvin. 2013. "The Pains of Imprisonment Revisited: The Impact of Strain on Inmate Recidivism." *Justice Quarterly* 30:144–168.

Loeber, Rolf, and David P. Farrington, eds. 2012. *From Juvenile Delinquency to Adult Crime: Criminal Careers, Justice Policy, and Prevention.* New York: Oxford University Press.

Logan, Charles. 1993. "Criminal Justice Performance Measures for Prisons." Pp. 15–59 in *Performance Measures for the Criminal Justice System.* Washington DC: Bureau of Justice Statistics.

Lorie, A. L. Nicholas, and Gerard Bryant. 2013. "Mentally Ill Inmates: Jails and Prisons as the New Asylum." Pp. 155–202 in *Special Needs Offenders in Correctional Institutions,* edited by Lior Gideon. Thousand Oaks, CA: Sage.

Loughran, Thomas A., Edward P. Mulvey, Carol A. Schubert, Jeffrey Fagan, Alex R. Piquero, and Sandra H. Losoya. 2009. "Estimating a Dose-Response Relationship Between Length of Stay and Future Recidivism in Serious Juvenile Offenders." *Criminology* 47:699–740.

Lovell, David, Kristin Cloyes, David Allen, and Lorna Rhodes. 2000. "Who Lives in Super-Maximum Custody?" *Federal Probation* 64:33–38.

Lovell, David, L. Clark Johnson, and Kevin C. Cain. 2007. "Recidivism of Supermax Prisoners in Washington State." *Crime and Delinquency* 53:633–656.

Lowen, Matthew, and Caroline Isaacs. 2012. *Lifetime Lockdown: How Isolation Conditions Impact Prisoner Reentry.* Tucson, AZ: American Friends Service Committee.

Lutze, Faith E. 2014. *Professional Lives of Community Corrections Officers.* Thousand Oaks, CA: Sage.

Lynch, James P., and William J. Sabol. 2004. "Assessing the Effects of Mass Incarceration on Informal Social Control in Communities." *Criminology and Public Policy* 3: 267–294.

———. 2001. *Prisoner Reentry in Perspective.* Washington, DC: The Urban Institute.

Lynch, Michael J. 2007. *Big Prisons, Big Dreams: Crime and the Failure of America's Penal System.* New Brunswick, NJ: Rutgers University Press.

MacKenzie, Doris L. 2012. "The Effectiveness of Corrections-Based Work and Academic and Vocational Educational Programs." Pp. 492–520 in *The Oxford Handbook of Sentencing and Corrections,* edited by Joan Petersilia and Kevin R. Reitz. New York: Oxford University Press.

———. 2006. *What Works in Corrections: Reducing the Criminal Activities of Offenders and Delinquents.* New York: Cambridge University Press.

MacKenzie, Doris L., and Rachel Freeland. 2012. "Examining the Effectiveness of Juvenile Residential Programs." Pp. 771–798 in *The Oxford Handbook of Juvenile Crime and Juvenile Justice,* edited by Barry C. Feld and Donna M. Bishop. New York: Oxford University Press.

Makarios, Matthew, and Edward J. Latessa. 2013. "Developing a Risk and Needs Assessment Instrument for Prison Inmates: The Issue of Outcome." *Criminal Justice and Behavior* 40:1449–1471.

Mancini, Christina. 2014. *Sex Crime, Offenders, and Society.* Durham, NC: Carolina Academic Press.

Mancini, Christina, James C. Barnes, and Daniel P. Mears. 2013. "It Varies From State to State: An Examination of Sex Crime Laws Nationally." *Criminal Justice Policy Review* 24:166–198.

Mancini, Christina, and Daniel P. Mears. 2013. "U.S. Supreme Court Decisions and Sex Offender Legislation: Evidence of Evidence-Based Policy?" *Journal of Criminal Law and Criminology* 103:1115–1154.

Manza, Jeff, and Christopher Uggen. 2006. *Locked Out: Felon Disenfranchisement and American Democracy*. New York: Oxford University Press.

Marion, Nancy E., and Willard M. Oliver. 2009. "Congress, Crime, and Budgetary Responsiveness: A Study in Symbolic Politics." *Criminal Justice Policy Review* 20:115–135.

———. 2006. *The Public Policy of Crime and Criminal Justice*. Upper Saddle River, NJ: Prentice Hall.

Martinson, Robert. 1974. "What Works? Questions and Answers About Prison Reform." *Public Interest* 35:22–54.

Maruna, Shadd. 2011. "Reentry as a Rite of Passage." *Punishment and Society* 13:3–28.

———. 2001. *Making Good: How Ex-Convicts Reform and Rebuild Their Lives*. Washington, DC: American Psychological Association.

Marvell, Thomas B., and Carlisle E. Moody. 2006. "Specification Problems, Police Levels, and Crime Rates." *Criminology* 34:609–646.

Massoglia, Michael. 2008. "Incarceration, Health, and Racial Disparities in Health." *Law and Society Review* 42:275–306.

Matthews, Betsy and Dana Jones Hubbard. 2008. "Moving Ahead: Five Essential Elements for Working Effectively With Girls." *Journal of Criminal Justice* 36: 494–502.

Mauer, Marc. 2009. *The Changing Racial Dynamics of the War on Drugs*. Washington, DC: The Sentencing Project.

———. 1999. "Why Are Tough on Crime Policies So Popular?" *Stanford Law and Policy Review* 11:9–22.

Mauer, Marc, and Meda Chesney-Lind. 2002. *Invisible Punishment: The Collateral Consequences of Mass Imprisonment*. New York: New Press.

Maxson, Cheryl L. 2013. "Do Not Shoot the Messenger: The Utility of Gang Risk Research in Program Targeting and Content." *Criminology and Public Policy* 12:421–426.

May, David C., Peter B. Wood, Jennifer L. Mooney, and Kevin I. Minor. 2005. "Predicting Offender-Generated Exchange Rates: Implications for a Theory of Sentence Severity." *Crime and Delinquency* 51:373–399.

Mays, G. Larry, and Rick Ruddell. 2015. *Making Sense of Criminal Justice Policies and Practices*. 2nd ed. New York: Oxford University Press.

McCord, Joan. 2003. "Cures That Harm: Unanticipated Outcomes of Crime Prevention Programs." *Annals of the American Academy of Political and Social Science* 587:16–30.

McDaniels-Wilson, Cathy, and Joanne Belknap. 2008. "The Extensive Sexual Violation and Sexual Abuse Histories of Incarcerated Women." *Violence Against Women* 14:1090–1127.

McKenzie, Karen, Amanda Michie, Aja Murray, and Charlene Hales. 2012. "Screening for Offenders With an Intellectual Disability: The Validity of the Learning Disability Screening Questionnaire." *Research in Developmental Disabilities* 33:791–795.

McPherson, Miller, Lynn Smith-Lovin, and James M. Cook. 2001. "Birds of a Feather: Homophily in Social Networks." *Annual Review of Sociology* 27:415–444.

Meade, Benjamin, Benjamin Steiner, Matthew Makarios, and Lawrence Travis. 2013. "Estimating a Dose-Response Relationship Between Time Served in Prison and Recidivism." *Journal of Research in Crime and Delinquency* 50:525–550.

Meadows, Donella H. 2008. *Thinking in Systems: A Primer*. White River Junction, VT: Chelsea Green Publishing.

Mears, Daniel P. 2013. "Supermax Prisons: The Policy and the Evidence." *Criminology and Public Policy* 12:681–719.

———. 2012a. "The Front End of the Juvenile Court: Intake and Informal vs. Formal Processing." Pp. 573–605 in *The Oxford Handbook of Juvenile Crime and Juvenile Justice,* edited by Barry C. Feld and Donna M. Bishop. New York: Oxford University Press.

———. 2012b. "The Prison Experience." *Journal of Criminal Justice* 40:345–347.

———. 2010. *American Criminal Justice Policy: An Evaluation Approach to Increasing Accountability and Effectiveness.* New York: Cambridge University Press.

———. 2008a. "Accountability, Efficiency, and Effectiveness in Corrections: Shining a Light on the Black Box of Prison Systems." *Criminology and Public Policy* 7:143–152.

———. 2008b. "An Assessment of Supermax Prisons Using an Evaluation Research Framework." *The Prison Journal* 88:43–68.

———. 2007. "Towards Rational and Evidence-Based Crime Policy." *Journal of Criminal Justice* 35:667–682.

———. 2004a. "Identifying Adolescent Substance Abuse." Pp. 185–220 in *Juvenile Drug Courts and Teen Substance Abuse,* edited by Jeffrey A. Butts and John Roman. Washington, DC: Urban Institute Press.

———. 2004b. "Mental Health Needs and Services in the Criminal Justice System." *Houston Journal of Health Law and Policy* 4:255–284.

———. 2002. "Sentencing Guidelines and the Transformation of Juvenile Justice in the Twenty-First Century." *Journal of Contemporary Criminal Justice* 18:6–19.

———. 2001. "Critical Challenges in Addressing the Mental Health Needs of Juvenile Offenders." *Justice Policy Journal* 1:41–61.

Mears, Daniel P., and Laudan Y. Aron. 2003. *Addressing the Needs of Youth With Disabilities in the Juvenile Justice System: The Current State of Knowledge.* Washington, DC: The Urban Institute.

Mears, Daniel P., and Sarah Bacon. 2009. "Improving Criminal Justice Through Better Decisionmaking: Lessons From the Medical System." *Journal of Criminal Justice* 37:142–154.

Mears, Daniel P., and William D. Bales. 2010. "Supermax Housing: Placement, Duration, and Time to Reentry." *Journal of Criminal Justice* 38:545–554.

———. 2009. "Supermax Incarceration and Recidivism." *Criminology* 47:1131–1166.

Mears, Daniel P., and James C. Barnes. 2010. "Toward a Systematic Foundation for Identifying Evidence-Based Criminal Justice Sanctions and Their Relative Effectiveness." *Journal of Criminal Justice* 38:702–810.

Mears, Daniel P., and Jeffrey A. Butts. 2008. "Using Performance Monitoring to Improve the Accountability, Operations, and Effectiveness of Juvenile Justice." *Criminal Justice Policy Review* 19:264–284.

Mears, Daniel P., and Joshua C. Cochran. 2014. "Who Goes to Prison?" In *The Oxford Handbook on Prisons and Imprisonment,* edited by John D. Wooldredge and Paula Smith. New York: Oxford University Press.

———. 2013. "What Is the Effect of IQ on Offending?" *Criminal Justice and Behavior* 40:1280–1300.

———. 2012. "U.S. Prisoner Reentry Health Care Policy in International Perspective: Service Gaps and the Moral and Public Health Implications." *The Prison Journal* 92:175–202.

Mears, Daniel P., Joshua C. Cochran, and William D. Bales. 2012. "Gender Differences in the Effects of Prison on Recidivism." *Journal of Criminal Justice* 40:370–378.

Mears, Daniel P., Joshua C. Cochran, and Kevin M. Beaver. 2013. "Self-Control Theory and Nonlinear Effects on Offending." *Journal of Quantitative Criminology* 29: 447–476.

Mears, Daniel P., Joshua C. Cochran, and Francis T. Cullen. 2014. "Incarceration Heterogeneity and its Implications for Assessing the Effectiveness of Imprisonment on Recidivism." *Criminal Justice Policy Review*.

Mears, Daniel P., Joshua C. Cochran, Sarah J. Greenman, Avinash S. Bhati, and Mark A. Greenwald. 2011. "Evidence on the Effectiveness of Juvenile Court Sanctions." *Journal of Criminal Justice* 39:509–520.

Mears, Daniel P., Joshua C. Cochran, and Sonja E. Siennick. 2013. "Life-Course Perspectives and Prisoner Reentry." Pp. 317–333 in the *Handbook of Life-Course Criminology: Emerging Trends and Directions for Future Research,* edited by Marvin D. Krohn and Chris L. Gibson. New York: Springer-Verlag.

Mears, Daniel P., Joshua C. Cochran, Sonja E. Siennick, and William D. Bales. 2012. "Prison Visitation and Recidivism." *Justice Quarterly* 29:888–918.

Mears, Daniel P., Carter Hay, Marc Gertz, and Christina Mancini. 2007. "Public Opinion and the Foundation of the Juvenile Court." *Criminology* 45:223–258.

Mears, Daniel P., and Julie Mestre. 2012. "Prisoner Reentry, Employment, Signaling, and the Better Identification of Desisters: Introduction to the Special Issue." *Criminology and Public Policy* 11:5–15.

Mears, Daniel P., Justin T. Pickett, Kristin Golden, Ted Chiricos, and Marc Gertz. 2013. "The Effect of Interracial Contact on Whites' Perceptions of Victimization Risk and Black Criminality." *Journal of Research in Crime and Delinquency* 50:272–299.

Mears, Daniel P., Matthew Ploeger, and Mark Warr. 1998. "Explaining the Gender Gap in Delinquency: Peer Influence and Moral Evaluations of Behavior." *Journal of Research in Crime and Delinquency* 35:251–266.

Mears, Daniel P., and Michael D. Reisig. 2006. "The Theory and Practice of Supermax Prisons." *Punishment and Society* 8:33–57.

Mears, Daniel P., Caterina G. Roman, Ashley Wolff, and Janeen Buck. 2006. "Faith-Based Efforts to Improve Prisoner Reentry: Assessing the Logic and Evidence." *Journal of Criminal Justice* 34:351–367.

Mears, Daniel P., and Mark C. Stafford. 2002. "Central Analytical Issues in the Generation of Cumulative Sociological Knowledge." *Sociological Focus* 35:5–24.

Mears, Daniel P., Eric A. Stewart, Sonja E. Siennick, and Ronald L. Simons. 2013. "The Code of the Street and Inmate Violence: Investigating the Salience of Imported Belief Systems." *Criminology* 51:695–728.

Mears, Daniel P., and Jeremy Travis. 2004. "Youth Development and Reentry." *Youth Violence and Juvenile Justice* 2:1–20.

Mears, Daniel P., Xia Wang, and William D. Bales. 2014. "Does a Rising Tide Lift All Boats? Labor Market Changes and Their Effects on the Recidivism of Released Prisoners." *Justice Quarterly* 31:822–851.

Mears, Daniel P., Xia Wang, Carter Hay, and William D. Bales. 2008. "Social Ecology and Recidivism: Implications for Prisoner Reentry." *Criminology* 46:301–340.

Mears, Daniel P., and Jamie Watson. 2006. "Towards a Fair and Balanced Assessment of Supermax Prisons." *Justice Quarterly* 23:232–270.

Mears, Daniel P., Laura Winterfield, John Hunsaker, Gretchen E. Moore, and Ruth M. White. 2003. *Drug Treatment in the Criminal Justice System: The Current State of Knowledge.* Washington, DC: The Urban Institute.

Merlo, Alida V., Peter J. Benekos, and William J. Cook. 1997. "Waiver and Juvenile Justice Reform: Widening the Punitive Net." *Criminal Justice Policy Review* 8: 145–168.

Metraux, Stephen, and Dennis P. Culhane. 2004. "Homeless Shelter Use and Reincarceration Following Release." *Criminology and Public Policy* 3:139–160.

Milgram, Anne. 2012. "Moneyballing Criminal Justice." *Atlantic Monthly*, June 20. Available at http://www.theatlantic.com/national/archive/2012/06/money-balling-criminal-justice/258703/.

Miller, Bryan L., and Joseph F. Spillane. 2012. "Civil Death: An Examination of Ex-Felon Disenfranchisement and Reintegration." *Punishment and Society* 14:402–428.

Mitchell, Ojmarrh, David B. Wilson, and Doris L. MacKenzie. 2007. "Does Incarceration-Based Drug Treatment Reduce Recidivism? A Meta-Analytic Synthesis." *Journal of Experimental Criminology* 3:353–375.

Monahan, Kathryn C., Asha Goldweber, and Elizabeth Cauffman. 2011. "The Effects of Visitation on Incarcerated Juvenile Offenders: How Contact With the Outside Impacts Adjustment on the Inside." *Law and Human Behavior* 35:143–151.

Morash, Merry, Robin N. Haarr, and Lila Rucker. 1994. "A Comparison of Programming for Women and Men in U.S. Prisons in the 1980s." *Crime and Delinquency* 40: 197–221.

Morris, Norval. 2002. *Maconochie's Gentlemen: The Story of Norfolk Island and the Roots of Modern Prison Reform*. New York: Oxford University Press.

Morris, Norval, and David J. Rothman, eds. 1995. *The Oxford History of the Prison*. New York: Oxford University Press.

Mumola, Christopher J. 2000. *Incarcerated Parents and Their Children*. Washington, DC: Bureau of Justice Statistics.

Mumola, Christopher J., and Jennifer C. Karberg. 2006. *Drug Use and Dependence, State and Federal Prisoners, 2004*. Washington, DC: Bureau of Justice Statistics.

Mushlin, Michael B. 2002. *Rights of Prisoners*. 3rd ed. St. Paul, MN: Thomson/West.

Nadelmann, Ethan A. 2004. "Criminologists and Punitive Drug Prohibition: To Serve or to Challenge?" *Criminology and Public Policy* 3:441–450.

Nagin, Daniel S. 2013. "Deterrence: A Review of the Evidence by a Criminologist for Economists." *Annual Review of Economics* 5:83–105.

Nagin, Daniel S., Francis T. Cullen, and Cheryl L. Jonson. 2009. "Imprisonment and Reoffending." *Crime and Justice* 38:115–200.

Nagin, Daniel S., Alex R. Piquero, Elizabeth S. Scott, and Laurence Steinberg. 2006. "Public Preferences for Rehabilitation Versus Incarceration of Juvenile Offenders: Evidence From a Contingent Valuation Survey." *Criminology and Public Policy* 5:627–651.

Nagin, Daniel S., and Matthew Snodgrass. 2013. "The Effect of Incarceration on Re-Offending: Evidence From a Natural Experiment in Pennsylvania." *Journal of Quantitative Criminology* 29:601–642.

O'Keefe, Maureen L., Kelli J. Klebe, Jeffrey Metzner, Joel Dvoskin, Jamie Fellner, and Alysha Stucker. 2013. "A Longitudinal Study of Administrative Segregation." *Journal of the American Academy of Psychiatry and the Law* 41:49–60.

Oliver, Willard M., and Nancy E. Marion. 2008. "Political Party Platforms: Symbolic Politics and Criminal Justice Policy." *Criminal Justice Policy Review* 19:397–413.

Pager, Devah. 2007. *Marked: Race, Crime, and Finding Work in an Era of Mass Incarceration*. Chicago: University of Chicago Press.

———. 2003. "The Mark of a Criminal Record." *American Journal of Sociology* 108:937–975.

Parsons, Jim. 2014. "Addressing the Unique Challenges of Jail Reentry." Pp. 105–123 in *Offender Reentry: Rethinking Criminology and Criminal Justice*, edited by Matthew S. Crow and John O. Smykla. Burlington, MA: Jones and Bartlett.

Paternoster, Raymond. 2010. "How Much Do We Really Know About Criminal Deterrence?" *Journal of Criminal Law and Criminology* 100:765–824.

Peffley, Mark, and Jon Hurwitz. 2010. *Justice in America: The Separate Realities of Blacks and Whites*. New York: Cambridge University Press.

———. 2002. "The Racial Components of 'Race Neutral' Crime Policy Attitudes." *Political Psychology* 23:59–75.

Pelissier, Bernadette M. M., Scott D. Camp, Gerald G. Gaes, William G. Saylor, and William Rhodes. 2003. "Gender Differences in Outcomes From Prison-Based Residential Treatment." *Journal of Substance Abuse Treatment* 24:149–160.

Petersilia, Joan. 2005. "From Cell to Society: Who Is Returning Home?" Pp. 15–49 in *Prisoner Reentry and Crime in America*, edited by Jeremy Travis and Christy Visher. New York: Cambridge University Press.

Petersilia, Joan. 2003. *When Prisoners Come Home: Parole and Prisoner Reentry*. New York: Oxford University Press.

———. 1997. "Probation in the United States." *Crime and Justice* 22:149–200.

———. 1991. "Policy Relevance and the Future of Criminology." *Criminology* 29:1–16.

Petersilia, Joan, and Francis T. Cullen. 2014. "Liberal but Not Stupid: Meeting the Promise of Downsizing Prisons." *Stanford Journal of Criminal Law and Policy* 2:1–44.

Petersilia, Joan, and Susan Turner. 1993. "Intensive Probation and Parole." *Crime and Justice* 17:281–335.

Peterson, Ruth D., Lauren J. Krivo, and John Hagan. 2006. *The Many Colors of Crime: Inequalities of Race, Ethnicity, and Crime in America*. New York: New York University Press.

Pettit, Becky. 2012. *Invisible Men: Mass Incarceration and the Myth of Black Progress*. New York: Russell Sage Foundation.

Pettit, Becky, and Bruce Western. 2004. "Mass Imprisonment and the Life Course: Race and Class Inequality in U.S. Incarceration." *American Sociological Review* 69:151–169.

Pew Charitable Trusts. 2013. *Leading on Public Safety: Four Governors Share Lessons Learned From Sentencing and Corrections Reform*. Philadelphia: Pew Charitable Trusts. Available online at http://www.pewtrusts.org/our_work_report_detail .aspx?id=85899495846.

———. 2012a. *Public Opinion on Sentencing and Corrections Policy in America*. Philadelphia: Pew Charitable Trusts. Available online at http://www.pewstates.org/ research/analysis/public-opinion-on-sentencing-and-corrections-policy-in-america-85899380361.

———. 2012b. *Time Served: The High Cost, Low Return of Longer Prison Terms*. Philadelphia: Pew Charitable Trusts. Available online at http://www.pewtrusts.org/ our_work_report_detail.aspx?id=85899396348.

———. 2011. *Risk/Needs Assessment 101: Science Reveals New Tools to Manage Offenders*. Philadelphia: Pew Charitable Trusts.

Pfeiffer, Steven I. 2013. *Serving the Gifted: Evidence-Based Clinical and Psychoeducational Practice*. New York: Taylor and Francis.

Phelps, Michelle S. 2013. "The Paradox of Probation: Community Supervision in the Age of Mass Incarceration." *Law and Policy* 35:51–80.

———. 2011. "Rehabilitation in the Punitive Era: The Gap Between Rhetoric and Reality in U.S. Prison Programs." *Law and Society Review* 45:33–68.

Piehl, Anne M., and Stefan F. LoBuglio. 2005. "Does Supervision Matter?" Pp. 105–138 in *Prisoner Reentry and Public Safety in America,* edited by Jeremy Travis and Christy Visher. New York: Cambridge University Press.

Piquero, Alex R., David P. Farrington, and Alfred Blumstein. 2007. *Key Issues in Criminal Career Research: New Analyses of the Cambridge Study in Delinquent Development.* New York: Cambridge Studies in Criminology.

Pizarro, Jesenia, and Vanja M. K. Stenius. 2004. "Supermax Prisons: Their Rise, Current Practices and Effect on Inmates." *The Prison Journal* 84:248–262.

Pollack, Harold, Eric Sevigny, and Peter Reuter. 2013. "How to Make Drug Courts Work." *The Washington Post,* April 26. Available at http://www.washingtonpost .com/blogs/wonkblog/wp/2013/04/26/how-to-make-drug-courts-work/.

Pratt, Travis C., and Francis T. Cullen. 2000. "The Empirical Status of Gottfredson and Hirschi's General Theory of Crime: A Meta-Analysis." *Criminology* 38:931–964.

Provine, Doris M. 2007. *Unequal Under Law: Race in the War on Drugs.* Chicago: University of Chicago Press.

Pryor, Marie, and Douglas E. Thompkins. 2013. "The Disconnect Between Education and Social Opportunity for the Formerly Incarcerated." *American Journal of Criminal Justice* 38:457–479.

Ramirez, Mark D. 2013. "Punitive Sentiment." *Criminology* 51:329–364.

Raphael, Steven. 2011. "Incarceration and Prisoner Reentry in the United States." *Annals of the American Academy of Political and Social Science* 635:192–215.

Raphael, Steven, and Michael A. Stoll. 2009. "Why Are So Many Americans in Prison?" Pp. 27–72 in *Do Prisons Make Us Safer? The Benefits and Costs of the Prison Boom,* edited by Steven Raphael and Michael A. Stoll. New York: Russell Sage Foundation.

Ramakers, Anke, Johan van Wilsem, Paul Nieuwbeerta, and Anja Dirkzwager. 2014. "Down Before They Go In: A Study of Pre-Prison Labour Market Attachment." *European Journal of Crime Policy Research* (forthcoming).

Rand, Michael R. 2009. *Criminal Victimization, 2008.* Washington, DC: Bureau of Justice Statistics.

Rand, Michael, and Shannan Catalano. 2007. *Criminal Victimization, 2006.* Washington, DC: Bureau of Justice Statistics.

Reaves, Brian. 2010. *Local Police Departments, 2007.* Washington, DC: Bureau of Justice Statistics.

Reisig, Michael D. 2010. "Community and Problem-Oriented Policing." *Crime and Justice* 39:1–53.

Republican National Committee. 2012. *2012 Republican Party Platform.* Washington, DC: Republican National Committee.

Rhine, Edward E., Tina L. Mawhorr, and Evalyn C. Parks. 2006. "Implementation: The Bane of Effective Correctional Programs." *Criminology and Public Policy* 5:347–357.

Rhodes, Dusty. 2009. "Tougher Than Guantanamo: Illinois Supermax Prison With No Way Out." *Illinois Times,* June 18. Available at http://illinoistimes.com/ article-6047-tougher-than-guantanamo.html.

Rhodes, Lorna A. 2004. *Total Confinement: Madness and Reason in the Maximum Security Prison.* Los Angeles: University of California Press.

Rhodes, William. 2013. "Machine Learning Approaches as a Tool for Effective Offender Risk Prediction." *Criminology and Public Policy* 12:507–510.

———. 2011. "Predicting Criminal Recidivism: A Research Note." *Journal of Experimental Criminology* 7:57–71.

Rice, Marnie E., and Grant T. Harris. 1995. "Violent Recidivism: Assessing Predictive Validity." *Journal of Consulting and Clinical Psychology* 63:737–748.

Ridgeway, Greg. 2013. "Linking Prediction and Prevention." *Criminology and Public Policy* 12:545–550.

Ridgeway, Greg, and John M. MacDonald. 2014. "A Method for Internal Benchmarking of Criminal Justice System Performance." *Crime and Delinquency* 60:145–162.

Ritter, Nancy. 2013. "Predicting Recidivism Risk: New Tool in Philadelphia Shows Great Promise." *NIJ Journal* 271:4–13.

Riveland, Chase. 1999a. "Prison Management Trends, 1975–2025." Pp. 163–204 in *Prisons,* edited by Michael H. Tonry and Joan Petersilia. Chicago: University of Chicago Press.

———. 1999b. *Supermax Prisons: Overview and General Considerations.* Washington, DC: National Institute of Corrections.

Riviere, Lyndon A., Athena Kendall-Robbins, Dennis McGurk, Carl A. Castro, and Charles W. Hoge. 2011. "Coming Home May Hurt: Risk Factors for Mental Ill Health in U.S. Reservists after Deployment in Iraq." *British Journal of Psychiatry* 198:136–142.

Roberts, Julian V. 1992. "Public Opinion, Crime, and Criminal Justice." *Crime and Justice* 16:99–180.

Roberts, Julian V., and Mike Hough. 2005a. "The State of the Prisons: Exploring Public Knowledge and Opinion." *Howard Journal* 44:286–306.

———. 2005b. *Understanding Public Attitudes to Criminal Justice.* Maidenhead, UK: Open University Press.

Roberts, Julian V., and Loretta J. Stalans. 1998. "Crime, Criminal Justice, and Public Opinion." Pp. 31–57 in *The Handbook of Crime and Punishment,* edited by Michael H. Tonry. New York: Oxford University Press.

Roberts, Julian V., Loretta J. Stalans, David Indermaur, and Mike Hough. 2003. *Penal Populism and Public Opinion: Lessons From Five Countries.* New York: Oxford University Press.

Rocque, Michael, Brandon C. Welsh, and Adrian Raine. 2012. "Biosocial Criminology and Modern Crime Prevention." *Journal of Criminal Justice* 40:306–312.

Roman, John K., and Christine DeStefano. 2004. "Drug Court Effects and the Quality of Existing Evidence." Pp. 107–135 in *Juvenile Drug Courts and Teen Substance Abuse,* edited by Jeffrey A. Butts and John Roman. Washington, DC: The Urban Institute.

Roman, John K., Terence Dunworth, and Kevin Marsh, eds. 2010. *Cost-Benefit Analysis and Crime Control.* Washington, DC: The Urban Institute Press.

Rose, Dina R., and Todd R. Clear. 2003. "Incarceration, Reentry, and Social Capital: Social Networks in the Balance." Pp. 313–341 in *Prisoners Once Removed: The Impact of Incarceration and Reentry on Children, Families, and Communities,* edited by Jeremy Travis and M. Waul. Washington, DC: The Urban Institute Press.

———. 1998. "Incarceration, Social Capital and Crime: Implications for Social Disorganization Theory." *Criminology* 36:441–478.

Ross, Jeffrey I., ed. 2013. *The Globalization of Supermax Prisons.* New Brunswick, NJ: Rutgers University Press.

Ross, Jeffrey I., and Stephen C. Richards. 2009. *Beyond Bars: Rejoining Society After Prison.* New York: Penguin Group.

Rossi, Peter H. 1980. "The Presidential Address: The Challenge and Opportunities of Applied Social Research." *American Sociological Review* 45:889–904.

Rossi, Peter H., and Richard A. Berk. 1997. *Just Punishments: Federal Guidelines and Public Views Compared.* New York: Aldine de Gruyter.

Rossman, Shelli B., John K. Roman, Janine M. Zweig, Michael Rempel, and Christine H. Lindquist, eds. 2011. *The Multi-Site Adult Drug Court Evaluation: The Impact of Drug Courts.* Washington, DC: The Urban Institute.

Rothman, David J. 1971. *The Discovery of the Asylum: Social Order and Disorder in the New Republic.* Boston: Little, Brown.

Rudes, Danielle S., Jennifer Lerch, Jill Viglione, and Faye S. Taxman. 2014. "Cultural Challenges: Implementing Reentry Reform at a Correctional Facility." Pp. 29–50 in *Offender Reentry: Rethinking Criminology and Criminal Justice,* edited by Matthew S. Crow and John O. Smykla. Burlington, MA: Jones and Bartlett.

Sabol, William J. 1999. *Prison Population Projection and Forecasting: Managing Capacity.* Washington, DC: Office of Justice Programs.

Salisbury, Emily J., and Patricia Van Voorhis. 2009. "Gendered Pathways: A Quantitative Investigation of Women Probationers' Paths to Incarceration." *Criminal Justice and Behavior* 36:541–566.

Sampson, Robert J. 2013. "The Place of Context: A Theory and Strategy for Criminology's Hard Problems." *Criminology* 51:1–32.

———. 2012. *Great American City: Chicago and the Enduring Neighborhood Effect.* Chicago: University of Chicago Press.

———. 2009. "Racial Stratification and the Durable Tangle of Neighborhood Inequality." *Annals of the American Academy of Political and Social Science* 621:260–280.

Sampson, Robert J., Christopher Winship, and Carly Knight. 2013. "Translating Causal Claims: Principles and Strategies for Policy-Relevant Criminology." *Criminology and Public Policy* 12:587–616.

Samuels, Julie, Nancy La Vigne, and Samuel Taxy. 2013. *Stemming the Tide: Strategies to Reduce the Growth and Cut the Cost of the Federal Prison System.* Washington, DC: The Urban Institute.

Schnittker, Jason, and Andrea John. 2007. "Enduring Stigma: The Long-Term Effects of Incarceration on Health." *Journal of Health and Social Behavior* 48:115–130.

Schlager, Melinda D. 2013. *Rethinking the Reentry Paradigm: A Blueprint for Action.* Durham, NC: Carolina Academic Press.

Sevigny, Eric L., and Jonathan P. Caulkins. 2004. "Kingpins or Mules: An Analysis of Drug Offenders Incarcerated in Federal and State Prisons." *Criminology and Public Policy* 3:401–434.

Sevigny, Eric L., Harold A. Pollack, and Peter Reuter. 2013. "Can Drug Courts Help to Reduce Prison and Jail Populations?" *Annals of the American Academy of Political and Social Science* 647:190–212.

Shalev, Sharon. 2009. *Supermax: Controlling Risk Through Solitary Confinement.* London: Willan.

Sherman, Lawrence W. 2004. "Research and Policing: The Infrastructure and Political Economy of Federal Funding." *Annals of the American Academy of Political and Social Science* 593:156–178.

———. 1993. "Defiance, Deterrence and Irrelevance: A Theory of the Criminal Sanction." *Journal of Research in Crime and Delinquency* 30:445–473.

Sherman, Lawrence W., David P. Farrington, Brandon C. Welsh, and Doris Layton MacKenzie, eds. 2002. *Evidence Based Crime Prevention.* London: Routledge.

Sherman, Lawrence W., Denise C. Gottfredson, Doris L. MacKenzie, John Eck, Peter Reuter, and Shawn Bushway, eds. 1997. *Preventing Crime: What Works, What Doesn't, What's Promising*. Washington, DC: Office of Justice Programs.

Siennick, Sonja E. 2014. "Parental Incarceration and Intergenerational Transfers to Young Adults." *Journal of Family Issues* (forthcoming).

Siennick, Sonja E., Daniel P. Mears, and William D. Bales. 2013. "Here and Gone: Anticipation and Separation Effects of Prison Visits on Inmate Infractions." *Journal of Research in Crime and Delinquency* 50:417–444.

Silver, Nate. 2012. *The Signal and the Noise: Why So Many Predictions Fail—But Some Don't*. New York: Penguin.

Simon, Jonathan. 2012. "Mass Incarceration: From Social Policy to Social Problem." Pp. 23–52 in *The Oxford Handbook of Sentencing and Corrections*, edited by Joan Petersilia and Kevin R. Reitz. New York: Oxford University Press.

———. 2007. *Governing Through Crime*. New York: Oxford University Press.

Skogan, Wesley G., ed. 2003. *Community Policing: Can It Work?* Belmont, CA: Wadsworth.

———. 1995. "Crime and the Racial Fears of White Americans." *Annals of the American Academy of Political and Social Science* 539:59–71.

Slobogin, Christopher. 2012. "Risk Assessment." Pp. 196–214 in *The Oxford Handbook of Sentencing and Corrections*, edited by Joan Petersilia and Kevin R. Reitz. New York: Oxford University Press.

Smith, Paula, Claire Goggin, and Paul Gendreau. 2002. *The Effects of Prison Sentences and Intermediate Sanctions on Recidivism: General Effects and Individual Differences*. Ontario: Solicitor General of Canada.

Smith, Peter S. 2006. "The Effects of Solitary Confinement on Prison Inmates: A Brief History and Review of the Literature." *Crime and Justice* 34:441–528.

Snodgrass, Matthew G., Arjan A. J. Blokland, Amelia Haviland, Paul Nieuwbeerta, and Daniel S. Nagin. 2011. "Does the Time Cause the Crime? An Examination of the Relationship Between Time Served and Reoffending in the Netherlands." *Criminology* 49:1149–1194.

Solinger, Rickie, Paula C. Johnson, Martha L. Raimon, Tina Reynolds, and Ruby C. Tapia. 2010. *Interrupted Life: Experiences of Incarcerated Women in the United States*. Berkeley: University of California Press.

Solomon, Amy L., Vera Kachnowski, and Avinash S. Bhati. 2005. *Does Parole Work? Analyzing the Impact of Postprison Supervision on Rearrest Outcomes*. Washington, DC: The Urban Institute.

Sorensen, Jon, and Mark D. Cunningham. "Conviction Offense and Prison Violence: A Comparative Study of Murderers and Other Offenders." *Crime and Delinquency* 56:103–125.

Sparks, Richard, Anthony E. Bottoms, and Will Hay. 1996. *Prisons and the Problem of Order*. Oxford, UK: Oxford University Press.

Spelman, William. 2009. "Crime, Cash, and Limited Options: Explaining the Prison Boom." *Criminology and Public Policy* 8:29–77.

———. 2008. "Specifying the Relationship Between Crime and Prisons." *Journal of Quantitative Criminology* 24:149–178.

———. 2006. "The Limited Importance of Prison Expansion." Pp. 97–129 in *The Crime Drop in America*, edited by Alfred Blumstein and Joel Wallman. New York: Cambridge University Press.

———. 1995. "The Severity of Intermediate Sanctions." *Journal of Research in Crime and Delinquency* 32:107–135.

Spiegel, Sarah. 2007. "Prison 'Race Riots': An Easy Case for Segregation?" *California Law Review* 95:2261–2293.

Spohn, Cassia. 2014. "Racial Disparities in Prosecution, Sentencing, and Punishment." Pp. 166–193 in *The Oxford Handbook of Ethnicity, Crime, and Immigration*, edited by Sandra M. Bucerius and Michael H. Tonry. New York: Oxford University Press.

Stafford, Mark C., and Daniel P. Mears. 2014. "Causation, Theory, and Policy in the Social Sciences." Chapter in *Emerging Trends in the Behavioral and Social Sciences*, edited by Robert A. Scott and Stephen M. Kosslyn. Hoboken, NJ: Wiley (forthcoming).

Stafford, Mark C., and Mark Warr. 1993. "A Reconceptualization of General and Specific Deterrence." *Journal of Research in Crime and Delinquency* 30:123–135.

Stahler, Gerald J., Jeremy Mennis, Steven Belenko, Wayne N. Welsh, and Matthew L. Hiller. 2013. "Predicting Recidivism for Released State Prisoners: Examining the Influence of Individual and Neighborhood Characteristics and Spatial Contagion on the Likelihood of Reincarceration." *Criminal Justice and Behavior* 40:690–711.

Stal, Marina. 2012. "Treatment of Older and Elderly Inmates Within Prisons." *Journal of Correctional Health Care* 19:69–73.

Steffensmeier, Darrell, and Emilie Allan. 1996. "Gender and Crime: Toward a Gendered Theory of Female Offending." *Annual Review of Sociology* 22:459–487.

Steiner, Benjamin. 2009. "Assessing Static and Dynamic Influences on Inmate Violence Levels." *Crime and Delinquency* 55:134–161.

Steiner, Benjamin, and Benjamin Meade. 2014. "The Safe Prison." Pp. 129–150 in *The American Prison: Imagining a Different Future*, edited by Francis T. Cullen, Cheryl L. Jonson, and Mary K. Stohr. Thousand Oaks, CA: Sage.

Steiner, Benjamin, and John Wooldredge. 2014. "Sex Differences in the Predictors of Prisoner Misconduct." *Criminal Justice and Behavior* 41:433–452.

———. 2013. "Implications of Different Outcome Measures for an Understanding of Inmate Misconduct." *Crime and Delinquency* 59:1234–1262.

Stockdale, Keira C., Mark E. Olver, and Stephen C. P. Wong. 2014. "The Validity and Reliability of the Violence Risk-Scale—Youth Version in a Diverse Sample of Violent Young Offenders." *Criminal Justice and Behavior* 41:114–138.

Stolz, Barbara A. 2002. *Criminal Justice Policy Making: Federal Roles and Processes.* Westport, CT: Praeger.

Streiner, David L., and John H. Cairney. 2013. "What's Under the ROC? An Introduction to Receiver Operating Characteristics Curves." Pp. 304–317 in *A Guide for the Statistically Perplexed*, edited by David L. Streiner. Toronto: Canadian Psychiatric Association.

Stuntz, William J. 2011. *The Collapse of American Criminal Justice.* Cambridge, MA: Harvard University Press.

Sugie, Naomi F. 2012. "Punishment and Welfare: Paternal Incarceration and Families' Receipt of Public Assistance." *Social Forces* 90:1403–1427.

Swanson, Cheryl G., Courtney W. Schnippert, and Amanda L. Tryling. 2014. "Reentry and Employment: Employers' Willingness to Hire Formerly Convicted Felons in Northwest Florida." Pp. 203–224 in *Offender Reentry: Rethinking Criminology and Criminal Justice*, edited by Matthew S. Crow and John O. Smykla. Burlington, MA: Jones and Bartlett.

Sweeten, Gary. 2012. "Scaling Criminal Offending." *Journal of Quantitative Criminology* 28:533–557.

Sykes, Gresham M. 1958. *The Society of Captives*. Princeton, NJ: Princeton University Press.

Tapley, Lance. 2010. "The Worst of the Worst: Supermax Torture in America." *Boston Review*. Available at https://www.bostonreview.net/tapley-supermax-torture-in-america.php.

Taxman, Faye S. 2012. "Probation, Intermediate Sanctions, and Community-Based Corrections." Pp. 363–388 in *The Oxford Handbook of Sentencing and Corrections*, edited by Joan Petersilia and Kevin R. Reitz. New York: Oxford University Press.

Tietz, Jeff. 2012. "Slow-Motion Torture." *Rolling Stone*, December 6, pp. 58–66.

Tonry, Michael H. 2012. "Race, Ethnicity, and Punishment." Pp. 53–82 in *The Oxford Handbook of Sentencing and Corrections*, edited by Joan Petersilia and Kevin R. Reitz. New York: Oxford University Press.

———. 2011. *Punishing Race: A Continuing American Dilemma*. New York: Oxford University Press.

———. 2009a. "Explanations of American Punishment Policies." *Punishment and Society* 11:377–394.

———, ed. 2009b. *The Oxford Handbook of Crime and Public Policy*. New York: Oxford University Press.

———. 2008. "Crime and Human Rights—How Political Paranoia, Protestant Fundamentalism, and Constitutional Obsolescence Combined to Devastate Black America: The American Society of Criminology 2007 Presidential Address." *Criminology* 46:1–34.

———. 2004. *Thinking About Crime: Sense and Sensibility in American Penal Culture*. New York: Oxford University Press.

———. 1997. *Intermediate Sanctions in Sentencing Guidelines*. Washington, DC: National Institute of Justice.

———. 1995. *Malign Neglect: Race, Crime, and Punishment in America*. New York: Oxford University Press.

Travis, Jeremy. 2005. *But They All Come Back: Facing the Challenges of Prisoner Reentry*. Washington, DC: The Urban Institute Press.

Travis, Jeremy, and Sarah Lawrence. 2002. *Beyond the Prison Gates: The State of Parole in America*. Washington, DC: The Urban Institute.

Travis, Jeremy, Amy L. Solomon, and Michelle Waul. 2001. *From Prison to Home: The Dimensions and Consequences of Prisoner Reentry*. Washington, DC: The Urban Institute.

Travis, Jeremy, and Christy Visher, eds. 2005. *Prisoner Reentry and Crime in America*. New York: Cambridge University Press.

Travis, Jeremy, and Michelle Waul, eds. 2004. *Prisoners Once Removed: The Impact of Incarceration and Reentry on Children, Families, and Communities*. Washington, DC: The Urban Institute Press.

Travis, Jeremy, Bruce Western, and Steven Redburn, eds. 2014. *The Growth of Incarceration in the United States*. Washington, DC: The National Academies Press.

Trulson, Chad R., Matt DeLisi, and James W. Marquart. 2011. "Institutional Misconduct, Delinquent Background, and Rearrest Frequency Among Serious and Violent Delinquent Offenders." *Crime and Delinquency* 57:709–731.

Trulson, Chad R., James W. Marquart, Craig Hemmens, and Leo Carroll. 2008. "Racial Desegregation in Prisons." *The Prison Journal* 88:270–299.

Truman, Jennifer, Lynn Langton, and Michael Planty. 2013. *Criminal Victimization, 2012.* Washington, DC: Bureau of Justice Statistics.

Turanovic, Jillian J., Nancy Rodriguez, and Travis C. Pratt. 2012. "The Collateral Consequences of Incarceration Revisited: A Qualitative Analysis of the Effects on Caregivers of Children of Incarcerated Parents." *Criminology* 50:913–959.

Tyler, Tom R. 1990. *Why People Obey the Law.* New Haven, CT: Yale University Press.

Uggen, Christopher, Jeff Manza, and Angela Behrens. 2004. "'Less than Average Citizen': Stigma, Role Transition, and the Civic Reintegration of Convicted Felons." Pp. 261–293 in *After Crime and Punishment: Pathways to Offender Reintegration,* edited by Shadd Maruna and Ross Immarigeon. Cullompton, UK: Willan.

Uggen, Christopher, Sarah Shannon, and Jeff Manza. 2012. *State-Level Estimates of Felon Disenfranchisement in the United States, 2010.* Washington, DC: The Sentencing Project.

Uggen, Christopher, and Sara Wakefield. 2005. "Young Adults Reentering the Community From the Criminal Justice System: The Challenge." Pp. 114–144 in *On Your Own Without a Net,* edited by Wayne D. Osgood, Michael E. Foster, Constance Flanagan, and Gretchen P. Ruth. Chicago: University of Chicago Press.

Uggen, Christopher, Sara Wakefield, and Bruce Western. 2005. "Work and Family Perspectives on Reentry" Pp. 209–243 in *Prisoner Reentry and Crime in America,* edited by Jeremy Travis and Christy Visher. New York: Cambridge University Press.

Unnever, James D. 2014. "Race, Crime, and Public Opinion." Pp. 70–106 in *The Oxford Handbook of Ethnicity, Crime, and Immigration,* edited by Sandra M. Bucerius and Michael H. Tonry. New York: Oxford University Press.

———. 2008. "Two Worlds Far Apart: Black-White Differences in Beliefs About Why African-American Men are Disproportionately Imprisoned." *Criminology* 46:511–538.

Unnever, James D., and Francis T. Cullen. 2010. "The Social Sources of Americans' Punitiveness: A Test of Three Competing Models." *Criminology* 48:99–129.

Useem, Bert, and Anne M. Piehl. 2008. *Prison State: The Challenge of Mass Incarceration.* New York: Cambridge University Press.

Van Voorhis, Patricia. 2012. "On Behalf of Women Offenders: Women's Place in the Science of Evidence-Based Practice." *Criminology and Public Policy* 11:111–145.

Van Voorhis, Patricia, Emily M. Wright, Emily Salisbury, and Ashley Bauman. 2010. "Women's Risk Factors and Their Contributions to Existing Risk/Needs Assessment: The Current Status of a Gender-Responsive Supplement." *Criminal Justice and Behavior* 37:261–288.

Vermink, Hilde, Robert Apel, Paul Nieuwbeerta, and Arjan A. J. Blokland. 2013. "The Incapacitation Effect of First-Time Imprisonment: A Matched Samples Comparison." *Journal of Quantitative Criminology* 29:579–600.

Vieno, Alessio, Michele Roccato, and Silvia Russo. 2013. "Is Fear of Crime Mainly Social and Economic Insecurity in Disguise? A Multilevel Multinational Analysis." *Journal of Community and Applied Social Psychology* 23:519–535.

Villettaz, Patrice, Martin Killias, and Isabel Zoder. 2006. *The Effects of Custodial versus Non-Custodial Sentences on Re-offending: A Systematic Review of the State of Knowledge.* Report to the Campbell Collaboration Crime and Justice Group. Lausanne, Switzerland: University of Lausanne, Institute of Criminology and Criminal Law.

Visher, Christy A., Sara A. Debus-Sherrill, and Jennifer Yahner. 2011. "Employment After Prison: A Longitudinal Study of Former Prisoners." *Justice Quarterly* 28:698–718.

Visher, Christy A., and Daniel J. O'Connell. 2012. "Incarceration and Inmates' Self Perceptions About Returning Home." *Journal of Criminal Justice* 40:386–393.

Visher, Christy A., and Jeremy Travis. 2012. "The Characteristics of Prisoners Returning Home and Effective Reentry Programs and Policies." Pp. 684–706 in *The Oxford Handbook of Sentencing and Corrections,* edited by Joan Petersilia and Kevin R. Reitz. New York: Oxford University Press.

———. 2011. "Life on the Outside: Returning Home After Incarceration." *The Prison Journal* 9:102S–119S.

———. 2003. "Transitions From Prison to Community: Understanding Individual Pathways." *Annual Review of Sociology* 29:89–113.

Vitiello, Michael. 2013. "Still Between a Rock and a Hard Place: Sentencing Reform in California." *Federal Sentencing Reporter* 25:233–235.

von Hirsch, Andrew, and Andrew Ashworth, eds. 1992. *Principled Sentencing.* Boston: Northeastern University Press.

Vose, Brenda, Paula Smith, and Francis T. Cullen. 2013. "Predictive Validity and the Impact of Change in Total LSI-R Score on Recidivism." *Criminal Justice and Behavior* 40:1383–1396.

Vrieze, Scott I., and William M. Grove. 2010. "Multidimensional Assessment of Criminal Recidivism: Problems, Pitfalls, and Proposed Solutions." *Psychological Assessment* 22:382–395.

Wacquant, Loïc. 2009. *Punishing the Poor.* Durham, NC: Duke University Press.

———. 2002. "The Curious Eclipse of Prison Ethnography in the Age of Mass Incarceration." *Ethnography* 3:371–397. Walmsley, Roy. 2013. *World Prison Population List.* 10th ed. London: International Centre for Prison Studies.

Wang, Xia, and Daniel P. Mears. 2010. "A Multilevel Test of Minority Threat Effects on Sentencing." *Journal of Quantitative Criminology* 26:191–215.

Wang, Xia, Daniel P. Mears, and William D. Bales. 2010. "Race-Specific Employment Contexts and Recidivism." *Criminology* 48:201–241.

Warren, Patricia, Donald Tomaskovic-Devey, William Smith, Matthew Zingraff, and Marcinda Mason. 2006. "Driving While Black: Bias Processes and Racial Disparity in Police Stops." *Criminology* 44:709–738.

Washington, Harriet A. 2008. *Medical Apartheid: The Dark History of Medical Experimentation on Black Americans From Colonial Times to the Present.* New York: Doubleday.

Weiman, David F., Michael A. Stoll, and Shawn Bushway. 2007. "The Regime of Mass Incarceration: A Labor-Market Perspective." Pp. 29–79 in *Barriers to Reentry? The Labor Market for Released Prisoners in Post-Industrial America,* edited by Shawn Bushway, Michael A. Stoll, and David F. Weiman. New York: Russell Sage Foundation.

Weisburd, David, Cynthia M. Lum, and Anthony Petrosino. 2001. "Does Research Design Affect Study Outcomes in Criminal Justice?" *Annals of the American Academy of Political and Social Science* 578:50–70.

Weisburd, David, Cynthia M. Lum, and Sue-Ming Yang. 2003. "When Can We Conclude That Treatments or Programs 'Don't Work'?" *Annals of the American Academy of Political and Social Science* 587:31–48.

Weiser, Benjamin. 2011. "A Judge's Education, One Sentence at a Time." *New York Times,* October 9, p. A31.

Weiss, Harald D., and Lauren M. Vasquez. 2013. "Immigrants Under Correctional Supervision: Examining the Needs of Immigrant Populations in a Criminal Justice

Setting." Pp. 405–430 in *Special Needs Offenders in Correctional Institutions,* edited by Lior Gideon. Thousand Oaks, CA: Sage.

Welsh, Brandon C., and David P. Farrington, eds. 2006. *Preventing Crime: What Works for Children, Offenders, Victims and Places.* New York: Springer-Verlag.

Welsh, Brandon C., and Rebecca D. Pfeffer. 2013. "Reclaiming Crime Prevention in an Age of Punishment: An American History." *Punishment and Society* 15:534–553.

Welsh, Brandon C., and Michael Rocque. 2014. "When Crime Prevention Harms: A Review of Systematic Reviews." *Journal of Experimental Criminology* 10:245–266.

Welsh, Wayne N., and Philip W. Harris. 2008. *Criminal Justice Policy and Planning.* 3rd ed. Dayton, OH: LexisNexis, Anderson Publishing.

Wermink, Hilde, Robert Apel, Paul Nieuwbeerta, and Arjan A. J. Blokland. 2013. "The Incapacitation Effect of First-Time Imprisonment: A Matched Samples Comparison." *Journal of Quantitative Criminology* 29:579–600.

Western, Bruce. 2006. *Punishment and Inequality in America.* New York: Russell Sage Foundation.

Western, Bruce, and Christopher Muller. 2013. "Mass Incarceration, Macrosociology, and the Poor." *Annals of the American Academy of Political and Social Science* 647:166–189.

Western, Bruce, and Christopher Wildeman. 2009. "The Black Family and Mass Incarceration." *Annals of the American Academy of Political and Social Science* 621:221–242.

White, Helene R., and Dennis M. Gorman. 2000. "Dynamics of the Drug-Crime Relationship." Pp. 151–218 in *The Nature of Crime: Continuity and Change,* edited by Gary LaFree. Washington, DC: National Institute of Justice.

White, Michael D., Philip Mulvey, Andrew M. Fox, and David Choate. 2012. "A Hero's Welcome? Exploring the Prevalence and Problems of Military Veterans in the Arrestee Population." *Justice Quarterly* 29:258–286.

Wildeman, Christopher. 2014. "Parental Incarceration, Child Homelessness, and the Invisible Consequences of Mass Imprisonment." *Annals of the American Academy of Political and Social Science* 651:74–96.

———. 2009. "Parental Imprisonment, the Prison Boom, and the Concentration of Childhood Disadvantage." *Demography* 46:265–280.

Wilkins, William W., Jr., Phyllis J. Newton, and John R. Steer. 1991. "The Sentencing Reform Act of 1984: A Bold Approach to the Unwarranted Sentencing Disparity Problem." *Criminal Law Forum* 2:355–380.

Wilson, David B., Catherine A. Gallagher, and Doris L. MacKenzie. 2003. "A Meta-Analysis of Corrections-Based Education, Vocation, and Work Programs for Adult Offenders." *Journal of Research in Crime and Delinquency* 37:347–368.

Wilson, David B., Doris L. MacKenzie, and Fawn N. Mitchell. 2005. *Effects of Correctional Boot Camps on Offending.* A Campbell Collaboration systematic review. Available online at http://www.campbellcollaboration.org.

Wilson, David B., Ojmarrh Mitchell, and Doris L. MacKenzie. 2006. "A Systematic Review of Drug Court Effects on Recidivism." *Journal of Experimental Criminology* 2:459–487.

Wilson, William Julius. 1987. *The Truly Disadvantaged: The Inner City, the Underclass and Public Policy.* Chicago: University of Chicago Press.

Windzio, Michael. 2006. "Is There a Deterrent Effect of Pains of Imprisonment? The Impact of 'Social Costs' of First Incarceration on the Hazard Rate of Recidivism." *Punishment and Society* 8:341–364.

Winterfield, Laura, and Jennifer Castro. 2005. *Returning Home Illinois Policy Brief: Treatment Matching.* Washington, DC: The Urban Institute.

Wolf, Angela M., Fabiana Silva, Kelly E. Knight, and Shabnam Javdani. 2007. "Responding to the Health Needs of Female Offenders." Pp. 182–213 in *What Works With Women Offenders,* edited by Rosemary Sheehan, Gill McIvor, and Chris Trotter. London: Willan.

Wolff, Nancy, and Jing Shi. 2011. "Patterns of Victimization and Feelings of Safety Inside Prison: The Experience of Male and Female Inmates." *Crime and Delinquency* 57:29–55.

Wolff, Nancy, Jing Shi, and Brooke E. Schumann. 2012. "Reentry Preparedness Among Soon-to-Be-Released Inmates and the Role of Time Served." *Journal of Criminal Justice* 40:379–385.

Wooditch, Alese, Liansheng L. Tang, and Faye S. Taxman. 2014. "Which Criminogenic Need Changes Are Most Important in Promoting Desistance From Crime and Substance Use?" *Criminal Justice and Behavior* 41:276–299.

Woolard, Jennifer L. 2012. "Adolescent Development, Delinquency, and Juvenile Justice." Pp. 107–122 in *The Oxford Handbook of Juvenile Crime and Juvenile Justice,* edited by Barry C. Feld and Donna M. Bishop. New York: Oxford University Press.

Wooldredge, John D. 1999. "Inmate Experiences and Psychological Well-Being." *Criminal Justice and Behavior* 26:235–250.

Wooldredge, John, Timothy Griffin, and Travis Pratt. 2001. "Considering Hierarchical Models for Research on Inmate Behavior: Predicting Misconduct With Multilevel Data." *Justice Quarterly* 18:203–231.

Wright, Emily M., Patricia Van Voorhis, Emily J. Salisbury, and Ashley Bauman. 2012. "Gender-Responsive Lessons Learned and Policy Implications for Women in Prison: A Review." *Criminal Justice and Behavior* 39:1612–1632.

Wright, Kevin A., and Gabriel T. Cesar. 2013. "Toward a More Complete Model of Offender Reintegration: Linking the Individual-, Community-, and System-Level Components of Recidivism." *Victims and Offenders* 8:373–398.

Yahner, Jennifer, and Christy Visher. 2008. *Illinois Prisoners' Reentry Success Three Years after Release.* Washington, DC: The Urban Institute.

Zahn, Margaret A., Robert Agnew, Diana Fishbein, Shari Miller, Donna-Marie Winn, Gayle Dakoff, . . . Meda Chesney-Lind. 2010. *Causes and Correlates of Girls' Delinquency.* Washington, DC: Office of Juvenile Justice and Delinquency Prevention.

Zimring, Franklin E. 2007. *The Great American Crime Decline.* New York: Oxford University Press.

———. 2005. "Penal Policy and Penal Legislation: Recent American Experience." *Stanford Law Review* 58:323–338.

Index

Note: page numbers followed by "n" refer to endnotes.

⑤SAGE research**methods**

The essential online tool for researchers from the world's leading methods publisher

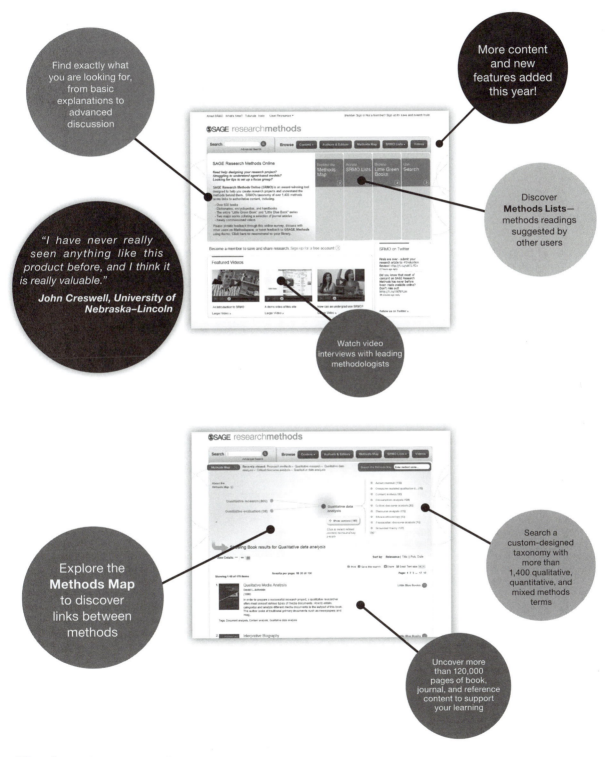

Find exactly what you are looking for, from basic explanations to advanced discussion

More content and new features added this year!

"I have never really seen anything like this product before, and I think it is really valuable."
John Creswell, University of Nebraska–Lincoln

Discover **Methods Lists**— methods readings suggested by other users

Watch video interviews with leading methodologists

Explore the **Methods Map** to discover links between methods

Search a custom-designed taxonomy with more than 1,400 qualitative, quantitative, and mixed methods terms

Uncover more than 120,000 pages of book, journal, and reference content to support your learning

Find out more at
www.sageresearchmethods.com